SOMERSET PARKS and GARDENS

A LANDSCAPE HISTORY
by JAMES BOND

PREFACE by STEFAN BUCZACKI

This volume is dedicated to
JOHN HARVEY (1911-1997),
a pioneer of the study of garden history.

First published in Great Britain in 1998
© JAMES BOND, 1998
   and the several authors in respect of their individual contributions.

British Library Cataloguing in Publication Data
A CIP record for this book is available from the British Library

ISBN   0 86183 465 8

Design and artwork by PETER WEBB.

SOMERSET BOOKS
Official Publisher to Somerset County Council
Halsgrove House
Lower Moor Way
Tiverton EX16 6SS
T: 01884 243242
F: 01884 243325
www.halsgrove.com

Printed and bound in Singapore by UIC Printing & Packaging Pte Ltd

Frontispiece:
The Eastern Forecourt at
MONTACUTE HOUSE.

CONTENTS

FOREWORD

Public interest in parks and gardens continues to grow and expand as more of us recognise and appreciate the importance of our historic landscapes. This study brings together a wide range of examples from across the historic county of Somerset covering almost two thousand years of landscape creation from Roman times up to the present century.

Many of the famous parks and gardens owe a great deal to the generations of local landowners and their garden staff who have nurtured and developed the gardens, often over several centuries. Their future care requires expertise, funding and consideration for the long-term management of the landscape.

I warmly support the publication of this book and can say the County Council is no stranger to supporting the parks and gardens on its own estate at Hestercombe and in partnership with the Somerset Building Preservation Trust, English Heritage and others at Halswell Park near Bridgwater.

This book presents a survey of current knowledge and illustrates how historic parks and gardens in Somerset are an asset for this and subsequent generations to appreciate and enjoy.

RALPH CLARK,
CHAIRMAN, SOMERSET COUNTY COUNCIL

PREFACE

It has been my pleasure over the past twenty or so years to travel the length and breadth of Britain, meeting gardeners, answering their questions and seeing a significant cross-section of British gardens. Somerset has featured of course in my journeys and Somerset has featured too when I have been asked, rather frequently, 'Which is your favourite garden?' Really being put on the spot and forced to give a response to this impossible question, 'Hestercombe near Taunton' has been my consistent answer. The frequency with which I have said it has served to reinforce my relationship with the county and it is now my privilege to be a Trustee of the Hestercombe Gardens Trust, whose concern embraces not just the Lutyens/Jekyll garden to which I so often referred but also Philip White's compelling project to restore the adjoining eighteenth-century Bampfylde landscape garden.

My acquaintance with these gardens has served to whet my appetite, however, and whilst the Hestercombe site is in a special category, it has become evident that there is a richness and diversity to the gardens of this beautiful county that I certainly had not appreciated. By and large, Somerset's gardens are not the gardens of the great and grand country houses such as I have become used to in my own native Derbyshire; rather they are treasures of smaller scale to be sought out and cherished. And in that respect, Somerset is more typical of the type of gardening that Britain as a whole can offer.

My task in seeking out Somerset gardens will be immeasurably easier with the publication of this quite splendid volume, and I am sure it will encourage others to do likewise. It is a remarkably thorough and perceptive piece of research. But it is certainly no dry and scholarly tome; rather it is a compelling read that reveals much of fascination and interest, not just about Somerset, but about the whole breadth and eclecticism of British gardening. I know of no comparable study, in such depth, for any other British county and this book will be the envy of gardeners, garden historians and lovers of Britain everywhere.

PROFESSOR STEFAN BUCZACKI

Acknowledgements

This book has been a long while in its preparation. Not only has the time I have been able to devote to it been restricted by the predictable demands of earning a living, but it has also been disrupted by two unexpected and prolonged spells of illness, a move of house and a number of other pressures outside my control. I owe a profound debt to the Somerset County Council publications group and its successive chairmen, Ray Hyde and David Cawthorne, and to Steven Pugsley of Somerset Books for their patience and forbearance during the delay between my taking on the commitment and delivering the final manuscript. I am particularly appreciative of the unfailing support and encouragement of Bob Croft and Russell Lillford - if their faith in the project has ever wavered, they have concealed it from me with great tact. I am most grateful to Tom Mayberry and the staff of the Somerset Archive and Record Service and to David Bromwich for assistance with illustrations. It has been a pleasure to work with Peter Webb, whose design has enormously enhanced the appearance of this volume. Thanks are also due to WS Atkins South West for helping with the production of this book.

I owe a considerable debt to the generations of antiquarians, historians, archaeologists and garden writers whose works are listed in the footnotes. I have tried my best to give proper acknowledgement in the appropriate place to all the books, articles and unpublished sources I have used, but I am also conscious that over the years things read, or heard in lectures, or communicated to me by colleagues and students may have become absorbed into my own memory-bank without any clear recollection of their source. If any reader should recognise something of his own here which has not been properly attributed, I can only offer my apologies and plead that the borrowing was by default rather than intent. Every effort has been made to secure permission to use copyright material, but in some cases it has proved difficult to identify or locate copyright owners.

Ken Brown, Paul Stamper, Tom Mayberry and Robert Dunning have read the final draft of the text, and I am grateful for their comments, and also for the inspiration of their own publications, which will be very evident. I am also indebted to the following for a wide range of information, advice, assistance and encouragement: Mark Angliss, Mick Aston, Joe Bettey, Mike Chapman, Nick Corcos, Ed Dennison, Janice Grove, Joan Hasler, Charles and Nancy Hollinrake, Andrew Holder, Hazel Hudson, Rob Iles, Norma Knight, Michael McGarvie, Tim Mowl, Frances Neale, Stan and Joan Rendell, Abigail Shepherd, Mary Stacey, Julian Watson, Jan Woudstra, and Rob Wilson-North. Any errors which have escaped notice are my responsibility alone. I am particularly grateful to Professor Stefan Buczacki for contributing the preface to this volume.

My wife, Tina, has suffered innumerable uncommunicative evenings and weekends when I have been glued to the front of a word-processor, and has accompanied me round many sites, often in the pouring rain, without a murmur of complaint. She has read my early drafts, translated most of my more tortured sentences into English, saved me from numerous bizarre spelling errors, and made many other helpful and constructive suggestions.

My final, and perhaps greatest, debts are to the designers and labourers of past centuries who have left us such a magnificent legacy of parks and gardens, and to those many owners who have been willing to open their grounds today for us all to enjoy them.

Contributors

Robert Ladd BSc, DipArchCons, DipTP, MRTPI, IHBC
Bob works for Mendip District Council as Conservation and Design Manager. After an early career in civil engineering he has spent the last twenty years working for local planning authorities. Away from the office Bob is actively interested in wildlife conservation.

Russell Lillford MA, DipArchCons, DipTP, ARICS, MRTPI, FRSA, IHBC
Russell is the Manager of the Architectural and Historic Heritage Group for Somerset County Council and as such is responsible for the Lutyens/Jekyll garden at Hestercombe. He is also an advisor to the Somerset Building Preservation Trust and contributed to *Aspects of the Medieval Landscape of Somerset* (edited by Michael Aston, 1988).

Philip White BSc
Philip studied zoology before working for the family dairy farming business for seventeen years. From 1991-97 he was a conservation Officer with the Somerset Wildlife Trust, and is now Director of the Hestercombe Gardens Project, for which he published *A Gentleman of Fine Taste - The Watercolours of Coplestone Warre Bampfylde* (1995). *Country Life* magazine voted Philip 'Gardener of the Year' for 1997 for his restoration of the eighteenth-century pleasure grounds at Hestercombe.

Editorial Notes

The historic county of Somerset endured for over a thousand years until 1974, when the portion north of the Mendip Hills was lopped off and incorporated into the new county of Avon. Avon itself lasted just twenty years until it was broken up in its turn, its two southern districts recognising their former Somerset allegiance in their new titles as unitary authorities. Who knows how long the present system will last and what the results of the next round of central government interference will be? Most people still think of Somerset as a unit within its ancient bounds, and in view of the ephemeral nature of modern administrative divisions, I have preferred to adopt the historic county as my frame of reference. In making this decision, I acknowledge some inevitable overlap with Stewart Harding and David Lambert's excellent recent publication on the *Gardens of Avon*, and my indebtedness to their survey will be obvious.

Several other editorial decisions may require explanation. For the sake of clarity most quotations from early documents have been rendered into modern spelling. After some agonising I have decided to quote all measurements in imperial dimensions, in preference to using the metric system. Even in the 1990s I suspect that most people still think in feet or yards rather than metres and have a better impression of what an acre looks like than a hectare. Finally, since this book is not specifically aimed at botanical specialists, I have preferred to refer to plants by the common names that most people will recognise, only quoting their scientific name where this seemed important for identification.

Imperial units have been used throughout this volume.
1 acre = 0.405 hectares
1 yard = 3 feet = 0.9144 metres
1 foot = 12 inches = 0.3048 metres
1 mile = 1,760 yards = 1.609 kilometres
£1 = 20 shillings(s), 1 shilling(s) = 12 pence(d)

PUBLIC ACCESS

Reference to individual houses, parks and gardens in this book is not intended to imply that there is any right of public access to them. Although a few of the sites described are now in some form of public or institutional ownership, most of them remain in private hands. Some are not accessible to visitors, while others may be open only for very limited periods. Opening arrangements may be subject to change at any time. Up-to-date information on opening dates, times and admission charges can be obtained from local tourist board offices, or can be found in the following annual publications:
GARDENS OF ENGLAND AND WALES OPEN FOR CHARITY - THE NATIONAL GARDENS SCHEME CHARITABLE TRUST (popularly known as the 'Yellow Book')
HISTORIC HOUSES, CASTLES AND GARDENS IN GREAT BRITAIN AND IRELAND

ABBREVIATIONS USED IN REFERENCES

CAL.CLOSE R.: Calendar of Close Rolls (Public Record Office)
CAL.INQ.P.M.: Calendar of Inquisitiones Post Mortem and other analogous documents (Public Record Office)
CAL.PAT.R.: Calendar of Patent Rolls (Public Record Office)
P.S.A.N.H.S.: Proceedings of the Somerset Archaeology and Natural History Society
SOMERSET C.R.O.: Somerset Archive and Record Service, Obridge Road, Taunton
S.D.N.Q.: Somerset and Dorset Notes and Queries
S.R.S.: Somerset Record Society
V.C.H.: The Victoria History of the County of Somerset

ILLUSTRATION ACKNOWLEDGEMENTS and COPYRIGHT

Michael Aston: *figs. 4.15, 5.15, 5.16*
Rob Bell: *fig. 6.18*
James Bond: *figs. 3.3 (redrawn P. Webb), 3.4, 4.8, 4.9, 4.10, 4.11 (redrawn P. Webb), 5.3, 5.8 (redrawn P. Webb), 5.10, 5.13, 6.5, 6.9 (redrawn P. Webb), 6.15, 7.2 (redrawn P. Webb), 7.3, 7.4, 7.7, 8.4, 8.5, 8.7, 8.8, 8.11, 8.12, 8.13, 8.14, 8.16, 8.18, 8.19, 8.20, 8.21, 8.23, 8.26, 8.29, 8.32, 8.35, 8.37, 9.3, 9.4, 9.15, 9.16, 9.17*

Tina Bond: *figs. 4.1, 9.2*
Cambridge University Collection of Air Photographs: *fig. 4.13*
Martin Charles, © Philip White: *cover, figs. 9.1, 9.6, 10.9, 10.10, 10.11*
David and Charles: *fig. 8.2*
Lady Gass: *fig. 6.1*
Frances Griffith: *fig. 4.12*
John Harvey: *fig. 4.6 (redrawn P. Webb)*
Kit Houghton: *fig. 8.22*
Russell Lillford: *figs. 7.17, 8.9, 9.8, 9.14, 9.18, 10.6*
Tom Mayberry: *figs. 8.1, 8.28*
National Portrait Gallery: *figs. 7.10, 7.23, 9.5*
National Trust: *fig. 6.14*
Ordnance Survey: *figs. 3.6, 7.22, 8.31, 10.7*
RCHME: *figs. 5.14 (redrawn P. Webb), 6.8*
RCHME National Monuments Record: *fig. 8.33, 9.7*
Geoff Roberts: *fig. 10.8*
Somerset Archaeological and Natural History Society: *figs. 2.1, 3.2, 4.3, 4.4, 4.5, 4.7, 5.5, 5.6, 5.7, 6.2, 6.7, 6.17, 7.19, 8.3, 8.6, 8.10*
Somerset County Archive and Record Service: *figs. 3.5, 3.7, 5.18, 6.1, 6.3, 6.12, 6.16, 7.5, 7.13, 7.18, 7.21, 7.26, 8.24, 8.25, 8.27, 8.30*
Somerset County Council: *fig. 7.14*
Somerset County Council Studies Library: *figs. 5.9, 5.19, 6.6, 6.13*
Iris Hardwick, © Somerset County Council Studies Library: *page 2 (frontispiece), figs. 7.1, 7.6, 7.15, 8.15, 9.9, 9.10, 10.1, 10.2, 10.3*
Peter Webb: *figs. 1.2, 10.5*
West Air Photography: *figs. 8.17, 10.13, 10.14*
Robert Winn: *page 1, figs. 1.1, 3.1, 3.8, 4.14, 6.21, 6.22, 7.12, 8.36, 9.12, 9.13, 10.4, page 171*
Whitworth Art Gallery, The University of Manchester: *fig. 7.9*

Chapter 1

An INTRODUCTION to the HISTORY of SOMERSET PARKS and GARDENS

A COUNTY OF
CONSIDERABLE
NATURAL BEAUTY ...
IN ITS RICH VARIETY
OF NATURAL
LANDSCAPE AND
SOILS, SOMERSET
OFFERS AN
ENORMOUS RANGE
OF PLANT HABITATS
AND THE POTENTIAL
FOR AN EQUALLY
WIDE RANGE OF
GARDEN STYLES.

The NATURE of PARKS and GARDENS

There are few parts of England where gardens and parks do not make a significant contribution to the landscape. To many visitors from abroad the loving care devoted to colourful, fragrant cottage gardens, manicured suburban lawns and even window-boxes and hanging baskets seems a peculiarly English characteristic; while at the other end of the scale, the great Georgian landscape park, mimicking natural scenery but never to be mistaken for it, was one of England's most distinctive contributions to European culture, widely imitated but never surpassed.

Is this delight in gardens and parks a comparatively recent phenomenon developed over the last couple of centuries, or does it have its roots in a more distant past? Certainly attitudes towards gardens and parks have always reflected the needs and aspirations of society as a whole; and as the tastes and requirements of all classes, from great landowner to small cottager, have evolved and changed, so has the form and character of the parks and gardens in their care.

What is the difference between parks and gardens? Today we would perhaps make three distinctions. One criterion is size: there is a general assumption that a park is bigger than a garden, though most of us would be hard pressed to define a precise threshold between the two. A second distinction might be that we feel a garden somehow to be more intensively cultivated than a park, with a greater variety of plant species, though again this assumption might prove difficult to justify if specific examples were examined. Finally there is the question of ownership and accessibility: parks tend to be thought of today as public grounds available for the recreation of all, whereas gardens seem to be more private, designed for the intimate enjoyment of their owners.

None of these distinctions necessarily applies over a longer time-span. If we examine the development of parks and gardens over a period of centuries, their sheer variety of form and function may surprise us. The very purpose of the park, in particular, has undergone some major transformations. Today we tend to think of parks as public open spaces in towns and suburbs, with playing-fields and lawns, ornamental exotic trees and brightly-coloured flower beds, gravel paths, wooden seats and municipal waste-paper baskets. In the eighteenth century, however, the park was essentially an expanse of private ground providing a 'natural' landscape setting for a great house of the aristocracy or gentry, with sloping pastures, clumps and belts of native deciduous trees, and perhaps a lake. In the Middle Ages the park was even more exclusive and even less visibly managed, an uncultivated tract of rough wooded pasture enclosed within a paling fence to provide sustenance, cover and protection for the lord's herd of deer; and woe betide any trespasser or poacher discovered therein.

Gardens embrace an even greater variety, from the basic subsistence plot of the medieval peasant growing a few vegetables and herbs for the pot, to the Victorian pleasure-garden with its eclectic mix of architectural elements and exotic plants garnered from all corners of the globe. Between these two extremes there is a whole range of specialised gardens - physic gardens growing medicinal herbs, botanic gardens developed for the scientific study of plants, nursery gardens distributing trees and shrubs to customers, kitchen gardens supplying fruit and vegetables to the great house, allotments providing the same for the town-dweller, pleasure-grounds designed for the dalliance of the wealthy.

Cutting across these manifold functions are the ever-changing concepts of design, with the tide of fashion alternating between the imitation of nature and the imposition of strict formality. Although Britain is an island, it has never been immune to influences from abroad, and at various times France, Italy, the Low Countries and even India, China and Japan have contributed something of their own distinctive styles to the design of parks and gardens in England.

The SOMERSET LANDSCAPE

A visitor eager to see something of the greatest English parks and gardens would probably not immediately head for Somerset. It is not a county dominated by great estates, and it contains nothing comparable in scale with Blenheim, Stowe or Chatsworth. Nevertheless, it has a wealth of more modest mansions and country houses, and it contains gardens and parks of virtually every style and period, including some outstanding examples which deserve to be much better known.

Somerset is a county of considerable natural beauty, with a long and varied coastline. Its inland scenery is characterised by several ranges of hills, each of very different character, separated by flat lowland basins. In its rich variety of natural landscape and soils, Somerset offers an enormous range of plant habitats, and the potential for an equally wide range of garden styles.

In the north the principal range of hills is the Mendip upland, a windswept plateau of Carboniferous Limestone 3-6 miles wide from north to south, extending from the coast at Brean Down inland for some 30 miles. The Mendip Hills rise steeply from near sea level to an average height of 800-900ft, the highest point being Beacon Batch above Burrington at 1,065ft. They are honeycombed with natural caves, and the edges of the hills are etched by gorges, the most spectacular and best-known of which is at Cheddar. North of Mendip more limited outcrops of the same limestone form the hills between Congresbury and Backwell, the Failand ridge and the coastal hills along the western side of the Gordano valley between Portishead and Clevedon. The intervening lowlands, which include the flat moors of the northern levels, are for the most part based upon the red Triassic marls, but there are also important outcrops of Pennant Sandstones and Coal Measures around Nailsea, Keynsham, Pensford and Clutton.

The middle part of Somerset is predominantly flat, but is divided into two separate basins by the low but persistent ridge of the Polden Hills. Between Mendip and the Poldens the central levels are a vast area of reclaimed marshland, drained by the Rivers Axe and Brue, with a few islands of higher ground, including Wedmore and Glastonbury. The Polden ridge itself runs westwards from Street to the Parrett estuary at Down End. It is formed by a south-facing scarp of Liassic limestone, never rising more than 330ft above sea level, and never more than a couple of miles wide. South of the Polden Hills the Southern Levels, which include Sedgemoor, are drained by the River Parrett and its tributaries, the Cary, Yeo, Isle and Tone. Here too there

Fig. 1.1
An old oak tree at DUNSTER.

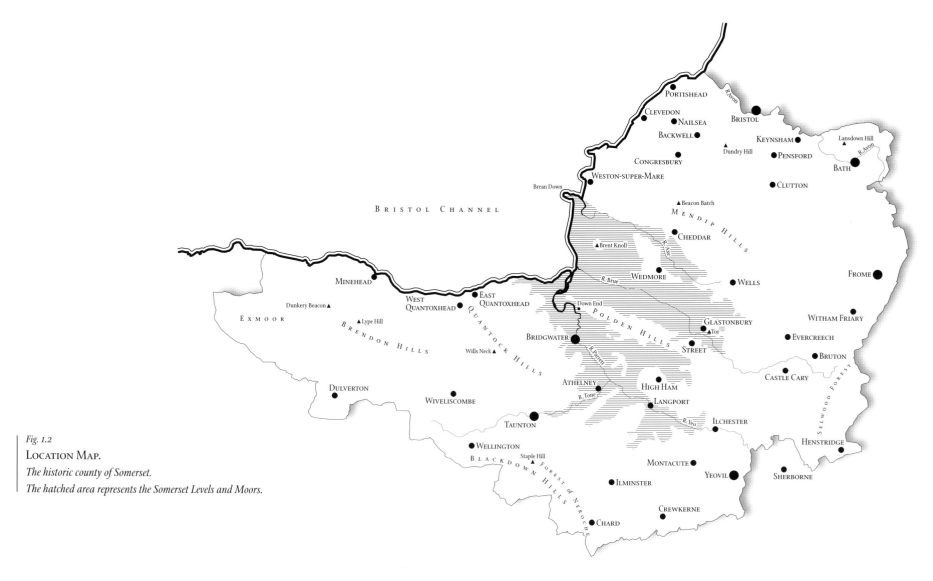

Fig. 1.2
LOCATION MAP.
The historic county of Somerset.
The hatched area represents the Somerset Levels and Moors.

are a few islands of higher ground, including the hills around High Ham and the low ridge of Athelney. The waterlogged nature of the Levels is the product of a combination of factors, including the high rainfall and runoff from the surrounding hills and the constricted outlet to the sea caused by the exceptionally high tidal range within the Bristol Channel. Deposits of marine clay along the coast rise up to 20ft higher than the peat moors further inland. Despite the best efforts of drainage engineers from Roman times through to the present day, winter floods still regularly drown thousands of acres of land in this region.

West of the River Parrett the landscape is dominated by three successive ranges of hills, all based upon the Devonian Old Red Sandstone. First, the Quantock Hills run north-westwards from near Taunton to the coast at East and West Quantoxhead. The Quantocks are a range of attractive rolling hills, part cultivated, part wooded and part open, rising to 1,260ft at Will's Neck near West Bagborough. The Doniford valley separates the Quantocks from the Brendon Hills, a region of magnificent natural scenery with its highest summit at 1,390ft on Lype Hill. In the far west, beyond the wooded valley of the River Exe, extending into Devon, lies Exmoor, the highest and bleakest part of Somerset, rising to 1,705ft above sea level on Dunkery Beacon.

South of the Quantock Hills lies the rich and fertile Vale of Taunton Deane, underlain by red Triassic marls, drained by the River Tone. The southern bounds of Taunton Deane are limited by the steep wooded face of the Blackdown Hills, a ridge of infertile Greensand

rising to 1,035ft on Staple Hill. The Blackdowns more or less form the Somerset boundary between Wellington, Chard and Crewkerne.

East Somerset is more like a miniature version of the scarplands of the English midlands. The clays of the Lower Lias form a shelf of good farming country south and east of the Southern Levels extending from the Forest of Neroche through Ilchester north-eastwards as far as Evercreech. These clays are overlain further east by the Middle Liassic Marlstone, an orange-brown iron-rich stone outcropping between Castle Cary and Montacute, where the villages resemble those of parts of north Oxfordshire and Northamptonshire. Around Yeovil the soft yellow Yeovil Sands form a particularly distinctive type of scenery, with the roads sunk into hollow ways 15ft or more deep. The Cotswold Hills reach their southern limit on Lansdown Hill, rising some 753ft above the northern suburbs of Bath, but the creamy-grey Oolitic Limestone which gives such a distinctive character to the field walls and buildings of the Cotswolds continues in a narrower band southwards through Frome and Bruton towards Sherborne. Outliers of these rocks, isolated by erosion, form several prominent detached hills further west amongst the levels and lowlands. The largest is Dundry Hill, south of Bristol, 764ft high, which is capped by the Inferior Oolite, while the smaller hills of Brent Knoll and Glastonbury Tor are formed by outliers of the Middle and Upper Lias. Further east still, the dip slope of the Oolitic Limestone hills gives way to a narrow band of Cornbrash, then to a wider belt of Oxford Clay extending from Henstridge to Witham Friary. Somerset's eastern boundary abuts Wiltshire along the high, infertile Greensand ridge forming the core of Selwood Forest.

The variety of natural scenery is matched by an equivalent variety of soil types, in particular a wide range of pH values (a measure of the degree of acidity). Broadly the sandstones of west Somerset provide a range of dry acid soils, turning to wet acid soils on the higher ground of Exmoor and the Blackdowns. Dry calcareous soils are more common in north and east Somerset, especially on the Mendip and Cotswold Hills and the outcrops of Lower Lias Limestone. The soils of the clay belts in the south-east are mainly neutral. Acid peat soils occur on the low-lying peat moors of the Levels.

The range of plants which can be grown on this variety of soils is further enhanced by the mild winters. Somerset enjoys a maritime climate without extremes of temperature. Air frosts are rare after April or before late October. Warm winds blowing off the Atlantic and the influence of relatively warm coastal waters mean that winter temperatures remain significantly higher than in the eastern counties where cold winds blow in from continental Europe. It is rare for snow to lie on the ground for more than five or six mornings in the year at sea level, though this may increase to ten or twenty mornings on Exmoor, where the average temperature may be colder by three degrees Celsius. In common with other western regions, it is relatively wet. Some 20-30ins of annual rainfall can be expected over much of Somerset, though on Mendip the total may rise to over 50ins, and on the higher parts of Exmoor it may be as much as 100ins. At the same time the orientation of the coast protects it from the worst of the south-westerly gales, though gales can still be expected on average between five and ten days a year, and on occasions can be savage. The worst natural disaster ever recorded in Somerset was the great storm of 26th-27th November 1703, when a combination of gale force winds, torrential rain and high tide devastated much of the county, tearing up trees and flooding thousands of acres. In more recent years, the famous hurricane of 16th October 1987, which ravaged other southern counties, left this region relatively less damaged; but Somerset's parks and gardens suffered much more in the late January and late December gales of 1990, which brought down hundreds of trees and smashed glasshouses.

The CHANGING GARDEN

With all its natural advantages of soil and climate, much of the Somerset landscape has been settled and cultivated for thousands of years, and so we should anticipate a correspondingly long and varied history of gardening and parkland management. However, parks and gardens represent a particularly specialised form of land use and, compared with agricultural landscapes, many of their features are relatively ephemeral. The dominant components of most gardens are their individual plants and trees, and these have a finite life. In an agricultural landscape a limited range of field crops may be planted and harvested year after year, and over a period of decades or even centuries there may be little significant change in its appearance. Within the smaller and more specialised compass of a garden, the cycle of plant growth, maturity and eventual death exerts a much more profound visual impact. No garden ever stands still. However

carefully tended it may be, the inevitable growth and loss of critical trees and plants cannot avoid altering its appearance in fundamental ways. Yet, even if it were possible to achieve stability, new ideas and fashions would still dictate that gardens respond to change.

As in so many other aspects of life, the pace of change has been greater within the past two hundred years than at any earlier time. We would not expect to find any Roman or medieval gardens surviving and still cultivated in the same way. The formal gardens of the Tudor and Stuart periods likewise are widely believed to have suffered total destruction at the hands of Capability Brown and his imitators in the later eighteenth century. It is difficult today even to find good surviving examples of Victorian and Edwardian garden schemes. If the present character of gardens is so dominated by relatively recent changes, is there any hope of being able to discover or to reconstruct their appearance at earlier periods?

SOURCES for GARDEN HISTORY

In fact a whole cornucopia of methods of investigation is now available to us, and we should consider their possibilities and limitations before moving on to apply them to the study of gardens in Somerset.

1. MANUSCRIPT and PRINTED SOURCES. One important group of written sources is concerned with the nature and uses of individual plants. Herbals describing the supposed medicinal virtues of plants had been compiled in classical antiquity, and the early Greek and Roman sources were repeatedly copied and modified in the medieval monasteries. With the advent of printing such information could be disseminated much more widely. The earliest printed herbal in Europe was published in Naples in 1477, the first English example in 1525. Two of the most important English printed herbals of the sixteenth century were produced by authors with strong Somerset connections, William Turner, Dean of Wells, and Henry Lyte of Lytes Cary (see Chapter 5). The advent of the new technology was soon followed by the awakening of a new interest in the science of botany. The hackneyed repetition of medical recipes and the recital of the healing powers of plants as an article of faith slowly gave way to more objective and scientific modes of study and description.[1]

The sixteenth century also saw an outpouring of treatises on the theory and practice of gardening and landscaping, which sometimes include valuable, if idealised, illustrations of contemporary garden layouts. In the early eighteenth century architectural pattern-books began to provide models for garden buildings and ornaments. By the later eighteenth century gardening journals were beginning to appear, providing information on plants and practical tips on their cultivation.[2]

Collections of private estate papers may include original garden designs, building accounts, bills of purchases from nurseries and planting records. Antiquarians and historians such as the Somerset writers Gerard, Collinson and Phelps sometimes provide incidental historical information on parks and gardens in the county, though this was not their primary interest.[3] Travellers such as John Leland in the mid-sixteenth century, Celia Fiennes in the late seventeenth century, and Dr Richard Pococke in the mid-eighteenth century recorded their subjective impressions of the parks and gardens which they visited on their journeys.[4] Garden guidebooks also provide a valuable source of information: the earliest English example was a guide to Stowe issued in 1744.

2. MAPS. Maps do not become a prolific source of information until after the late sixteenth century. The early county maps of Somerset produced by Christopher Saxton (1575) and John Speed (1611) are on too small a scale to show gardens, but they do show numerous parks, many of them deer parks surviving from the Middle Ages. The later county maps, such as those of Day & Masters (1782) and Christopher Greenwood (1822) provide greater accuracy and more detail.[5]

Larger-scale privately-commissioned estate maps also begin to appear in the late sixteenth century, reflecting the rise of the professional surveyor and the contemporary technical advances in surveying equipment. These sometimes include very detailed portrayals of park and garden layouts, though with varying standards of accuracy.[6]

The Ordnance Survey maps, which were first published for Somerset at a scale of one inch to one mile in 1809-30, provide through their successive editions a valuable record of changes in the extent and internal design of parks over the past century and a half; a service greatly enhanced with the first appearance of maps on a scale of six inches and twenty-five inches to the mile in 1882-8.

3. ILLUSTRATIONS. The tradition of making illustrations of houses set in their gardens can be traced back to Renaissance Italy. From there the fashion spread to France and, more particularly, the Low Countries. By the mid-sixteenth century Dutch artists were beginning to make some contribution in England. The outbreak of the Civil War interrupted progress, but after the Restoration there was a considerable influx of Dutch artists. Particularly important were Leonard Knyff (1650-1721), who produced well over 70 bird's-eye prospects of English country seats, including several in Somerset, and Johannes Kip (1653-1722), who made engravings from many of Knyff's drawings. Their pictures often provide a vivid and graphic impression of great formal gardens which have since entirely vanished. Such sources need to be used with some caution, since there must have been a temptation for the artist to flatter his patron by making the gardens appear even grander than they were in reality. However, where Knyff's or Kip's illustrations can be checked against independent evidence, they often appear remarkably accurate.

By the 1720s English owners were coming to appreciate the prestige which the depiction of their property could give them, and English artists such as John Harris, Thomas Robins, John Wootton and George Lambert came into their own. Several later artists worked in Somerset, including William Tomkins (d.1792), John Inigo Richards (d.1810) and Samuel Jackson (1794-1869). The historical value of garden paintings is almost in inverse proportion to the reputation of the artist: local men of modest ability tended to illustrate what they saw, whereas those of greater fame and accomplishment, like Gainsborough, Constable and Turner, were more interested in producing fine works of art.[7]

4. ARCHAEOLOGICAL SURVEY. Abandoned parks and gardens are not always wholly expunged from the landscape, and their remains are susceptible to investigation by a wide range of archaeological techniques Although the garden flora are the most transient component, some of the more vigorous plants may survive as naturalised escapes for years, decades or even centuries after their deliberate cultivation has ceased. Sooner or later subsequent land use is likely to eliminate such plants, but in special circumstances, such as the island environment of Steep Holm, a case can be made for a relict vegetation surviving in part from the Middle Ages. Trees have a longer life-span than shrubs and flowering plants, and themselves provide a habitat for other species such as lichens, which themselves can provide information about the age and stability of their environment, a technique of special value in the investigation of old parkland.[8]

The framework of a formal garden was often made by substantial earth-moving operations to create prospect mounts, parterres, terraces and ponds. Long after formal gardens fell out of fashion and ceased to be maintained, these features are likely to survive as grassy earthworks which can be surveyed on the ground.[10] Such sites were hardly recognised by archaeologists before the late 1960s, but Somerset contains some notable examples (see Chapter 5). Park walls, gates, lodges, garden buildings and other associated structures may also survive, and will repay detailed examination and recording.[11]

Aerial photography is another technique which can be used to discover and to record the remains of abandoned gardens. Low-level oblique photographs taken under conditions of early morning, evening or winter sunlight are especially valuable in the recording of earthwork sites. A light dusting of snow, or drought conditions, may provide additional information. High-level vertical photographs, often taken initially for non-archaeological purposes, are of special value in the study of the wider landscape of parks, enabling the site to be appreciated as a whole in a way never possible from ground level.[12]

Geophysical prospection techniques such as resistivity survey or magnetometry provide a means of detecting sub-surface structures and disturbances such as large flower-beds, surfaced paths, foundations of garden buildings and infilled ponds without excavation. Experiments have also been carried out with a variety of soil analysis techniques.[13]

5. ARCHAEOLOGICAL EXCAVATION. The potential of archaeological excavation as a technique for the investigation of garden history has also only recently been realised. High costs mean that excavation can only be undertaken in exceptional circumstances, but its value has already been demonstrated locally by the excavation of the Georgian garden of no.4 The Circus, Bath, prior to its restoration (see Chapter 6).

Excavation can provide a wide range of information. Elements of the garden plan - paths, bedding trenches, bed edging, statue bases, ponds - can be recovered. A chronology and sequence can be established for changes in layout. The artefacts of garden cultivation - tools and equipment, ceramic articles such as drains and plant pots, lead plant markers - can also be recovered and studied, along with domestic refuse which may throw considerable light upon the social and economic status of the garden's owners.[14] Conventional dating techniques through artefact evidence can in some circumstances be reinforced by scientific techniques such as dendrochronology.

Finally, environmental sampling has enormous potential. The study of bones, invertebrate and insect remains can provide a picture of the past ecology of a garden. Pollen, seeds, fruit stones and other plant remains which may be preserved in waterlogged conditions or by carbonisation or mineralisation can be recovered and identified. The hazards of survival and contamination and the problems of recovery and identification do, nevertheless, present many difficulties in interpretation. Acidic soil conditions likely to preserve pollen do not favour the survival of bones, snailshells or insect remains. Cultivated plants were often discouraged from seeding while the garden was in use, so weeds tend to predominate in the seed record. Pollen deposits also often give a misleading impression, being dominated by the prolific dispersion from wind-pollinated trees which may be some distance outside the garden, whereas brightly-coloured garden flowers are usually insect-pollinated and produce little pollen.[15]

APPROACHES to PARK and GARDEN HISTORY

Like any other aspect of landscape study, the understanding of parks and gardens requires a multi-disciplinary approach. The skills of the plantsman, the landscape architect, the documentary historian and the archaeologist offer quite different perspectives, and the synthesising of their different approaches is not always easy. As the most recent, and often the most expensive contributor (because of the range of scientific back-up required), the garden archaeologist has been faced with a particular need to justify his existence, especially when working upon apparently well-documented sites. Yet the excavator is in closer touch with the physical reality of his subject than any theoretician, and has on more than one occasion shown that the detailed plans drawn up on paper by the designer were modified in significant ways by the builders and gardeners working on the ground. For the earlier centuries of garden development, archaeology may be the only effective source we have. All the approaches described above have something to contribute, and in our exploration of the evolution of Somerset parks and gardens we shall, therefore, employ as wide a range of sources and techniques as are available to us.

Garden history and garden archaeology are still relatively new and lively fields of study. The following chapters attempt to summarise our present state of knowledge, but it can be anticipated with confidence that some parts of this book will soon become out of date. Historical research, notably by the staff of the Victoria County History, and archaeological field work by local groups and individuals, will continue to produce more information on known sites and to identify further sites which had not previously been recognised, while the work of the Somerset Gardens Trust now provides a new focus for the promotion of interest in the protection, conservation and management of local gardens.

REFERENCES - Chapter 1

1.   Wilfrid Blunt & Sandra Raphael, THE ILLUSTRATED HERBAL (1979).
2.   Early works on the theory and practice of gardening include Thomas Hill, A MOSTE BRIEFE AND PLEASAUNT TREATYSE TEACHING HOW TO DRESS, SOWE AND SET A GARDEN (1563) and THE PROFITABLE ART OF GARDENING (1568); the same author, under the pseudonym Didymus Mountain, THE GARDNER'S LABYRINTH (1571, 1586); Gervase Markham, THE ENGLISH HUSBANDMAN (1613); William Lawson, A NEW ORCHARD AND GARDEN (1618); John James, THE THEORY AND PRACTICE OF GARDENING (1728); Batty Langley, NEW PRINCIPLES OF GARDENING (1728) and POMONA, OR THE FRUIT GARDEN ILLUSTRATED (1729). Early gardening journals include William Curtis's BOTANICAL MAGAZINE (1787-1984), Henry Andrews's BOTANIST'S REPOSITORY (1797-1815), John Claudius Loudon's GARDENER'S MAGAZINE AND REGISTER OF RURAL AND DOMESTIC IMPROVEMENT (1826-44), Joseph Paxton & Joseph Harrison's HORTICULTURAL REGISTER AND GENERAL MAGAZINE (1831-6) and George Glenny's GARDENER'S GAZETTE (1837-44)
3.   The PARTICULAR DESCRIPTION OF THE COUNTY OF SOMERSET DRAWN UP BY THOMAS GERARD OF TRENT IN 1633, ed. E.H. Bates (S.R.S. Vol.15, 1900); John Collinson, THE HISTORY AND ANTIQUITIES OF THE COUNTY OF SOMERSET (3 vols, Bath, 1791); William Phelps, THE HISTORY AND ANTIQUITIES OF SOMERSETSHIRE (2 vols,1836, 1839).
4.   LELAND'S ITINERARY IN ENGLAND AND WALES, ed. Lucy Toulmin Smith, 5 vols (1907); THE JOURNEYS OF CELIA FIENNES, ed. Christopher Morris (1947); THE TRAVELS THROUGH ENGLAND OF DR RICHARD POCOCKE, ed. James Joel Cartwright (2 vols, Camden Soc., 1888, 1889). Daniel Defoe and John Byng, who left valuable accounts of their journeys elsewhere in Britain, travelled little in Somerset.
5.   The Day & Masters and Greenwood maps have been reprinted as SOMERSET MAPS, ed. J.B. Harley & R.W. Dunning, S.R.S. Vol.76.
6.   Maps of the northern part of Somerset are conveniently listed in Avon County Council's CATALOGUE OF HISTORIC MAPS IN AVON (undated). Somerset Record Office holds an unpublished catalogue of its own map collections.
7.   John Harris, THE ARTIST AND THE COUNTRY HOUSE (1979).
8.   C. Taylor, THE ARCHAEOLOGY OF GARDENS (Princes Risborough, 1983).
9.   F. Rose, 'Lichenological indicators of age and environmental continuity in woodlands', in D.H. Brown, D.L. Hawksworth & R.H. Bailey (eds), PROGRESS AND PROBLEMS IN LICHENOLOGY (1976); for a local example of this approach, see Francis Rose & Pat Wolseley, 'Nettlecombe Park: its history and its epiphytic lichens: an attempt at correlation', FIELD STUDIES, Vol.6 (1984), pp.117-148.
10. Paul Everson, 'Field survey and garden earthworks', in A.E. Brown (ed.), GARDEN ARCHAEOLOGY (Council for British Archaeology, Research Report no.78, 1991), pp.6-19.
11. Paul Woodfield, 'Early buildings in gardens in England', in Brown (ed.), GARDEN ARCHAEOLOGY, pp.123-137.
12. D.R. Wilson, 'Old gardens from the air', in Brown (ed.), GARDEN ARCHAEOLOGY, pp.20-35; Robert Croft & Michael Aston, SOMERSET FROM THE AIR: AN AERIAL GUIDE TO THE HERITAGE OF THE COUNTY (Somerset County Council, 1993).
13. A useful review of archaeological techniques is provided by C.K. Currie & M. Locock, 'An evaluation of archaeological techniques used at Castle Bromwich Hall, 1989-90', GARDEN HISTORY, Vol.19, no.1 (1991), pp.77-99.
14. Stephen Moorhouse, 'Ceramics in the medieval garden', in Brown (ed.), GARDEN ARCHAEOLOGY, pp.100-117.
15. Peter Murphy & Robert G. Scaife, 'The environmental archaeology of gardens', in Brown (ed.) GARDEN ARCHAEOLOGY, pp.83-99.

Fig. 2.1
A Tessellated Pavement
*of a Roman villa near Nunney
showing plant pots.*

Chapter 2

PREHISTORIC and ROMAN GARDENS

THE CONCEPT OF THE PLEASURE GARDEN WAS WELL ESTABLISHED IN THE ROMAN WORLD ...
EVEN IN THIS FAR-FLUNG CORNER OF THE EMPIRE, GARDENS WERE REGARDED AS PART OF
THE ESSENTIAL EQUIPMENT OF THE MOST ELABORATE VILLAS.

Prehistoric Cultivation

Somewhere around 5000 BC the beginnings of a significant change to the natural vegetation can be detected in many parts of Britain, as intermittent clearances appeared within the primeval forest, accommodating grazing domesticated livestock and the first cultivated crops. By about 1000 BC the landscape had been cleared of much of its virgin woodland, and a network of scattered settlements with extensive field systems had developed.

Before the beginnings of farming man had fed himself by hunting, fishing and collecting wild fruits and nuts, and these activities continued to supplement the diet long after the raising of crops and livestock had become established. Hazelnuts have been found in several neolithic contexts in Somerset.[1] The first important cultivated crops were varieties of wheat and barley: cereal pollens appear in peat deposits in the Levels from the late Bronze Age, and carbonised grain has been recovered from Iron Age hill forts such as Worlebury near Weston-super-Mare and Small Down near Evercreech.[2]

The fullest record of man's exploitation of the local vegetation comes from the waterlogged sites of the Somerset Levels and Moors. Here the Iron Age lake villages of Meare and Glastonbury have produced evidence for the collection and cultivation of a wide variety of plants [3] Wheat and barley were the principal cereal crops. Oats, rye, chess (*Bromus secalinus*), vetches and edible plants of the goosefoot family such as melde or fat hen (*Chenopodium album*) and common orache or ironfoot (*Atriplex patula*, useful also for orange dye) are also present, though it is not clear whether these were deliberately planted or whether they occurred as cultivation weeds. Celtic bean (*Vicia faba minor*) has been reported not only from the Meare and Glastonbury lake villages, but also from the Worlebury hill fort and from Wookey Hole. Plants of the cabbage family are often difficult to tell apart from their archaeological remains, but the Glastonbury lake village has produced traces of what may be the native annual black mustard (*Brassica nigra*) which may have been used as a green vegetable or grown for the oil obtainable from its seeds. Wild fruits such as apple, sloe, wild cherry, blackberry, dewberry, elderberry, strawberry and wild rose hip were collected, along with hazel nuts; acorns could also have been eaten in times of need. Other wild plants like mint, thyme or watercress would have been available to give flavouring to otherwise unappetising meals.

While many of the plants used in Britain before the Roman invasion were native species, some were certainly introductions. None of the cultivated cereals have any native forebears, and all have an ultimate source in Anatolia and the Fertile Crescent. Flax is also a native of the middle east, but the large-seeded summer annual form appears in Britain in the Iron Age, and is known from the Meare lake village. It was probably cultivated initially for the food value of its oily seeds rather than for its fibre. By the early first century BC wine was regularly imported through southern coastal settlements like Hengistbury (Dorset), and the depiction of vine-leaves on certain Iron Age coins raises the possibility that the grape itself had already been introduced successfully before the Roman invasion.

Almost as soon as man began to make permanent settlements, the thought of growing a few useful plants close at hand to supplement the crops brought in from the fields may have occurred to him. Many prehistoric settlements include small enclosed plots adjoining the houses, some of which might bear interpretation as gardens. It has to be admitted that the evidence for gardening remains slender. Most of the plants used were either field crops or fruits and nuts collected from the wild. However, the planting of a few valuable food plants and dye plants conveniently near the dwelling remains an attractive notion; and who can say whether their growers may not also have found some enjoyment in the colours and foliage that they produced?

Roman Villa Gardens

The concept of the pleasure garden was well-established in the Roman world. The settled conditions which prevailed over much of the empire by the first century AD allowed those in favoured social positions more time for leisure and entertainment. The climate of the Mediterranean, with its reliable long warm summers, encouraged people to spend their leisure time out of doors, and gardens came to be furnished with as much care as interior rooms. The Roman skill in water engineering made possible the introduction of ornamental ponds and fountains and irrigation pipes for watering gardens. The works of Roman writers such as Varro (116-27 BC), Columella (1st century AD), the elder Pliny (c.AD 23-79) and younger Pliny (c.AD 61-113), provide much information on contemporary gardens, which can be amplified by the pictorial record of wall-paintings and the evidence from excavations at Pompeii, Herculaneum and the villas destroyed by the eruption of Vesuvius in AD79. Roman gardens on the continent tended to be formal in layout, with a strongly architectural character, using rows of trees, low hedges, statues, and ponds.[4]

While some adjustments had to be made for the harsher climate of Britain, there are signs that, even in this far-flung corner of the empire, pleasure-gardens were regarded as part of the essential equipment of the most elaborate villas. Archaeological excavations carried out at Fishbourne (Sussex) revealed an elaborate formal garden laid out within the collonaded courtyard during the second half of the first century AD. This early date is, however, exceptional. Elsewhere in the province, up until the late third century, most villas appear to have been little more than superior farmhouses. While they may have had small kitchen gardens, orchards and even flower-gardens, such features have left little trace and have rarely been detected.

In the late third and early fourth centuries, however, there is widespread evidence for the investment of new capital in country houses and rural estates. The courtyard villa plan, in which the residential ranges are grouped around an inner court, then makes its appearance. It seems likely that in many cases, as at Fishbourne, the open space thus enclosed would have been used as an ornamental garden rather than a farmyard, and several examples have come to light in southern Britain.[5]

North and north-east Somerset have one of the densest concentrations of villas in Britain, especially around Bath, in the Avon valley and the Vale of Wrington, and there are also significant

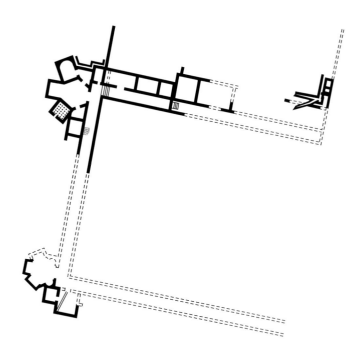

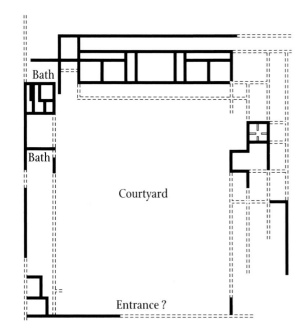

Bath

Bath

Courtyard

Entrance ?

left: Fig. 2.2
KEYNSHAM *Roman courtyard villa*
(after Bulleid, 1925).
right: Fig. 2.3
WELLOW *Roman courtyard villa*
(after VCH).

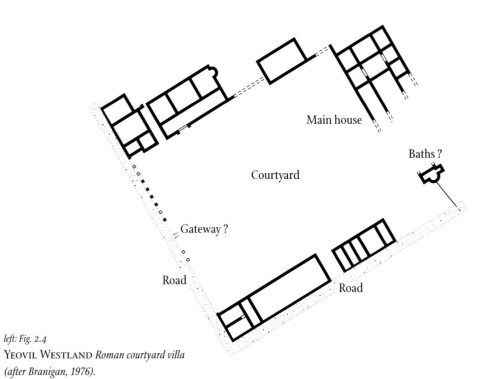

Main house

Baths ?

Courtyard

Gateway ?

Road

Road

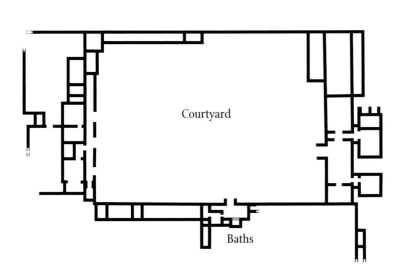

Courtyard

Baths

left: Fig. 2.4
YEOVIL WESTLAND *Roman courtyard villa*
(after Branigan, 1976).
right: Fig. 2.5
PITNEY *Roman courtyard villa*
(after VCH).

North

Scale 0   10   20   30   40   50   60   70 feet

concentrations elsewhere in Somerset, notably around Ilchester.[6] The courtyards of some Somerset villas were very large indeed: the biggest, at the palatial villa at Keynsham, measured 217ft by 170ft, but this is rivalled by others at Pitney (210ft x 150ft) and Wellow (200ft x 160ft).[7] Unfortunately, though understandably, most excavations carried out in the past have concentrated upon the villa buildings; their courtyards either remain wholly unexplored, or were dug before the potential for the survival of garden details was realised.

Even when garden features were excavated, their true identity may not have been recognised at the time. The Pitney villa had a large courtyard with the house at the west end and two long narrow ranges flanking either side of the courtyard, that on the north 75ft long x 8ft wide internally, that on the south 12ft wide. In both cases the thickness of the walls suggests that these ranges were of two storeys. They have provisionally been interpreted as farmhands' and slaves' quarters or as pigsties. However, more recently Christopher Taylor has questioned this view on the grounds that the placing of such unsavoury structures in such a position relative to the main front of the house seems inherently unlikely. As an alternative he suggests that their interpretation as some sort of garden pavilions should be considered.[8]

Several Roman villas in other parts of Britain have produced evidence for long rectangular ornamental fishponds aligned parallel with or perpendicular to the main wing of the house; more purely functional examples for storing and breeding fish for the table have also been recognised.[9] No examples have so far been noted on any of the Somerset villas, but their presence as garden features may yet come to light in future surveys or excavations.

In addition to their ornamental gardens, Roman villas are also likely to have had kitchen gardens, orchards and perhaps vineyards. A number of villas lay within larger enclosures which seem likely to have included orchards and vegetable plots. Examples include the Lye Hole villa in the Vale of Wrington, which stood within a rectangular enclosure of a little over 4 acres, and Gatcombe, where the gardens are

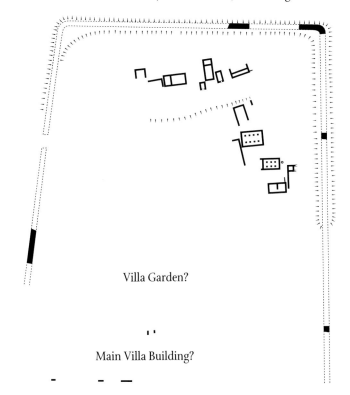

Villa Garden?

Main Villa Building?

presumed to have lain between the supposed villa and its service outbuildings, all within a walled enclosure of at least 18 acres.[10]

ROMAN TOWN GARDENS

Ornamental gardens were not limited to rural villas. Many Roman towns in Britain contained sufficient space for private gardens, and there is both structural and environmental evidence for town gardens in London and Silchester.

Of the Roman towns in Somerset the spa and religious centre of Bath and the cantonal capital of Ilchester both contain the sort of spacious and well-appointed town houses with tessellated pavements and hypocausts which one might expect to have been set within pleasure-gardens. Unfortunately many of the older archaeological discoveries are inadequately recorded, both towns (unlike Silchester) are complicated by medieval and later occupation, and even recent excavations have rarely been on a sufficiently extensive scale to stand much chance of recovering structural evidence of gardens.

The smaller towns, such as Camerton, Charterhouse-on-Mendip and Shepton Mallet, all included houses set within enclosures, some of which which may be gardens of a more workaday character. Again, however, there is as yet no positive evidence for this interpretation.

GARDEN PLANTS of ROMAN BRITAIN

Finally, the evidence from palaeobotanical studies must be considered. In favourable conditions waterlogged sediments may preserve a range of macroscopic plant remains, fruit stones, nut shells, seeds and pollen. A well at the Low Ham villa contained fragments of hazel and pear or crab-apple wood, hazelnuts, walnuts, cones of the stone pine (*Pinus pinea*), stones of wild plum, sloe and common hawthorn, and seeds which include culinary herbs and drug plants such as marjoram, vervain and opium poppy as well as common weeds of cultivated ground such as knotgrass, field woundwort and chickweed.[11] At the Chew Park villa plant remains from the well and elsewhere included wood and charcoal from hazel, ash, oak, beech, sweet chestnut, hawthorn, holly, dogwood and maple, leaves and bark of box, seeds of elder and pear, cherry and plum stones, stone pine cones, walnut shells and twigs and thorns of rose.[12] Neither at Chew Park nor at Low Ham is there any direct evidence for an orchard or garden. While it seems likely that most of the plants listed were grown locally, the possibility that some of the plant material was imported also has to be taken into account. Kernels of the stone pine, for example, which were used in cooking, have turned up on other Roman sites in Britain. However, the tree itself is a native of southern Europe, and it is not known precisely when it was first grown in this country, where it remains uncommon. Similar doubts surround the significance of the fig seeds and almond stones found on Roman sites elsewhere in Britain. For some of the fruit species it is not easy to distinguish introduced cultivated varieties from wild forms already present before the Roman occupation.

By contrast with the two villa sites, the plant remains from the 1974-5 excavations in the town of Ilchester and the 1979 excavations

Fig. 2.6
A plan of GATCOMBE *villa showing the extent of the enclosure (after Branigan, 1976).*

Scale 0   50   100 150 200 250feet

in the rural village of Catsgore were almost exclusively of cereals, weeds of cultivated ground and wild plants associated with hedges and ditches, and there was little evidence for the garden crops which might have been expected.[13]

The local evidence is insufficient to provide any adequate picture of the plants available for garden use in the third and fourth centuries, and to achieve this we need to cast our net wider. The first attempt to provide a scientific overview of the plant data for Roman Britain was included in Sir Harry Godwin's magisterial survey, the economic implications of the newly-introduced species have been discussed by Shimon Applebaum, while an assessment of the environmental data for garden and orchard crops from Roman Britain has recently been provided by Murphy & Scaife.[14] New flowering plants probably included the violet, recorded as a wild plant in early post-glacial levels but then apparently lost until it was reintroduced for garden use during the Roman occupation. Varieties of rose, the madonna lily, columbine, ox-eye daisy and pansy may also have been grown. Kitchen-garden vegetables included radish, pea, celery, cucumber, cabbage, white mustard, parsnip, turnip and carrot, possibly also onion and leek. Several pot-herbs of Mediterranean origin, including marigold, coriander, fennel and dill, are known from Roman contexts in Britain. Opium poppies seem to have been grown for their seed.

Britain was relatively well-endowed with native wild fruits before the Roman conquest. Apple, pear, cherry, plum, damson, bullace, sloe and raspberry are all represented in prehistoric contexts. However, in several instances the Romans may have introduced improved domesticated varieties. Pliny, for example, records that cherry was introduced into Britain in AD 47, and cherry wood or cherry stones have been found on a number of Roman sites in Britain, including Chew Park. Medlar and mulberry, identified at Silchester, may be new introductions of the Roman period. Blackberry is well-represented in Roman contexts, but was probably then, as now, collected from the wild rather than cultivated. As suggested above, the grape may have made its first appearance in southern Britain even before the Roman conquest. Grape pips have been found on a number of Roman sites, sometimes in contexts which suggest that they were cultivated locally.

Trees and shrubs known from Roman sites and often claimed as Roman introductions include the walnut, the sweet or Spanish chestnut, the horse chestnut, the holm oak, the plane and the box, though in several cases the evidence remains controversial. The walnut does particularly well in west Somerset, and one specimen near Cothelstone had achieved a height of nearly 95ft, a spread of 81ft and a girth of 18ft shortly before 1897, when it was blown down.[15] Particular problems surround the date of introduction of the sycamore, which has been claimed as a Roman import on the basis of some rather insecure recognitions of its remains in archaeological contexts. There are occasional oblique and inconclusive indications that the tree was known in England in the Middle Ages. However, sycamore does not appear in the documentary record until 1578, when Henry Lyte of Lytes Cary listed it as a garden tree in his *Herball*. Most authors today accept it as a sixteenth-century introduction and dismiss any possibility of its being present in the Roman period.[16]

Although it is impossible as yet to produce any definitive plant list, it seems certain that the native flora was considerably enriched by imported species during the Roman occupation, and that the new plants were grown for both practical and ornamental purposes. Further enlargement of our understanding of Roman gardens will depend upon future archaeological work.

The End of Roman Britain

Around the end of the first decade of the fifth century Britain's links with the imperial government were finally sundered, and the administration of the province devolved upon local communities. Western Britain escaped the first brunt of the Anglo-Saxon incursions, and there is every reason to suppose that the basic fabric of local Roman society suffered little immediate disturbance. Certainly there is no evidence for the wholesale destruction of the local Roman towns and villas, or for the mass slaughter of their inhabitants. For a generation or more Roman gardens may still have been tended by the descendants of those who had enjoyed the last years of imperial rule, and in some cases the basic framework of Roman estates may have survived considerably longer. However, the style of life which had permitted the leisure for enjoyment of elaborate gardens, and the opportunities for the replenishment of garden stock were both breaking down. Gradually the ornamental grounds were abandoned and the less hardy plant introductions probably soon disappeared from cultivation.

REFERENCES - Chapter 2

1. Leslie Alcock, *'By South Cadbury is that Camelot': Excavations at Cadbury Castle, 1966-70* (1972), p.112; Bryony & John Coles, *Sweet Track to Glastonbury: the Somerset Levels in Prehistory* (1986), pp.59-60.

2. Harry Godwin, 'Correlations between climate, forest composition, prehistoric agriculture and peat stratigraphy in Sub-Boreal and Sub-Atlantic peats of the Somerset Levels', *Philosophical Trans.*, B.233 (1948), 275; Hans Helbaek, 'Early crops in southern England', *Proc.Prehistoric Soc.*, new ser., Vol.18 (1952), pp.194-233.

3. A. Bulleid & H. St.George Gray, *The Glastonbury Lake Village* (2 vols, Glastonbury, 1911, 1917); A. Bulleid & H. St.George Gray, *The Meare Lake Village*, Vol.1 (Taunton, 1948); H. St.George Gray & A. Bulleid, *The Meare Lake Village*, Vol.2 (1953); G. Jones, 'The carbonised plant remains', in B.J. Orme, J.M. Coles, A.E.Caseldine & G.N. Bailey, 'Meare Village West, 1979', *Somerset Levels Papers*, no.7 (1981), pp.33-36; G. Jones, 'The carbonised plant remains from Meare West, 1979: 2', in *Somerset Levels Papers* no.12 1986), pp.57-60; R.A. Housley, 'The carbonised plant remains from Meare, 1984', in J.M. Coles (ed.), Meare Village East: the Excavations of A. Bulleid and H. St.George Gray, 1932-1956, *Somerset Levels Papers*, no.13 (1987), pp.226-228.

4. Elisabeth Blair MacDougall & Wilhelmina F. Jashemski (eds), *Ancient Roman Gardens* (Dumbarton Oaks Colloquium on the History of Landscape Architecture, no.7, Washington, 1981); E.B. MacDougall (ed.), *Ancient Roman Villa Gardens* (Dumbarton Oaks Colloquium no.10, Washington, 1987).

5. Barry Cunliffe, 'Roman gardens in Britain: a review of the evidence', in MacDougall & Jashemski, *Ancient Roman Gardens*; R.J. Zeepvat, 'Roman gardens in Britain', in A.E.Brown (ed.), *Garden Archaeology*, pp.53-59.

6. K. Branigan, 'Villa settlement in the West Country', in Keith Branigan & P.J. Fowler (eds), *The Roman West Country: Classical Culture and Celtic Society* (Newton Abbot, 1976), pp.120-141; Keith Branigan, *The Roman Villa in South-West England* (Bradford-on-Avon, 1977); Roger Leech & Peter Leach, 'Roman town and countryside, 43-450 AD', in Michael Aston & Ian Burrow (eds), *The Archaeology of Somerset* (Somerset County Council, 1982), pp.62-81; Stephen Bird, 'Roman Avon', in Michael Aston & Rob Iles (eds), *The Archaeology of Avon* (Avon County Council, 1987), pp.52-71.

7. Arthur Bulleid & Dom Ethelbert Horne, 'The Roman house at Keynsham, Somerset', *Archaeologia* Vol.75 (1924-5), pp.109-138; for Wellow and Pitney see F.J. Haverfield, 'Romano-British Somerset', *V.C.H.* Vol.2 (1906), pp.312-4, 326-7.

8. Shimon Applebaum, 'Peasant economy and types of agriculture', in C.Thomas (ed.), *Rural Settlement in Roman Britain* (Council for British Archaeology, Research Report no.7, 1966), p.102; Christopher Taylor, *The Archaeology of Gardens* (Princes Risborough,1983), p. 8.

9. R.J. Zeepvat, 'Fishponds in Roman Britain', in M. Aston (ed.) *Medieval Fish, Fisheries and Fishponds in England* (British Archaeological Reports, British Series no.182.i, Oxford,1988), pp.17-26.

10. P.J. Fowler, 'Fieldwork and excavation in the Butcombe area, North Somerset', *Proc.Univ.Bristol Spelaeological Soc.*, Vol.12, pt.ii (1970), pp.169-194; K. Branigan, *Gatcombe: the Excavation and Study of a Romano-British Villa Estate, 1967-78* (British Archaeological Reports no.44, Oxford, 1977).

11. H. Godwin, 'Plant remains from a well at Low Ham', *S.D.N.Q.*, Vol.27 (1957), p.157.

12. P.A. Rahtz & E. Greenfield, *Excavations at Chew Valley Lake, Somerset* (Dept.of the Environment, Archaeological Report no.8, 1977), pp.363-9.

13. Peter Murphy, 'Plant remains from Roman deposits at Ilchester', in Peter Leach, *Ilchester, Vol.1: Excavations, 1974-1975* (Western Archaeological Trust, Excavation Monograph no.3, 1982), pp.286-290; Martin Bell, 'Environmental Report', in Peter Ellis, *Catsgore, 1979: Further Excavation of the Romano-British Village* (Western Archaeological Trust, Excavation Report no.7, 1984), pp.37-41.

14. Sir Harry Godwin, *The History of the British Flora: a Factual basis for Phytogeography* (Cambridge University Press, 1956, 2nd edn, 1975); Shimon Applebaum, 'Roman Britain', in H.P.R. Finberg (ed.), *The Agrarian History of England and Wales*, Vol.1 part ii: AD 43-1042 (Cambridge, 1972), esp.pp.108-21; Peter Murphy & Robert G. Scaife, 'The environmental archaeology of gardens', in A.E. Brown (ed.), *Garden Archaeology*, esp.p.88, table 8.2

15. E. Chisholm-Batten, 'The forest trees of Somerset', *P.S.A.N.H.S.* Vol.36 (1890), ii, pp.186-9; J.C. Cox & W.H.P. Greswell, 'Forestry', *V.C.H.* Vol.2 (1911), p.571

16. E.W.Jones, 'Biological flora of the British Isles: Acer L.', in *Jnl.of Ecology*, Vol.32 pt.ii (1944), p.215; Oliver Rackham, *The History of the Countryside* (1986), pp.56-7.

Chapter 3

MEDIEVAL DEER PARKS in SOMERSET

HUNTING CAME TO ASSUME A NEW
IMPORTANCE AMONG THE ARISTOCRACY
IN THE EARLY MIDDLE AGES ...
INCREASING NUMBERS OF DEER PARKS ARE
RECORDED DURING THE TWELFTH
CENTURY, THE PEAK PERIOD OF CREATION
FALLING WITHIN THE SECOND HALF OF
THE THIRTEENTH CENTURY.

THE REVIVAL OF HUNTING

Although remnants of Roman provincial culture lingered on for some decades after the withdrawal of the imperial administration, the economy became disrupted by barbarian raids and political uncertainty, and the population appears to have been reduced by pestilence. Some tracts of land which had formerly been under cultivation, particularly in marginal locations, now began to fall out of use. As Roman coastal defences and drainage works broke down through lack of maintenance, reclaimed parts of the Levels reverted to marshland. Elsewhere scrub and woodland recolonised abandoned fields. In such areas of secondary wilderness deer, boar and other game flourished.

Hunting had long since ceased to be essential for subsistence purposes, but it had remained popular as a recreation throughout the Roman period. Depictions of the chase appear on certain types of Roman pottery. The villa at East Coker included two tessellated pavements, one portraying two dogs chasing a deer and a hare, another depicting two men returning from a successful hunt, both carrying spears, with a dead deer slung from a pole carried across their shoulders, and a dog barking at their feet.[1]

Hunting came to assume a new importance among the aristocracy in the early Middle Ages, largely because it served as a training for another aristocratic pursuit which required the same skills of strength, stamina, horsemanship, use of weapons and eye for country - the art of warfare.

ROYAL FORESTS, CHASES and WARRENS

There were four distinct types of hunting preserve in the Middle Ages. Our main concern here will be with *parks*, pieces of wooded pasture usually less than 1,000 acres in extent, which were enclosed as private deer preserves. However, these need to be seen against a background of more extensive hunting grounds, unenclosed but nevertheless delimited by defined boundaries.

The most important of these were the *royal forests*, areas administered by crown officials under the special code of Forest Law, which was designed to protect the king's right to hunt certain beasts like deer and wild boar. There were five royal forests in Somerset: Exmoor in the far west, North Petherton in the Parret valley, (perhaps a remnant of a once larger upland hunting preserve centred on the Quantock Hills), Mendip in the north, Neroche in the south and Selwood in the east, extending into Wiltshire. Some forests, like Selwood, did contain extensive woodland within their bounds, but others, like Exmoor and Mendip, were largely open. The precise area of land under Forest Law fluctuated, reaching its greatest extent under Henry II (1154-89), but progressively contracting between the early thirteenth and mid-fourteenth centuries. The designation of a royal forest did not eliminate other forms of land use, cultivated fields and whole villages frequently being included within its bounds.[2]

Chases were also extensive areas reserved for hunting, the distinction being that chases belonged not to the king, but to great nobles or ecclesiastical magnates. Often they were former royal forests where the king had granted away his hunting rights to others.

Fig. 3.2
Return from a successful hunt: a tessellated pavement from the Roman villa at EAST COKER.

Keynsham and Filwood Chases in north Somerset had been taken out of the Gloucestershire forest of Kingswood in the thirteenth century and were held as a perquisite of the office of constable of Bristol Castle.[3]

Finally, *warrens* were areas where local lords were licensed by the king to hunt small game on their own estates: hare, rabbit, woodcock, pheasant and partridge could be hunted for the pot, while fox, wildcat, badger, marten, otter and squirrel could be hunted as vermin. The hare was the principal beast of the warren and, in one unique case, the royal warren of Somerton was administered under Forest Law because, in that open, cultivated countryside, the hare had the status of a sort of honorary deer.[4] Sometimes the acquisition of rights of warren seem to be a prelude to emparking: in 1256, for example, a charter of free warren for Wiveliscombe was obtained by Bishop William Bitton, followed in 1330 by an emparking licence granted to the prebend. Elsewhere in Somerset emparkment followed grants of free warren at Castle Cary, Huish Episcopi, Chaffcombe, Aley, Nettlecombe, Stockland Lovell and Staple Fitzpaine.[5]

The hunting of wild birds with hawks cannot be explored here in detail; but it is of some passing interest that one of the earliest western European treatises on falconry covering the training and care of hawks was compiled in the twelfth century by the Somerset-born cleric Adelard of Bath.[6]

PARKLAND DEER

Three species of deer were available for stocking parks in the Middle Ages. *Red deer* were the larger and more widespread of the two native species. They thrive as well on open moor as in wooded countryside, and in the Middle Ages they were numerous on the upland forest of Exmoor, where they survive today. They are also recorded from some of the larger royal parks, such as North Petherton. Elsewhere, however, their numbers appear to be in sharp decline after the thirteenth century, perhaps as a result of agricultural encroachment into the waste and woodland and consequent reduction in their natural habitats.

The other native species, *roe deer*, were also occasionally found in parks. In 1232, for example, Godfrey de Crocombe was given six roebucks from Powerstock Forest and six more from Newton Park for stocking the park of Beercrocombe.[7] Roe deer, too, had become scarce in southern England by the fifteenth century, partly because the spread of coppicing restricted access to the hazel which formed an important part of their diet, and perhaps also because of their exclusion from the protection of Forest Law in 1338.

The *fallow deer* is a native of southern Europe, and there is little evidence for its presence in Britain before the late eleventh century. Documentary records indicate its rapid spread after the Norman Conquest, and faunal remains from kitchen middens underline its increasing importance in the aristocratic diet. Fallow deer were especially suited to being kept in parks: they are gregarious by nature, able to fatten on poor land, need little attention, breed readily, are less dangerous than red or roe deer in the rutting season, will graze alongside cattle, and produce excellent venison. Fallow deer also soon escaped from parks to establish themselves in the wild in most parts of Somerset, failing only to colonise the bleaker uplands of Exmoor.

The MANAGEMENT and EXPLOITATION of DEER

Parks, if properly managed, were able to support large herds of deer, and were efficient producers of venison. A later writer recommends two bucks and one doe to three acres of parkland, though in practice ratios of a half to two head per acre were commonly used.[8] The numbers could be increased by a variety of means: reducing the woodland cover, improving the quality of the grass, bringing in supplementary feed and regular restocking with deer imported from elsewhere.

Red and roe deer were normally hunted on horseback across the open country of forests, chases and warrens. Royal parks sometimes served as reserves to ensure that game was available when needed, with individual deer being released into the forest whenever the king wished to hunt. Relatively few parks were large enough to permit the fallow deer to be hunted on horseback within their bounds. Parkland deer were more regularly killed by beaters driving them past archers standing on foot. In fact the use of parks as live larders was generally far more important than their occasional use for recreational hunting. The culling of the deer was frequently carried out by professional servants charged with the duty of supplying their employers with venison as and when required. Venison was valued as an item in the aristocratic diet, for it rarely appeared on sale in the open market, and its exclusiveness proclaimed the high social status of its consumer. It was probably always more important as a special item for feast days than as regular fare.

The royal records show that venison was regularly packed in barrels and salted by the crown servants and sent to the king wherever he happened to be. In 1238 and 1239 venison from Taunton Park was sent to the royal larder at Winchester for the Christmas feast. In 1248 the keeper of Newton Park received an order to allow the king's huntsmen to take five stags to be salted and sent to Winchester for Whitsuntide, the first of a string of similar orders over the next twenty-five years.[9] Occasionally considerable quantities were involved: in 1247 25 does taken in Bridgwater Park were carried to Westminster for the feast of St Edward.[10] Harts and bucks were usually taken between June and September, when at their fattest before the autumn rut, while hinds and does were usually taken in the winter. Conspicuously the king often failed to use the nearest source to the point of consumption, which may hint at increasing difficulties in ensuring a satisfactory supply.

All English kings hunted as a recreation, but they would also grant presents of surplus deer to their magnates and officials as a sign of favour. Live deer from the forests were often granted for the stocking of parks. In 1230-1 Bishop Jocelin was allowed eleven fallow does and one buck from Selwood Forest and further deer from Cheddar for his park at Bath. In 1252 Robert Musgrove received five bucks and ten does from Selwood to stock Brewham Park. In 1280 Roger de Amery was granted five bucks from Mendip Forest to replace five bucks which had escaped from his park at Ubley.[11] Less frequently transfers were made from park to park. Bridgwater Park on occasions supplied considerable numbers, including 50 bucks and 25 does destined for the various parks of Richard of Cornwall in 1234.[12] In 1281 Edward I granted the Bishop of Bath & Wells 20 bucks and does from Neroche Forest to stock his park at Buckland St Mary, but the keeper of Neroche failed to comply with the order, and on learning of this later in the year, the king granted him instead fifteen does and five bucks from Dunster Park for the same purpose.[13]

Grants of live deer involved catching them in nets and carrying them by cart, sometimes over considerable distances. King John had deer sent to replenish the depleted herd in Taunton Park from Hereford, a distance of over 110 miles by road. Even more remarkably, in 1225 Henry III granted William de Marisco ten live does and two bucks from Cheddar to take to the island of Lundy, a minimum of 10 miles overland and 75 miles by sea, or over 60 miles overland for the shortest sea crossing of 25 miles; whether this transfer was ever actually achieved remains a mystery.[14]

Poaching was a constant threat to parkland deer, and gave rise to numerous investigations, records of which are enrolled in the Patent Rolls. In 1355, for example, Sir John de Mohun lodged a complaint against nine individuals, including the parson of Selworthy and a man who had recently been his own parker at Minehead, for poaching deer and taking sparrowhawks from his parks at Dunster, Marshwood and Minehead and poaching hares, rabbits, partridges and pheasants from his warrens.[15] Even conviction did not always result in a fine: in 1311 William le Sengle of Somerton was pardoned for breaking into Cecily de Beauchamp's park at Compton Dundon because of his recent good service to the king in Scotland.[16]

ORIGINS and CHRONOLOGY of PARK CREATION

Although deer parks are usually held to be a product of Norman feudal society, the Anglo-Saxon landscape contained some provisions for trapping and enclosing deer: for example, a charter of King Athelstan granting land at Pitminster in 938 has attached to it a boundary perambulation which includes features named as the *haga* ('game enclosure') and *ealden haga* ('old game enclosure').[17] It has yet to be demonstrated whether any of these pre-Conquest game enclosures were the direct precursors of post-Conquest deer parks.

The only Somerset park to find mention in the Domesday survey is the park at Donyatt, held by Drogo from the Count of Mortain. What has sometimes been claimed as a remarkable record of 20 park-keepers (*parcarii*) at North Petherton in fact results from a misreading of the word *porcarii*, meaning 'swineherds'. However, a royal servant named Ansketil the Parker did hold land in Newton in North Petherton, so there is a case for including this important royal park also amongst the Domesday parks.[18]

The total number of medieval deer parks will probably never be known. Leonard Cantor, who undertook the first systematic modern enquiry, identified 72 examples in Somerset, 1900 examples in England as a whole. Subsequently Oliver Rackham has estimated that by 1300 there may have been something like 3,200 parks in England, occupying some 640,000 acres or two per cent of the entire land surface.[19] Investigations in Somerset have now pushed the total up to 105 examples which can be identified with reasonable confidence, but further local research will undoubtedly yield even more.

It was, in theory, necessary to obtain royal permission to enclose a park, since deer were held to be the property of the king; and it was especially advisable to do so if the park lay within or near an area designated as royal forest. Many emparking licences were enrolled in the Pipe Rolls and Close Rolls. However, in Somerset licences account for less than ten per cent of the total number of parks known in the Middle Ages. There were also large numbers of unlicensed parks which have been identified only through chance references in later documents, or by the evidence surviving in the landscape today. Imparking and disparking went on throughout the Middle Ages, and if it is difficult to determine the overall total, it is almost impossible to ascertain the number in use at any one time.

Increasing numbers of parks are recorded during the twelfth century, but the peak period of creation appears to have fallen within the second half of the thirteenth century, continuing up to the time of the Black Death. This increase to some extent corresponds with a contraction in the extent of countryside under Forest Law. The number of new parks created then tails off to the beginning of the sixteenth century.

As we have seen, licences form only a minority of first records of parks, and even these need to be used with caution as dating evidence. Sometimes they are clearly retrospective attempts to legalise a park already in existence, as at Nether Stowey in Somerset, where Peter de Columbariis received permission to have a park in 1248, which other sources show was already there by 1222.[20] Conversely, sometimes the licence represents a declaration of intent which might be long delayed in its fulfilment. When the manor of Cheddar was disafforested in 1337, Bishop Ralph and his successors were given licence to enclose its woods and to hold them as a park 'at their will'.[21] Emparking licences are most frequently encountered within the royal forests because they represent, in effect, a form of local disafforestation. In 1231, for example, Henry III permitted the Bishop, Dean and Chapter of Bath and Wells to disafforest the manor of North Curry so that its inhabitants should be quit of forest pleas and to

enclose its woods as parks, while in 1237 Henry de l'Orti acquired a licence to impark his woods of Curry Rivel in order to be exempt from the regard of the foresters of Neroche.[22] They provided a source of revenue to the Crown: in 1251 when Robert de Musgrove acquired a licence to enlarge Brewham Park, the charter records that William de Montacute had held this park in King John's time, but had allowed it to fall into decay because the price asked for the licence was too expensive.[23]

DISTRIBUTION and OWNERSHIP

Parks were particularly numerous in south Somerset, in the Vale of Taunton Deane, and along the coastal belt of west Somerset, particularly between the Quantock Hills and the River Parrett. There were lesser concentrations along the eastern and northern borders of the county. By contrast there were few examples on the open uplands of Exmoor, the Brendon Hills, Mendip, or on the flat lands of the Somerset Levels. It was the intermediate land in the vales, below the uplands and above the marshes, particularly where there were also significant extents of woodland and wood-pasture, which tended to attract the greatest concentrations of parks. The legal restraints of Forest Law are sometimes said to have inhibited park creation, and in North Petherton Forest the only parks were those belonging to the king. However, in less intensively used forests with more private demesnes, such as Neroche, the density of park distribution was not markedly reduced.

At parochial level the parks were often located on the most marginal land available, on the edge of the estate, distant from the manor-house, where they did not conflict with the needs of agricultural production; they were, therefore, often at some distance from the castle, palace or manor-house to which they belonged. The park of the Bishop of Winchester's manor of Taunton was actually located at Poundisford, some three miles south of the town and castle. There were, however, some conspicuous exceptions. The Bishop of Bath and Wells had sufficient power to commandeer much of the best-quality land at Westbury-sub-Mendip for his park, thereby forcing the inhabitants of the village to extend their cultivated fields by terraced strips high up over the southern face of the hills.

The king owned at least 150 parks in England at one time or another during the Middle Ages, though two-thirds of these lay within a radius of a hundred miles of London. The largest and most important royal park in Somerset was Newton or North Petherton Park, with a circuit of four miles. Other parks in royal hands for significant periods included Bridgwater and Queen Camel. The crown also had intermittent custody of many other parks, through confiscation, minority of heirs and other factors.

Episcopal owners were also prominent. The Bishop of Bath and Wells had at least ten parks in Somerset, the most important of which were at Bath, Banwell, Evercreech and Huish Episcopi. The Bishop of Winchester's manor of Taunton included the valuable park of Poundisford. Bishop Walter Stapledon of Exeter had a park at Norton Fitzwarren.

Glastonbury Abbey was the major monastic owner, with parks at Sharpham, Wirrall, Norwood, Pilton and Mells. The Abbot of

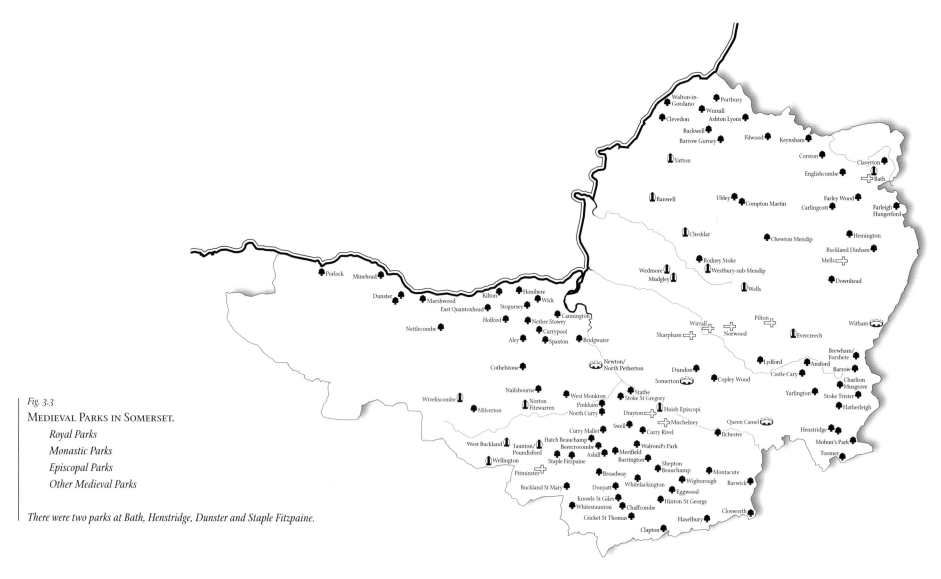

Fig. 3.3

MEDIEVAL PARKS IN SOMERSET.
  Royal Parks
  Monastic Parks
  Episcopal Parks
  Other Medieval Parks

There were two parks at Bath, Henstridge, Dunster and Staple Fitzpaine.

Muchelney had parks at Muchelney itself and at Drayton. The Prior of Bath acquired the western third of the bishop's park south-east of the town in the thirteenth century and the Prior of Taunton had a park on the edge of the Blackdown Hills above Pitminster, both reflected in modern place-names. The former home estate of Keynsham Abbey in 1544 contained a park and a pasture called the Coneyger.[24] There is little doubt that most of these were genuine deer parks. The involvement of clergy and monks in hunting was frowned upon by the church authorities and venison, in theory, found no place upon the monastic table. Many such institutions justified their ownership of parks by the entertainment they provided for important visitors, but it is evident that many abbots kept their own hawks and hounds and were not above indulging in the chase themselves. The abbot of Glastonbury was exempted by charter from the requirement to have his hounds lawed (deprived of three toes of the right foot) within the bounds of the forest of Gillingham.[25] The visitation of Keynsham Abbey carried out by Bishop Ralph of Wells in 1348 resulted in an order that canons who kept sporting dogs inside the monastery were to be punished by being deprived of meat for a month and of fish for a fortnight.[26] Sometimes, however, the passing of a deer park into monastic ownership did result in the cessation of its original function: at Montacute the park enclosed by the Count of Mortain before 1100 was granted to the Cluniac priory in 1192, but finds no mention in a survey of 1302-3.[27]

The secular nobility also owned numerous parks. John de Warenne, Earl of Surrey and Sussex, held two parks near Henstridge in 1347. The Earls of Salisbury had parks at Donyatt, Knowle St Giles and Yarlington in the fourteenth century.[28] However, the estates of the great barons had less stability, as their lands were more liable to change hands through marriage, confiscation and other factors. The majority of parks, particularly in the later Middle Ages, were held by minor local lords with modest estates.

SIZE AND SHAPE OF MEDIEVAL PARKS

Deer parks were very variable in size. Clarendon Park in Wiltshire, at 4,200 acres the greatest royal park in the south-west of England, would have dwarfed the largest parks in Somerset. North Petherton Park was a little over 1,000 acres, Witham about 790 acres and the larger of the two parks at Staple Fitzpaine about 740 acres. Most were of the order of 100-300 acres. The larger parks were clearly more economical in terms of maintenance costs per head of deer, and some authors see parks of less than 50 acres as status symbols rather than items of practical utility. Nevertheless, even a very small park could, with careful management, contain a worthwhile herd. Hatch Beauchamp Park, only 8½ acres in 1892 and much contracted since the Middle Ages, still then supported 40 head of fallow deer.[29]

Many parks were enlarged during their lifespan, some of them on more than one occasion. In 1251 Robert Musgrove acquired a licence to enlarge Brewham Park in Selwood Forest by the addition of two acres, which was to be enclosed by a hedge and ditch 120 perches long. The bounds are described in some detail, and have been reconstructed by Michael McGarvie using a combination of documentary research and fieldwork.[30] The park at Minehead, only 51 acres in extent in 1383, was enlarged by the Luttrells to 150 acres in 1428, and was estimated at 200 acres in 1551.[31] Another park which came into the hands of the Luttrells, that at Dunster, initially covered only the area known as 'the Hanger', the sloping ground north-east of the castle between the town and the River Avill, and part of the flat land beyond the river known as 'the Lawns'. The present deer park, covering a much larger area on the rising ground beyond the river south of the castle, is first mentioned in 1366, when both the Hanger and the 'New Park' were leased out for four years by Sir John de Mohun for the nominal annual rent of a rose. Some extension to the Hanger Park seems to have been carried out by Sir Hugh Luttrell, so that it contained 100 acres of pasture and wood worth 20s a year at his death in 1428.[32]

The creation or enlargement of parks frequently interfered with the course of pre-existing roads, a recurring problem through the centuries. In 1207, for example, Bishop Jocelin of Bath was permitted to enclose two parts of the king's highway within his park at Wells.[33] At Dunster the line of the old road from Gallox Bridge to Carhampton, blocked by the creation of the new deer park, can still be traced as a track and footpath. New parks might also have a significant impact upon the settlement pattern: Robert Dunning has pointed to the creation of the park at Nether Stowey as a likely reason for the isolation and decline of the Domesday vill of Budley.[34]

Archaeologically the most striking remains of deer parks are likely to be their boundary earthworks. Deer are capable of leaping considerable obstacles, so the park fences needed to be up to 6-10ft high, depending upon the slope of the ground, and needed to be well-maintained to prevent escapes. The maintenance of fencing was expensive. In older parks this was sometimes carried out by tenants as a labour service. In the early thirteenth century, for example, various tenants of Glastonbury Abbey had to put in so many days' work each year on repairing the ditch and palings of the abbot's park at Pilton, or had responsibility for maintaining specified lengths of the pale.[35] Tenants of the Bishop of Bath & Wells owed similar services for the maintenance of the park of Westbury-sub-Mendip in the same period.[36] In both cases the services were owed, not just by tenants in the immediate vicinity, but by the inhabitants of villages up to 18 miles distant.

The classic form of deer-proof boundary consisted of cleft-oak palings set on top of a bank and fastened to a rail, with a ditch inside the bank to inhibit deer inside the park from leaping the fence. In 1289 Queen Eleanor obtained a grant of 20 oaks from Selwood Forest in order to make palings to enclose her park at Queen Camel.[37] The burgage tenements on the east side of Dunster High Street were separated from the Hanger Park by a continuous paling in the fourteenth century, and in 1486 the borough court ordered "*that nobody shall henceforth break the palings of the lord's park, or carry them away, or have any gates or footpaths in the lord's park without licence, save the parker of the same*".[38] Remains of the banks and ditches can still be seen in many Somerset parks. Few examples have been examined by

excavation, although a section of the Poundisford Park boundary recorded in a water pipe trench revealed a severely truncated bank 20-26ft wide and 3-4ft high.[39] Massive boundary earthworks were by no means universal, however, and probably became less common in the later Middle Ages as labour costs increased. Marshwood Park was enclosed partly by a ditch and hedge and partly by a paling fence in the mid-sixteenth century, while ditch and hedge were specified in the emparking licences for Brewham in 1251 and Ashton Lyon in 1392.[40]

Sometimes the pale was set back from the boundary of the property, leaving a narrow band known as a 'freeboard', which was used to give access for inspection and repair. In 1279 a strip 7½ feet wide between the parks of Huish Episcopi and Drayton was the subject of a dispute between their respective owners, Bishop Burnell of Bath and the Abbot of Muchelney; this was resolved by an agreement that the strip was owned by the bishop, with rights of access to repair his park wall, but that the abbot's beasts would be permitted to graze there. A 1687 map of Marshwood Park notes the owners' rights to a 'verge' of 18ft outside the park.[41]

Stone walls were a more ostentatious form of boundary, and they were particularly favoured by the crown and by episcopal and monastic owners. However, they were even more costly to build and maintain, and did not become at all common until late in the Middle Ages. The expenses of the communar of Wells in 1448-9 included the hire of a labourer for three days and three waggonloads of stone to

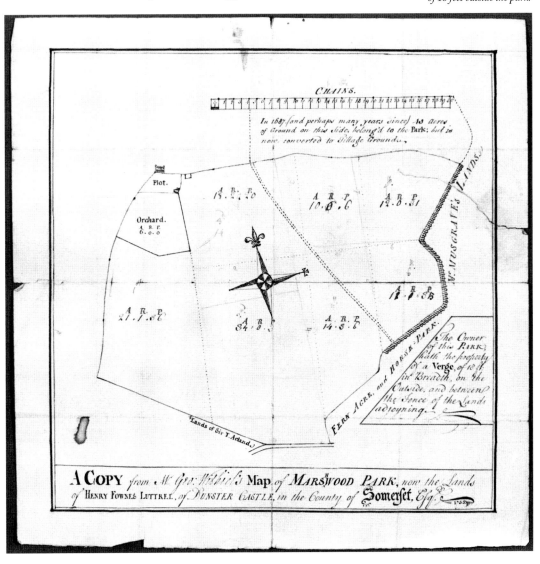

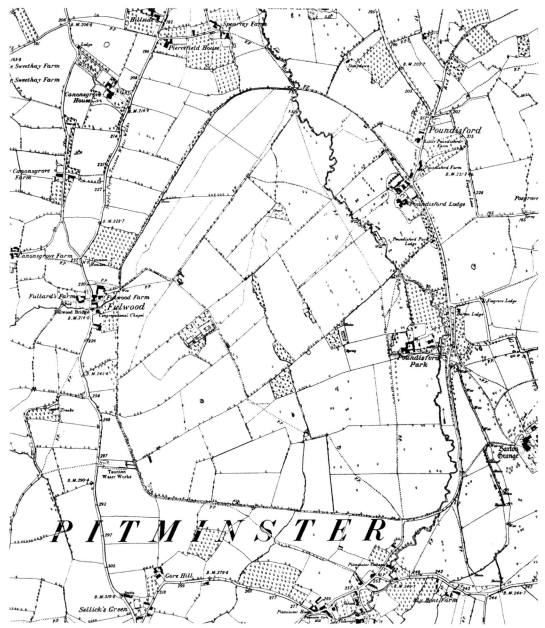

Fig. 3.6

POUNDISFORD PARK.
1st edition Ordnance Survey map of 1888 showing the oval park boundary.

make two ropes (1 rope = 20 feet) of park wall at Westbury-sub-Mendip. The paling fence separating the old park at Dunster from the town was replaced by a stone wall after the fifteenth century.[42] John Leland saw the two conjoined parks of the Bishop and Prior outside Bath in the sixteenth century, both then derelict and with their stone walls ruinous. Some fragments of the medieval boundary walls may survive along Popes Lane and below Rainbow Wood.[43]

The labour and expense involved in making and maintaining any sort of boundary meant that the optimum shape for a deer park was a perfect circle, to maximise the area of grazing while minimising the length of boundary. Parks laid out on the waste where there were no topographical constraints, such as the Bishop of Winchester's park at Poundisford, sometimes came close to this ideal. Extensions to the original circuit are often betrayed by sharp angles in the boundary. Examples with a more rectilinear outline, such as Mohun's Park at Henstridge, are often lesser manorial parks, created in the later Middle Ages and accommodated within an existing framework of agricultural boundaries.

Deer-leaps allowed deer to enter a park from the surrounding countryside, but not to leave it again. Their possession was a special privilege for which royal permission was normally required. In 1324 the Bishop of Bath & Wells received confirmation of an earlier charter permitting him two deer-leaps in each of his parks of Evercreech and Wellington, both of which lay outside the royal forest.[44] Deer-leaps were rarely permitted in private parks within or even near royal forests. An interesting case is recorded in 1367, when William Montagu, Earl of Salisbury, was requested to take deer from Neroche Forest for the king's table. During the hunt one buck escaped from the forest and entered Matthew Gurney's park at Curry Mallet, where there were two deerleaps. The forester followed it into the park to take it for the king, but was prevented from doing so by five local men, including the parson, who carried off the venison for their own use.[45]

PARKLAND PASTURE

The parks' primary purpose of raising deer was not incompatible with other forms of exploitation. Domestic livestock such as cattle and pigs could share the feed with the deer, provided that overgrazing did not occur, and income could therefore be obtained from agistments and pannage. Elsewhere in Britain, notably at Chillingham in Northumberland and Chartley in Staffordshire, there are distinctive strains of white cattle thought to be descended from native wild herds which had become confined to parks by the thirteenth century. At Leigh Court in north Somerset a white or fawn breed claimed to have descended from a herd owned by the canons of St Augustine's Abbey in Bristol survived up to 1806. The beasts were so savage that the owner then had them all shot, exterminating the only herd of wild park cattle known from south-west England.[46]

PARKLAND TIMBER and WOOD PRODUCTION

Despite the demand for grazing, timber production from parks appears to have increased in importance during the thirteenth century. As the extent of unmanaged woodland diminished through clearance, and as conserved woodlands became managed as coppices, it was only under the wood-pasture regime of parks that very large trees could still be found. Newton Park in North Petherton was the source of much timber granted away by the king : six *furcas* (? pairs of cruck blades) went to Godfrey de Crocombe for building a barn in 1230; a total of 70 oaks to the sisters of the Order of St John at Minchin Buckland in 1234 and 1236 to help with the rebuilding of their house after its destruction by fire; a total of 18 oaks to the Blackfriars of Ilchester in 1261; three oaks for the townspeople of Somerton to repair their belfry in 1278; and in the same year five oaks to the Greyfriars of Bridgwater towards the building of their dormitory.[47] In 1423 a row of shambles was built along the middle of the High Street in Dunster using timber from the Hanger Park there; these survived at least until 1800.[48] Timber was also supplied from Newton Park for fine woodwork: two oaks in 1232 for choirstalls at Cleeve Abbey, three oaks for making images for the abbey church of Glastonbury in 1250.[49]

Dead trees, windfallen wood and undergrowth provided fuel.

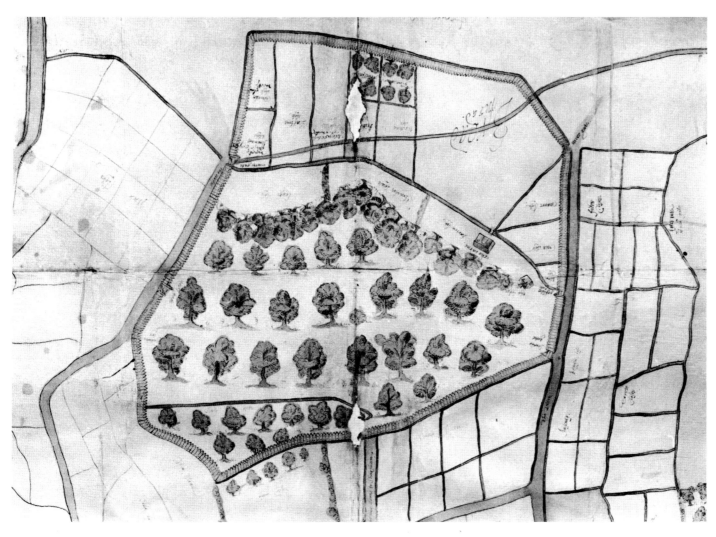

Fig. 3.7
SHARPHAM PARK, *near Glastonbury,*
from an early 17th century map.

In 1229 the sisters of Minchin Buckland received a series of grants of dead wood, thorn, buckthorn and maple from Newton Park for this purpose, grants often repeated in later years.[50] In August 1342 John de Mohun granted 12 cartloads of windfallen wood for fuel from Marshwood Park and the woods of Dunster to the monks of Bath, provided that the carts were not too large to be drawn by a pair of horses.[51] Similar grants could be documented from many other parks.

Vestiges of the ancient wood-pasture regime can still be identified in many former deer parks. Massive old pollard oaks with girths of 20ft or more, such as survive in the parks of Long Ashton, Dunster and Mells, are particularly characteristic. Parkland trees were often pollarded at 50- to 80-year intervals. This process not only produced a regular crop of wood while allowing new shoots to grow out of range of grazing livestock, but also had the effect of prolonging the life of the tree, sometimes to a great age. Another distinctive feature is their richness in lichen species: 122 different epiphytic lichen taxa have been recorded in Mells Park, 150 in Nettlecombe Park, including many which appear to be restricted to 'ancient' woodlands. By contrast, parks dominated by eighteenth- or nineteenth-century planting, such as Montacute or Orchardleigh, have only 50-60 different species of lichens and hardly any of the species believed to be diagnostic of ancient woods.[52]

Contrary to earlier opinions which viewed planted woodland as a sixteenth-century innovation, John Harvey has been able to document examples from a much earlier date, including some parkland planting. The Bishop of Winchester's pipe roll of 1210-11 records the expenditure of 2s on wages for 12 weeks' work in planting brook willows in Taunton (presumably Poundisford) Park.[53]

PARKS in the LATER MIDDLE AGES

In the immediate aftermath of the Black Death high labour costs may have restricted new emparking activities to the wealthiest landowners. On the other hand, the reduced population allowed more land to be taken out of cultivation. Two new trends may be observed. Enterprising individuals now had the opportunity to better themselves in a way that had never been possible before and, as a reflection of new patterns of landownership, new parks were created by people rising up the social scale. The later medieval parks were also characterised by more varied and flexible forms of land use. The reduction in rent income through famine and plague in the early fourteenth century had forced many landowners to reappraise the ways in which their estates were managed. The preservation of tracts of wood-pasture solely for deer may increasingly have seemed an unaffordable luxury, and some parks were abandoned entirely. However, if the deer could be accommodated alongside pasture for fattening farm stock and even some arable, the park could still be maintained. As early as the first half of the fourteenth century it was suggested that the 'launds' of Marshwood Park, comprising some 400 acres, should be ploughed and sown, with the remainder enclosed to contain the deer; and the writer expressed the view that if cowhouses and storehouse were established there, the park might be made to

Fig. 3.8
A pollarded oak tree at
SANDHILL, *near Taunton.*

yield more profit than the entire demesne of Dunster. Certainly grazing of cattle and horses could be accommodated alongside the raising of deer fairly easily. A case of poaching at Aley Park in Over Stowey in 1357 recorded that the malefactors had not only carried off most of the deer but also killed a steer, a foal, four oxen and two cows in the park.[54]

Oliver Rackham has estimated that about half the parks of medieval England included some form of compartmentation, reserving some areas for pasture and others for woodland.[55] In late medieval parks this is sometimes implicit in the original licence, as in 1412 when Thomas Beauchamp was allowed to impark 250 acres of land and wood in 'le Shawe' on his manor of Ashill by Neroche Forest, or in 1448 when William Carent imparked 80 acres of wood and 300 acres of land in Toomer and Henstridge.[56] The surveys of some of the Glastonbury Abbey parks at the Dissolution imply that they were compartmented: Norwood Park contained 800 deer and 172 acres of wood felled and sold on a sixteen-year rotation, while Sharpham Park included 160 deer, pasture for horses, 80 acres of oak, ash and maple coppice felled on a fourteen-year rotation, and 200 timber oaks.[57]

FISHPONDS

Deer needed water, and watercourses were often diverted to feed fishponds as an additional resource within the park. In the Hanger Park at Dunster a fishpond one acre in extent is mentioned several times in the fifteenth century: in 1417 Philip the Carpenter and his mate were paid 18s 4d for cutting stakes to enclose the stews, in 1420 live fish were brought from Bridgwater to stock the pond at a cost of 3s 9d, and again in 1423, live fish brought from Woolavington at a cost of 4s.[58] Many other examples are documented: a sixteenth-century map of Queen Camel shows a small moat and pond within the park.[59] The earthwork remains of fishponds can be seen in many other medieval parks, for example at Castle Cary, Merifield, Sharpham, Staple Fitzpaine and Stoke Trister, though their precise date often remains uncertain.[60]

RABBIT WARRENS

The rabbit is a native of the western Mediterranean, and in the eleventh century had only recently arrived in northern France. Like fallow deer, rabbits were almost certainly introduced to England after the Norman Conquest, and may not have appeared in Somerset before the thirteenth century. Rabbits were an attractive proposition for many landowners, because both their flesh and fur were of value, and they could be raised on a wide variety of terrain. The establishment of rabbit warrens inside parks offered another way of increasing their productivity in the late Middle Ages.

The most characteristic feature of the rabbit warren is the long rectangular artificial burrow for which the term 'pillow-mound' has been coined by archaeologists, but more widely known in the west country by the name 'rabbit buries'. Pillow mounds sometimes survive singly or in groups in parkland landscapes. There is an unusual cruciform example in Banwell Park.[61]

Fig. 3.9
A plan of BANWELL
cruciform pillow mound
(after Iles, 1984).

PARK LODGES

As mentioned earlier, the deer park could be up to three miles distant from the manor-house to which it belonged, so it was often equipped with a lodge which provided occasional shelter, storage and sometimes permanent accommodation for a parker. The lodge might be located by the entrance to the park, in its centre, or at the highest point within it, wherever a resident parker was best able to oversee the deer and defend them against poachers. The parker was a relatively minor official, so his accommodation was rarely very elaborate. Often all that survives of the lodge is a small moated site, such as can be seen at Forshete Park in Brewham.

However, in the later Middle Ages park lodges on larger estates were sometimes taken over by the lord and enlarged into sumptuous residences which were used as country retreats. In the mid-fourteenth century Ralph of Shrewsbury, Bishop of Bath and Wells, built what amounted to a full-scale palace in the park at Evercreech. Similarly, Abbot Richard Beere of Glastonbury rebuilt the lodges of Sharpham and Norwood Parks and used them as country residences.[62] In some respects this development anticipates the eighteenth-century concept of the grand country house surrounded by its landscaped grounds. Even in the Middle Ages it can be argued that the deer park, with its great trees, open glades, watercourses and fishponds, was appreciated for its scenic qualities as much as its practical and prestige value. By the later fifteenth century more and more landowners were coming to perceive their parks as an important amenity as well as an economic resource and status symbol. The older manor-houses, hemmed in by other properties in villages, with little room for the further development of gardens and ornamental grounds, seemed increasingly cramped and unattractive; whereas the isolated park lodge offered considerable potential for enhancement as a more important residence within its own grounds.

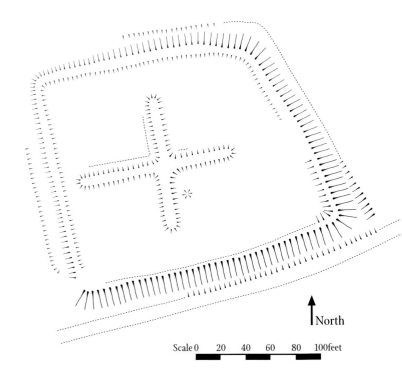

North

Scale 0   20   40   60   80   100feet

REFERENCES - Chapter 3

1. F.J. Haverfield, 'Romano-British Somerset', in *V.C.H.* Vol.1 (1906), pp.329-331).
2. W.H.P. Greswell, *The Forests and Deer Parks of the County of Somerset* (1905); J.C. Cox & W.H.P. Greswell, 'Forestry', in *V.C.H.* Vol.2 (1911), pp.547-572. Much of this chapter is adapted from James Bond, 'Forests, chases, warrens and parks in medieval Wessex', in Michael Aston & Carenza Lewis (eds) *The Medieval Landscape of Wessex* (Oxbow Monograph no.46, Oxford, 1994), pp.115-157, which offers a wider regional perspective.
3. Cox & Greswell, 'Forestry', p.567).
4. Cox & Greswell, 'Forestry', pp.552-3).
5. Wiveliscombe: Greswell, *Forests and Deer Parks*, p.249; *Cal.Pat.R.*, 1330-34, p.6; Castle Cary: W. Phelps, *The History and Antiquities of Somersetshire* (1839), i, p.379; *Cal.Inq.P.M.*, ix, no.665; Huish Episcopi: *Cal.Chart.R.*, i, 1226-57, p.469; Chaffcombe: *Cal.Chart.R.*, ii, 1257-1300, p.76; *V.C.H.* Vol.4, p.121; Aley: *Cal.Chart.R.*, iii, 1300-26, p.388; *Cal.Pat.R.*, 1354-8, p.616; Nettlecombe: Cox & Greswell, 'Forestry', p.570; Greswell, *Forests and Deer Parks*, pp.246-7; Stockland Lovell: *Cal.Chart.R.*, iii, 1300-26, p.45; *V.C.H.* Vol.4, p.112; Staple Fitzpaine: *Cal.Close.R.*, 1231-4, p.212; *Cal.Chart.R.*, i, 1226-57, p.391; R.A. Sixsmith, *Staple Fitzpaine and the Forest of Neroche* (Taunton, 1958), pp.7, 9-10, 14.
6. Louise Cochrane, *Adelard of Bath* (1994), pp.53-61.
7. *Cal.Close R.*, 1231-4, p.15.
8. E.P. Shirley, *Some Account of English Deer Parks, with Notes on the Management of Deer* (1867).
9. *Cal.Lib.R.*, i, 1226-40, pp.355, 431; iii, 1245-51, pp.183, 233; iv, 1251-60, pp.125, 291, 370, 467; v, 1260-67, p.100; vi, 1267-72, p.171.
10. *Cal.Close R.*, 1247-51, pp.11-12.
11. *Cal.Close R.*, 1227-31, pp.459, 572; 1251-3, p.144; 1279-88, p.32.
12. *Cal.Close R.*, 1231-4, p.494.
13. *Cal.Close R.*, 1279-88, pp.97, 143.
14. Greswell, *Forests and Deer Parks*, pp.9, 38; Cox & Greswell, 'Forestry', p.559.
15. Sir H.C.Maxwell Lyte, *A History of Dunster and of the Families of Mohun and Luttrell* (1909), ii, p.343.
16. *Cal.Pat.R.*, 1307-13, p.326.
17. The Pitminster charter bounds are recited in full in G.B. Grundy, 'The Saxon charters of Somerset', *P.S.A.N.H.S.* Vol.73-4 (1927-8), Supplement, pp.30-34.
18. *Domesday Book, Somerset*, ed. Caroline and Frank Thorn (Chichester, 1980), 19.24, 46.17.
19. Leonard Cantor, *The Medieval Parks of England: a Gazetteer* (Loughborough, 1983); Oliver Rackham, *Ancient Woodland: its History, Vegetation and Uses in England* (1980), p.191.
20. *Cal.Chart.R.*, i, 1226-57, p.330; R.W. Dunning, 'The origins of Nether Stowey', *P.S.A.N.H.S.* Vol.125 (1981), p.126 .
21. *Cal.Chart.R.*, iv, 1327-41, p.428.
22. *Calendar of the Manuscripts of the Dean and Chapter of Wells*, Vol.1, ed. W.H.B. Bird (1885), p.8; *Cal.Chart.R.*, i, 1226-57, p.104; *Cal.Close R.*, 1234-7, p.433.
23. *Cal.Pat.R.*, 1247-58, p.107; *Cal.Chart.R.*, i, 1226-57, p.357.
24. F.W. Weaver, 'Keynsham Abbey', *P.S.A.N.H.S.*, Vol.53 (1907), ii, p.52.
25. Quoted in T.H.M. Bailward's Presidential Address in *P.S.A.N.H.S.* Vol.50 (1904), i, p.21.
26. Weaver, 'Keynsham Abbey', p.45.
27. R.W.Dunning, 'Montacute', in *V.C.H.* Vol.3 (1974), pp.210, 216.
28. *Cal.Inq.P.M.*, ix, no.54, p.47, no.244, p.245; viii, no. 532, p.387.
29. Joseph Whitaker, *A Descriptive List of Deer Parks and Paddocks of England* (1892); Cox & Greswell, 'Forestry', p.570.
30. *Cal.Pat.R.*, 1247-58, p.107; *Cal.Chart.R.*, i, 1226-57, p.357; Michael McGarvie, 'Brewham: a Lost Park', *S.D.N.Q.* Vol.30 (1974), pp.60-63.
31. Lyte, *History of Dunster*, i, pp.159-60, ii, p.344; Hilary Binding & Douglas Stevens, *Minehead: a New History* (Minehead, 1977), pp.31, 44).
32. Lyte, *History of Dunster*, i, p.318; ii, pp.343-4.
33. Greswell, *Forests and Deer Parks*, p.249.
34. Dunning, 'Origins of Nether Stowey', *P.S.A.N.H.S.* Vol.125 (1981), p.126.
35. *Rentalia et Custumaria Michaelis de Ambresbury, 1235-1252, et Rogeri de Ford, 1252-1261*, ed.C.J. Elton & E. Hobhouse (S.R.S. Vol.5, 1891), pp.7-8, 36-7, 45-7, 49, 148, 150-3, 157, 163.
36. *Cal. of MSS of Dean & Chapter of Wells*, Vol.1, pp. 62, 78-9, 100, 104, 136, 144-5.
37. *Cal.Close R.*, 1288-96, p.3.
38. Lyte, *History of Dunster*, i, p.285, 307; ii, p.343.
39. John Hawkes, 'Poundisford park pale, ST.21762035', *P.S.A.N.H.S.* Vol.135 (1991), p.158.
40. Lyte, *History of Dunster*, i, p.160; Cal.Pat.R., 1247-58, p.107; Greswell, *Forests and Deer Parks*, p.261.
41. *Two Cartularies of the Benedictine Abbeys of Muchelney and Athelney in the County of Somerset*, ed.H.E. Bates (S.R.S. Vol.14, 1899), no.21, pp.56-7; S.C.R.O., DD/L1/10/35A.
42. *Calendar of the Manuscripts of the Dean and Chapter of Wells*, Vol.2, ed.W.P.Baildon (1914), p.76; Lyte, *History of Dunster*, ii, p.343.
43. *Leland's Itinerary in England and Wales*, ed. Lucy Toulmin Smith (1907), v, p.86; Mike Chapman, *A Guide to the Estates of Ralph Allen around Bath* (Bath,1996), p.17.
44. *Cal.Chart.R.*, iii, 1300-26, p.474.
45. Cox & Greswell, 'Forestry', pp.562-3).
46. Shirley, *Some Account of English Deer Parks*, p.99; J.E. Harting, *British Animals Extinct within Historic Times, with Some Account of British Wild White Cattle* (1880), pp.239-240; D.P. Kirby, 'The Old English forest: its natural flora and fauna', in T. Rowley (ed.), *Anglo-Saxon Settlement and Landscape* (British Archaeological Reports no.6, Oxford, 1974), p.126.
47. *Cal.Close R.*, 1227-31, p.308; 1231-4, p.402; 1234-7, p.282; *Cal.Lib.R.*, v, 1260-67, pp.18, 48; *Cal.Close R.*, 1272-9, p.451.
48. Lyte, *History of Dunster*, ii, p.331.
49. *Cal.Close R.*, 1231-4, p.77; 1247-51, p.312.
50. *Cal.Close R.*, 1227-31, pp.166, 176, 211-12, 214.
51. Lyte, *History of Dunster*, ii, p.392.
52. Francis Rose & Pat Wolseley, 'Nettlecombe Park: its history and its epiphytic lichens: an attempt at correlation', *Field Studies*, Vol.6 (1984), pp.117-148.
53. John Harvey, *Mediaeval Gardens* (1981), p.72.
54. Lyte, *History of Dunster*, i, p.324; *Cal.Pat.R.*, 1354-8, p.616.
55. Rackham, *Ancient Woodland*, p.195.
56. *Cal.Pat.R.*, 1408-13, p.471; *Cal.Chart.R.*, vi, 1427-1516, p.101.
57. William Dugdale, *Monasticon Anglicanum*, ed. J. Caley, H. Ellis & B. Bandinel, i, p.10; Cox & Greswell, 'Forestry', p.568).
58. Lyte, *History of Dunster*, i, p.97; ii, pp.357-8.
59. Somerset C.R.O., DD/MI c/86.
60. M. Aston & E. Dennison, 'Fishponds in Somerset', in Michael Aston (ed.), *Medieval Fish, Fisheries and Fishponds in England* (British Archaeological Reports, British Series, no.182.ii (Oxford, 1988), pp.391-400.
61. Rob Iles, 'Avon archaeology, 1983', *Bristol & Avon Archaeology* Vol.3 (1984), p.57. For a general background to rabbits in medieval England see E.M. Veale, 'The rabbit in England', *Agricultural History Review*, Vol.5.ii (1957), pp.85-90; John Sheail, *Rabbits and their History* (Newton Abbot, 1971); and James Bond, 'Rabbits: the case for their medieval introduction into Britain', *The Local Historian*, Vol.18.ii (1988), pp.53-57.
62. Phyllis M. Hembry, *The Bishops of Bath and Wells, 1540-1640: Social and Economic Problems* (1967), p.22; *Leland's Itinerary*, i, p.290; Phelps, *History and Antiquities of Somersetshire*, i, pp.560-1.

Chapter 4

SOMERSET GARDENS in the MIDDLE AGES

EVEN FROM THE ELEVENTH CENTURY PLANTS WERE GROWN AND GARDENS
DESIGNED FOR THEIR BEAUTY AS WELL AS FOR THEIR USEFULNESS ...

Fig. 4.1
A section of glass from
BRISTOL CATHEDRAL CLOISTER
showing a medieval wooded pasture or
garden enclosed within a wattle fence.

The Rediscovery of the Medieval Garden

Until relatively recently little was known about medieval gardens in England. No examples survive intact, and we have virtually no contemporary descriptions or plans to tell us what they were like. It was generally assumed that, if gardens existed at all in the Middle Ages, they must have been small, utilitarian and without much interest. Our understanding of the subject was transformed in 1981 by the publication of John Harvey's classic book, *Mediaeval Gardens*.[1] Harvey was able to show how, even from the eleventh century, plants were grown and gardens designed for their beauty as well as for their usefulness, and he has emphasized the continental traditions from which medieval English gardens drew their inspiration. In fact, although detailed descriptions are lacking, an enormous amount of miscellaneous information does lie scattered through a wide range of medieval written sources, while the potential for archaeological investigation has as yet hardly begun to be realised.

The Survival of the Classical Tradition

Despite the ruin of the Roman empire throughout western Europe, it would be a mistake to assume that all the rich heritage of classical horticulture was entirely forgotten. The works of Greek herbalists like Dioscorides of Anazarbos were copied in Constantinople and other Byzantine centres, and from there transmitted to the Islamic world. As the tide of Moslem conquest swept into Spain, Sardinia, Sicily and Apulia between AD 711 and 840, new palace gardens were made and Islamic scholars kept alive the horticultural knowledge of many classical authors. Greek sources were also used by southern European writers such as Apuleius Platonicus (c.AD 400) and Bishop Isidore of Seville (c.AD 560-636), whose work became very influential in the west. The first direct records of garden cultivation from northern Europe come from Carolingian sources of the eighth and ninth centuries.

Copies of some of the classical herbals are known to have found their way into English monastic libraries as early as the seventh century. Bede was familiar with Pliny the Elder's encyclopedia, and there is some evidence that the herbal of Apuleius was translated into Anglo-Saxon around AD 1000 [2]. A late seventh- or early eighth-century Irish copy of Bishop Isidore's *Etymologiae*, a celebrated early medieval encyclopaedia which includes a notable section on the properties of plants, may have been brought to Glastonbury Abbey by Irish monks in the ninth or tenth century. This ancient manuscript had been discarded, either because its archaic Irish script was no longer understood or because it had been damaged in the great fire of 1184; but fragments were recycled to bind the survey of Glastonbury properties compiled in 1189 when Henry of Sully became abbot.[3] It was evidently replaced, since the 1247-8 catalogue of the abbey library records two copies of Isidore's work. John Leland lists in the library of Wells Cathedral another copy of Isidore of Seville's encyclopedia, also a copy of the herbal of Rhabanus Maurus of Fulda.[4]

The Glastonbury library also contained one of the most remarkable Anglo-Saxon herbals, the *Leech Book* of Bald, which appears to have been compiled at Winchester around the end of the ninth century. A note in the colophon names its original owner, Bald, who was perhaps some sort of medical practitioner, and also the author or scribe, Cild. An approximate date is provided by a citation in the text that some of the medical recipes were sent to King Alfred by Helias, Patriarch of Jerusalem. Written in Anglo-Saxon, it draws extensively but selectively, not only from the classical Greek and Roman medical literature, but also from Scandinavian and Irish sources. Although references to perishable exotic ingredients which could not have been available in England were generally omitted, the book nevertheless mentions an astonishing range of drug plants from as far away as China, Indonesia, India, the Near East and Africa, including aloes, balsam, cassia, cinnamon, galbanum, ginger, incense, mastic, mercury, myrtle, olive, pepper and 'swailsapple', probably malabathrum, a spicy leaf of the cinnamon family. It is not clear when or how the text came to Glastonbury, but the abbey library catalogue of 1247-8 includes a volume entitled *Medicinale Anglicanum*, and the flyleaf of the surviving manuscript bears the same inscription.[5]

Clearly in abbeys like Glastonbury there was already considerable knowledge of the classical European literature on plants and their uses well before the Norman Conquest. Cultural contacts were extended after the eleventh century. Many of the Norman barons who acquired English estates after 1066 had close family links with the Normans who had conquered Apulia and Sicily, and would there have come into direct contact with the Islamic gardening tradition. Bishop Geoffrey of Coutances, who held many Somerset manors at the time of the Domesday survey, himself visited southern Italy and returned, impressed with what he had seen, to create a new garden, park and ponds on his property in Normandy. During the Crusades many more Englishmen saw for themselves the gardens of the Byzantine and Islamic worlds. Later medieval English scholars such as Alexander Neckam (1157-1217) and Bartholomew de Glanville (c.1200-1260) drew extensively upon classical and continental herbals in their own writing. It would be wrong, therefore, to see English gardening in the Middle Ages as wholly backward and insular.

The Form of Medieval Gardens

There were many different types of garden in the Middle Ages. Some were little more than pasture closes, perhaps with a few fruit trees, valued mainly for their herbage. Others were fairly basic cultivated plots producing a limited range of herbs, green vegetables or industrial crops. However, there were also many more ambitious gardens, deliberately designed for pleasure and enjoyment. Utilitarian gardens occurred at all levels of society, but pleasure-gardens were only likely to exist on royal and baronial properties, at episcopal palaces and in the larger monasteries.

While we lack detailed contemporary plans or descriptions of medieval English gardens, French and Flemish illuminated manuscripts give us some idea of the standard components of the pleasure-garden. The whole garden was ideally surrounded by a high wall or, failing that, by a bank and hedge or paling fence to provide shelter and privacy. Internally it was often divided into square or rectangular compartments by trelliswork fences and further subdivided by intersecting gravel paths. Within this framework plants were often grown in raised beds one or two feet above path level, edged with planks. Trelliswork arbours or pergolas with climbing roses, honeysuckle or grape vines, used in classical Roman gardens, had reappeared by the twelfth century. There was often a compartment given over to grass with daisies and other flowers, imitating the sward of a meadow. Seats were commonly set against walls or around trees, and often consisted of raised banks of turf revetted at the front with wattle, planks, bricks or stone. Orchards were often an intrinsic component of larger gardens.[6]

Such garden features are, by their nature, relatively ephemeral, and we would not expect much evidence to survive from them. Only when significant quantities of earth were moved is there likely to be some visible trace remaining, and this was done primarily in connection with water features. Some gardens were surrounded by moats, which had no defensive purpose but served as stockproof boundaries and were perhaps also intended to be seen as an attractive feature in their own right. Some of the many moats in Somerset, including those at Kenn Court, Marston Magna and Sock Dennis, probably surrounded gardens attached to the manor house. The remains of separate fishponds can also be seen on many sites, for example at Kenn Court, Banwell, Chaffcombe, Cothay and Brympton d'Evercy.[7] While many of these may have served as store ponds or breeding tanks, providing the occasional pike or bream for the lord's table, even the most complex layouts are never of sufficient size to ensure a year-round supply. Indeed, most of the fish eaten in the Middle Ages were of marine origin, freshwater fish being reserved for special feast days and the entertainment of important guests. The fishponds, therefore, have to be seen more as status symbols and visual amenity features than as providers of basic subsistence.

PLANT INTRODUCTIONS
of the MIDDLE AGES

At the end of the tenth century a Benedictine monk named Aelfric compiled a vocabulary which included the names of around two hundred different plants and trees then known in England. Less than a hundred of those were regularly cultivated, about half of them being grown for food or flavouring, another quarter for medicinal use, and most of the remainder for industrial purposes (including teasles for raising the nap on cloth, and woad and madder for dyeing). However, some flowering plants, such as the madonna lily and several varieties of rose, were already being grown primarily for their attractive appearance, while other medicinal and culinary plants such as flag iris, marsh mallow, poppy, sage and sweet bay, were also of ornamental value in the flower garden.[8]

Increasing contacts with continental Europe resulted in many new plant introductions during the course of the Middle Ages, and some plants whose cultivation had lapsed since the Roman period were reintroduced. Although the precise date and source of the new introductions is rarely known with any precision, the works of English herbalists such as Alexander Neckam in the twelfth century and Henry Daniel in the fourteenth century provide some idea of the general sequence of their appearance. One difficulty with the medieval sources is that the Latin and vernacular names used then did not invariably apply to the plants which bear those same names today, and in some cases the identification of the precise species mentioned in the documents remains uncertain.[9] Despite the problems, however, it seems likely that by the end of the Middle Ages the number of plants available for garden cultivation in England had doubled or tripled.

Flowering plants grown primarily for ornamental purposes included many native species brought into cultivation from the wild. These included dog rose, daisy, buttercup, cowslip, chamomile, speedwell, lily-of-the-valley, forget-me-not, campion, cranes-bill, mallow, foxglove, mullein, single pinks, lesser periwinkle, honeysuckle, and perhaps also daffodil and bluebell. Medieval introductions probably included hollyhock (possibly introduced from Spain in the mid-thirteenth century), peony, yellow wallflower, black hellebore and carnation.[10]

Recipes and medical texts provide evidence for the cultivation of a wide range of culinary and medicinal herbs. Native wild plants such as agrimony, alexanders, betony, chicory, sweet cicely and tansy were brought into cultivation after the Norman Conquest, if they had not been used before. Pot marigold had already been reintroduced from central Europe and the Mediterranean before the Norman Conquest. Hyssop, from the Mediterranean, first appears in the eleventh century. Parsley was also introduced from the Mediterranean, chervil from the Caucasus and the Middle East. Borage, a native of the Middle East, was cultivated in England by about 1200. Lavender had appeared by the middle of the thirteenth century. Balm, clary and liquorice (all natives of southern Europe) came in during the fourteenth century, and the annual lupin a little later. Other herbs, like fenugreek (from the Mediterranean), costmary (from the Near East), basil (from India) and caraway (a native of temperate Europe, Asia Minor and Persia), do not seem to have

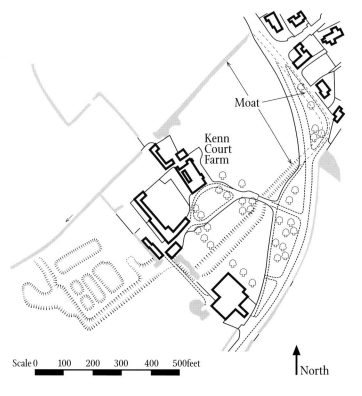

Fig. 4.2
A plan showing the complex
fishpond layout at KENN COURT
(after Dennison and Iles, 1988).

Moat

Kenn
Court
Farm

Scale 0   100   200   300   400   500feet

↑ North

reached England before the fifteenth century.[11]

The saffron crocus (*Crocus sativus*), a native of Greece and Asia Minor, had long been cultivated in Mediterranean regions, and was much prized in medieval cooking for its flavour and yellow colouring. It is said that the first saffron corm planted in Britain was smuggled in by a returning pilgrim in the 1320s or 1330s. Records of its cultivation appear in eastern England around the middle of the fourteenth century, and by the fifteenth century it was grown in gardens at both Wookey and Taunton (see below). However, it is an uncertain crop in the English climate, and is laborious to harvest, so much of the saffron used in medieval English kitchens continued to be imported, although it remained extremely expensive.

A slightly later introduction from the Mediterranean was rosemary. Queen Philippa acquired some rosemary plants in 1338, and by 1342 was growing it successfully in her own gardens in England. Although vulnerable to wind and frost in some regions, it flourishes in the milder south-west in all but the hardest winters.[12]

Garden vegetables were fairly limited in range in the early Middle Ages, but nevertheless provided a vital contribution to the diet. Indeed, pottage consisting of cereal grains, colewort leaves, leeks, peas and beans boiled in water enriched with stock and flavoured with parsley and other herbs provided a staple meal for aristocrat, monk and peasant alike. Leeks were perhaps the commonest of all medieval vegetables. Onions, garlic and shallots were widely grown in gardens, but it was still necessary to import considerable quantities from France and Spain. Although garlic does better in a warmer climate and could never be produced in sufficient quantity to meet the demand, it was still much more widely grown in England in the Middle Ages than in later times. Both the native black mustard and the Mediterranean white or yellow mustard were grown, their leaves eaten as greens and their seeds ground as a condiment. Broad beans and peas were cultivated as field crops and dried for keeping through the year, but there is little evidence that either were grown in gardens or eaten green before the fourteenth century. Medieval broad beans were somewhat larger than the Celtic bean mentioned in Chapter 2, but were of the same family (*Vicia faba*). Green peas of an early-ripening variety called 'hastyngez' were grown in the great garden of St Augustine's Abbey in Bristol in 1491. Horse-beans and the larger grey peas were used primarily as fodder for horses, but were also eaten by the poor and by others in times of famine. Colewort was sown several times a year and its leaves plucked as needed to ensure a constant supply. Improved varieties of cabbage were becoming available in the fourteenth century, but it was another century before they were

widely cultivated. Spinach and cauliflower did not appear before the fifteenth century. Globe artichokes and lettuce first appeared in England after 1500. Root crops were hardly known before about 1300, and for long were restricted to the gardens of the wealthy: carrots, skirrets, parsnips and turnips were not widely grown in England before the fifteenth century.[13]

Certain soft fruits such as strawberry, raspberry, blackberry, sloe and elderberry were readily available in the wild, and while they were certainly collected and eaten, there is little evidence that they were deliberately planted. Others, like the cultivated gooseberry, had been introduced from France by the thirteenth century, though never extensively grown in England in the Middle Ages.[14]

Trees from Gerard's
HERBALL of 1636.
left: Fig. 4.4
MEDLAR (Mespilus sativa).
right: Fig. 4.5
MULBERRY (Morus).

Of the native fruit trees, apple, pear, cherry, plum and bullace were often found in medieval gardens along with introduced species such as the medlar and mulberry. By the thirteenth century new varieties of apple, the Pearmain, Costard and Blandurel, and new varieties of pear such as the Warden, had appeared, along with peach and quince.[15] Fig pips are sometimes found in medieval sewage deposits, and fig trees were certainly grown in the early Middle Ages in sheltered spots in the warmer southern counties, though their yield was unpredictable; customs records show that figs were generally imported dried in the later Middle Ages, and were relatively expensive - one pound of figs cost 1½d, equivalent to a full day's pay for a contemporary labourer. The native hazel also grew alongside early introductions such as walnut and sweet chestnut. Almond, a native of the eastern Mediterranean and long cultivated in Spain and Italy, was being grown in England from the beginning of the sixteenth century.

Timber trees such as oak, elm, ash, and beech were sometimes grown in gardens or on garden boundaries. There were relatively few tree introductions in the Middle Ages, though the oriental plane (*Platanus orientalis*), a native of Persia and the Near East, finds occasional mention in English sources after the twelfth century.[16]

A few native evergreen shrubs were available. Holly was sufficiently widespread to be a valuable hedgerow tree. Box and

Fig. 4.3
BUSH VETCH (Vicia maxima
dumetorum) as illustrated in
Gerard's HERBALL of 1636.

Fig. 4.6

The LIST OF SPECIES *identified by John Harvey from 'OF OTHER MANNER OF HERBS' in Master Jon Gardener's 'THE FEAT OF GARDENINGE'.*

'Adderstongue'	*March* (Smallage)
(?Cuckoo-pint)	*Mints*
Agrimony	*Motherwort*
Alexanders	(Mugwort)
Avens	*Mouse-Ear*
Betony	*Nepp*
'Bigold'	*Oculus Christi*
(?Corn Marigold)	(Wild Clary)
Borage	*Onion*
Brooklime	*Orach*
Bugle	*Orpine*
Calamint	*Parsley*
Camomile	*Pellitory*
Campion	*Peony*
Caraway	*Periwinkle*
Centaury (Lesser)	*Pimpernel*
Clary	*Plantain*
Colewort	(Ribwort)
Comfrey	*Plantain*
Coriander	(Waybread)
Cowslip	*Polypody*
Cress	*Primrose*
Cress, Water	*Radish*
Daffodil	'Red Knees'
Daisy	'Red Mayweed'
(Bruisewort)	*Rose, Red*
Dill	*Rose, White*
Dittander	*Rue*
'Dittany'	*Saffron*
Elecampane	*Sage*
(Horseheal)	*St John's Wort*
Felwort, Gentian	*Sanicle*
Fennel	*Savory*
Feverfew	'Scabious'
Foxglove	*Senevy* (Mustard)
Garlic	*Southernwood*
Gladwin	'Spearwort'
(Flag Iris)	'Spinach'
Gromwell	*Stitchwort*
Groundsel	*Strawberry*
'Half-wood'	*Tansy*
(?Bittersweet)	*Teasel, Wild*
Hartstongue	*Thistle, 'Wolf's'*
Henbane	*Thyme*
Herb Robert	*Tutsan*
'Herb Walter'	*Valerian*
Hollyhock	*Vervain*
'Honeysuckle'	*Violet*
Horehound,	*Wallwort*
White	*Waterlilly*
Hyssop	*Woodruff*
Langdebeef	*Wood Sage*
Lavender	(Hindheal)
Leek	*Wood Sorrel*
Lettuce	*Wormwood*
Lily	*Yarrow*
'Liverwort'	

juniper also grew in the wild in a few localities, though there is little evidence that they were much cultivated in gardens. Cypress was introduced in the fourteenth century.[17]

Finally, industrial crops must be considered. Fibre plants such as flax and hemp were widely grown in the Middle Ages, both as a field crop and in gardens. Plants which could produce dye were also cultivated. A dye-works operating in the Bristol suburb of Redcliffe during the late thirteenth and fourteenth centuries was using madder to produce red cloth and woad to produce blue cloth.[18] Both crops could have been grown in Somerset. Woad is mentioned in the will of Agnes Lyte of Lytes Cary in 1428. Bequests of woad were made by many other clothiers, weavers and merchants in Glastonbury, Bridgwater, Wells and elsewhere throughout the late Middle Ages. Ralph Hunt of Bath left to his servant in 1432 a quantity of undressed cloth, fulling equipment and a bale of madder. Cisterns, furnaces and vats for processing woad figure in the wills of Simon Lacy of Leigh-on-Mendip (1481), John Attwater of Wells (1500) and Thomas Street of Mells (c.1520).[19] However, large quantities of woad were also being imported at this period from Bordeaux.

MONASTERY GARDENS

The cultivation of gardens is associated with the earliest years of hermit monasticism in the deserts of Egypt and Syria. The importance of gardens in monastic life is emphasized in the Rule drawn up by St Benedict around AD 530, which ultimately emerged as the most influential of all monastic rules in western Europe.[20] As early as the ninth century monastic precincts could contain several different kinds of garden. The famous plan made around AD 820 for the abbot of St Gall in Switzerland shows a kitchen garden with eighteen beds of named crops arranged in two utilitarian rows of nine beds each; a smaller infirmary garden, comprising sixteen beds of named medicinal herbs; and a cemetery garden laid out in more ornamental form and including fruit and nut trees.[21] A similar range of herb and vegetable gardens, with orchards, vineyards and ornamental components, developed at many English monasteries.

Monastic libraries were important repositories of horticultural information, and some of the pre-Conquest herbals at Glastonbury have already been mentioned. The Glastonbury Abbey library contained another text of great interest, an account of horticultural techniques written in doggerel English verse by one 'Master Jon Gardener'. The existing manuscript dates from around 1440, but John Harvey has argued convincingly that this is probably a copy of a document compiled fifty to a hundred years earlier. The identity of its author is not certain, but the most likely candidate is John de Standerwyk, one of the royal gardeners, who died in 1345. His name suggests that he came originally from the village of Standerwick near Frome, so he may have had some connection with Glastonbury Abbey earlier in his career. The most striking aspect of his poem is that it contains sound advice on manuring, sowing, grafting, training vines, and harvesting, which is clearly based upon practical experience rather than derived from other written authorities. The introductory section, rendered here into modern English, will give something of its character:

"Who so will a gardener be,
Here he may both hear and see,
Every time of the year and of the moon.
And how the craft shall be done,
In what manner he shall delve and sett,
Both in drought and in wet,
How he shall his seeds sow;
Of every month he must know,
Both of worts and of leek,
Onions and of garlick,
Parsley, clarey, and eke sage,
And all other herbage."

There follow sections advising on the setting and rearing of trees, the grafting of apples and pears, the cutting and setting of vines, the setting and sowing of garlic, leeks, onions and worts, and notes on parsley, other herbs, and finally saffron which, as a recent introduction, may have been appended to the original text. The seventh section, 'Of Other Manner of Herbs' is of particular interest for the list of species which might be encountered in a monastic garden like Glastonbury, or indeed, any large contemporary kitchen garden. Some of the medieval names are ambiguous, and a small number have defied identification, but most of the plants have been identified by John Harvey, who has listed them alphabetically in *fig. 4.6* (uncertain or unknown identifications within inverted commas).

While vegetables and potherbs predominate in the list, there is also a significant number of plants - cowslip, daffodil, daisy, foxglove, hollyhock, iris, lavender, lily, peony, periwinkle, primrose, rose, violet and waterlily - which suggest an interest in attractive and ornamental plants.[22] Such instructions give a valuable insight into what was possible, but we also have more direct evidence of the monastic gardens from other Glastonbury records.

Glastonbury Abbey occupied a large rectangular walled precinct which would have contained ample room for both gardens and orchards. There are intermittent references to the abbey's gardens throughout its history. John of Glastonbury's Chronicle, probably compiled in the 1340s, records of Æthelwold, a Glastonbury monk in Dunstan's time who went on to become Abbot of Abingdon and then Bishop of Winchester, that "*Such was his humility that he laboured daily in tending the garden with his own hands, and at the noon meal he prepared fruits and various sorts of vegetables for the brothers, serving them himself*".[23]

The account of the abbey gardener, Thomas Keynsham, survives for the year 1333-4, detailing receipts from sales of garden produce and purchases of seeds and equipment. This shows that there were at least two separate gardens within the precinct, the Great Garden and the Little Garden, in addition to an orchard and vineyard. Large parts of both gardens were then down to pasture and were grazed by horses, at other times being mown for hay or providing winter pasture for sheep. The nettles were valued, along with the herbage, and may have been used as fodder, boiled as a vegetable in pottage, used in cheese-making or dried for their fibre. Several kinds of crops are recorded from the cultivated areas. Firstly, the gardens were producing a range of pot vegetables, including onions, leeks, beans and garlic (in that year they produced three quarters of onions and provided 2,000 heads of garlic for the abbey kitchen, also 6,000 heads of garlic for the larderer, with a further 3,000 heads being kept for seed). Secondly, they were producing dyeing plants, specifically *gallium*, which may be either madder or bedstraw. Thirdly, fibre-producing plants like flax and hemp were being cultivated. Finally there were fruit trees, particularly cider apples and pears. Garden pests are represented by a payment of 3d for the capture of ten moles. 2d was spent on the repair of a bolt to the garden door. Several new tools were purchased, including a sickle for 8d and new iron shoes for the wooden spades for 10d, five old spade irons being sold for 2½d. Other equipment mentioned included an axe and four iron hoes.[24] Records of purchases and sales inevitably emphasize the commodities of economic value produced by the gardens rather than the common subsistence crops. Such accounts also generally ignore the aesthetic qualities of the garden, only occasionally providing hints of ornamental features. Shortly before the Dissolution, the sacrist's account of 1538-9 provides an incidental mention of a flower-garden, which could have provided flowers for decorating the shrines and chapels in the church; and we find Richard Whiting, the last abbot (1525-39), receiving payment of a debt from John Lyte of Lytes Cary in an 'erber of bay' in his garden.[25]

Excavations in 1938 to the south-east of the existing Abbot's Kitchen revealed foundations of a wall enclosing an area about 54 yards square which was probably the abbot's private garden.[26] The precise location and extent of the other gardens mentioned is not known, but they presumably lay further to the south and east, where slight banks, scarps and cultivation ridges have been surveyed. The existing oval pond in the southern part of the abbey grounds is probably, in its present form, no older than the eighteenth century, but the dam of an abandoned medieval fishpond survives further to the east.[27]

From the Benedictine abbey of Muchelney we have a series of medical and other recipes inserted into a two-volume breviary, which complements the plant records from Glastonbury. Some of the ingredients are exotic imports: for example, a cure for stomach chill contains galingale (from Indonesia or south China), ginger (from Indonesia or Indo-China), 'cinnamon' (probably cassia from Burma, since it is doubtful whether true cinnamon was known outside Ceylon at this time), liquorice (from southern Europe or the Middle East) and sugar (probably from Spain or Sicily). Other recipes use herbs and wild plants which could have been grown locally. Juice of pennyroyal in warm water was also recommended for stomach-ache. A cure for costiveness included mallow, violet, 'mercury' (allgood, or Good King Henry), borage, 'langue-de-boeuf' (a culinary form of bugloss), 'rodes' (culinary marigold), hyssop and stitchwort. The other extreme could be treated with a mixture of sorrel, plantain, cinquefoil, shepherd's purse, ribwort and dried roses. A fifteenth-century dietary in the same volume recommends flavouring pottage, the staple monastic meal of boiled coleworts, with sage, borage, 'langue-de-boeuf', parsley, marigold, rosemary, thyme, hyssop, summer savoury, or Good King Henry. Ale could be flavoured with sage, rosemary or something which may be rowan. A sauce to be served with fish included sorrel, alecost, 'dittany' (oreganum), 'peleter' (wild thyme), parsley and avens or Herb Bennet. A further drink recipe includes scabious, fumitory,

sorrel, sowthistle, dandelion, devil's-bit, lettuce, borage, mouse-ear and white water-lily, in addition to liquorice, Spanish spikenard and white Cyprus sugar. Finally there are instructions for growing and making dye from woad.[28]

The other local Benedictine abbeys, Bath and Athelney, would certainly have had similar gardens within their precincts, though little is known of them. So too would the smaller houses of various orders. The initial endowment of the Cluniac priory of Montacute by the Count of Mortain in c.1102 included orchards and vineyards, and by 1303 the priory's demesne estate included gardens, though by then the vineyards and orchards are no longer recorded.[29]

The group of monks most closely associated with gardening were the Carthusians, a hermit order founded in 1084. Unlike the Benedictines and similar orders, where the monks used communal refectories and dormitories, the Carthusian monks were solitaries, spending most of their time working and praying in individual cells, to which gardens were attached in order to provide them with a place for manual labour and outdoor meditation. The cells and gardens normally surrounded a large grassed cloister garth. The two earliest Carthusian houses in England are both in Somerset. Witham Charterhouse (the English name is a corruption of the French Chartreuse) was founded by Henry II in Selwood Forest in 1178 as part

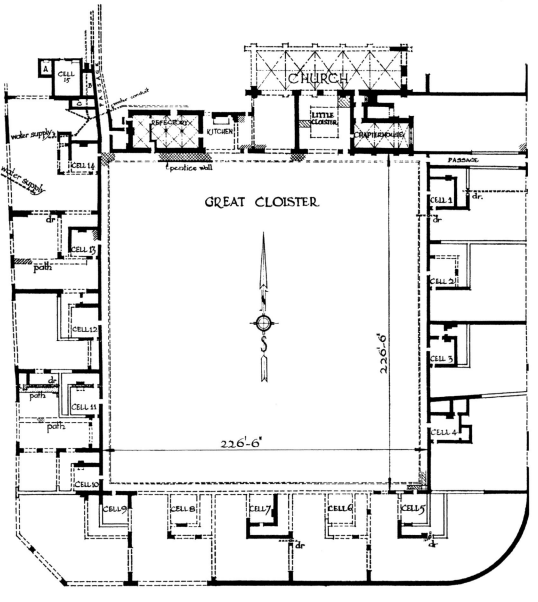

Fig. 4.7
HINTON CHARTERHOUSE
as revealed in excavations of the 1950s.

Scale 0   20   40   60 feet

A selection of plants from
STEEP HOLM*'s unique flora:*
top: Fig. 4.8 SINGLE PINK PEONY.
centre: Fig. 4.9 ALEXANDERS.
bottom: Fig. 4.10 WILD LEEK.

of his penance for the assassination of Thomas Becket. Small-scale excavations took place here between 1965 and 1969, locating the church, one cell and part of the outline of the cloister, and further information has come from a recent geophysical survey.[30] Hinton Charterhouse, near Bath, was founded in 1226, and here the layout is more completely known: a large cloister, 75 yards square, was surrounded by fifteen individual cells, each with its own L-shaped garden and paved walk, with piped water for drinking, washing and irrigation being supplied from a conduit-house. A treatise on gardening appears among a list of books loaned out from the library of Hinton Priory in 1343.[31] Unfortunately both of the Somerset Charterhouses were excavated before the potential of garden archaeology was realised. More recent excavations at the Mount Grace Charterhouse in Yorkshire have demonstrated how detailed plans of the monks' gardens can be recovered from the evidence of paths bordered by stones set on edge, planting-pits and cultivation trenches; it has also been shown how varied the layouts of individual gardens can be.

One further site where evidence of a different kind may survive is on the island of Steep Holm in the Bristol Channel, where a small, short-lived community of Augustinian canons was settled in the thirteenth century.[32] The present flora of the island includes a number of rarities and long-established exotics, some of which have been claimed as monastic introductions. The most striking is the Mediterranean single pink peony (*Paeonia mascula*), seeds of which are said to have been found on at least one other west-country monastic site, Winchcombe Abbey in Gloucestershire.[33] Unfortunately, however, the first record of this plant on the island occurs as recently as 1803, and if such a striking flower had been present since the Middle Ages, it would surely have occasioned some comment before then. A better case could be made for some of the edible plants: alexanders (*Smyrnium olustratum*) was growing there before 1562, and the wild leek (*Allium ampeloprasum*), which appears to be identical with the medieval cultivated variety, was also present before 1562. Other island plants of possible medicinal use which might have been escapes from monastic cultivation, such as caper spurge, henbane and hemlock, are not documented before the late eighteenth or early nineteenth centuries.[34]

CASTLE and PALACE GARDENS

The best-documented of all medieval gardens are those which belonged to the crown. However, the king had relatively few houses in Somerset apart from the palace at Cheddar, which had been a royal residence from the ninth century until it was given up by King John to Bishop Jocelin of Bath in 1213. Although excavations on this site have revealed a great deal of the layout of the Saxon timber halls and the medieval palace and hunting-lodge, little archaeological evidence for a garden was found, and the site had passed out of royal hands before the commencement of the classes of records which might have provided detailed information.

The Bishops of Bath and Wells had several splendid residences elsewhere within the county, notably the great moated house at Wells itself, but also at Banwell, Evercreech, Wookey, Chew and Wiveliscombe. Most of these will have included some sort of garden, and for a couple of them we have fuller details.

Fragments of the moated palace at Wookey are preserved in the present Court Farm. Some records of the garden appear in the bishop's accounts of 1461-2, when wages were paid to three men for "*digging and cleaning the chapel garden*"; there are also payments to eleven men for three days' work each in digging and thinning crocus for the lord's table; seven payments for six and a half days' work in digging and setting crocus; payments for paring 14 *pannae* of garden crocus at 20d per *panna* (the medieval Latin word '*panna*' has many meanings, but here may refer to a square bed, i.e. shaped like a 'pane' of glass). Further payments are recorded of 1s 4d for cutting the garden and 1s 2d to William Hicks for levelling the crocus-bed The references to crocus are clearly to the introduced culinary saffron crocus (*Crocus sativus*) rather than to the poisonous native autumn crocus or meadow saffron (*Colchicum autumnale*). A survey of the Wookey property in 1557-8 mentions the garden containing half an acre to the rear of the house, an orchard also containing half an acre, a rabbit-warren containing one acre, a dovecote, and a long orchard containing four acres with apple trees.[35]

At Banwell Bishop Thomas Beckington is said to have laid out a most beautiful orchard with many wonderful fruits.[36] Inventories of the goods and chattels of the recently-deceased Bishop Thomas Godwin at the Banwell palace taken in 1590 and 1591 recorded that a peacock and three peahens were kept in the garden, which included an orchard with a great walnut tree and a hop yard.[37]

Taunton Castle was held by the Bishops of Winchester throughout the Middle Ages after its first construction in the twelfth century. In 1210-11 the garden was planted with apple trees, 30 trees being purchased for 5s It also produced leeks and garlic.[38] The outline of another castle garden can still be seen at Farleigh Hungerford, where the earlier manor house had been rebuilt and fortified by Sir Thomas Hungerford after his purchase of the property in 1369-70. Sandwiched between the main domestic range and the curtain wall in the north-eastern quarter of the inner ward is an open rectangular area some 30 yards x 20 yards in extent, with a pitched stone path slightly off-centre, parallel with the north wall of the hall. This was secluded from the entrance courtyard on the southern side of the domestic buildings, and was overlooked only from the hall and private chambers, and it can reasonably be interpreted as the private garden of Sir Thomas and his successors. While the hall would have shaded the southern portion of the enclosure, the curtain wall would have provided shelter and warmth to the part north of the path, while water for irrigation would have been available from a well in the kitchen courtyard nearby. Unfortunately no record of the content of this garden is known.[39]

MANORIAL GARDENS

Manor-houses were often surrounded by small closes used as gardens, orchards and vineyards. These often receive a brief mention in the manorial extents attached to inquisitions post mortem (descriptions of the property of a recently-deceased landowner drawn up to evaluate what dues were owed to the crown and to identify the heir), but such surveys rarely provide any details of what the garden was actually like. For example, the inquisition drawn up on the death of John de Mandeville in 1276 records merely that he held at East Coker a house, a garden, dovecotes and a vineyard with 105 acres of pasture in the park; later on, in 1474-5, the bailiff's accounts of this manor note 33s 4d being spent on "*the great garden and a close under the court*".[40] In 1325 Sir Peter d'Evercy held at Brympton d'Evercy "*a capital messuage with gardens and closes adjoining*"; a few more details are given in 1343 in the inquisition taken on the death of his successor, Peter de Glamorgan, where the garden is described as two acres in extent and said to have been "*planted with divers and many apple trees*".[41]

Assignments of land in dower to the lord's widow are sometimes a little more informative. After the death of Robert de St Clare in 1336 his wife, Sibyl, was allocated various portions of his property on condition that she would not remarry without the king's licence. These comprised parts of the manor-house at Stapleton in Martock, including both domestic and farm buildings, a plot called 'Chapelheye' with the vines growing there (to be held with Robert's heir in common), one-third of the garden on the north side of the house with one-third of the profits of the fishpond and dovecote there, and a *virgultum*, a term which may imply a nursery of young trees; also a house at Butleigh with a third part of the garden on the east side; and buildings at Somerton, including one-third of two gardens on either side and of the profits of the dovecote.[42]

The general impression from the written sources is that many manorial gardens were not particularly intensively cultivated. A survey of the Denebaud estate at Hinton St George in 1362 records two dovecotes and two gardens which were worth little that year because the apple trees had been blown down.[43] When an assignment of dower in the manor of Wigborough in South Petherton was made to Isabel Cogan in 1382, it included "*one several garden, wherein are no trees, containing 4½ acres of pasture*".[44] In another case we are given a strong hint that the manorial gardens had ceased to be cultivated, perhaps because the lord was no longer resident: at Portbury in 1514 a new bailiff was appointed "*with custody of the mansion-house therein, and of three gardens called le gret and lytyll Conyger*", with the clear implication that these gardens were now used only as a rabbit warren.[45]

Fuller details tend to be more readily available for the gardens of manor-houses which happened to be in episcopal or monastic ownership. The Bishop of Winchester held the manor of Rimpton, north-east of Yeovil, and his account rolls record the enclosure and planting of a new garden here in 1264-6, apparently to extend a much smaller existing garden. The new enclosure was surrounded by a substantial bank and ditch, five feet high, seven feet broad, planted with a hedge on the top, and 113 perches in circuit, which implies an area of something between three and six acres. It was planted with apple and pear trees and vines, also with flax, beans and other unspecified vegetables; there was also a part given over to orchard with grazing. 248 fruit tree grafts cost a total of 18s. A specialist gardener supervised the making of the new garden, earning around 1s a week.[46] The Dean of Wells had a house and garden at Mudgley near Wedmore. In 1378 it was estimated that £6 13s 4d was required for the repair of the garden wall and the wall round the fishponds there.[47] Some earthworks remain in this site.

The abbots of Glastonbury had numerous manor-houses, scattered throughout their extensive estates, many of them with gardens and orchards attached. A survey of Shapwick manor in 1327 mentions a garden five acres in extent attached to the court, which must lie beneath the closes and paddocks north and north-west of the present Shapwick House, where there is an ornamental moat, traces of fishponds and other earthworks.[48]

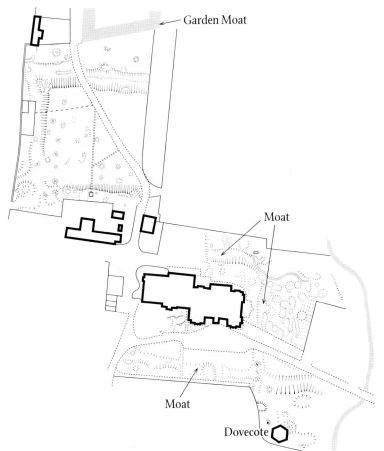

Fig. 4.11
A plan showing the moat and earthworks around SHAPWICK HOUSE.

Scale 0   50   100   150 feet

North

The abbey accounts of 1333-4 reveal considerable quantities of apples being sent in to the abbey gardener from Marksbury (8 quarters), Pilton (43 quarters, 2 bushels), Batcome (11 quarters, 2 bushels), Ditcheat (10.5 quarters), Meare (10 quarters, 6 bushels), Godney (8 quarters) and Shapwick (8 quarters, 7 bushels). By contrast, apples from the Sowy orchards were apparently made into cider on the spot rather than sent to Glastonbury. The gardener also received quantities of leeks from the gardens of Meare and Pilton for the use of the abbot when he visited those manors.[49] Later, Abbot Selwood (1456-92) is recorded as having planted on his manor of East Brent an orchard over three acres in extent with apples and pears of the finest fruit, as well as elms and oaks.[50]

Adam Sodbury, Abbot of Glastonbury, built an important manor-house at Meare in the second quarter of the fourteenth century, centred around a first-floor hall which still survives in modified form. It was enclosed within a courtyard, which Abbot Adam had fortified with stonework. The house was improved in the sixteenth century: the terrier of Abbot Richard Beere made in 1516 describes it as "*a very handsome and ample Manor-House, founded long ago, and adorned by the present Abbot with new chambers*". Abbot

Fig. 4.12
An aerial view of MEARE *manor house with walled enclosures, fish house and fishponds.*

Adam's enclosure wall still stood "*of great height and thickness, surrounding it strongly with stone, enclosing within the said walls 3 acres and 1 perch*", and fragments of it survive even today. The customs of Meare in 1235-52 mention the garden and dovecote, and the 1516 terrier also records in addition to the walled precinct an outer garden and orchard occupying two and a half acres to the east, along with fisheries and stews. There was also a vineyard here as early as the eleventh century, the site of which was very probably on the plateau of high ground towards the road, between the manor-house and the fish-house. The fish-house was surrounded by three small fishponds which probably served as a store-pond for freshwater fish awaiting transfer to the abbot's table; but they may also have fulfilled some ornamental function.[51]

The skeleton of another late medieval garden belonging to Glastonbury Abbey, probably dating to the time of Abbot Beere (1493-1524) or Abbot Whiting (1525-1539), survives at Mells. Behind and to the north of the Elizabethan mansion built by the Horners, who acquired the manor at the Dissolution, is an earlier high stone wall, supported internally by semicircular buttresses enclosing a square garden. A four-centred arch provides an additional entry from the village churchyard, and there were formerly mounts at each end of the northern terrace, providing viewpoints over raised parapets.[52]

PEASANT GARDENS

Most of the existing villages in Somerset are of medieval origin, and in most cases continuing occupation has destroyed all evidence of medieval peasant cultivation. However, a significant minority of villages and hamlets were depopulated by a variety of factors towards the end of the Middle Ages, and in some cases these abandoned settlements have left clear traces in the present landscape in the form of grass-grown hummocks and hollows in the fields. Aerial photography or ground-level survey can often reveal from these slight earthworks the complete plan of the village just prior to its final abandonment. At Nether Adber, one of the clearest sites in Somerset, the mounds representing the individual peasant cottages lie within larger ditched enclosures which can be interpreted as gardens.[53] There is very little documentation for how these parcels were used. Some may be no more than tiny plots of enclosed pasture. Others could have produced a variety of potherbs and vegetables like leeks, onions, garlic and coleworts, and fruit from apple or pear trees, and while their yield may not have been great, they could have made a significant contribution to the nutritional value and flavour of the medieval peasant diet of bread and pottage. A few may even have yielded a cash income from crops like flax or hemp.[54]

Fig. 4.13
NETHER ADBER *deserted medieval village showing closes around peasant houses.*

Few sites of this type have yet been excavated locally, but preliminary reports from the excavations at Eckweek, a hamlet near Peasedown St John which was abandoned in the fourteenth century, indicate the recovery of remains of a number of food plants in addition to the common cereals, including cabbage, carrots, peas, beans, lentils, fat hen and a single plum stone.[55]

TOWN GARDENS

In the popular imagination medieval towns are often envisaged as congested rookeries of narrow lanes and tottering timber houses. In reality this picture is generally more representative of the sixteenth or seventeenth century than of earlier centuries. Many medieval towns were well-planned, containing a good deal of open space, much of which was used as private orchards and gardens. The Domesday survey records one garden (*ortus*) in the borough of Langport which belonged to the Count of Mortain's manor of Staple Fitzpaine.[56] Public open space in towns was provided by churchyards, and these were often adorned by the planting of trees. A cathedral close might be planted up on a grander scale. In 1243 rows of elm trees had been planted outside the southern part of the west front of Wells Cathedral. These may be the same trees that were the subject of a dispute involving the cathedral treasurer over the pollarding and lopping of trees in the churchyard in 1487.[57]

Details of private gardens in medieval towns are often elusive, but we have a few glimpses of high-status urban gardens from the documents of Wells Cathedral. During the Middle Ages this cathedral was staffed by secular canons, each living in their own private house within the Close or Liberties, and each house was set in its own garden. Lands and houses in the locality known as Mountroy, north and north-east of the cathedral, included in the early thirteenth century a garden belonging to Walter of Downhead. Nearby, John & Mirabel Cardevill granted to the chaplain Elias some land on the east side of their garden, beyond the ditch, including a dovecote with the land around it. Mountroy Lane led to a plot called Sareorchard, mentioned in several medieval records; the name may imply that this orchard had become derelict (from Old English *sear*, meaning 'withered'), and it was described in lease of 1696 as a close of about two acres used as meadow or pasture. In 1397 another lane linked Sareorchard to a site called Purymulle, implying a mill for crushing pears for making perry.[58]

On 4th June 1326 a canon named Michael de Eston acquired a piece of land in the bishop's garden adjoining his own garden in order to enlarge it. The plot is described as adjoining Eston's garden 50 feet to the east of the newly-built Lady Chapel, extending southwards for 28 feet from Eston's old wall towards St Andrew's Well. The grant specifically excluded a medlar tree growing near a well and a path eight feet wide between the tree and well; both the tree, which was clearly valued for its fruit, and the path were to remain in the possession of the bishop. This plot appears to be represented now by the southern part of the lawn behind the large medieval house now called 'The Rib'.[59] The Deanery on the north side of Cathedral Green now stands in an extensive plot, and in 1361 Dean John de Carleton petitioned the bishop for permission to acquire a derelict neighbouring house and curtilage in order to enlarge his own house, and the bishop allowed him to demolish the house and convert the ground to a garden.[60] Many other gardens are mentioned incidentally in records of sales and leases of the canons' houses. In 1381-2 the escheator's accounts record an income of 7s 4d from sale of stone and pasture of the garden of the archdeacon's houses, and a later account of 1417-18 includes a payment for the making of two gardens.[61]

We also find some valuable glimpses of town and suburban gardens amongst the medieval churchwardens' accounts of St Michael outside the North Gate in Bath. These accounts deal with the costs of upkeep and income from various houses and lands belonging to the parish as well as the ordinary expenses of the church itself. In the fifteenth century many of the gardens were enclosed by walls, fences or hedges which required maintenance. In 1459-60, for example, 3d was spent on thorn bushes and 2d on stakes for the repair of the hedge of a garden in the tenure of Richard Rede, while in 1531-2 20d was spent on making a thorn hedge around a close containing a dovecote. Occasionally materials were purchased for making or repairing garden gates. Income was derived from sales of pasture, apples and hedge wood, and in 1400 Lawrence Webbe paid 2d for nettles (used for food or fibre).[62]

Some town gardens were evidently used for the production of subsistence crops. In 1463-4 expenses amounting to 6d were paid to William Aylesbury for 200 'quykfrytte' (live plants) in the garden lately in the tenure of John Court in Bath. Another garden in Bath included a crop of leeks in 1477-8, while green beans used for pottage are mentioned in 1509 and 1533.[63] Simon Fisher, a Taunton merchant, left to his son Alexander his saffron garden in his will dated September 4th 1505.[64] Industrial crops were probably also a significant yield from many town gardens. The Bath accounts record payments of 3d for setting 70 teazle plants in the tenement of William Abingdon, 6d for the purchase of the plants and 3d for weeding them in 1459-60, while another garden in Bath included teazles in 1477-8. At Yeovil Syon Abbey took tithes of flax growing in yards and gardens in the town.[65]

NURSERY GARDENS

The frequent records of purchases of substantial quantities of tree stocks and other plants show that there was already a flourishing nursery trade in the Middle Ages. In 1369 the widow of Sir John de Merriott inherited lands which included a plot called 'la noresirie' (the earliest known use of this word in the arboricultural or horticultural sense) adjoining the garden and park of Merriott manor near Crewkerne.[66]

VINEYARDS

As already mentioned, vineyards are sometimes recorded in medieval sources alongside orchards and gardens. It is evident that vines were not always cultivated in rows together in a specialised vineyard, but could sometimes be scattered in odd corners of the garden. At Rimpton the accounts of 1264-6 record payment of 2s 2d for "*planting vines in various places*".[67]

The origins of vine cultivation in England remain unclear. As

Fig. 4.14
Vines on a carved benchend in the
CHURCH OF ST THOMAS
OF CANTERBURY, COTHELSTONE.

mentioned in Chapter 2, it is likely that the Romans cultivated the vine in the southern part of the country, but there is no evidence that any Roman vineyards survived beyond the end of the fourth century. However, vine cultivation had resumed on monastic estates well before the Norman Conquest. The earliest Somerset reference occurs at Panborough near Wedmore, where a vineyard was confirmed to Glastonbury Abbey in a charter of AD 956. Slight terraced earthworks on the shelving land immediately south-east of Barrow Hill may mark its site.[68]

The Domesday survey records vineyards at three places on the Glastonbury estates, three arpents at Panborough, three arpents at Glastonbury itself and two arpents at Meare (an arpent was a measure of land roughly equivalent to an acre). A single arpent of vines belonged to Muchelney Abbey; and there were seven acres on the royal estate of North Curry.[69] Another early record comes from Dunster where, before 1100, William de Mohun had given the tithe of his vines to the monks of Bath. The costs of cultivating this vineyard and the income from sales of wine are recorded in 1177.[70]

The Glastonbury vineyards continue to find occasional mention in the documentary record over the next two or three centuries. In the middle of the thirteenth century many of the abbey's tenants from villages as widely scattered as Butleigh, South Brent, Berrow, Lympsham and Shapwick, owed services of several days' work in the abbey vineyards at Glastonbury or Panborough while all inhabitants of Meare had to contribute the considerable sum of 12d each towards the costs of digging the vineyard there.[71] Similar services applied on the Mohuns' manor of Dunster, where in 1266 34 of the peasant tenants were obliged to dig half a perch apiece in the lord's vineyard each year, each of these works being valued at one halfpenny; the vineyard at this time occupied seven acres. By 1279 its produce was valued at 18s. Its position is identified in a deed of 1419, which locates it on the slope above the present Luttrell Arms Hotel.[72] In 1245 the prior of Bath granted a furlong of vineyard at Timberscombe near Dunster to one Richard le Tort. Vineyards belonging to the Bishop of Wells are also mentioned intermittently through the thirteenth and fourteenth centuries.[73]

Two factors seem to have led to the eventual decline of the English vineyards. One was a deterioration of the climate through the late thirteenth and fourteenth centuries, with harder winters, later spring frosts and duller and wetter summers, which made vine cultivation increasingly marginal even in the south. The other was the competition from better-quality Gascon wines imported in increasing quantities by Bristol traders after the middle of the thirteenth century. One by one the English vineyards were abandoned. By 1355 that at Meare was described as comprising two acres of arable and one of meadow, implying that vine cultivation had ceased. The Panborough vineyard was still apparently functioning at that date, but by the time of Abbot Beere's survey in 1516-17, the three acres known as 'Wineland' were down to arable. The Dunster vineyard was grubbed up and converted to pasture by Sir Hugh Luttrell, who inherited the estate from the Mohuns in 1404. The Meare vineyard was still remembered at the end of the nineteenth century, when Canon Ellacombe described what he believed to be its ruined back wall, with stone projections to which the vines were fixed.[74]

Fig. 4.15
The vineyard site at PANBOROUGH.

REFERENCES - Chapter 4

1. John Harvey, MEDIAEVAL GARDENS (1981).
2. Wilfrid Blunt & Sandra Raphael, THE ILLUSTRATED HERBAL (1979), pp.32-3.
3. James P. Carley & Ann Dooley, 'An early Irish fragment of Isidore of Seville's ETYMOLOGIAE', in Lesley Abrams & James P. Carley (eds), THE ARCHAEOLOGY AND HISTORY OF GLASTONBURY ABBEY (Woodbridge, 1991), pp.135-161.
4. James P. Carley, 'John Leland at Somerset Libraries', *P.S.A.N.H.S.* Vol.129 (1985), pp.141-54.
5. O. Cockayne, LEECHDOMS, WORTCUNNING AND STARCRAFT OF EARLY ENGLAND 3 parts, Rolls Series, Vol.35 (1864-6); see also M.L. Cameron, 'Bald's "Leechbook" and cultural interactions in Anglo-Saxon England', in ANGLO-SAXON ENGLAND, Vol.19 (1990), pp.5-12.
6. For a fuller discussion see Harvey, MEDIAEVAL GARDENS, and Sylvia Landsberg, THE MEDIEVAL GARDEN (1995), pp.11-73.
7. E. Dennison & R. Iles, 'Medieval fishponds in Avon' and M.A. Aston & E. Dennison, 'Fishponds in Somerset', in Michael Aston (ed.), MEDIEVAL FISH, FISHERIES AND FISHPONDS IN ENGLAND, British Archaeological Reports, British Series no.182.ii (Oxford, 1988), pp.205-28, 391-408.
8. Aelfric's vocabulary is published in T. Wright & R.P. Wülcker, ANGLO-SAXON AND OLD ENGLISH VOCABULARIES (1884), Vol.1, pp.133-49, and many of the plants listed are identified by Harvey, MEDIAEVAL GARDENS, Appendix 3, pp.163-80. See also John Harvey, 'The medieval garden before 1500', in John Harris (ed.), THE GARDEN: A CELEBRATION OF ONE THOUSAND YEARS OF BRITISH GARDENING (1979), p.7
9. Tony Hunt, PLANT NAMES OF MEDIEVAL ENGLAND (Cambridge, 1989) provides an interpretation of some 1,800 names, covering 600 species.
10. Harvey, MEDIAEVAL GARDENS, pp.126-133.
11. Tom Stobart, HERBS, SPICES AND FLAVOURINGS (1977); Harvey, MEDIAEVAL GARDENS, p.131.
12. Stobart, HERBS, SPICES AND FLAVOURINGS, pp.215-9; John H. Harvey, 'Mediaeval plantsmanship in England: the culture of rosemary', GARDEN HISTORY Vol.1 no.1 (1972), pp.14-21.
13. Harvey, MEDIAEVAL GARDENS, pp.120-1; John H. Harvey, 'Vegetables in the Middle Ages', GARDEN HISTORY Vol.12 no.2 (1984), pp.89-99.
14. F.A. Roach, CULTIVATED FRUITS OF BRITAIN: THEIR ORIGIN AND HISTORY (Oxford,1985), pp.23-24, 50-52).
15. Roach, CULTIVATED FRUITS OF BRITAIN, pp.15-25.
16. Harvey, MEDIAEVAL GARDENS, pp.122-4.
17. Harvey, MEDIAEVAL GARDENS, pp.124-5.
18. B. Williams, EXCAVATIONS IN THE MEDIEVAL SUBURB OF REDCLIFFE, BRISTOL, 1980 (Bristol, 1981)
19. SOMERSET MEDIEVAL WILLS, 1383-1500, ed. F.W. Weaver (S.R.S.Vol.16, 1901), pp.126, 228, 233, 234, 237, 247, 248, 255, &c ; SOMERSET MEDIEVAL WILLS (SECOND SERIES), 1501-1530, ed. F.W. Weaver (S.R.S. Vol.19, 1903), pp.269, 333, 389.
20. THE RULE OF ST BENEDICT, transl. Justin McCann (1952). In Chapter 66 it is advised that the garden should be contained along with other necessary resources within the monastic enclosure, so that the monks should not be compelled to wander outside it.
21. Walter Horn & Ernest Born, THE PLAN OF ST GALL: A STUDY OF THE ARCHITECTURE AND ECONOMY AND LIFE IN A PARADIGMATIC CAROLINGIAN MONASTERY (3 vols, University of Berkeley, California, 1979).
22. The extant manuscript is at Trinity College, Cambridge, MS 0.9.38. The full text in medieval English is published in A.G. Rigg, A GLASTONBURY MISCELLANY OF THE FIFTEENTH CENTURY (Oxford, 1968), pp.103-111, and discussed by John H. Harvey, 'The first English garden book', GARDEN HISTORY Vol.13, no.2 (1985), pp.83-101.
23. THE CHRONICLE OF GLASTONBURY ABBEY, ed. James P. Carley (Woodbridge, 1985), ch.65, pp.124-5.
24. Ian Keil, 'The garden at Glastonbury Abbey', *P.S.A.N.H.S.*, Vol.104 (1959-60), pp.96-101.
25. Keil, 'The garden at Glastonbury Abbey, p.97, n.4; H.C. Maxwell Lyte, 'The Lytes of Lytescary', *P.S.A.N.H.S.*, Vol.38 (1892), p.36.
26. Sir Charles R. Peers, Alfred W Clapham & Prior E. Horne, 'Glastonbury Abbey excavations, 1938: interim report', *P.S.A.N.H.S.*, Vol.84 (1938), pp.134-136.
27. Peter Ellis, 'Glastonbury Abbey fishpond, Somerset, ST.501386', *P.S.A.N.H.S.*, Vol.124 (1980), p.133; Ian Burrow, 'Earthworks in the south-eastern part of the abbey precinct, Glastonbury', *P.S.A.N.H.S.* Vol.126 (1982), pp.39-42.

28. *Muchelney Memoranda*, ed. B. Schofield (S.R.S. Vol.42, 1927), nos.11, 12, 15, 55, 62, 65.

29. *Two Cartularies of the Augustinian Priory of Bruton and the Cluniac Priory of Montacute*, ed. Members of the Council (S.R.S. Vol.8, 1894), p.119; R.W. Dunning, 'Montacute', *V.C.H.* Vol.3 (1974), pp.210, 216.

30. Ian Burrow & Cathe B. Burrow, 'Witham Priory: the first English Carthusian monastery', *P.S.A.N.H.S.* Vol.134 (1990), pp.141-182; Robert Wilson-North, 'Witham: from Carthusian monastery to country house', *Current Archaeology* Vol.13 no.iv (1996), pp.151-8).

31. E.T.D. Foxcroft, 'The Carthusian priory of Hinton', *Proceedings of Bath Natural History & Antiquarian Field Club*, Vol.7 no.iii (1891), pp.293-307; Philip C.Fletcher, 'Further excavations at Hinton Priory', *P.S.A.N.H.S.* Vol.103 (1958-9), pp.76-80.

32. Stan & Joan Rendell, *Steep Holm: the Story of a Small Island* (Stroud, 1993), pp.31-57).

33. Teresa McLean, *Medieval English Gardens* (1981), pp.156-7.

34. R.G.B. Roe (1981) 'Vascular Plants', in Somerset Archaeological & Natural History Soc., *Steep Holm, a Survey* (Taunton, 1981), pp.57-63.

35. Thomas Scott Holmes, *The History of the Parish of Wookey* (1886), p.47; Joan Hasler & Brian Luker, 'The site of the Bishop's Palace, Wookey', *P.S.A.N.H.S.* Vol.137 (1993), pp.111-8.

36. William Worcestre, *Itineraries*, ed. John H. Harvey (Oxford, 1969), pp.296-7.

37. Phyllis M. Hembry, 'The death of Thomas Godwin, Bishop of Bath and Wells (1549-90)', *P.S.A.N.H.S.* Vol.96 (1951), pp.102-3.

38. Harvey, *Mediaeval Gardens*, p.72; T.J. Hunt, 'A thirteenth-century garden at Rimpton', *P.S.A.N.H.S.* Vol.104 (1959-60), p. 95.

39. Anon., *Farleigh Hungerford Castle* (English Heritage guide book, 1986).

40. Robert Dunning, *Some Somerset Country Houses* (Wimborne, 1991), pp.27-8.

41. Quoted in Dunning, *Some Somerset Country Houses*, p.17.

42. *Cal.Inq.P.M.* , viii, p.45, no.75.

43. R.W. Dunning, 'Hinton St George', *V.C.H.* Vol.3 (1978), p.45.

44. *Cal.Close R.*, 1381-5, pp.579-80.

45. Quoted in Eve Wigan, *The Tale of Gordano* (Taunton, undated), p.72.

46. T.J. Hunt, 'A thirteenth-century garden at Rimpton', *P.S.A.N.H.S.* Vol.104 (1959-60), pp.91-95.

47. *Calendar of the Manuscripts of the Dean and Chapter of Wells*, Vol.1, ed. W.H.B. Bird (1885), pp.284-5.

48. James Bond, 'Earthwork surveys around Shapwick House', in *The Shapwick Project: an Archaeological, Historical and Topographical Study: 7th Report* (in press, 1996)

49. Keil, 'The garden at Glastonbury Abbey', pp. 99-101.

50. Harvey, *Mediaeval Gardens*, p.136.

51. William Phelps, *The History and Antiquities of Somersetshire*, Vol.1 (1836), pp.569-71; Harvey, *Mediaeval Gardens*, p.136; I am grateful to Hazel Hudson and Frances Neale for further information from unpublished sources.

52. Harvey, *Mediaeval Gardens*, pp.136, 140-2; John Harvey, 'Parks, gardens and landscaping', in Michael Aston (ed.), *Aspects of the Medieval Landscape of Somerset* (Taunton, 1988), p.30.

53. M.A. Aston, 'Deserted settlements in Mudford parish, Yeovil', *P.S.A.N.H.S.* Vol.121 (1977), pp.41-53.

54. Christopher Dyer, *Standards of Living in the Later Middle Ages: Social Change in England, c.1200-1520* (Cambridge, 1989), pp.115, 157-8.

55. Andrew Young, *Eckweek Medieval Settlement, Peasedown St John* (1995), pp.12, 14-15; the full report on this excavation is in preparation.

56. *Domesday Book, Somerset*, ed. Caroline and Frank Thorn (Chichester, 1980), 19.26.

57. *Cal. of MSS of Dean & Chapter of Wells*, Vol.1, pp.73-4 *Cal.of MSS of Dean & Chapter of Wells*, Vol.2, ed. W.P. Baildon (1914), pp.108-9; Harvey, *Mediaeval Gardens*, pp.16, 140.

58. *Cal.of MSS of Dean & Chapter of Wells*, Vol.1, p.29, ch.91, 93; Vol.2, p.548, ch.12; *Wells City Charters*, ed. Dorothy O. Shilton & Richard Holworthy (S.R.S. Vol.46, 1931), p. 101; Sherwin Bailey, *Canonical Houses of Wells* (Gloucester, 1982), pp.41, 43, 49-50.

59. *Cal.of MSS of Dean & Chapter of Wells*, Vol.1, p.214; Bailey, *Canonical Houses of Wells*, p.137.

60. *Cal.Pat.R.*, 1361-4, p.131; Bailey, *Canonical Houses of Wells*, p.103.

61. *Cal.of MSS of Dean & Chapter of Wells*, Vol.2, pp.17, 57; Bailey, *Canonical Houses of Wells*, pp.90, 91.

62. *The Churchwardens' Accounts of the Church and Parish of St Michael without the North Gate, Bath, 1349-1575*, part i (*P.S.A.N.H.S.* Vol.23 (1877), pp.2,5, 16; part ii (*P.S.A.N.H.S.* Vol.24, 1878), pp.37, 38; part iii (*P.S.A.N.H.S.* Vol.25, 1879), pp.55, 56, 64, 71, 74-5, 80-81, 86; part iv (*P.S.A.N.H.S.* Vol.26, 1880), pp.110-11, 118.

63. *Churchwardens' Accounts of St Michael without North Gate, Bath*, part i, v; part iii, pp.61,73.

64. *Somerset Medieval Wills (Second Series), 1501-1530*, p.90.

65. *Churchwardens' Accounts of St Michael without North Gate, Bath*, part iii, pp.56, 73; flax and hemp are frequently mentioned as valuable garden crops in medieval tithe records; see Christopher Dyer, *Everyday Life in Medieval England* (London, 1994), pp.119-120.

66. *Cal.Close R.*, 1374-7, p.264; Harvey, *Mediaeval Gardens*, pp.17, 103.

67. Hunt, 'A thirteenth-century garden at Rimpton', p.92.

68. Hazel Hudson & Frances Neale, 'The Panborough Saxon charter, A.D. 956', *P.S.A.N.H.S.*, Vol.127 (1983), pp.55-69.

69. *Domesday Book, Somerset*, 1.19; 8.1; 9.1.

70. *Two Chartularies of the Priory of St Peter at Bath*, ed. William Hunt (S.R.S. Vol.7, 1893), p.38, no.34.

71. *Rentalia et Custumaria Michaelis de Ambresbury, 1235-1252, et Rogeri de Ford, 1252-1261*, ed. C.J. Elton & E. Hobhouse (S.R.S. Vol.5, 1891), pp.7-8, 36-7, 47, 49, 148-150).

72. Sir H.C. Maxwell Lyte, *A History of Dunster and of the Families of Mohun and Luttrell* (1909), i, pp.324-5.

73. Hugh Barty-King, *A Tradition of English Wine* (1977), p.40.

74. Lyte, *History of Dunster*, i, 325; Canon Henry E. Ellacombe, 'The vineyards of Somerset and Gloucestershire', *Proceedings of Bath Natural History & Antiquarian Field Club* Vol.7 no.i (1890), p.35

Chapter 5

PARKS and GARDENS under the TUDORS and EARLY STUARTS

THE ARISTOCRACY WERE NOW ABLE TO DISPLAY AND ENJOY THEIR WEALTH. THE EXPANSION OF THE SMALL ENCLOSED GARDENS OF THE MIDDLE AGES INTO MORE ELABORATE PLEASURE GROUNDS BECAME ONE OF THE WAYS IN WHICH THE SOCIAL CHANGES OF THE PERIOD WERE MADE MANIFEST ...

Fig. 5.1
The title page from
TURNER'S *NEW HERBALL of 1551.*

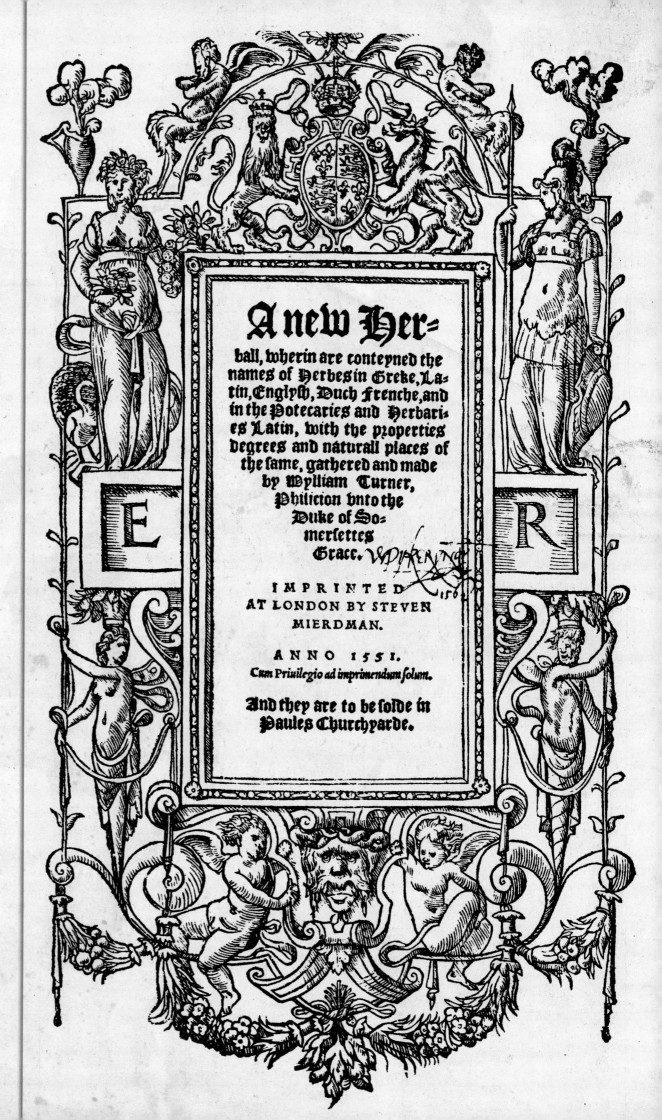

INTRODUCTION

The accession to the throne of Henry Tudor in 1485 marked the end of the Wars of the Roses and the beginning of a period of greater political stability. The court and aristocracy, no longer so preoccupied with internal conflict, were now able to display and enjoy their wealth. Just over fifty years later the Dissolution of the Monasteries brought to an abrupt end another tradition of medieval life, and some 30 per cent of the land area of England changed hands, the biggest upheaval in landownership since the Norman Conquest. The expansion of the small enclosed gardens of the Middle Ages into more elaborate pleasure grounds became one of the many ways in which the social changes of the period were made manifest, as the royal court replaced the monasteries as the leading patrons of gardening. Other developments with profound implications for the future included the invention of the printed book, superseding the laboriously hand-copied herbals of the Middle Ages; and the ever-widening circle of trade and exploration, resulting in the first important plant introductions to Britain from outside Europe.

This was a time when people of relatively humble background had unprecedented opportunities to become wealthy in the service of the Crown, and thereby to climb up the social ladder. Many of the nouveau-riche took advantage of the Dissolution of the Monasteries to acquire landed estates to reflect their new status. Ralph Hopton, soldier and royal official, acquired the site of Witham Charterhouse and was subsequently able to buy the rich Glastonbury manor of Ditcheat. William Petre, another royal official, obtained the site of Montacute Priory. Sir William Portman, lawyer and close associate of Thomas Cromwell, purchased extensive properties from the lands of Taunton Priory and three other dissolved houses in Somerset to add to his small ancestral estate at Orchard Portman. Thomas and John Horner, previously tenant farmers of Glastonbury Abbey, purchased the abbey manors of Mells, Leigh-on-Mendip and Nunney after its suppression. John Smyth, a Bristol merchant, bought one of the manors of Long Ashton, which had belonged to Bath Abbey.[1] Most of these properties subsequently developed as great estates with important parks and gardens.

New opportunities for travel abroad gave some Englishmen a keen interest in garden developments on the continent. William Knight, who became Bishop of Bath and Wells in 1541, had earlier in his career been a civil servant and ambassador for the first two Tudor kings, and in 1527 had travelled to Rome to negotiate Henry VIII's divorce from Catherine of Aragon. There he saw at first hand some of the great Italian renaissance gardens and, much impressed, tried to imitate the style on a small scale at his own home at Horton Court in Gloucestershire.[2]

The first printed ENGLISH HERBALS and BOOKS on GARDEN DESIGN

Underlying the developing fashion for herb and flower-gardens in the sixteenth century were the beginnings of a more scientific study of botany, based upon original observation rather than the transmission of knowledge inherited from the classical world. The introduction of printing at the end of the fifteenth century revolutionised the dissemination of knowledge of plants and gardening techniques, and by the sixteenth century the first printed herbals in English had made their appearance. Significant contributions were made by two men with Somerset connections.

William Turner, a Northumbrian by birth, had a turbulent career. He published his first brief work on herbalism in 1538 while at Cambridge, but because of his fervent protestant views he found it prudent to leave England in 1540. He took refuge in Italy, pursuing his botanical and medical studies at the University of Bologna for a year, and then travelled through Switzerland to the Rhineland, where he lived for the next three years. He spent four more years in East Friesland before returning to England after the accession of Edward VI to take up an appointment as physician and chaplain to the Duke of Somerset. During this period he was able to publish a more extensive botanical work, the *Names of Herbes*, in 1549. In 1551 Turner became Dean of Wells. His appointment caused considerable resentment, and it was some years before he was even able to gain entry to the Deanery House or to secure the emoluments that went with the post. Despite his difficulties, he succeeded in bringing out the first volume of his greatest botanical work, the *New Herball*, in 1551. He was again forced to flee back to Germany on the accession of Mary Tudor, living a second period in exile until 1558. Returning to Wells in 1560, he published the second volume of his *Herball* two years later. His last years continued to be dogged by religious controversy and friction with his colleagues in the Wells chapter, and he retired in ill-health to London, where he died in 1568, shortly after the publication of the third and final volume of the *Herball*.[3]

Some of the descriptions in Turner's great herbal were derived, following medieval precedent, from classical authors such as Dioscorides and Pliny, and he also drew upon the works of contemporary Italian and German herbalists who he had encountered during his travels, using many woodcuts from continental sources. However, he was much more than a mere copyist, being always critical of his sources and concerned for accuracy. He was a keen observer of plants, both in the wild and in the garden, and was particularly concerned to quote their natural habitats; therein lies his most original contribution. He describes many plants which he had seen in Somerset. The narrow-leaved flax grew wild within a mile of Wells so prolifically that Turner expressed surprise that the cultivated form was not grown locally on a commercial scale. Meadow saffron grew near Bath. Alexanders grew (as its still does) on Steep Holm. White mustard grew in the cornfields near Glastonbury. Common hyssop and black horehound also grew locally. The common hare's ear (*Bupleurum rotundifolium*) grew abundantly between Somerton and Martock. Navelwort or pennywort (*Umbilicus rupestris*) Turner describes as especially prolific in local walls. Plants of the Somerset Levels included the marsh mallow (*Althaea officinalis*), which grew by the mere a mile from Wells, and sweet gale or bog myrtle (*Myrica gale*), both now generally uncommon, though the latter is prolific north of Shapwick and Ashcott. He describes many varieties of fruits, and distinguished between the garden bullace and the wild hedgerow bullace, saying of the latter "*I never saw in all my life more plenty of this*

Fig. 5.3
*Wall plaque commemorating
William Turner at the*
OLD DEANERY, WELLS.

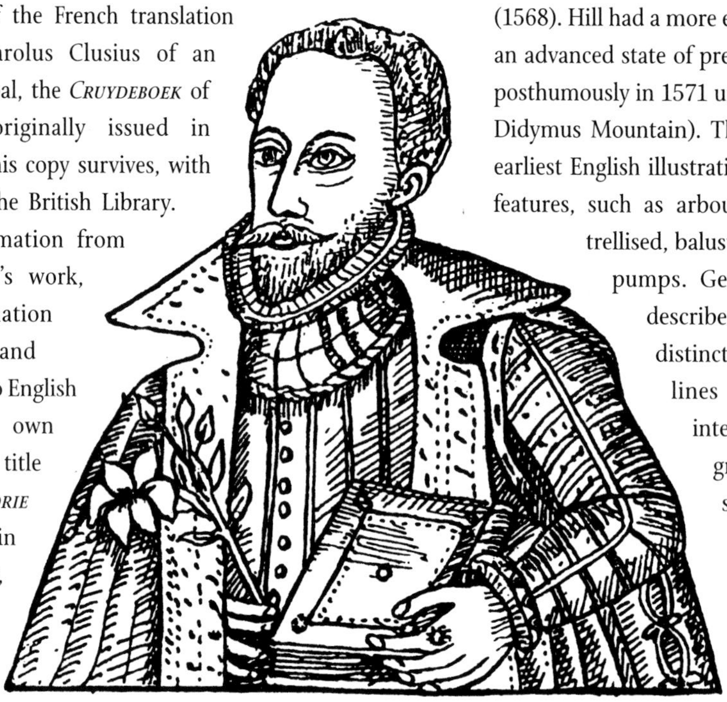

Fig. 5.4
Portrait of HENRY LYTE
from family pedigree.

sort of bullace trees than in Somersetshire"; they are still common today in many local hedgerows. Plants growing in his own garden at the old Deanery in Wells included the 'scorpion's tail' heliotrope (*Heliotropum europaeum*), which Turner had seen nowhere else in England. The partly-medieval embattled wall of Dean Turner's garden at Wells still remains, and now bears a plaque in memory of the 'Father of English Botany'.

Somerset's other great herbalist was Henry Lyte. Unlike Dean Turner, Lyte was a local man, whose family had held land around the manor of Lytes Cary since the thirteenth century. He was born around 1529 and studied at Oxford before travelling abroad. He acquired a copy of the French translation made in 1557 by Carolus Clusius of an important Flemish herbal, the *CRUYDEBOEK* of Rembert Dodoens, originally issued in Amsterdam in 1554. This copy survives, with Lyte's annotations, in the British Library. He collated the information from Dodoens with Turner's work, adding some information from other sources, and translated the whole into English with some of his own observations under the title *NIEWE HERBALL OR HISTORIE OF PLANTS*, published in 1578. Like Dean Turner, he was interested in plants which grew locally, mentioning for example the white Solomon's seal, which grew plentifully by Harridge Wood near Ashwick on the Fosse Way, and the rustyback fern (*Asplenium ceterach, al. Ceterach officinarum*) commonly seen around Wells. Further editions of Lyte's herbal were issued in 1586, 1595 and 1619. Clearly the gardens at Lytes Cary flourished in his time. His son Thomas recorded the many varieties of apple, pear and plum still growing there in 1618, in addition to cherry, peach, bullace, sloe, quince, grape, fig, hazel, walnut and almond. John Aubrey noted the remnants of this garden later in the century, when a few of Henry Lyte's original plants still lived.[4]

Later English herbals included John Gerard's *HERBALL, OR GENERALL HISTORIE OF PLANTES*, published in 1597, with revised editions issued in 1633 and 1636. Gerard's text was partly plagiarised from a translation of another work of Dodoens, but he also had extensive personal experience of gardening, and included many of his own observations. Gerard's *HERBALL* represents the most exhaustive catalogue of western European plants attempted up to that date. Gerard knew of Dean Turner's work and quoted a number of Somerset locations in his own text. A yellow variety of star of Bethlehem grew as a weed in Somerset cornfields. Solomon's seal grew wild on Mendip near Shepton Mallet. Meadow saffron grew abundantly in the meadows around Bath, Bristol and Shepton Mallet, and the cuckoo-flower also grew near Bath. He reports the dwarf Mediterranean

cyclamen growing in Somerset by the house of one Mr Hales (this is probably Highfield near Hemington), and on the Bampfyldes' estate at Hardington. Navelwort or pennywort grew on stone walls in Bristol, Bath, Wells and other west country localities.[5]

Practical manuals on cultivation techniques were also beginning to appear, although the earliest examples were more concerned with agricultural improvements, horticulture remaining a relatively minor concern.[6] The first printed English book to concern itself specifically with garden design was Thomas Hill's *A MOST BRIEFE AND PLESAUNTE TREATISE, TEACHYNG HOW TO DRESSE, SOWE AND SET A GARDEN* (1563), later revised as *THE PROFFITABLE ARTE OF GARDENING* (1568). Hill had a more extensive book, *THE GARDENER'S LABYRINTH*, in an advanced state of preparation at the time of his death (published posthumously in 1571 under the grander-sounding nom-de-plume of Didymus Mountain). The woodcuts in Hill's books are among the earliest English illustrations we have of many contemporary garden features, such as arbours, turf seats, raised beds, knot gardens, trellised, balustraded and palisaded boundaries and garden pumps. Gervase Markham, another prolific author, describes in *THE ENGLISH HUSBANDMAN* (1613) two distinct types of knot garden, the 'open knot' using lines of rosemary, thyme or hyssop with the intervening spaces filled with coloured earths or gravel, and the 'closed knot' using flowers of a single colour to fill up the spaces. William Lawson, a Yorkshire parson and author of *A NEW ORCHARD AND GARDEN* (1618) and *THE COUNTRY HOUSEWIFE'S GARDEN* (1638), describes the more modest orchards, kitchen gardens and flower gardens of the minor gentry and yeoman farmers lower down the social scale, yet still illustrates the use of topiary, knots, fountains, prospect mounts, summerhouses, fruit trees and fishponds. To what extent the ideas of these authors were applied in practice, only archaeology can answer.

PLANT INTRODUCTIONS of the 16th and EARLY 17th CENTURIES

Until 1560 most new plant introductions to England continued to come from mainland Europe, but there was an increasing emphasis on flowers grown purely for ornamental purposes, as opposed to those with culinary or medicinal uses. As long as the garden relied upon northern European plants, the colour range remained generally limited to pastel shades, blues, purples and yellows, and the flowering season remained relatively short. Slowly, however, the new introductions extended both the colour range and the length of the season later into the autumn.[7]

An influx of Huguenot refugees may have been responsible for some introductions from France after 1572, including the French marigold (*Tagetes patula*), cotton lavender (*Santolina incana*), fair maids of Kent (*Ranunculus aconitifolius*), sweet rocket (*Hesperis matronalis*), bear's ears (*Primula auricula*) and double crimson peony

(*Paeonia officinalis*). Honesty (*Lunaria annua*) was introduced from Sweden at about the same time.

One of the results of the renaissance was the awakening of a new interest in the plants described in the classical herbals and grown in the gardens of the classical world, and this led to a number of collectors exploring the Mediterranean and the Levant between 1550 and 1620. The snapdragon (*Antirrhinum majus*) was recommended by Dioscorides as a shield against witchcraft, and Dean Turner imported from Italy seeds of a variety he called 'broad calf's snout'; Henry Lyte knew of a yellow variety which he compared with the related native toadflax. The white jasmine from the Near East (*Jasminum officinale*) is first mentioned by Turner. Other introductions from these regions included ornamental trees such as the white-flowered horse chestnut (*Aesculum hippocastanum*), laburnum (*Laburnum anagyroides*) and lilac (*Syringa vulgaris*), bulbs and tuberous plants such as the tulip (*Tulipa gesneriana*), oriental hyacincth (*Hyacinthus orientalis*), crown imperial (*Fritillaria imperialis*), martagon lily (*Lilium martagon*) and Persian crowfoot (*Ranunculus asiaticus*), and annuals such as candytuft (*Iberis umbellata*).

Voyages out into the Atlantic brought back the sweet-smelling yellow wallflower from the Azores. The rediscovery of America did not produce an immediate influx of new species, but subsequent explorations through the late sixteenth and seventeenth centuries resulted in the recognition of many valuable plants. The establishment of the English colonies in Virginia and Canada began to produce more of an influx of new herbaceous species from North America after 1620, including the perennial sunflower (*Helianthus multiflorus*), spiderwort or trinity-flower (*Tradescantia virginiana*), bee-balm (*Monarda didyma*), red and yellow columbine (*Aquilegia canadensis*), garden golden-rod (*Solidago canadensis*), and goat's-beard (*Aruncus dioicus*). The michaelmas daisy (*Aster novae-belgae*), the aster *Aster tradescantii*, the yellow cone-flower *Rudbeckia laciniata* and the sneezeweed (*Helenium autumnale*) extended the blooming season into October, previously a bleak period in the garden. Some of the North American species quickly became garden favourites, others had to wait until more attractive hybrid forms were bred successfully.

Although the greatest innovations affected the range of flowering plants, food plants were not neglected. Improved grafts of apples, pears and cherries were imported from France and the Low Countries. Dean Turner provides the first English record of several fruits. The apricot was a recent introduction from France, and Turner records that he had seen many growing near Cologne. The gooseberry was also commonly grown in Germany, but Turner regarded it still as a rare garden plant in England; similarly the cultivated garden raspberry, which he had also observed growing above Bonn and in Eastern Friesland; and the redcurrant, which he had seen growing by the waterside at 'Clouer' on Mr Horner's land (this must be Cloford near Nunney, rather than Clewer near Wedmore). He implies that figs were quite common, countering the widely-believed myth that they were reintroduced to England in 1525. Turner also recorded almonds, black mulberries, quinces and pomegranates as commonly grown in suitably sheltered locations. Peaches and nectarines were further sixteenth-century introductions from France, while melons and greengages were introduced from Italy. Lyte's herbal advises growing

melons in dry, sunny, well-manured ground to achieve adequate fruiting.

The spiked star of Bethlehem, *Ornithogalum pyrenaicum*, which is relatively abundant in the woods around Bath (though rare elsewhere), was grown commercially as a pot-herb there from the later sixteenth century, its flower spikes sold in bundles under the name of 'Bath asparagus'. There was a general increase in the available range of vegetables. Turner describes spinach as a plant which had only recently come into use, having probably been introduced from Spain. The Mediterranean globe artichoke also finds its first notice in Turner. Other sixteenth-century introductions from Europe included Swiss chard, broccoli and cauliflower, though these did not enjoy immediate popularity. Gerard experimented with planting aubergines, which he called the 'mad apple', but the plant could not stand the English climate, and it was not even grown as a greenhouse crop until the nineteenth century.[8]

Some of the new crops from the Americas were initially regarded with considerable suspicion. Henry Lyte said of the tomato that "*the complexion, nature, and working of this plant is not yet known, but ... it should be cold of nature, especially the leaves, somewhat like unto mandrake, and therefore, also it is dangerous to be used*". The potato was not widely cultivated in England before the late eighteenth century, while it was the nineteenth century before the tomato and marrow found much favour. Lyte had grown maize successfully in hot summers, but it was hardly cultivated at all on any scale before the present century. A variety of nasturtium was introduced from central America during the sixteenth century, but it enjoyed little success until a superior garden variety was introduced in the 1680s. Others, like the Jerusalem artichoke, kidney bean and runner bean, were a little more popular, even if their cultivation was not always fully understood. John Evelyn quotes a remarkable letter dated 1679 from Mr Gifford, minister of Montacute, in which he described a technique for growing runner beans, first steeping them in sack for five days, then in salad oil for five days, then in brandy for four days, before setting them in a hot-bed and pouring the liquor around the holes. According to the ingenuous Gifford, whose gardeners were clearly pulling his leg, the plants had grown a foot within three hours, flowered on the third day, and produced ripe pods a week later! [9]

Hops had grown wild in Britain for centuries, but they do not seem to have been cultivated for flavouring ale until the 1520s, when the first hopyards were planted in Kent. Small hop gardens began to appear on estates in many parts of southern England during the later sixteenth century. In the 1560s four Dutchmen went from Glastonbury to make the new hop garden at Longleat House in Wiltshire. Records of tithes on crops payable to Somerset churches from the second decade of the seventeenth century onwards occasionally include hops, while hopyards or hop gardens are recorded at Nether Stowey vicarage before 1613, at Combe Sydenham in 1626-7, at Compton Pauncefoot in the 1640s and at Enmore in 1656.[10]

The Mediterranean was the main source of tree introductions in the sixteenth century. These included the evergreen holm oak (*Quercus ilex*), which soon became naturalised in the coastal regions of Somerset; the half-hardy Italian cypress (*Cupressus sempervirens*)

Plant introductions of the 16th and early 17th centuries as illustrated in Gerard's HERBALL *of 1636.*
top: Fig. 5.5
RANUNCULUS ASIATICUS.
above: Fig. 5.6
PRIMULA AURICULA.
below: Fig. 5.7
RANUNCULUS ACONITIFOLIUS.

Walton-in-Gordano
Clevedon Wraxall Long Ashton
St. Catherine's Court
Backwell Filwood
Kelston
Claverton
Sutton
Banwell
Farleigh Hungerford
Eastwood
Chilcompton Hardington
Rodney Stoke
Westbury-sub-Mendip
Wedmore
Wells
Witham Charterhouse
Fairfield
Dunster Marshwood East Quantoxhead Stogursey Knowle Witham
Nether Stowey Norwood Pilton
Nettlecombe Crowcombe Over Stowey Currypool Shapwick Sharpham Evercreech
Combe Sydenham
Cothelstone Huntworth
North Petherton
Combe Florey High Ham Castle Cary
Low Ham Stoke Trister
Lytes Cary Hazelgrove
Pixton Queen Camel
Isle Brewers
Orchard Portman Merifield Barrington Montacute
Wellington Staple Fitzpaine Brympton d'Evercy
Whitelackington East Coker
Donyatt Hinton St George
Chard

which also became relatively common in Somerset; the oriental plane (*Platanus orientalis*); and the stone pine (*Pinus pinea*). Some of these may have been grown in Britain in Roman times, but died out during the Dark Ages.

EARLY TUDOR GARDENS

Tudor palace gardens were characteristically situated below the main state rooms of the house, so that they could be enjoyed from the windows; they were usually square, divided into quarters containing elaborate 'knots' made out of clipped shrubs, often with a fountain at the centre, and often surrounded by raised or covered walks. All these ideas were borrowed from France, but a distinctive English invention was the use within the garden of painted and gilded wooden heraldic decorations mounted on posts or pedestals. Free-standing sundials also became popular.[11]

The style of the great royal gardens was imitated by the aristocracy, thereby spreading out from the environs of London into the western provinces. Some elements can yet be seen of the Duke of Buckingham's great new palace-castle at Thornbury in south Gloucestershire, abandoned uncompleted in 1521 when the duke was executed.[12] Somerset had no gardens of this period on the scale of Thornbury, but there are several sites which would warrant further investigation. When the premises of the dissolved Carthusian

monastery at Witham were taken over in 1544 by Ralph Hopton, they already included gardens and orchards, and Hopton may well have altered and extended them. Leland tells us that Sir John Newton pulled down the remains of the medieval castle of Richmont at East Harptree in order to build a new mansion at Eastwood (not on the site of the present Eastwood Manor, but further east near the magnificent Victorian model farm). The tithe map of 1839 shows a chain of seven ornamental pools called 'The Waterworks' which clearly belong to former gardens, though whether these are of Tudor or later date is uncertain. The earthworks of their dams still remain.[13]

ELIZABETHAN GARDENS

During the 1580s there was a phenomenal proliferation of great private houses all over England. This prodigal building spree continued throughout Elizabeth I's reign and on into the 1620s.[14] Most of these splendid new country houses were accompanied by formal pleasure-grounds.

There were few major innovations in style, as the French court continued to be the main source of influence. Characteristic features included the plat, a great flat parterre normally divided into four compartments with a statue or fountain at the centre; a raised terraced walk around one or more sides of the plat; arbours; knot gardens; prospect mounds giving a view down over the gardens; water features, particularly moats; a banqueting-hall, usually at some distance from the house, where *al fresco* meals could be taken during a walk or ride around the estate; and a bowling green for more active recreation. Elaborate forms of symbolism and allegory became more popular.

The greatest of the new gardens created in Somerset in the second half of the sixteenth century was that at Montacute. Here a great new mansion of Ham Hill stone was built in the 1590s for Sir Edward Phelips, whose family had lived in Somerset for at least four generations. Phelips had trained as a lawyer and was called to the Bar in 1579. An able and energetic man, he had already amassed considerable wealth when he inherited Montacute in 1587. He entered Parliament in 1584, and was knighted in 1603, subsequently becoming Speaker of the House of Commons in 1604 and Master of the Rolls in 1611. He is noted for opening the prosecution of Guy Fawkes after the failure of the Gunpowder Plot in 1605.

It is not known precisely when the gardens of Montacute were begun, but they were well-established by 1633 when Gerard commented on the "*large and spacious courts, gardens, orchards, a park &c*".[15] There is a fuller description of the grounds in 1667, which describes how the east porch of the house led out to four steps descending to a terrace walk "*paved with freestone and rails and*

balusters with very large high pillars of freestone and pyramids between". From the terrace walk six steps led down into "*a fair court with a freestone walk in the midst leading to a gatehouse, which court is walled about with freestone ashlar wall topped with rails and balusters and pyramids and turrets of ornament*". In the middle of the east wall of this court was the "*fair gatehouse with lodging chambers of freestone*", and at each corner of the court "*2 fair turrets with lodging chambers, all built with freestone*". Beyond the gatehouse was another "*fair large court walled about and coped with freestone set with several walks and rows of trees, on the north side of which court is a fair bowling green set about with goodly rows of trees, and variety of pleasant walks, arbours and coppices full of delight and pleasure*". The principal garden lay north of the house, "*a very fair spacious garden walled about and furnished with all sorts of flowers and fruits and divers mounted walks*". Outside this garden ten steps descended to "*private walks walled about and furnished with store of fruit*". At the end of the east walk of the main garden was a "*fair banqueting house built and arched with freestone, wainscotted within and leaded on the top thereof*", while beyond the west walk was a "*fair orchard furnished with good fruit and divers pleasant walks*". South of the house beyond the woodyard, dairy, laundry, brewhouse, bakehouse and pigeon-house were "*several orchards of cherries, pears, plums, others*

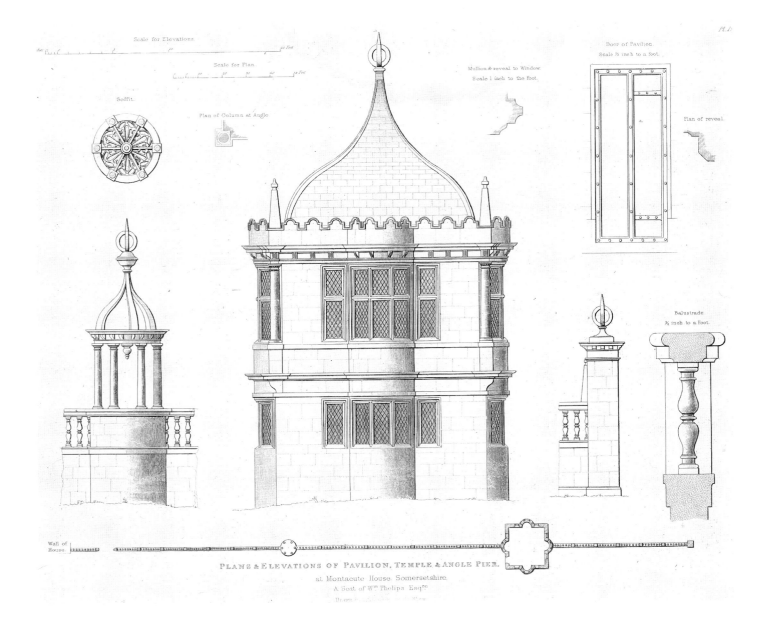

Fig. 5.9
An engraving showing plans and elevations of the 'Pavilion, Temple and Angle Pier' around the Eastern Forecourt at MONTACUTE HOUSE.

of apples, and also good kitchen-gardens with two fish-ponds, all encompassed with a wall". West of the house was yet another "large void court set with rows of trees in order, of elms and walnuts", leading to the stables, barns, stalls and granaries. By the farm buildings were several fishponds and a hop garden occupying an acre and a half.[16]

Although much of the Montacute garden has changed, several important components of its late Elizabethan layout survive. The outline of the eastern forecourt, about 57 yards square, still remains, with its walls balustraded and punctuated with obelisks. At the mid-point of both flanking walls is a small rotunda, capped with an ogee tripod spire and pierced finial. From some directions the three curved legs of the cap give a decidedly lop-sided appearance, but they are clearly designed to be viewed from a point immediately in front of the house. At the two outer corners of the east court are two larger, square pavilions with bay windows, battlemented parapets with corner obelisks, and ogee roofs surmounted by pierced finials; these were subsequently used as game larders. Today this court has been converted to a pleasant garden with lawns and flower borders, but originally it was no more than an enclosed yard for the reception of horses and carriages using the main approach from the east. The stone gate lodges mentioned in 1667 were removed in the late eighteenth century. The principal walled garden to the north was about 98 yards square; the broad terrace overlooking it from the house side and the raised perimeter walks are probably both original, but the internal layout was changed in the 1840s and all trace of the prospect mound and banqueting hall have disappeared.

The concept of larger, more elaborate formal gardens was beginning to percolate down from the provincial nobility to the gentry. Some of the smaller manor houses of this period still retain elements of their Elizabethan formal surroundings today, although it can be difficult to ascertain how much of their layout is original and how much a recreation of more recent times. At Lytes Cary the basic form of the raised terrace walk around the orchard east of the house is probably of Tudor origin, but in all other respects the layout of the gardens has undergone much change in later centuries. The skeleton of the Elizabethan layout at Cothelstone Manor on the Quantocks can still be discerned, though the fine details are lost. The courtyard on the south-eastern front of the house is closed off by a gatehouse giving access to a straight drive, which leads to an outer gate in a short screen wall. North-east of the house are the outlines of a bowling-green with a loggia of three arches and of another formal garden, both since converted to vegetable plots. A banqueting-hall was added beyond the formal garden in the early seventeenth century.[17] Fairfield House near Stogursey was remodelled for Elizabeth Verney around 1580, and this too is said to have had an important late Elizabethan garden.[18]

Archaeologically, the best evidence for the nature of Elizabethan gardens comes not from those examples which have remained in use (and have therefore been subject to many later changes), but rather from those which were abandoned at a relatively early date. This tended to occur when the house itself was superseded by a new house elsewhere. The earthworks of abandoned formal gardens were hardly recognised in Somerset before the 1970s, yet the county contains some fine examples, and more probably await discovery.

Fig. 5.11
Plan of the garden earthworks at
KELSTON COURT.

Fig. 5.10
LYTES CARY.
The raised terrace walk.

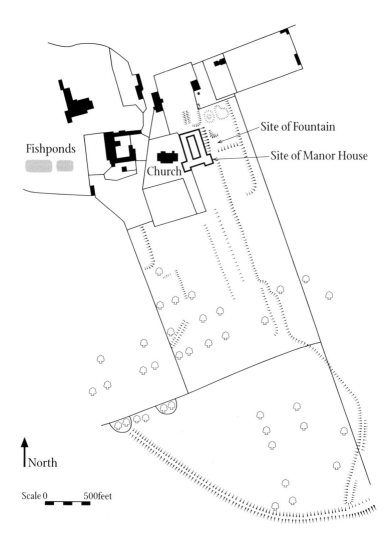

Kelston Court, west of Bath, was begun by John Harington in 1574, and completed in 1589 by his son, also named John. Both men were courtiers, and the second John Harington, a godson of Queen Elizabeth, was knighted in 1599. The family later ran into financial difficulties and were forced to sell the estate in 1759. Their old house, which stood on rising ground immediately east of Kelston church, was demolished by the new owner and replaced by a grander mansion in a more secluded location overlooking the Avon valley. Of the old manor-house little trace remains, but considerable earthworks of its gardens do survive. Directly south of the church are the remains of a large walled orchard. Further south and east of the church are the scarps of several long garden terraces, the most prominent of which flanked the eastern side of the house itself. On the flat top of the terrace above this scarp, overlooking the site of the house, are several low banks and rectilinear depressions which clearly represent former walks and flower-beds. Further south the principal scarp breaks back in two sharp dog-legs, and there are further, slighter terraces below. A central feature of the garden on the main terrace above the house was a fountain designed by the younger Sir John Harington. Sir John was noted as the inventor of the water-closet, described in his 1596 publication, THE METAMORPHOSIS OF AJAX, and he installed a complex water system at Kelston, whereby a spring-fed reservoir, higher up the hill to the east, worked the fountain, supplied the house, operated the water-closet, and fed the fishponds on the further side of the farm buildings. An estate map of 1744 shows an area of parkland extending southwards to the site of a summerhouse where the new mansion was shortly to rise. The park was crossed by several straight double avenues, one of which led from the old house to the summerhouse vantage-point. The alignments of these avenues can still be discerned from a few surviving trees.[19]

Claverton Manor and its gardens, east of Bath, were probably begun around 1580. In 1608 Sir Thomas Estcourt sold Claverton, complete with its newly-built manor-house, the park and vineyard, to Sir William Bassett of Uley. Some alterations may then have been carried out, since a lead rainwater-head from the site bears the date 1625. As at Kelston, a later owner demolished the old house in 1823 following completion of the new Claverton House higher up the hill. His successor seems to have had some regrets about this decision, and took care to preserve something of the gardens which had belonged to the old house. These consist of a series of five terraces cut into the rising ground. The higher terraces are merely grass slopes. The middle terrace was broader and, from the evidence of parch marks in dry summers, contained the house itself. The two lower terraces are still enclosed by stone walls. The easternmost wall, fronting the road, has a balustrade of openwork panels and a central gateway with Montacute-style openwork obelisks above the piers. There is a similar wall above the next terrace, with a flight of steps to its centre, fanning out at the bottom. Little survives of the house itself, unless the existing Manor Cottage preserves some part of its service wing in much-altered form. The Bassett arms were incorporated into the south end wall of this cottage and many finials and other architectural details were reused in it . High stone walls east of the church also survive from the former kitchen garden.[20]

Earthworks at Hardington, north-west of Frome, which included the remains of the gardens of the Bampfyldes' great house, were unfortunately bulldozed and levelled in 1977. A survey made by Michael Aston before their destruction revealed a complex series of platforms, lynchets and hollow-ways of medieval date around the isolated church, remains of the village of Hardington which had already been depopulated by 1538. The village earthworks were traversed by a long bank passing from one straight length to another through a series of obtuse angles. This latter feature appears to be a park or garden boundary, and within it were three rows of planting mounds, one above and two below a terrace. At the west end of the uppermost row is a keeper's lodge with a first-floor banqueting chamber. The date 1581 carved over the doorway of this building may point to the general period of the whole garden layout. The Bampfyldes' house at Hardington was in ruins by Collinson's time, and only a fragment remains.[21]

Vestiges of other gardens attached to late Tudor houses can be seen elsewhere in Somerset. At Combe Florey the remains, including a substantial prospect mound, stand across the road from the gatehouse of the old manor-house, built for the Frаunceis family in 1593. South of Chilcompton Manor, visible from the churchard, are a series of low, angled terraces which must also relate to a former garden layout. Greenwood's map of 1822 shows this area still set in a small park bounded by a row of trees on the western side.

Some garden earthworks are not directly related to any known great house, and their origin remains a puzzle. A recent discovery by Charles and Nancy Hollinrake in the orchard north of Parsonage Farm

at Over Stowey consists of a rectangular plat or parterre cut into the south-facing slope with three prominent terraces above, turning around the western side, with a stream and former pond below. There are some irregularities on the surface of the parterre itself, in addition to the overgrown remains of a possible small prospect mound in the middle of its eastern side. A long bank and ditch continues up towards the top of the slope from the western corner of the terraces; it appears to be cut by them and may therefore be of earlier date. The general character and scale of these earthworks are typical of Elizabethan gardens, and the rebuilding of the parsonage house around the end of the sixteenth century may have been the occasion for their development; yet they seem almost too lavish for a rectory estate owned by an absentee landlord (the property belonged to the mayor and commonalty of Bristol from 1541 to 1840). Whatever their origin, some vestiges of a formal layout seem to have survived at least up to 1744, when a survey of the rectory lands owned by the Corporation of Bristol shows a pattern of rectangular beds, apparently above the terraces rather than on the parterre itself; but the site was used only as an orchard by 1822.[22]

Similar problems surround a set of earthworks in Henhills Copse in Shapwick surveyed in 1992. Here a rectangular pond about 65 yards long by 22 yards wide occupies the lowest of three terraces cut into the hillside, facing north-west. On three sides the pond is fringed by a narrow flat strip of ground which would have provided a suitable habitat for water-loving plants. A more substantial terrace cut into the slope above the pond to the south-east has been much damaged, but retains traces of internal banks and platforms which may represent the remains of boundary walls or fences, flower beds and possibly garden buildings.[23] This site lies at a considerable distance from either manor-house in the village, and its historical context at present remains entirely unknown.

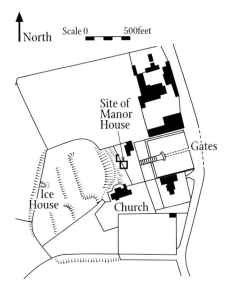

CLAVERTON MANOR.
above: Fig. 5.12
Plan of the garden earthworks
(after Iles, 1984).

below: Fig. 5.13
Gates and garden terraces.

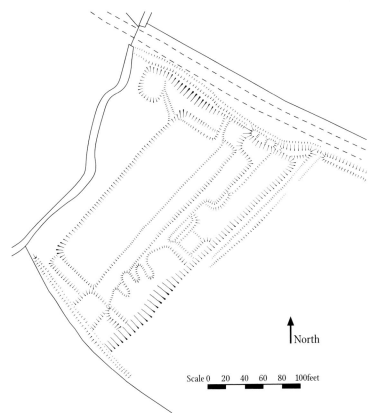

Fig. 5.14
Plan of garden earthworks in
HENHILLS COPSE, *Shapwick.*

JACOBEAN GARDENS

When James I came to the English throne in 1603 peace prevailed throughout western Europe, and for almost the first time since the 1530s the way was reopened for continental fashions to influence English garden design through direct personal contacts. The new queen and the prince of Wales both employed a French Huguenot hydraulic engineer and garden designer, Salomon de Caus, to redesign the grounds of their several houses near London. De Caus had himself studied in Italy in the 1590s and was familiar with some of the gardens made by Buontalenti for the de Medici family around Florence. The French influence was reinforced by more direct contact with renaissance Italy when Inigo Jones returned from his second tour there in 1615.

Somerset's Jacobean houses, such as East Quantoxhead and Newton Surmaville, remain architecturally conservative, and it is unlikely that local garden design underwent any immediate transformation. Plats, terraces, topiary, water features and banqueting-houses continued to be employed in formal array as had been the case in Elizabeth's time. The existence of gardens is noted in numerous early seventeenth-century documents, but these records rarely give much evidence of their character. A survey of Clevedon Court made in 1629 during the last years of the Wake family's occupancy described a *"fair, ancient and large stone-built house ... with two gardens, an orchard, a fair court, a strong and large barn and other outhouses, besides 60 acres of wood and coppice of 30 or 40 years"*.[24] The house of Brympton d'Evercy was described by Gerard in 1633 as *"daintily seated and furnished with all manner of conveniences as gardens, orchards, groves &c."*, and the basic early seventeenth-century pattern of forecourt, southern terrace and bowling-green can still be discerned, though much modified by later developments.[25] Shapwick House was remodelled in the early seventeenth century, and this may have been the occasion for elaborating and extending the medieval gardens there: it was perhaps at this time that the moat surrounding the house was filled in and some of the banks and ditches to the north were created.[26] Other elaborate gardens appear to have been developed during the early seventeenth century at Long Ashton Court, St Catherine's Court and East Coker Court, but little is known of them.[27]

Once again abandoned gardens are potentially more informative than those which have remained in use. The most spectacular of all the lost gardens in Somerset are those at Low Ham, first recognised and described by Michael Aston in 1978.[28] Here the extensive earthworks belong to at least two separate periods of garden construction, related to two successive vanished mansions.

In 1588 the manor of Low Ham was purchased by Sir Edward Hext, and within five years he had completed the first mansion, regarded as one of the finest in the west of England.[29] In about 1620 he began the strangely anachronistic Gothic church, which sits in a field at the foot of Hext Hill with no surrounding churchyard. Sir Edward's great house was thought to have stood some 330 yards south of the church, on top of the hill, where earthworks and parchmarks of walls and foundations are clearly visible. Immediately to the southwest a hollowed-out area resembling an abandoned quarry was, nevertheless, sufficiently regular in shape to prompt the initial speculation that it might represent a small uncompleted formal garden attached to the rear of the house. The hilltop site would have commanded fine views over the valley to the north-east, and it was thought that the main gardens and approach lay down the slope facing in this direction. However, a new survey of the site by the Royal Commission on Historical Monuments suggests that some of these early thoughts need revision.[30] The relatively slight earthworks down the north-east-facing slope now seem to represent agricultural closes rather than garden terraces. Instead of occupying different faces of the slope, as was first thought, it is now believed that the two sets of gardens were both terraced down the northern slope, the Jacobean garden being partly overlain by the gardens of the later period (see Chapter 6). By this interpretation the Hext garden would have lain directly between the hilltop and the church, broadening out fanwise from top to bottom, with a line of trees (now represented by shallow pits) along its eastern limit. Re-examination of the foundations on the hilltop has suggested that they represent a series of small buildings and yards, a farmyard complex or group of outbuildings rather than a great house. The Hext mansion itself, therefore, remains unlocated. Could its foundations have been robbed away entirely by the shallow quarrying on the hilltop? There are some problems with this interpretation also, since the general alignment of the quarry lies skew to that of the gardens, and placing the mansion here would allow neither the gardens nor the church to be visible from its lower floor. Wherever precisely it stood, the Hext mansion lasted only about a century before it was demolished.

CAROLEAN GARDENS

During the second quarter of the seventeenth century Henrietta Maria, Charles I's queen, provided a new lead in garden design. Daughter of Henri IV of France and Maria de' Medici, she had been brought up in French palaces whose gardens had been shaped directly by Florentine influences. When she first came to England she brought with her a gardener from Fontainebleau named André Mollet, who introduced at St James's Palace and Wimbledon Manor the French form of *parterre de broderie*. This consisted of scrolled or flowing plant-like designs outlined in box, the intervening spaces filled with a variety of coloured earths or gravels - chalk to make white, brick

Fig. 5.15
An aerial photograph showing the earthworks of the abandoned gardens at LOW HAM. *For a detailed plan see fig. 6.8.*

dust to make red, coal to make black. This form of parterre never became widely popular in England; however, it influenced the development of a distinctively English version, the so-called *parterre a l'anglaise*, in which the designs were made out of cut turf, sometimes also filled with coloured gravels. Through the influence of Inigo Jones, Palladian villas set in Italianate gardens were beginning to appear in the countryside around London. Salomon de Caus had left England in 1613 and never returned; but in his place his brother or nephew Isaac arrived, working in a similar style with a new emphasis upon perspectives and upon the architectural alignments of house and garden, using grottoes, fountains and other hydraulic effects. In the west country Isaac de Caus carried out major works for Philip Herbert, 4th Earl of Pembroke, at Wilton House, which included *parterres de broderie* in the style of Mollet and elaborate sculptured fountains.

Little is known of gardens of this period in Somerset, and probably no local examples came into the top rank exemplified by Wilton. The most elaborate were probably those created by the Pouletts at Hinton St George in the 1630s. Duke Cosimo III de' Medici, soon to become Grand Duke of Tuscany, visited Hinton in 1669 and was impressed with the provision of gardens there, with their wide variety of plants and fruits, "*both for utility and pleasure*"; and he commented in particular on the parterre which, he says, was unlike the usual contemporary English version with turf and rolled gravel walks; instead, it was "*a meadow with different beds having borders of bricks on end, filled with flowers*".[31] This sounds more like an example of the cutwork parterre or *parterre de pieces coupées* pioneered by the Dutch gardener Hans Vredeman de Vries (1527-1606), which only became popular in Europe after his lifetime.

In the 1620s Witham Charterhouse was held by Ralph Hopton, Baron Hopton of Stratton, who was created a Knight of the Order of the Bath on the coronation of Charles I. It seems likely that he was responsible for the enlargement of the gardens there. Recent survey work has shown that the remains of the medieval monastery were overlain by a formal garden, the outline of which still survives in earthwork form. At the centre, adjoining the southern side of the residence which occupied part of the monastic premises, the roofed alley around the former priory's great cloister seems to have been maintained into the seventeenth century as a sheltered walk around a privy garden. Beyond the privy garden, occupying the whole of the

existing rectangular field, was an outer garden, its margins defined by broad terraced walks, with a square mound at the south-west corner marking the site of a pavilion.[32]

SMALLER COUNTRY GARDENS

The best written evidence for gardening activites on a smaller scale comes from parsonages. Adrian Schaell, who arrived for his induction as rector of High Ham in 1570 to find the rectory house in a severe state of decay, annotated the parish register in 1598 with a record of his achievements. In addition to his work on the house, he tells us "*concerning the orchards and gardens, what wisdom and diligence I have used in fencing and stopping them, in grafting of trees and planting of diverse sorts of herbs with great diligence sought out of sundry places*".[33] The vicarage at Nether Stowey had a garden and orchard in 1571, and a hopyard by 1613.[34]

TOWN GARDENS

Gardens attached to town houses are frequently mentioned in surveys of the early seventeenth century, but usually little is known of their layout or contents. A survey of the manor of Chard made in 1602 mentions many gardens but provides little information about them, apart from occasional references to their size and to timber trees growing on them. A few examples will serve to give the flavour of the record. Thomas Every held an inn called the Lion in the High Street, the property including a garden one rod in extent, a bowling alley, a kitchen garden, and a meadow of four acres adjoining the back of the house, plus two further meadows on the edge of the town, the whole containing 60 elms and ashes. Robert Selwood held two garden plots in the middle of the High Street next to the Sessions hall one rod in extent, with two adjoining meadows, one of two acres, another of five acres, the whole containing six ash trees. Nicholas Wall held a newly-built tenement in the High Street, divided into two, with an orchard of half an acre and a meadow of one acre, containing six ashes. Anne Pincher had a large house in the High Street occupied by four tenants, with gardens occupying half an acre and one acre of meadow adjoining. Margaret Channen had a tenement on the north side of the High Street with a garden one acre in extent and a pasture close also of one acre.[35]

TUDOR & STUART DEER PARKS - Sources

As noted in Chapter 3, the distribution and character of deer parks underwent several significant changes towards the end of the Middle Ages. Since the middle of the fourteenth century fewer new parks had been created, while many older parks were abandoned and converted to agricultural use. Those parks that remained were managed with greater flexibility, accommodating more profitable forms of land use alongside the traditional grazing of deer, and increasingly incorporating ornamental plantations and avenues.

The decline in the number of parks since the high-water mark of the early fourteenth century was not particularly apparent to contemporary commentators. Indeed, chroniclers in the sixteenth

Fig. 5.16
WITHAM CHARTERHOUSE. *Earthworks of the abandoned gardens overlying the remains of the Medieval monastery.*

Fig. 5.17

SOMERSET PARKS in the
1569 MUSTERS CERTIFICATES

Location	Occupier	Compass in miles	No. of Mares
BARRINGTON	Sir J Clifton	2	2
CASTLE CAREY	John Yownge esq.	1	2
CURRYPOOL (Spaxton)	Thomas Mallet esq.	1	2
DONYATT	Robert Cuffe, gent.	2	2
DUNSTER	Thomas Luttrell esq.	2	2
EAST QUANTOXHEAD	Dame Joan Luttrell	1	2
EVERCREECH	Tristram Pister, gent.	2	2
HINTON ST GEORGE	Sir Hugh Paulet, kt.	4	4
KNOWLE (Shepton Montague)	Sir James FitzJames, kt.	1	2
MARSHWOOD	Thomas Luttrell esq.	2	2
MERIFIELD	John Wadham esq.	1	2
NETHER STOWEY	Humphrey Colles esq.	3	2
NETTLECOMBE	John Trevelyan, gent.	1	2
NORWOOD (Glastonbury)	Sir Maurice Berkeley, kt.	4	4
NORTH PETHERTON	Sir Maurice Berkeley, kt.	4	4
PILTON	George Rogers, esq.	2	2
SHARPHAM (Glastonbury)	Edward Dyer, esq.	2	2
SUTTON	John Bushe, gent.	2	2
WHITELACKINGTON	Sir George Speke, kt.	2	2
WRAXALL	Edward Gorges, esq.	2	2

and seventeenth centuries sometimes expressed amazement at the numbers of parks they saw. In 1507 Polidore Vergil, a scholar of European reputation who had come to England as a collector of papal dues and had just been appointed Archdeacon of Wells through the agency of its absentee Italian bishop, still thought of England as having one-third of its area devoted to forests and parks: "*almost everywhere a man may see clausures and parks paled and enclosed and fraught with venery*", to the detriment of tillage. John Leland noted at least twenty parks during his travels through Somerset in 1540-42. Moryson's ITINERARY of 1617 reckoned that there were more fallow deer in one English county than in the rest of Europe, and "*every gentleman of £500-£1000 rent by the year hath a park for them inclosed with payles of wood for two or three myles compass*".[36] Gerard's description of Somerset in 1633 also mentions many parks.

The muster rolls for the County Militia made in 1569 include records of enquiries into the number of parks made by the sheriff. This information was sought in order to assess their capacity for the breeding and rearing of horses required for military purposes.[37] The results can be tabulated, as shown in fig. 5.17.

Most of these parks are shown on Christopher Saxton's county map, published in 1575, which in addition shows seven more parks not listed in the musters certificates: Backwell, Banwell, Filwood, Stogursey, Stoke Trister, Walton-in-Gordano and Witham. Saxton normally showed parks by a conventional symbol of a few trees within a circular paling fence, but North Petherton Park is shown significantly larger than average, and there seems to be some attempt to portray its actual shape. Evercreech Park is shown with its lodge or palace. Filwood, Banwell, Castle Cary, Donyatt and Merrifield are shown without trees, while Walton-in-Gordano Park is named but shown without a pale.

The 1569 returns may be compared with similar records from the 1583 musters certificates, though these are less complete. Nine of the parks listed in 1569 - Castle Cary, Donyatt, Evercreech, Knowle, Nether Stowey, Nettlecombe, Norwood, Sutton and Wraxall - find no mention in 1583. According to the later record, the parks at Barrington, Dunster and Marshwood had all contracted in the intervening fourteen years from circuits of two miles to one, while Hinton St George had declined from four to two miles in circumference, though it is doubtful whether these estimates are reliable. However, two new parks, Cothelstone and Huntworth, appear in the records for the first time in 1583.[38]

Pictorial evidence begins to supplement the written record. A survey made of Stoke Trister in 1566-7 includes a sketch of the manor-house, with a walled courtyard in front, deer grazing in the foreground, and a wooden paling fence and gate to the rear.[39] Saxton's county map was followed by the products of other cartographers such

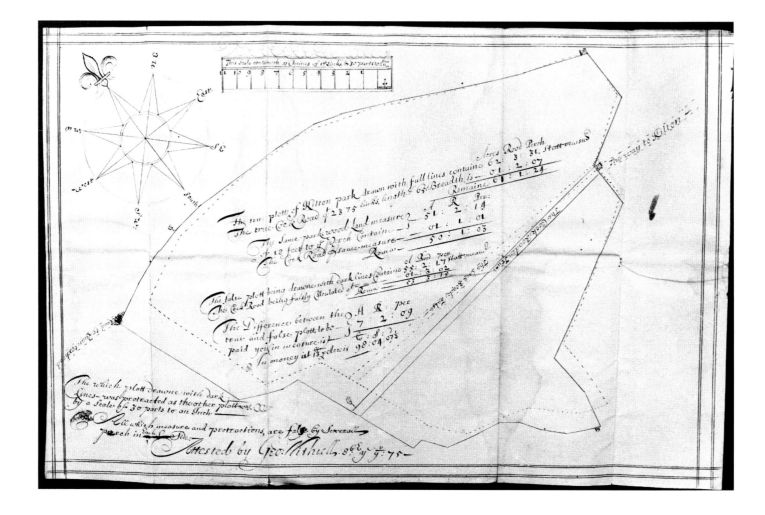

Fig. 5.18

KILTON PARK. *A map of 1675 surveyed by George Withiel illustrating the importance increasingly accorded to having accurate measurements and records of landholdings.*

as John Speed (1610), John Janssen (1646), John Blaeu (1648), Richard Blome (1673) and Robert Morden (1695), but these generally plagiarised older surveys without adding much new information, and it was not until the eighteenth century that there were further advances in mapping at the county scale. However, large-scale estate maps also begin to appear in the sixteenth century, and these become increasingly detailed, accurate and useful. One of the earliest Somerset examples shows the park of Queen Camel in 1573.[40] The outline of Castle Cary park with its lodge is shown on another map of c.1650.[41]

OLD DEER PARKS -
a CONTINUING TRADITION

Although their numbers had decreased, some of the older deer parks continued to be maintained for their original purpose. For example, the park attached to Farleigh Hungerford Castle is mentioned in 1654 in Anthony Hungerford's will, and a survey describes it as as 2¾ miles in circumference, containing 26 antlered deer and 44 rascal deer (i.e. harts with antlers of less than ten tines).[42]

Continuity of ownership was the factor most likely to produce some degree of stability in the form and use of parks. The 1569 musters certificates identify three ancient parks in west Somerset which had long been the property of the Luttrells, at Dunster, East Quantoxhead and Marshwood, and all three continued in use into the seventeenth century. However, they did not survive without some changes.

The park at Dunster was really two parks, the Hanger or Old Park on either side of the River Avill north of the castle, and the New Park covering the rising ground to the south. The Old Park was already subject to flexible management. Sir John Luttrell (d.1551) retained in hand 72 acres there, containing 50 deer and *"divers great oaks, elms and ashes"*. In 1556 Thomas Luttrell permitted the temporary use of the Hanger in the Old Park for pasturing *"ten rother beasts or kine and three geldings"*. When George Luttrell came of age in 1581 he was confronted with a list of claims from his grasping father-in-law, Hugh Stewkley, the lay rector and a London lawyer, which included agistment fees for all cattle feeding in Dunster Park and the shoulder of every deer killed there. The basis of this claim appears to be that the South Lawn in the Old Park had been arable land owing tithes earlier that century. The Old Park had lost all its deer by the early eighteenth century. However, the New Park on the higher ground continued to serve as a deer park. In 1584 George Luttrell allowed his mother two deer a year, a buck in summer and a doe in winter, either from Dunster park or from East Quantoxhead. In 1597 two poachers tried in the Star Chamber Court confessed to hunting and killing some deer in Dunster Park, and were fined £100 apiece and sentenced to three months in the Fleet Prison. The Dunster deer park was estimated at 416 acres in 1892, and still then contained about 300 fallow deer, though it was reduced in size soon afterwards.[43]

Although parts of the Luttrells' park at East Quantoxhead had gone down to arable in 1408 and 1452-3, it still contained deer. By the middle of the sixteenth century it comprised about 100 acres enclosed within a pale, containing about 100 deer. Shortly after 1630 Thomas Luttrell brought a lawsuit against his stepmother for damage to his deer and timber at East Quantoxhead. A glebe terrier of 1630 claimed tithes on deer taken in the park.[44]

The third of the Luttrell's parks at Marshwood in Carhampton had been reduced from 270 acres in 1428 to 100 acres by the middle of the sixteenth century, when it was leased to Thomas Wyndham, but it still contained 100 deer. Its circumference was estimated at one mile in 1583, when it was leased out. It is marked on the county maps of Saxton and Speed, and is depicted in more detail on an estate map of 1687, when it still contained deer.[45]

Episcopal parks, stable throughout the later Middle Ages, became more vulnerable during the upheavals of the Reformation, though some survived. The Bishop of Wells continued to reward his associates and servants with perquisites from his parks during the early sixteenth century. In 1500, for example, the keeper of Westbury-sub-Mendip Park, Thomas Weld, was to have all trees blown down by the wind, while in 1511-12 his successor, Thomas Broke, was to have the herbage and pannage from the park, subject to the reservation of sufficient pasture for the bishop's game. In 1546 another episcopal servant, Edward Upton, keeper of the palace and prison at Wells, was granted four loads of firewood from the park at Wells.[46] A brief break in ownership occurred in 1548, when Bishop Barlow was forced to 'sell' the parks and palaces of Wells, Evercreech and Banwell to Edward Seymour, Duke of Somerset, King Edward VI's uncle and Lord Protector. The parks of Westbury-sub-Mendip and Wedmore also came into the Duke's hands soon after. In fact the bishop never seems to have received any cash for these transactions, and the Duke proceeded to plunder the bishopric's estates unmercifully. Most of these properties were recovered, however, following Somerset's attainder and execution in 1552. In 1590 agreement was reached with the lessee of Westbury Park that no timber trees should be cut down there for repairs to the park or buildings without the bishop's consent.[47] Immediately after the death of Bishop Godwin that same year John Sawyer of Wulfarshill was said to have made off with six waggonloads of timber cut out of Banwell Park, part of a calculated attempt to pre-empt the seizure of the bishop's effects by the sheriff in the name of the Crown.[48] There is a clear impression that the timber, wood and grazing of the bishop's parks were of most value during this period, but Banwell Park at least still contained deer.

Poaching continued to concern many owners. In 1524 Bishop Clerk complained in the Westminster Court of Star Chamber that William St Loe of Knight Sutton and several of his associates had *"gathered and united to them other evil and riotous persons to the number of 16 persons in manner of war harnessed and arrayed, being of one confederacy to hunt in ... Banwell Park on 28th June last, about 11 o'clock of the same night, with force and arms, that is to say swords and bucklers, crossbows and other bows and arrows ... [they] broke and entered the said park, and hunted and killed four bucks and many other rascal deer, and carried them away ... and the said riotous persons, not satisfied with this misdemeanor, of their further malicious mind, on 17th August then next ensuing, in riotous manner assembled themselves as beforesaid to the number of 30 persons and above, and at 10 o'clock in the night ... with force and arms ... broke and entered the said park, and not only with bows and arrows and greyhounds, but also with nets, then and there did hunt and kill*

Fig. 5.19
CHRISTOPHER SAXTON'S MAP
of the COUNTY of SOMERSET.
*This version of the 1575 map, issued
in 1607, brings out the park enclosures
more clearly than the original.*

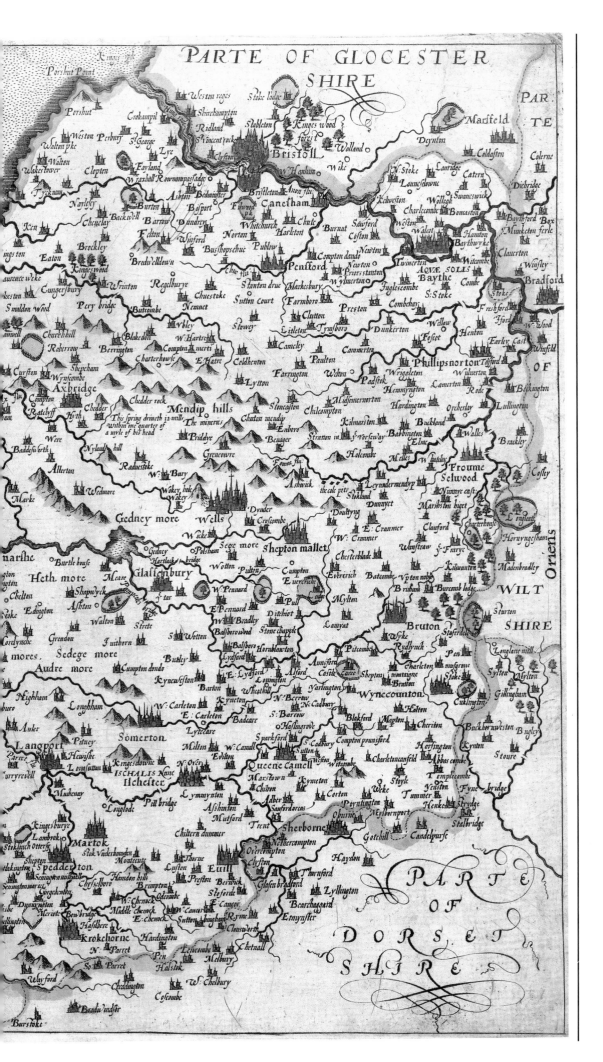

PARTE OF GLOCESTER SHIRE

deer of all sorts to the number of 20 deer and more; and in further despite did set the heads upon the pales of the same park, to the pernicious example and also to the great comfort and boldness to other malefactors...".[49] Interestingly, William St Loe subsequently obtained from the bishop a 21-year lease of land in Banwell together with the office of park keeper and the herbage and pannage of the park for life - perhaps a case of setting a thief to catch a thief.

A similar case is recorded in 1552-8, when William Clifton took action in the Star Chamber Court against Osmond Williams, barber of Ilminster, and six other "riotous and evil-disposed persons being arrayed with bows and arrows, pikes, staves, swords and other weapons" who entered the park of Barrington during Clifton's absence at the royal court in London and hunted his deer there until apprehended by the keepers. Walter Trott, one of the poachers, was pursued by the drawing of a hound to the house of Osmond Williams, but fled through the back door and leaped over a wall to escape.[50]

Where a single manor contained a pair of parks, this sometimes reflected the keeping of different types of deer in separate enclosures. Leland described Lord Audley's manor at Nether Stowey "having by it a park of red deer and another of fallow". Such double parks reflected the contemporary belief that it was unwise to mix the two species in the same park, "for the red deer is a masterful beast, and when the time of bellowing cometh, he grows fierce and outrageous and will kill the fallow deer if they but cross him in his walk".[51]

The rebuilding of park lodges continued to reflect the rising status of their occupiers and the general demands for greater comfort. William Wroth, resident keeper of North Petherton Park in the time of Henry VI, rebuilt the moated lodge on the edge of the park. In the 1580s this was partly demolished in its turn, the materials being reused to build Broad Lodge, subsequently known as Petherton Park, which continued to serve as the Wroth family's residence into the eighteenth century.[52]

NEW DEER PARKS of the 16TH and 17TH CENTURIES

In a period when many parks were falling into disuse or changing their function, it is easy to underestimate the contrary trend, the creation of new deer parks. The procedures for acquiring emparking licences were beginning to lapse into disuse by the early sixteenth century, though occasional examples can still be found. In 1524 Henry VIII granted a patent to Sir Nicholas Wadham licensing him to make a park at his manor of Merifield consisting of 200 acres of pasture and 40 acres of wood. Sir John Carew acquired a licence to create a park and warren at Crowcombe in 1616, though this may have been no more than an attempt to restore a derelict park which had for some time been used only as pasture.[53]

The identification of parks newly created during the Tudor and early Stuart periods often rests largely upon the absence of any earlier documentation. For example a deer park north-east of Nettlecombe Court is mentioned for the first time in 1532; its extent was estimated at 80 acres in 1556 and 70 acres in 1619, and its grazing was leased to the lord's tenants for their cattle and horses. There was also an extensive area of common wood-pasture to the south of the Court where the occurrence of the name 'Park Gate' in a lease of 1524 suggests an early attempt at enclosure, though emparkment of this area was not formalised before 1755. Nettlecombe Park became noted for the quality of its timber, which was being used for building projects as far away as Cornwall by 1591. The Great Park to the south still contains some mighty pollard oaks with girths of up to 23ft.[54] In 1539 the Dean of Wells appointed William Butler as keeper of a previously unrecorded park at Wedmore. This was clearly a genuine deer park, since in 1545 Thomas Clerk was permitted a buck from it every summer and a doe every winter, and a record of 1558 speaks of the 'New Park Wall'.[55] Saxton's map shows a previously unrecorded park called Filwood Park between Whitchurch and Bishopsworth, now in the southern suburbs of Bristol. According to Norden, this was created out of the rump of Filwood Chase, being enclosed with a pale and stocked with deer by Hugh Smyth.[56] Sir John Stawell's deer park at Cothelstone and Edward Popham's deer park at Huntworth in North Petherton both first appear in the 1583 muster rolls, when they were estimated at one mile in compass, sufficient for two mares each. The small park at Combe Sydenham had been established before 1626-7, and still contained a few red and fallow deer in the early years of the present century.[57] The deer park at Pixton near Dulverton is apparently first mentioned in a marriage agreement of 1658.[58]

Leland's *Itinerary* provides the first known reference for several parks. The most important of these was at Hinton St George, where Sir Hugh Poulett "*hath of late made a park not far from his house at Hinton on the side of a hill*". This was expanded on a piecemeal basis by exchanges with tenants and the absorption of old freeholds, until by 1569 it was estimated at four miles in circumference. As the park was slowly extended over the West Field and part of the South Field, agricultural enclosure proceeded elsewhere in the parish, till by 1600 open-field farming had been eliminated from Hinton entirely. Fifty years later the park had encroached beyond the parish boundary into Dinnington, and there are records of hedges being grubbed up, further fields taken in, and new hawthorn boundaries being planted around the edges of the park and warren. One area was known as the 'New Park' in 1718. A new entrance lodge had been made shortly before 1654, and there was a second entry called the White Lodge by 1680. Hinton St George exemplifies the multi-purpose role of the park in this period. Although it was recorded as a deer park in 1583 and 1669, the meadow and cattle pasture which it contained were equally important, if not more so. When Cosimo de' Medici visited Hinton in 1669, he saw the park as a backdrop to the house and gardens, "*three miles in circumference, shut in by a thick plantation of trees*", containing deer "*of two sorts, black and red, to which the mixture of plain, of hill, of coppice wood, and meadow land, together with two plentiful springs of water affords a most suitable abode*". Ornamental trees were also beginning to appear: in 1652 the estate purchased 2 cwt of cherry trees from London to plant in the park.[59] Travelling westwards from Hinton St George, Leland passed by Whitelackington Park, which he mentions as an appendage to Mr Speke's main residence. Whitelackington Park also appears on Saxton's county map, yet is curiously omitted from John Speed's map of 1610, though it reappears in later sources.

Gerard's survey of 1633 adds further examples. He mentions two parks belonging to the manor of Hazlegrove, the ancient park at Queen Camel and a previously unrecorded park at Hazlegrove itself. He also mentions the new gardens and parks at Montacute and Orchard Portman; and he describes how the mansion of Mr Walrond, Sheriff of Somerset, at Ile Brewers,"*seated in a park and environed with trees yields a goodly prospect to travellers*".[60] Again the visual appearance of the park as the setting for the great house was clearly now assuming a greater importance.

A few of the new parks may replace examples previously abandoned. At Walton-in-Gordano there are some hints of a medieval park, and the name 'Walton Park' without a pale symbol appears on Saxton's map north of the present village. A new park was made south of the village by the Pouletts of Hinton St George, who acquired the manor of Walton by marriage in 1614. Its enclosure may well have contributed to the disappearance of the older village above Ladye Bay, where the church survived as an isolated ruin until rebuilt in 1870 to serve the expanding villa suburbs of Clevedon. The first Lord Poulett built a new hunting lodge on the highest point of the park, which took the form of a mock castle with an octagonal central tower surrounded by an octagonal battlemented curtain wall with round towers at the angles.[61] This remarkable structure, completed in about 1620, was never a permanent residence, since the Pouletts' main interests were still centred upon their Hinton and Buckland estates; instead it seems to have served as a retreat for various indulgences which must be passed over here. Close by, Saxton's map also marks Wakes Tower on the hill above Clevedon Court, another early folly or hunting box, which was still standing when a painting was made of the court and its grounds around 1722.

Some older parks were considerably enlarged. In the 1550s Hugh Smyth greatly extended the deer park around Ashton Court.[62] Such actions could lead to conflict. Some of Hugh Smyth's tenants at Whitchurch brought a case against him in 1579 for making a new park out of their common and enclosing it with palings, but he denied this, claiming that his shepherd had simply repaired some railings which had collapsed.[63] In 1516 the tenants of Rodney Stoke brought a case in Star Chamber against Sir John Rodney who, they claimed, had added part of their common pasture in Stoke Moor to his park, enclosed 200 acres from the Royal Forest of Mendip, pulled down two tenements and enclosed them within his park, blocked up the public road, installed red deer in the park, and killed the hounds of any of his tenants who tried to drive the deer off their crops. For his part, he claimed that the action against him had been brought out of malice by certain ill-disposed persons who had already broken down his park pale and attacked him with a pitchfork; that his deer did little harm, and that he had every right to enclose a park on his own ground, provided that he left sufficient common for his tenants.[64] An armorial shield on Sir John Rodney's tomb in Rodney Stoke Church appears to depict a small park enclosed with wooden palings and a gate.

Disparkings

If establishing the precise date when deer parks were created is difficult, determining the date of their abandonment is even more so.

Many medieval parks simply fade from the record without any note of their passing. Often disparking was less the result of a deliberate decision at a particular point in time than a slow process of change and decay, with agricultural uses and subdivision by enclosure slowly advancing at the expense of the deer.

On manors where there had been two parks, it was often no great loss to relinquish one of them for farming purposes while maintaining the other for deer. At Staple Fitzpaine there had been two deer parks in the thirteenth century, but the musters certificate of 1583 records only one, belonging to Sir John Clifton. In 1595 Gervase Clifton sold the park, then estimated at 5,120 yards in circumference, with all its deer and its "*pale, rayles and postes*" recently made, to Hugh Portman. Clearly the Portman family continued to use the surviving park for some forms of hunting. One night in 1610 Sir John Portman's hawks were stolen from the park by an intruder. By 1690 a park lodge and kennels had been built in the small park (now Staple Park Farm), and in that year the 6th Baronet Portman willed his hounds and three of his best hunting horses to two relatives.[65] There had also been two parks at Castle Cary since the fourteenth century, the Home Park and Ansford Park. Both are mentioned in the inquisition on the property of the Duke of Somerset following his attainder in 1552, but Saxton's map shows only the Home Park. Gerard in 1633 describes the two ancient parks "*whereof the one remains unto this day and stored with deer; the other being a mile off at Almsford* (sic) *and leased out*".[66]

Episcopal and monastic parks were prominent among the early casualties. Muchelney Abbey's park had been partly converted from woodland to arable by 1451, when three tenants were presented for failing to undertake their ploughing services there, and by the sixteenth century it was divided into two parts and included meadow and pasture.[67] Cleeve Abbey, suffering increasing financial difficulties in the last few decades before the Dissolution, was leasing out its park at Stout Grange by 1507.[68] The park of the Bishop of Bath and Wells at Huish Episcopi was leased for pasture in the fifteenth century, though it was still then fenced and gated; sales of thickets and thorns from the park in 1490-1 suggest declining standards of management. Sales of underwood and pasture continued into the 1560s, but a century later the park had become the nucleus of the biggest farm in the parish.[69] John Leland recorded that the parks of the bishop and prior south-east of Bath were without deer, their walls ruinous.[70] Poundisford Park had been a valuable part of the Bishop of Winchester's manor of Taunton throughout the Middle Ages, but in 1534 Bishop Gardiner seems to have reached a decision that the deer park was no longer required, and leased it as two separate agricultural holdings to two Taunton merchants, Roger and William Hill. Each built his own substantial house within it, both of which survive today.[71]

Many secular parks tell the same story. Spaxton Park was partly ploughed by 1476, and all 74 acres had been converted wholly to farmland by the seventeenth century, although it was still then recognised as a discrete area of land.[72] Kilton Park had become a mere wood by 1553, about 100 acres in extent, "*well set with oaks and young ashes*".[73] Wick Park near Stogursey included 100 acres of 20-year-old coppice in 1527, ten acres of which had been cut in the last two years, and it was still producing underwood and timber in 1577-8, but was divided and leased for agricultural use soon after.[74] Currypool Park

near Spaxton was divided into fields in about 1618, though some fallow deer lingered on even after that date.[75] East Quantoxhead still had a deer park in the 1630s, but a survey of the manor in 1746 makes no mention of any park then surviving.[76] Aley Park, already divided and leased out by 1604, went under the plough for the first time in 1647.[77] In 1652 deer were removed from Wellington Park to Littlecote by Alexander Popham, though the park and warren at Wellington still figured in the marriage settlement of his son sixteen years later.[78] Chaffcombe Park, which had been leased out for long periods since 1582, returned to the Pouletts in 1759, and six years later was stocked with their cattle.[79] The red deer park at Nether Stowey, comprising 172 acres, was divided into closes by 1620, and by the following century the entire park had been split up into fields.[80]

Leland tells us that at Minehead "*there was a fair park...but Sir Andrew Luttrell of late time destroyed it*". In fact Sir Andrew had leased out the whole manor in 1538 in order to provide legacies for his children, and the park may well have lost its deer and been converted to agricultural use in his time. The park was recovered by Sir John Luttrell who undertook to pay the promised legacies, but to achieve this he was forced to mortgage it two months before his death in 1551 to his cousin, Hugh Stewkley, for £230 13s 4d. At that time the park was estimated at 200 acres. Sir Andrew's widow, Dame Margaret Luttrell, was unaware of the closing date set for its redemption, and Stewkley attempted to foreclose, whereupon Dame Margaret refused to relinquish the park until the legacies had been paid. This began an ownership dispute which was not finally settled until the early eighteenth century, by which time the park had long since ceased to have any recognisable existence.[81]

A few of the new parks described in the previous section were short-lived. Wedmore Park, held by the crown in 1553, was described as 'lately disparked', though the new purchaser was required to maintain its fences and ditches; four years later part of it was down to arable.[82] Another recent enclosure, Filwood Park, lasted only six years before it was disparked by Sir Hugh Smyth, nephew of its creator; the pales were carried to Long Ashton, and the 249 acres of the former park were divided into four enclosed grounds, a wood, a good pasture, a rougher pasture and a meadow.[83]

The greatest loss of the period was the ancient royal park of North Petherton. The 1583 musters certificate records the park as owned by absentee landlords living in London, and "*almost decayed*", being unable to provide pasture for any mares. Though the numbers of deer there seem to have declined, it was still producing an average income of about £150 per annum from sales of wood and pasture and up to £200 a year from timber. Part of the park was enclosed and leased out in 1584, and the resulting rents appear to have been more profitable. It was perhaps inevitable that disparkment would follow, though it was not until 1638 that the keeper, Sir Thomas Wroth, entered into any formal disafforestation agreement. From then on the disintegration of the park was rapid. About 140 of the best timber oaks were destroyed during the Civil War. By 1665 the park had been fragmented into eleven separate holdings, increased to 15 by 1676, all held on short leases, producing a total income of £889. Lime was being used to improve some of the pasture for sheep in 1660, while bricks were being made in the southern part of the park in 1670.[84]

When parks declined or disappeared from the landscape, the houses and lodges associated with them often followed. Leland records that the palace at Evercreech, which had fallen into ruin, was pulled down by Bishop Clerk (1523-41), though the park itself could still be recognised as an entity into the eighteenth century.[85] The Wadhams' house in Merifield Park, described by Gerard as "*a fair ancient house moated in and neighboured with a park*", was demolished by Sir John Wyndham some time after his acquisition of the manor in 1609.[86] Today only the moat and fragments of one tower, together with remains of a fishpond, can be seen.

Most of the abandoned parks went down to farmland, a few to woodland. However, in a couple of cases they provided the sites for projected settlements. Part of Mudgley Old Park was used by the Clifton family after the late sixteenth century to establish a new planned village comprising at least ten tofts, two of which are still occupied today.[87] In 1551 the Duke of Somerset attempted to settle a colony of Flemish weavers in Glastonbury, and the keeper of Wirrall Park, a man named Cornish, was required to provide each family with four acres of land out of the park, sufficient for two kine, for a term of three lives. The 140 deer in the park were to be removed. The park at that time comprised about 200 acres, but 60 acres of this was high wood, and the remainder did not provide sufficient pasture to permit the intended division, so the herbage was offered in common. Cornish seems to have attempted to retain possession of the park and its deer by offering to find accommodation for 36 families elsewhere, and nothing further is heard of this scheme.[88]

REFERENCES - Chapter 5

1. For further examples see J.H. Bettey, *Suppression of the Monasteries in the West Country* (Gloucester, 1989).

2. C.J. Bond & R. Iles, 'Early gardens in Avon and Somerset', in A.E. Brown (ed.), *Garden Archaeology* (Council for British Archaeology Research Report no.78, 1991), pp.38-9

3. Whitney R.D. Jones, *William Turner: Tudor Naturalist, Physician and Divine* (1988), pp.6-54).

4. H.C. Maxwell Lyte, 'The Lytes of Lytescary', *P.S.A.N.H.S.* Vol.38 (1892), pp.44-8.

5. John Gerard, *The Herball or Generall Historie of Plantes* (1636 edn.), i, pp.38, 40; ii, pp. 60, 121, 195-6, 217.

6. Examples relevant to garden history include Anthony Fitzherbert's, *Book of Husbandry* (1525), which includes a section on fruit propagation; Thomas Tusser's *Five Hundred Points of Good Husbandry* (1573), which gives in delightful doggerel verse many practical tips on the cultivation of fruit trees, flowers and herbs; Leonard Mascall's *The Book of Art and Manner, How to Plant and Graft all sorts of Trees* (1572); and John Parkinson's *Paradisi in Sole Paradisus Terrestris ('Park-in-Sun's Park on Earth')*(1629), which illustrates contemporary practices in the flower-garden, kitchen garden and orchard.

7. Introductions of flowering plants are to some extent covered by Roy Genders, *The Cottage Garden and the Old-Fashioned Flowers* (1969); and by Penelope Hobhouse, *Plants in Garden History* (1992).

8. For fuller details of fruit and vegetable introductions see F.A. Roach, *Cultivated Fruits of Britain: their Origin and History* (Oxford, 1985); Charles Lyte, *The Kitchen Garden* (Sparkford, 1984); David C. Stuart, *The Kitchen Garden: a Historical Guide to Traditional Crops* (Gloucester, 1987).

9. Quoted in Stuart, *The Kitchen Garden*, p.219.

10. M.C. Siraut, 'Nettlecombe', *V.C.H.* Vol.5 (1985), p.118; R.W. Dunning, 'East Quantoxhead', *V.C.H.* Vol.5, p.127; Siraut, 'Nether Stowey', *V.C.H.* Vol.5, p.198; *Sales of Wards in Somerset, 1603-1641*, ed. M.J. Hawkins (S.R.S. Vol.67, 1965), p.65; John Batten, 'Somersetshire Sequestrations', *P.S.A.N.H.S.* Vol.16 (1870), ii, p.18; *Quarter Sessions Records for the County of Somerset*, Vol.iii, 1646-1660, ed. E.H. Bates Harbin (S.R.S. Vol.28 (1912), p.309, no.1.

11. For a background to contemporary garden styles, see Roy Strong, *The Renaissance Garden in England* (1979); and John Anthony, *The Renaissance Garden in Britain* (Princes Risborough, 1991)

12. Bond & Iles, 'Early gardens in Avon & Somerset', pp.37, 39.

13. *Leland's Itinerary in England and Wales*, ed. Lucy Toulmin Smith (1907), v, p.85; Robin Atthill, *Old Mendip* (2nd edn, Newton Abbot, 1971), pp.36-7.

14. Aspects of this process are examined by Colin Platt, *The Great Rebuildings of Tudor and Stuart England* (1994); Malcolm Airs, *The Tudor and Jacobean Country House: a Building History* (Stroud, 1995).

15. *The Particular Description of the County of Somerset drawn up by Thomas Gerard of Trent, 1633*, ed. E.H. Bates (S.R.S. Vol.15, 1900), p.99.

16. Somerset C.R.O., DD/PH 226/16, quoted in Mark Girouard, *Montacute House* (1975), pp.33-4; Dudley Dodd, *Montacute House, Somerset* (1978), p.48; Michael Havinden, *The Somerset Landscape* (1981), pp.241-2.

17. *Country Life*, Vol.23 (11 January 1908), pp.54-61.

18. John Harvey, 'Parks, gardens and landscaping', in Michael Aston (ed.), *Aspects of the Medieval Landscape of Somerset* (Taunton, 1988), p.102.

19. J. Edgar & R.Iles, 'Kelston village, manor house and garden remains', *Bristol Archaeological Research Group Review* Vol.2 (1981), pp.66-72; Bond & Iles, 'Early gardens in Avon and Somerset', p.41.

20. R. Iles, 'Claverton manor-house and garden', in R. Iles & H. White (eds), 'Avon archaeology, 1984', *Bristol & Avon Archaeology* Vol.5 (1985), pp.61-2; Bond & Iles, 'Early gardens in Avon and Somerset', p.43.

21. M. Aston, 'Gardens and earthworks at Hardington and Low Ham, Somerset', *P.S.A.N.H.S.* Vol.122 (1978), pp.12-17; Michael McGarvie & John H. Harvey, 'The keeper's lodge in Hardington Park', *Trans. Ancient Monuments Soc.* Vol.24 (1980), pp.143-52.

22. Charles & Nancy Hollinrake, *Parsonage Farm, Over Stowey: Archaeological Landscape Survey* (Privately circulated, 1994). I am grateful to Charles Hollinrake for showing this site to me.

23. David McOmish & Graham Brown, 'Earthwork surveys at Shapwick', in M.A. Aston & M.D. Costen (eds), *The Shapwick Report: a Topographical and Historical Study*, 4th Report (Bristol, 1993), pp.43-4.

24. Quoted in Arthur & Margaret Ann Elton, *Clevedon Court* (9th edn, 1986), p.11.

25. Gerard, *Particular Description of Somerset, 1633*, p.105.

26. James Bond, 'Earthwork surveys around Shapwick House', in *The Shapwick Report: an Archaeological, Historical and Topographical Survey*, 7th Report (in press, 1996)

27. Harvey, 'Parks, gardens and landscaping', p.102.

28. Aston, 'Gardens and earthworks at Hardington and Low Ham, Somerset', pp.17-26; Aston's interpretation is followed by Bond & Iles, 'Early gardens in Avon & Somerset', pp.43-5.

29. John Collinson, *The History and Antiquities of the County of Somerset*, Vol.3 (Bath, 1791), pp.444-6.

30. I am grateful to Rob Wilson-North of the Royal Commission for discussing his ideas with me on a visit to the site.

31. Duke Cosimo's description is translated in full in Harvey, 'Parks, gardens and landscaping', p. 106.

32. Robert Wilson-North, 'Witham: from Carthusian monastery to country house', *Current Archaeology* Vol.13 no.4 (1996), pp.151-6.

33. C.D. Crossman, 'Adrian Schaell's memoir of High Ham church and rectory, AD 1598', *P.S.A.N.H.S.* Vol.40 (1894), ii, 119.

34. M.C. Siraut, 'Nether Stowey', *V.C.H.* Vol.5 (1985), p.198.

35. E. Green, 'On the history of Chard', *P.S.A.N.H.S.* Vol.28 (1882), ii, pp.35-8.

36. Vergil and Moryson are both quoted in W.H.P. Greswell, *The Forests and Deer Parks of the County of Somerset* (1905), p.242.

37. *Certificate of Musters in the County of Somerset, temp. Elizabeth, AD 1569*, ed. Emanuel Green (S.R.S. Vol.20, 1904).

38. J.C. Cox & W.H.P. Greswell, 'Forestry', *V.C.H.* Vol.2 (1911), pp.568-9.

39. R.G. Gilson, 'Three Somerset manor houses', *P.S.A.N.H.S.* Vol.129 (1985), p.139.

40. Somerset C.R.O., DD/MI c/186.

41. British Library, Add.MS 9050.

42. E.P. Shirley, *Some Account of English Deer parks, with Notes on the Management of Deer* (1867), p.98.

43. Sir H.C. Maxwell Lyte, *A History of Dunster and of the Families of Mohun and Luttrell* (1909). i, 160, 174-5; ii, 365, 415; Joseph Whitaker, *A Descriptive List of Deer Parks and Paddocks of England* (1892). Cox & Greswell, 'Forestry', in *V.C.H.* Vol.2 , p.569, estimate an area of 348 acres, containing about 150 fallow deer.

44. Lyte, *History of Dunster*, i, pp.160, 174, 179; Somerset C.R.O., D/D/Rg 268 (I owe the latter reference to Mick Aston).

45. Lyte, *History of Dunster*, i, p.160; Cox & Greswell, 'Forestry', p.568; Somerset C.R.O., DD/L 1/10/35A.

46. *Calendar of the Manuscripts of the Dean and Chapter of Wells*, Vol.2, ed. W.P. Baildon (1914), pp.160, 230, 263.

47. *Cal. of MSS of Dean & Chapter of Wells*, Vol.2, pp.267, 317.

48. Phyllis M. Hembry, 'The death of Thomas Godwin, Bishop of Bath and Wells (1549-90)', *P.S.A.N.H.S.* Vol.96 (1951), p.84.

49. *Proceedings in the Court of the Star Chamber in the Reigns of Henry VII and Henry VIII*, ed. G. Bradford (S.R.S. Vol.27, 1911), pp.81-3.

50. *Proceedings in Court of Star Chamber*, pp.293-4.

51. *Leland's Itinerary in England and Wales*, ed. Lucy Toulmin Smith (1907), i, p.164; Gervase Markham, *The Country Farme* (1616).

52. Collinson, *History and Antiquities of the County of Somerset*, Vol.3, pp.62, 67; R.W. Dunning & M.C. Siraut, 'North Petherton', *V.C.H.* Vol.6 (1991), p.286.

53. William Wyndham, 'The Wadhams and Merifield', *P.S.A.N.H.S.* Vol.80 (1934), ii, p.6; John Batten, 'Craucombe - Carew', *S.D.N.Q.* Vol.6.xlii (1898), p.55

54. Francis Rose & Pat Wolseley, 'Nettlecombe Park: its history and its epiphytic lichens: an attempt at correlation' *Field Studies* Vol.6 (1984), pp.125-30.

55. *Cal. of MSS of Dean & Chapter of Wells*, Vol.2, pp.251, 260; Hazel Hudson & Frances Neale, 'Wedmore, Sand Park', in C.J. Webster & R.A. Crofts (eds), Somerset Archaeology, 1991', *P.S.A.N.H.S.* Vol.135 (1991), pp.159-60.

56. Cox & Greswell, 'Forestry', p.567.

57. *Sales of Wards in Somerset, 1603-1641*, ed. M.J. Hawkins (S.R.S. Vol.67, 1965), p.65; Cox & Greswell, 'Forestry', p.570.

58. Highclere Castle, Box Q A1 xii; I am grateful to Julian Watson for this reference.

59. Leland, *Itinerary*, i, p.160; R.W. Dunning, 'Hinton St George', *V.C.H.* Vol.4 (1978), pp.38-40, 45; Colin G. Winn, *The Pouletts of Hinton St George* (Stroud, 1995), pp.158-9.

60. Gerard, *Particular Description of Somerset, 1633*, p.197.

61. Nikolaus Pevsner, *The Buildings of England: North Somerset and Bristol* (Harmondsworth, 1973), p.274; Robert Dunning, *Somerset Castles* (Tiverton, 1995), pp.77-8.

62. J.H. Bettey, 'Hugh Smyth of Ashton Court, 1530-1581: Somerset Landowner, Justice of the Peace and Trouble-maker', *P.S.A.N.H.S.* Vol.136 (1992), p.142.

63. Bettey, 'Hugh Smyth of Ashton Court', p.144.

64. *Proceedings in Court of Star Chamber*, pp. 34, 73-5, 79.

65. R.A. Sixsmith, *Staple Fitzpaine and the Forest of Neroche* (1958), pp.32, 59.

66. William Phelps, *The History and Antiquities of Somersetshire*, Vol.1 (1836), p.382; Gerard, *Particular Description of Somerset, 1633*, p.221.

67. R.W. Dunning, 'Muchelney', *V.C.H.* Vol.3 (1974), pp.40, 43.

68. R.W. Dunning, 'Old Cleeve', *V.C.H.* Vol.5 (1985), p.46.

69. R.W. Dunning, 'Huish Episcopi', *V.C.H.* Vol.3 (1974), pp.5-6.

70. Leland, *Itinerary*, v, p.98.

71. *Country Life* Vol.39 (1916), pp.758-63, 786-91; A.W. Vivian-Neal & H. St.George Gray, 'Materials for the history of Taunton castle', *P.S.A.N.H.S.* Vol.86 (1940), ii, p.78; Robert Dunning, *Some Somerset Country Houses* (Wimborne, 1991), pp.129-35.

72. R.W. Dunning & M.C. Siraut, 'Spaxton', *V.C.H.* Vol.6 (1992), pp.112, 114.

73. Lyte, *History of Dunster*, i, p.160.

74. Dunning & Siraut, 'Stogursey', *V.C.H.* Vol.6, pp.134, 150.

75. Dunning & Siraut, 'Charlinch', *V.C.H.* Vol.6, p.92.

76. A.W. Vivian-Neal, 'The Court House' [East Quantoxhead], *P.S.A.N.H.S.* Vol.92 (1946), i, p.37.

77. Dunning & Siraut, 'Over Stowey', *V.C.H.* Vol.6, p.166.

78. *Calendar of State Papers, Domestic, 1651-2*, Oct 14th, 1652, p.440; W.A. Seaby, 'Wellington House: the Elizabethan mansion of Sir John Popham, knight, Lord Chief Justice', *P.S.A.N.H.S.* Vol.97 (1952), p.160n.

79. R.J.E. Bush, 'Chaffcombe', *V.C.H.* Vol.4 (1978), p.125.

80. M.C. Siraut, 'Nether Stowey', *V.C.H.* Vol.5 (1985), p.191.

81. Leland, *Itinerary*, i, 167; Lyte, *History of Dunster*, i, pp.159-60, ii, p.344; Hilary Binding & Douglas Stevens, *Minehead: a New History* (Minehead, 1977), pp.43-5, 176.

82. Hazel Hudson & Frances Neale, 'Wedmore, Sand Park', in C.J. Webster & R.A. Croft (eds), 'Somerset Archaeology, 1991', *P.S.A.N.H.S.* Vol.135 (1991), pp.159-160.

83. Cox & Greswell, 'Forestry', p.567.

84. Cox & Greswell, 'Forestry', pp.568-9; Dunning & Siraut, 'North Petherton', *V.C.H.* Vol.6 (1992), pp.281, 286, 301, 304.

85. Leland, *Itinerary*, i, pp.149, 294; Collinson, *History and Antiquities of the County of Somerset* (1791).

86. Gerard, *Particular Description of Somerset, 1633*, p. 135; Wyndham, 'The Wadhams and Merifield', p.8.

87. Hazel Hudson, 'Wedmore, Oldwood, ST.4346', in C.J. Webster & R.A. Croft (eds), 'Somerset Archaeology, 1991', *P.S.A.N.H.S.* Vol.135 (1991), pp.162-3

88. Emanuel Green, 'On some Flemish weavers settled at Glastonbury, AD 1551', *P.S.A.N.H.S.* Vol.26 (1881), ii, pp.17, 19.

Chapter 6

LATER STUART and BAROQUE GARDENS

DUTCH INFLUENCES BECAME MORE IMPORTANT AFTER THE ACCESSION OF WILLIAM OF ORANGE, WITH ORNAMENTAL CANALS BECOMING INCREASINGLY POPULAR ... THE PARK WAS INCREASINGLY BROUGHT INTO THE GRAND DESIGN, WITH AVENUES RADIATING OUT FROM THE MAIN FRONT OF THE HOUSE.

Fig. 6.1
NETHER STOWEY. *An estate plan of 1750 showing the Manor House and its grounds, surveyed by Thos. England.*

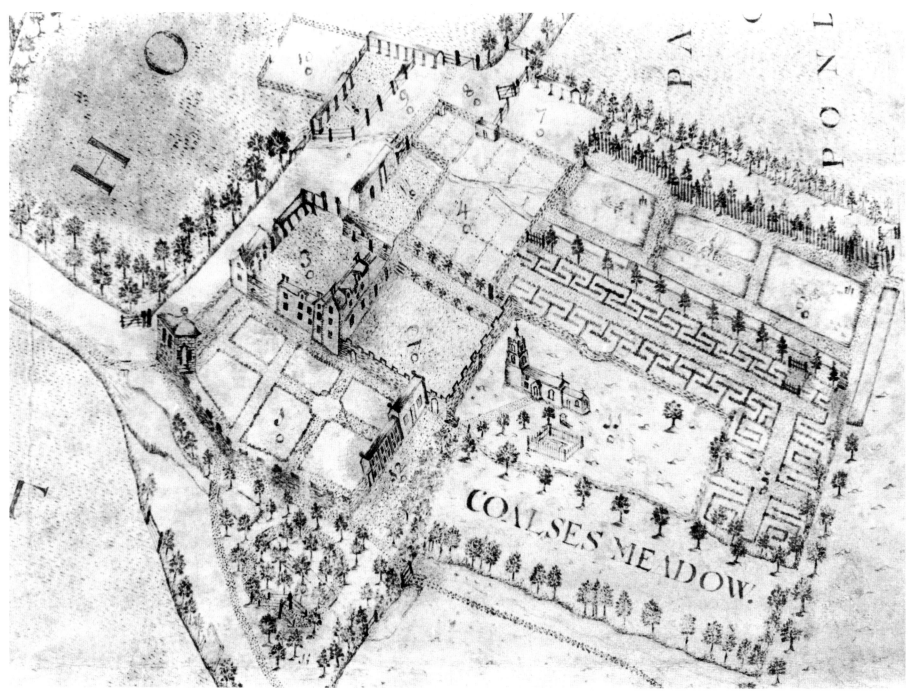

INTRODUCTION

The Civil War and the Parliamentary interregnum had not been propitious times for Somerset landowners who had supported the king, such as Lord Poulett of Hinton St George, Sir William Portman of Orchard Portman, Sir John Stawell of Cothelstone, Sir Ralph Hopton of Witham, George Trevelyan of Nettlecombe and Col. Edward Phelips of Montacute. All suffered through heavy fines, temporary exile or the seizure and plundering of their houses, while their parks and gardens fell into dereliction. Only after the restoration of Charles II in 1660 did the fortunes of the great estates recover.

Although the general character of gardens remained formal throughout the later seventeenth and early eighteenth centuries, it was far from static. Continuing introductions of new plant species from abroad offered an ever-widening range of possibilities. Immediately after the Restoration, French influence resumed its domination of garden design, with André Mollet returning to England, while English gardeners such as John Rose and George London went to train in France. Dutch influences became more important after the accession of William of Orange in 1689, with water features such as ornamental canals becoming increasingly popular; but by the early eighteenth century gardens were becoming more insular in style once again. The scale of planning was becoming ever more expansive. Although gardens were still divided from parks by walls, fences or hedges, the park was increasingly brought into the grand design, with crows-foot patterns of avenues radiating out from the main front of the house, or sight-lines focussing upon some distant vista. The earlier avenues normally made use of native trees like elm, but from the 1680s onwards the hybrid European lime or linden (*Tilia x europaea*) enjoyed enormous popularity for this purpose.[1]

SOURCES for PARK and GARDEN DESIGN

After the Restoration literature on the theory and practice of park and garden design once more proliferated. Advice on practical gardening continued to be dispensed by agricultural writers such as John Worlidge, while concern over the depletion of woodland resources led the diarist John Evelyn to become an influential advocate of timber plantations in parks.[2]

The swansong of the formal style was heralded by two writers in particular. Stephen Switzer (1682-1745) served an apprenticeship at the Brompton Park nurseries and went on to work both at Castle Howard and Blenheim, before taking on commissions of his own and eventually establishing a seedsman's business.

Although he produced some notable designs, including one in Somerset to be discussed later, he is better known for his books on gardening, the raising of timber trees and the setting out of park plantations, orchards and hopyards.[3] One of Switzer's maxims was that the whole estate should be subject to a uniform design, with great axial lines linking the house with other important features. Another of his recommendations, picked up by the early landscape gardeners such as Charles Bridgeman and William Kent, was that the garden should no longer be shut in behind high walls, but opened out to view the charms of the surrounding countryside. Equally influential was

Batty Langley, an architect, landscape gardener and nurseryman whose career similarly spanned the transition between the formal garden and the succeeding naturalistic styles. Langley was particularly concerned with the architectural embellishment of gardens, producing many designs for both classical and gothic temples and ruins. He stressed the importance of placing classical statues in their correct contexts, avoiding such *faux-pas* as displaying Neptune on a mount or Pan in a canal or fountain.[4]

Travellers' accounts often provide valuable information in this period, and Celia Fiennes and Daniel Defoe regularly mention estates seen on their journeys elsewhere in England. Unfortunately, although both travelled through Somerset, Defoe found nothing to say about local parks and gardens, while Celia Fiennes only noticed in passing avenues of trees on several unnamed estates in the north of the county and offered a few uncharacteristically laconic comments on the public walks in Bath, the park at Ashton Court and the grounds of the Bishop's Palace in Wells.[5]

Fig. 6.2
NETHER STOWEY MANOR HOUSE
and GAZEBO *painted by John Buckler in 1840.*

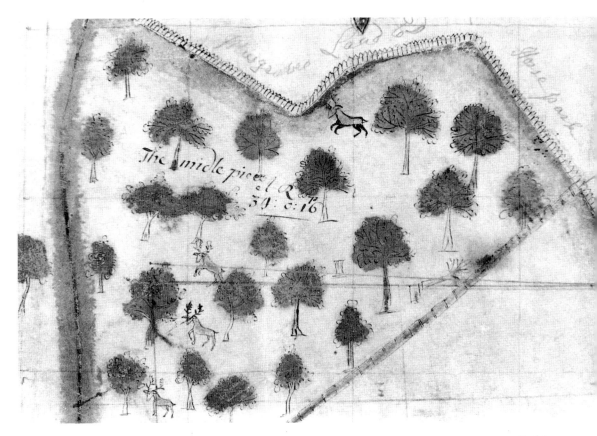

Fig. 6.3
MARSHWOOD PARK.
An estate plan of 1687 showing the continuing use of the park for deer; and the paling fence.

More accurate estate maps become increasingly numerous after the 1670s. The parks at Kilton and Toomer, for example, are shown in outline on maps of 1675 and 1689, while an interesting and colourful group of maps commissioned by Francis Luttrell in 1687 depicts the parks of East Quantoxhead, Marshwood in Carhampton and Heyfield in Dunster, all decorated with deer, rabbits and hunting scenes. Gardens are also represented, sometimes in considerable detail. An undated map depicts the "*Old garden under the Old Park at Dunster Castle, as first set out and built*", in formal style, with additions made shortly after 1750.[6] Other examples will be referred to below.

Above all, however, this period is distinguished by a new fashion for pictorial illustration of parks and gardens.[7] The first stirrings of this innovation in England had been stifled by the Civil

War, and for some decades after the Restoration the market was cornered by an influx of Dutch artists. The most important of these were Leonard Knyff (1650-1721), who made over 70 bird's-eye-view drawings of country estates in England, and Johannes Kip (1653-1722), who engraved many of Knyff's drawings.[8] Their vivid and complex illustrations are an invaluable source for assessing the appearance of the last generation of great formal gardens before they were swept away by the landscape movement. The temptation on the part of the artist to flatter the owner by making the house and gardens look even grander and more elaborate than they really were means that all such illustrative sources need to be used with some caution; nevertheless, where independent corroboration exists, the prospects of Knyff and Kip are often shown to be remarkably faithful representations of contemporary reality. English artists such as the brothers Samuel and Nathaniel Buck were also beginning to make some impact by the 1720s. Over the following fifty years the Bucks published well over 500 topographical prospects covering all parts of England and Wales. They tended to concentrate on towns, castles and abbeys rather than country houses but, as at Dunster Castle, they often showed incidental glimpses of the gardens and grounds attached.

Fig. 6.4
COURT OF WICK PIPPIN
from an illustration by William Hooker in 1816 for POMONA LONDINENSIS.

PLANT INTRODUCTIONS of the LATE 17TH and EARLY 18TH CENTURIES

Introductions of new plant species from Europe, western Asia and Mediterranean Africa continued. The first rhododendron grown in Britain, the pink evergreen *Rhododenron hirsutum* from central Europe, made its appearance in 1656. *Phlomis samia* was found growing in the mountains of North Africa in 1714. The great perennial scarlet oriental poppy (*Papaver orientalis*) was discovered in Armenia by a French collector in 1702, and was cultivated in England before 1741.

By the later seventeenth century the horizons of plant collectors had spread well beyond Europe. Three regions of the world became especially important as sources of new plants. English collectors continued to operate in Virginia, Carolina and the West Indies between the 1670s and 1720s, sending back plants such as the purple coneflower (*Echinacea purpurea*) and *Phlox paniculata*. The first explorations around the Cape of Good Hope towards the end of the seventeenth century began to reveal the enormous promise of the South African flora. Among the most spectacular and successful imports from that part of the world were the red hot poker, *Kniphofia uvaria*, and the first pelargoniums, *P. inquinans* and *P. zonale*. Finally, the opening up of trade links with the far east enabled a few collectors to begin the exploration of the flora of China and Indo-China in the 1690s; seeds sent back included the first specimen of camellia ever seen in Europe.[9]

Fig. 6.5
The London Plane tree at WALTON-IN-GORDANO *Manor House.*

On a more mundane level, significant advances in fruit cultivation can be discerned during the seventeenth century. Apples were always an important orchard and garden crop in Somerset, and local varieties can now be identified for the first time. The Court of Wick Pippin was first grown at Yatton in the seventeenth century and was widely cultivated in Somerset and beyond during the eighteenth century, though it has subsequently fallen from favour. The Red Quarrendon, first recorded in 1678, may be a native strain from the south-west of England or an import from the Carentan district of Normandy, and was popular in Devon and Somerset, though its poor storing qualities meant that it was rarely stocked by nurserymen or sold on the open market. The 'Meriott Ysnot' recorded in 1670, appears to have been a forerunner of the Somerset Redstreak. Despite developments in grafting elsewhere, most local cider orchards continued to consist mainly of seedling, ungrafted trees. Nevertheless, John Evelyn praised the local cider, "*strong, and of a generous vigour*". Celia Fiennes described how "*in most parts of Somersetshire it is very fruitful for orchards, plenty of apples and pears*", but she thought that the standards of production were inferior to those in Herefordshire because there was less care in selecting the best varieties of fruit to plant and, when used for cider, all sorts of apples were pressed together.[10]

Evelyn provides a contemporary account of exotic trees, showing several earlier introductions from the Mediterranean, including the Italian cypress, holm oak, and evergreen phillyrea now coming into more general use. Another tree mentioned by Evelyn, the Lebanon Cedar (*Cedrus libani*), had first arrived in Britain in 1638, but became more widely available later in the century as a popular garden and parkland evergreen.[11] The park at Hinton St George had a famous cedar lawn, planted in 1684, when similar plantings were carried out at Wilton House. The trees are said to have been brought back from the Holy Land by Margaret, Countess of Pembroke, who was related to the then Dowager Lady Poulett. The Hinton cedars were wrecked in the great storm of 3rd May, 1897.[12] Further Mediterranean species were introduced before the end of the seventeenth century; amongst them the cork oak (*Quercus suber*) did particularly well in parks and big gardens in the south-west. The oriental plane had been introduced in the sixteenth century, and there were notable examples in the vicarage garden at Lydeard St Lawrence, at Dunster and in Nettlecombe Park. Its American relative, the occidental plane, was hardly ever grown in England, though one specimen planted at Chipley near Nynehead in 1760 achieved a height of over 100ft and a spread of 120ft.[13] The London Plane (*Platanus x hispanica*), a hybrid which originated in southern Europe, was first raised successfully in England at the Oxford Botanic Garden by Jacob Bobart, and was becoming available to English growers by about 1680. One of the first specimens to be planted in Somerset still thrives in the garden of the manor-house at Walton-in-Gordano, and now stands 100ft high, with a girth of 20ft. Early introductions from the east coast of North America included the Weymouth pine (*Pinus strobus*), locust-tree (*Robinia pseudocacacia*) and tulip-tree (*Liriodendron tulipifera*).

NURSERY GARDENS

The marketing of the new plants brought in by collectors depended upon an effective nursery trade, and from the 1680s this was dominated by the great Brompton Park nursery in Kensington. Not only did this quickly become the foremost nursery garden in England, it also produced some notable garden designers, particularly George London, who designed planting schemes for Longleat, Chatsworth, Hampton Court and Kensington Palace, and Henry Wise, who worked at Kensington, Windsor Castle and Blenheim. Provincial nurseries were as yet small by comparison, but there are records of one local nursery garden at Mudgley near Wedmore in the seventeenth century, and another at Crewkerne reputedly founded in 1728.[14]

PARKS and GARDENS after the RESTORATION

Many Somerset estates, damaged and neglected during the Civil War and Commonwealth period, now required substantial reconstruction. Orchard Portman was recovered by Sir William Portman after its sequestration by Parliament. He repaired and extended the Tudor house between 1660 and 1690, and probably began the new gardens at the same time.[15] Sir William was a friend of John Evelyn, and seems to have taken his plea for new plantations to heart. Kip's 1707 engraving of Orchard Portman shows an elaborate formal parterre west of the house approached across the park by a long double avenue, with a bowling-green immediately to the north. Subsidiary avenues meet the main approach at right-angles in front of the parterre. Before the east front of the house is a gravelled forecourt with a circular lawn and beyond that further formal gardens extending up to the present road. A large walled kitchen garden and extensive

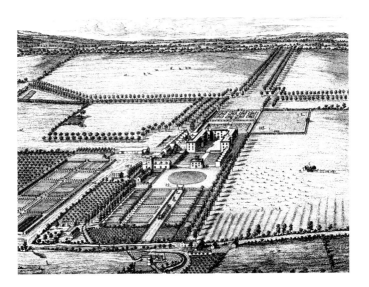

orchards lie to the south. Some of the buildings shown by Kip, including the church and rectory, survive, but otherwise there are only slight terraces and lines of some of the enclosure walls.

At Brympton d'Evercy Sir John Sydenham transformed the Tudor manor-house during the 1660s by the addition of an impressive new Palladian range, at the same time extending the gardens. Kip's engraving shows an extensive rectilinear layout, with a terrace, bowling-green and formal shrubbery below the new south front of the house, a rectangular fishpond and kitchen garden south of the church, a walled lawn west of the house, extensive formal orchards to north and east, and long formal avenues both north and south of the house. Some elements of this layout, including the south terrace and the western lawn, survive despite extensive later remodelling.[16]

The manor of Marston Bigot had been bought by Richard Boyle, 2nd Earl of Cork and Lord High Treasurer of Ireland, in 1641, when it was described as "*a fair house, with orchards, gardens and pleasant walks about it*". On his death two years later the earl left the property to one of his younger sons, Roger, who was created 1st Earl of Orrery in 1660. His principal seat was at Charleville in Co.Cork and, although he occasionally stayed at Marston, his real interests remained in Ireland. In 1669, embarrassed by the neglected condition of his grounds at Marston, Orrery employed a gardener to begin restoring them to order. Some records of the works survive, including the despatch of six bundles of trees in 1669, the repair of the garden walls in 1677 and 1678, and the planting of fruit trees in the orchard in 1678. Some distance to the north of the house, beyond the orchard and alongside the Frome-Shepton Mallet road, two prospect mounts were built, taking the form of circular stone-revetted bastions with viewing platforms approached by flights of steps, giving vistas southwards over the gardens and northwards over the Sharpshaw valley. After the death of the 1st Earl in 1679 the gardens of Marston Bigot again fell into neglect and the stonework of the two mounts was robbed. A survey taken in 1681 mentions 240 fruit trees in the orchard north of the house, with 97 more fruit trees against the walls, quinces, filberts and roses, also cherry trees and vines; but the gardener was said to be dishonest and unscrupulous, and by 1684 the steward was describing the garden as 'now all ruinous', advising that, unless urgent repairs could be made, the whole site would be better laid down to pasture. The following year some emergency repairs to the garden and orchard walks and the two mounts were put in hand. However, at least thirty years were to elapse before any further significant developments occurred there.[17]

Redlynch Park near Bruton has been described as the '*only first-class development (in Somerset) during the reign of Charles II*': the estate was purchased in about 1672 by Sir Stephen Fox, who rebuilt the mansion, and it is likely that some ornamental grounds were created at that time, along with the partial removal of the old village.[18] A fuller understanding of this important site must, however, await the publication of the next volume of the Victoria County History.

Among the smaller layouts of this period was Charlton House near Kilmersdon, begun in 1685 by James Twyford, a Bristol merchant who had married one of the heiresses of Kilmersdon manor. By 1694 the property was described as "*a new built Genteel mansion house*", complete with stable, coach-house, dovecote and other outbuildings,

Fig. 6.6
ORCHARD PORTMAN.
A 1707 Johannes Kip engraving from a drawing by Leonard Knyff.

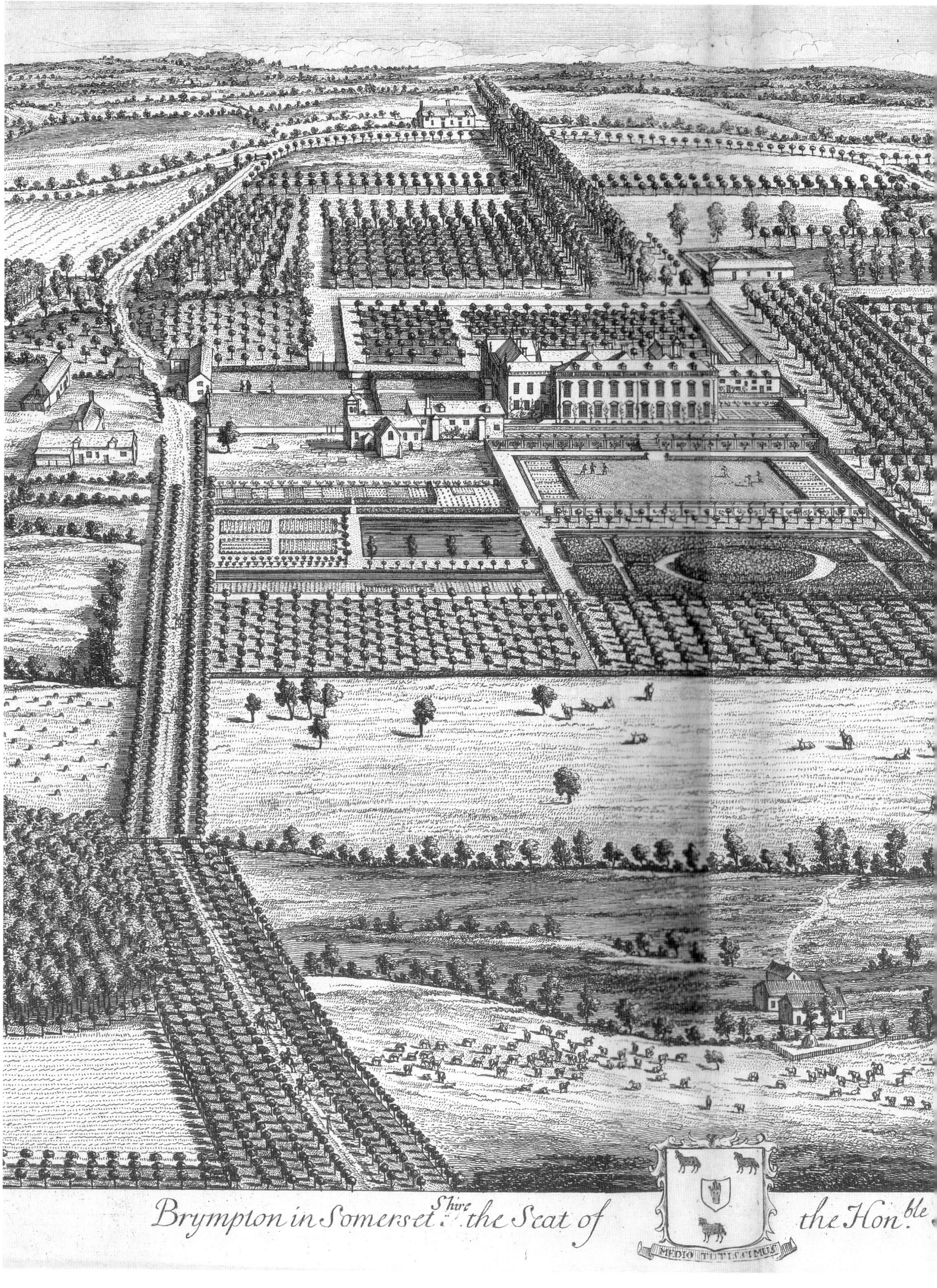

Fig. 6.7
BRYMPTON D'EVERCY.
A 1707 Johannes Kip engraving from a drawing by Leonard Knyff.

Brympton in Somerset Shire the Seat of the Hon.ble

MEDIO TUTISSIMUS

Philip Sydenham.

orchards, gardens and fishponds. The lodge gates, stables and fishponds survive, but the house fell into ruin in the nineteenth century and was eventually demolished. Gardens were also created at Crowcombe Manor by John Carew in 1676, but little is known of their form or extent.[19]

GARDENS and PARKS in the time of WILLIAM and MARY

The accession of William of Orange in 1689 opened up English gardens to new design influences from the Low Countries. Dutch gardens were typified by the use of formal canals, avenues and small enclosed plots placed without any special regard for symmetry. However, Daniel Marot, a French Huguenot emigré, had worked for William of Orange both at the Dutch palace of Het Loo and at Hampton Court, so at the top social level a sort of European court style was evolving, combining the ethos of several national styles.

Somerset has nothing left from this period to compare with the Gloucestershire gardens of William Blathwayt at Dyrham or Maynard Colchester at Westbury-on-Severn, both laid out in the 1690s and 1700s. However, the second phase of the gardens at Low Ham might have rivalled them had they ever reached maturity.

The short-lived gardens laid out here by Sir Edward Hext earlier in the century were described in the previous chapter. The property had passed by marriage from the Hexts to the Stawells in 1625. Collinson tells us that John, 2nd Lord Stawell, pulled down the Hext mansion in about 1690, and replaced it with "*a most sumptuous and expensive edifice, 400 feet in length and 1 hundred in breadth*".

Fig. 6.8
Garden earthworks of two periods at LOW HAM.

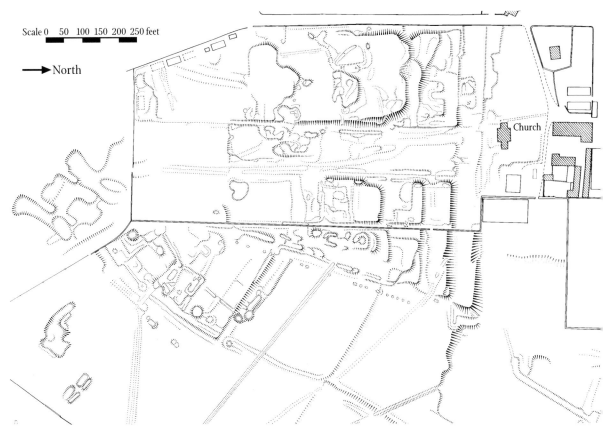

Scale 0   50 100 150 200 250 feet

➜ North

Church

Perhaps Sir Edward's house on the hilltop had been too exposed for comfort, but Collinson regarded the new site at the foot of the hill east of the church as "*a very low and bad situation*". No contemporary plans or prospects of this house have yet come to light, and although there is a rough sketch on an estate map of 1779, this is not wholly to be trusted. Stawell died in 1692 at the age of 24, by which time his new mansion had already cost him over £100,000, and he had been obliged to sell most of his other estates to pay for it. The uncompleted house was in ruins by 1823, and had disappeared entirely by 1838; fragments of three small half-columns belonging to a cellar at the rear of the house and quantities of reused stone amongst the farm buildings are all that remain.

New gardens had been commenced at the same time as the house, and a letter from Jacob Bobart, curator of the Oxford Botanic Garden, dated 26th July 1690, mentions some of the works then in hand. Near the foot of the hill a terrace 90ft broad was under construction, from which two flights of ten steps led up to a plot 262ft square. From here five steps led up to another terrace 74ft broad, within which a 'canal' was to be made: in reality this was more of a pond than a canal, 40ft long by 80ft broad, and Bobart queries whether this should be shaped like a parallelogram or "*whether an Octagonal figure would not keep cleaner, considering there is no great flux of water*". From this level two parallel flights of ten steps led up to a plot 260ft square, and finally ten more steps up to a Wilderness at the top,

also 260ft square. The length of the whole garden was estimated at about 980ft, rising 848 inches from top to bottom.

While it is difficult to identify all of the features mentioned by Bobart, part of the impressive series of terraces and banks set into the hill south of the church does accord quite well with the dimensions he describes. The axis of a vista was cut up the hill alongside the terraces due south of the new house. However, in the light of the recent re-examination of the site by the Royal Commission on Historical Monuments, it now seems likely that the gardens described by Bobart were not so much new works as a remodelling of the terraces of the abandoned gardens made by Sir Edward Hext three generations earlier. The massive stone wall overriding the east end of the terraces, which had tentatively been interpreted as a boundary wall built to enclose the rabbit and hare warren which occupied the abandoned site by 1779, now has to be reconsidered. If the somewhat splayed plan of the Hext gardens was now being regularised into a more rectangular form, as seems clear from the Bobart letter, the stone wall would fit well into the context of the Stawell gardens as an eastern boundary, hiding from view those portions of the Hext garden terraces which had now been abandoned. To the west of the vista axis, apparently outside the area documented by Bobart, a series of irregular quarry-pits and spoil tips interspersed between terraces show that further works were in hand on that part of the slope when the project was abandoned uncompleted. The 1779 map shows that more extensive plantations, including three avenues focussing on a point just east of the Stawell mansion, had begun to incorporate the fields to the south-east into a park.[20]

The increasing popularity of formal water features can be seen in two other Somerset parks. Halswell Park was probably created by Sir Halswell Tynte, who held the manor from 1667 until his death in 1702. A stream which flowed past the east side of the house was diverted into a straight canal, with a walk alongside it leading to a pavilion, while a formal parterre with terraces was formed in front of the new north range. To the west a triple gateway led to a broad, straight avenue. This formal landscape was all swept away in the following century.[21]

At Nettlecombe the Trevelyans had been raised to a baronetcy after the Restoration as a reward for their support for the royalist cause. During the 1690s Sir John Trevelyan, 2nd baronet, embarked upon a major campaign of improvement to the house and grounds. The old park to the north-east of the house was refenced. Four new gardens were made, enclosed with brick walls. Clearly some elaborate works were involved, including "*altering the Green Court front with iron gates and palisades opposite to which is a new canal-pond, and a new cascade of five falls or breaks about 26 feet perpendicular falling in the middle of the said canal*", also "*new making the garden in the front with a bason for water in the middle*". Part of the walled garden complex still survived in 1796, but the water features were remembered only in the name 'Canal Field'.[22]

BAROQUE GARDENS of the EARLY 18TH CENTURY

The term 'baroque' is traditionally used of an architectural style popular in England between about 1700 and 1730, based upon the elements of renaissance classicism used in an original way, deliberately breaking the rules of proportion and other conventions in order to achieve grand and striking effects. Some elements of this architectural style can be matched in new developments in garden design, characterised by monumental scale, theatrical conception, florid and elaborate detail, and heavy architectural frameworks often incorporating mock military features. The work carried out by George London and John Vanbrugh at Castle Howard, or by Henry Wise, John

Vanbrugh and Nicholas Hawksmoor at Blenheim, typify the style. Another exponent was Stephen Switzer, who carried out several commissions in the west of England, notably at Cirencester Park in Gloucestershire, where some elements of the design based upon his advice to Lord Bathurst in about 1718 can still be seen.

Formal gardens continued to be made and maintained in Somerset through the first half of the eighteenth century. Marston Bigot had become the principal seat of the Earls of Orrery after their great house at Charleville was burned down by James II's forces in 1690. Charles Boyle, 4th Earl of Orrery, extended the house and employed Stephen Switzer to update the gardens. Switzer's contribution at Marston is not well-documented, but he seems to have undertaken some fairly major works between 1715 and 1724 for the 4th Earl, to whom he dedicated his book THE PRACTICAL FRUIT GARDENER. He returned between 1738 and 1749 to work for John, 5th Earl of Cork & Orrery. New landscaping in the 1770s swept away Switzer's garden, but its appearance is known from a print made in 1739 by René Parr. From the south the main front of the house was approached through gatepiers in a projecting semicircular wall which gave access to a figure-of-eight drive around two circular pools probably containing *jets d'eau*. Immediately in front of the house's forecourt the ground was projected forward on a level in an extended semicircle around the upper basin. To the east was the old parish church and the stable court. Between the stables and the pleasure-gardens, immediately east of the house, there appears to have been a small walled kitchen garden. The old orchard to the rear had now been replaced by a large walled garden divided into four unequal compartments. Immediately behind the house the south-western compartment contained a small parterre with a complex pattern of six curvilinear steps leading up to the main walk beyond. This was flanked by two small square orchards. The south-eastern compartment, north of the kitchen garden, was occupied by a plantation or orchard containing serpentine and irregular walks. A cross walk traversed the slope above the fourth step. The biggest compartment, to the north-east, was a large lawn or bowling-green surrounded by a breast-wall. A few years earlier Samuel Bowden, a local poet, had described how

"..... *an Area of Enamel'd Green*
Displays its Robes, where Statues rise between,
And shine with features of a Roman mien";

but if there had been any classical statuary around the green it seems to have been removed by 1739. To the west of the lawn the main broad walk, lined by small standard trees, led on from the curvilinear steps towards the northern boundary, although there was no exit through the wall onto the Frome road. The north-western compartment was a larger rectangular walled orchard with another series of irregular, sinuous walks, leading to a small square garden in its centre. The two earlier mounts by the Frome road survived, linked by the northern boundary wall, which had fruit trees growing against its sheltered southern side. South-west of the house was a much larger kitchen garden, walled in front but hedged behind, divided into square beds containing randomly-scattered fruit trees. In the centre was an extraordinary gridiron pattern of high walls, four aligned east-west, two north-south, which closely resembles a scheme for heated fruit

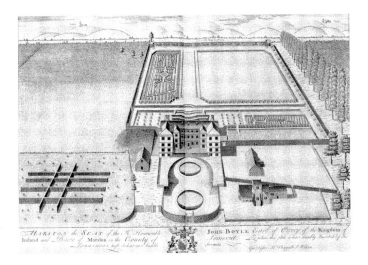

walls advocated by Switzer in the 1731 edition of his *Fruit Gardener*.[23] In some respects the enclosed nature of the Marston Bigot garden was at odds with Switzer's dictum of laying open the view beyond, but its bleak and exposed situation may have dictated this; indeed, lines of trees to the east provided a further windbreak. Although the general outline of the garden remained strictly geometrical, the irregular pattern of walks in two of the compartments heralded the approaching end of formality. The 5th Earl continued to extend the ornamental grounds at Marston Bigot well into the 1750s, but his later work will be more appropriately considered in the following chapter.

At Witham the ancient house of the Hoptons was acquired by the Wyndham family, and around 1710 William Wyndham decided to have it rebuilt. The elevation of the new mansion published in *Vitruvius Britannicus*, which shows a massive open portico facing the garden front, has been attributed to William Talman, but a recently-discovered plan links the design with James Gibbs. Building was completed by about 1717, and it is clear from the earthworks and from a recent geophysical survey that the house faced west, requiring a new approach from that direction The outline of part of the octagonal front courtyard can still be seen, now bisected by the railway. It is likely that the gardens were elaborated and perhaps extended during this period; the field containing the entrance court is still named 'Great Garden' on an 1812 sale map. To the north-west, where the approach drive crossed over the Frome by a bridge, the river may have been diverted to accommodate two ornamental lakes in the valley bottom. The Wyndham mansion was in decay by the later seventeenth century, and its gardens were abandoned. Sir Charles Wyndham sold the estate in 1762 to William Beckford of Fonthill, whose plans will be discussed in Chapter 7. The construction of the railway destroyed the last remains of the Wyndhams' great house.[24]

Ven House near Milborne Port is a splendid three-storey baroque mansion, of brick with stone dressings, ornamented with giant pilasters and a balustraded parapet complete with urn finials. The traditional belief is that it was built around 1698-1700 for James Medlycott, son of a lawyer-politician, grandson of a London dyer. However, its style seems much more adventurous than one would expect in the west of England at that time, and the recent rediscovery of the building accounts identifies the designer-builder as Nathaniel Ireson of Wincanton, working during the 1720s. When the house was almost completed, Richard Grange was called in to design a suitably baroque landscape to embellish its setting. The main approach was from the north, through gates set in semicircular railings and along a drive between a double avenue of trees and formal parterres to a second set of gates, where the drive divided to form an oval in front of the house. Below the south front there was a broad paved terrace extending beyond either flank of the house, with small pavilions at its corners and a set of splayed steps at its centre, leading down to a gravel walk and a long canal set in lawns with formal beds of ornamental trees. Beyond the gardens were formal wooded walks. The development of the gardens was still continuing as late as 1739, and some remains of the formal scheme can still be identified there, though much modified in the later eighteenth century. Phelps described the house merely as standing in a lawn, surrounded by a grove of venerable elms.[25]

The great park of Hinton St George acquired some baroque elements during the early eighteenth century. There was a statue of Diana in 1704, surrounded by oaks and thorn trees, with six radiating walks. Earl Poulett bought out some of his tenants between 1704 and 1721 in order to enlarge the park westwards by the addition of some 115 acres. John Loveday admired the gardens around the house in 1736, but his comments indicate an increasing interest in the outward view: "*By the help of an haw-haw you take in a good view for a low situation, particularly an hill at a proper distance beautifully clothed with trees. The Wilderness and Maze are in the park, the hedges of it are in great perfection, the building within serves as a banqueting room*". The 'banqueting room' referred to by Loveday may be the building more recently known as the Keeper's Lodge, about a mile west of the house. A drawing made by Edward Prideaux in 1735 shows the garden in front of the house separated from the park by stone pillars with ornamental gates and railings.[26]

Scanty remains of another extensive formal layout survived until relatively recently at Newton St Loe. This manor was purchased in 1666 by Joseph Langton of Brislington, a member of the Merchant Venturers of Bristol, and it was probably he who enclosed the ancient fortified house of the St Loes within a park, possibly removing part of the village in the process. Subsequent improvements are poorly documented, but an estate map of 1789 shows the remains of an asymmetrical pattern of six avenues, five of which focus upon the old house, therefore clearly antedating the building of the new mansion and the remodelling of the grounds in the 1760s. One avenue ran southwestwards from the old house towards a building on the edge of the park, the site of which is now marked by mounds, hollows and

Fig. 6.11
Ven House, Milborne Port.
left: Original plan of north side.
right: Original plan of south side.

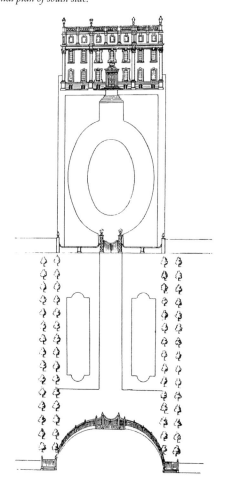

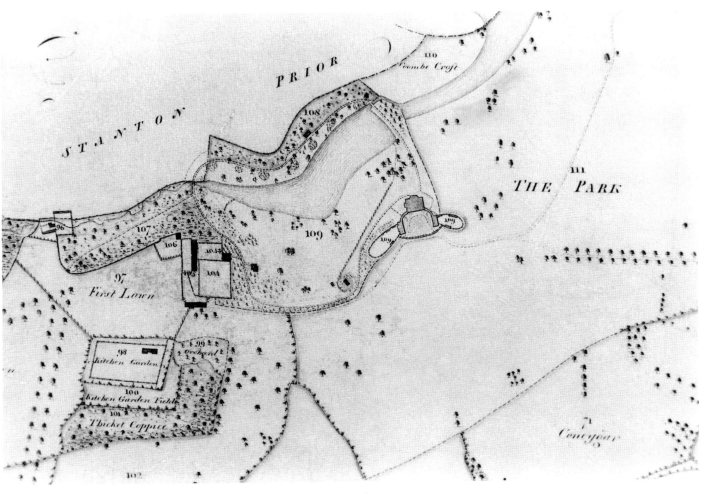

Fig. 6.12
NEWTON ST LOE.
*Part of estate plan of 1789
showing remains of avenues.*

scatters of rubble. This was probably some sort of gazebo or summerhouse, commanding fine views towards Stanton Prior. Two other avenues ran northeastwards towards Bath, looking northwards over the Corston Brook valley. The avenues are still recognisable on the Ordnance Survey map of 1888, and a few ancient elms on the line of the northern avenue survived until the onset of Dutch elm disease in the 1970s. This scheme could have been laid out at any time between the late 1660s and early 1760s, but the scale and pattern of the avenues would be most compatible with a baroque layout of the early eighteenth century.[27]

The medieval deer park at Mells was altered in the third quarter of the eighteenth century. Thomas Horner commissioned Nathaniel Ireson to build a new mansion in the middle of the park in 1725, and it was probably at this time that a formal garden south of the house was created in mock-military style, centred upon a temple and grotto, flanked by two clumps. Remains of a circular battlemented wall south of Melcombe Wood, straight rides within the wood, the 'Serpentine Plantation' in the south-east of the park and the screen of trees around the park perimeter may all be fragments of an elaborate baroque layout which has been obscured by later changes. The long pond in the valley north of the house is probably of industrial origin, but was later incorporated into the ornamental landscape with a waterfall, stepping stones and a duckery.[28]

The contemporary delight in imitating military features in landscape design was such that a genuine castle must have been an extra bonus. Dunster Castle had suffered siege and severe damage during the Civil War, and its defences were subsequently slighted, although the Luttrells continued to occupy the domestic quarters. The

family was beset by debts, and for fifty years after the Restoration little further development was possible. However, Alexander Luttrell's widow, Dorothy, who managed the estates between 1711 and 1723, achieved some improvement in their finances, and began improving the surroundings of the castle. The summit of the hill where the Norman keep had stood was flattened and converted to a bowling-green, and an octagonal summer house was built beside it. Regular rows of trees were planted up the steep slopes leading to the upper ward, with more extensive plantations on the slopes below the lower ward. In 1720 a new approach drive was made around the east flank of the hill up to the south-east gate, fenced and planted with small, evenly-spaced, standard trees. Above it a very regular plantation with three tiers of trees rose to the level of the south terrace, which was laid out with two rectangular flower beds, subsequently gravelled over. These features are clearly seen on the prospect made by Samuel and Nathaniel Buck in 1733.[29]

At Orchard Wyndham the small park near the house was extended up to the higher ground to the south in the early eighteenth century, taking in the wooded knoll of Black Down, where vistas were cut through the trees. The stream in the valley between the wood and house was dammed to make a chain of small ornamental ponds, and there are signs that the slope between the house and the valley were terraced. An avenue led from the house towards the Williton road.[30] Avenues continued to be planted through the early eighteenth century, the broad lime avenue approaching Montacute House from the east being a splendid surviving example. They were an effective way of making a relatively modest property seem more important. From the Leversedge family home at Vallis an avenue led eastwards for

Fig. 6.13
DUNSTER CASTLE *prospect made by Samuel and Nathaniel Buck in 1733.*

nearly a mile towards the outskirts of Frome. The site of Richmond House at East Harptree was once approached by a noted lime avenue, but the remaining trees were all felled after the Great War.[31]

LESSER FORMAL GARDENS of the EARLY 18TH CENTURY

The fully-fledged baroque style demanded above all the grand scale. It was difficult to achieve the same effect on smaller properties, and many newly-created gardens remained conservative in style. Clevedon Court provides a good example. This house and manor were bought up in 1709 by Abraham Elton, son of a humble scavenger and road-mender, who had made a considerable fortune in Bristol through shipping, trading in wool, wine, sugar and tobacco, mining coal, lead and calamine and copper works. His son, Sir Abraham Elton II (1679-1742), began to improve the Clevedon property soon after its purchase, altering the house and building new stables and a gamekeeper's cottage. He also enlarged and extended the existing garden terraces, supporting the lower one with a stone revetment wall and building another boundary wall higher up the slope. The terraces faced due south, providing an excellent location both for fruit and vegetable production and for sheltered walks. Two black mulberries were planted on the lawn in front of the house, one of them still bearing fruit today. Avenues were laid out over the ridge pointing towards Clevedon and Bristol, a great horse chestnut and lime tree

surviving from this planting. The boundary wall was pierced at the eastern end by an arched gateway giving access out onto the hill. The three long fishponds south-west of the house were cleaned out and restored. When the work was complete an unknown artist was commissioned to paint a bird's-eye view of the court and its grounds. This painting, which still hangs in the house, is a valuable source for its appearance prior to the later eighteenth-century alterations, showing fruit trees pleached against the brickwork of the lower terrace and planting just beginning on the bare slopes above the boundary wall. Sir Abraham was clearly very pleased with his achievements, but by the standards of Marston Bigot or Ven House, the works at Clevedon Court have a distinctly old-fashioned air.[32]

Fig. 6.14
CLEVEDON COURT *from an anonymous 18th century painting.*

Terraces, ponds and canals continued to dominate the scene elsewhere. Widcombe Manor near Bath, soon to provide a feature in the view from Ralph Allen's Prior Park, already had fine gardens of its own. Soon after 1727 the new squire, Philip Bennett, had two broad terraces made below the house, with a spring-fed bath-house below. Across the open ground to the west the view took in a circular pool, fed by a stepped cascade, and a prospect mount planted with yews and ascended by a spiral walk.[33] The Bacon family, who occupied Maunsel House in North Petherton from 1648 to 1726, had developed gardens and orchards on four acres of ground around the house, which included a large fishpond with an island. A formal canal was added in the early eighteenth century, perhaps incorporating the former fishpond.[34] The grounds of Fairfield House were also provided with a short canal, running parallel with the entrance front of the house but separated from it by the old road between Stogursey and Stringston, which must have reduced its aesthetic impact.[35] Thomas Carew, builder of the new Crowcombe Court in 1724, had ornamental gardens laid out to the south, at the same time extending the park and planting up woodlands of native trees on the hill to the east.[36] Only rarely, as at Standerwick Court near Beckington, where earthworks of an abandoned rectangular garden include a semicircular bastion-like projection at the front, do baroque innovations appear in these smaller grounds.

Many formal gardens cannot be dated within close limits. A mid-eighteenth-century estate map of Nether Stowey shows in considerable detail the walled gardens around the Court, some elements of which still survive. To the south was a lawn divided into six compartments by intersecting paths, enclosed within an embattled stone wall. An ogee-roofed gazebo, the lower portion of stone, the upper portion of brick, with paired sash windows on each face, still stands at its south-west corner. To the east a second embattled wall enclosed a square court, bordered by a terraced walk along its northern side, with fruit trees trained against the walls above and below it. A third walled enclosure to the north appears to have been a kitchen garden. A gate from the raised walk east of the house led to a further walk around two sides of the churchyard, flanked by a series of beds in key pattern, with a row of trees on the north separating them from three rectangular fishponds. Some of this layout could date from the later sixteenth century, when the Court was rebuilt, but the style of the existing gazebo would fit more readily into the 1730s or 1740s.[37]

Another undated estate map of the late seventeenth or early eighteenth century shows the small village of Ston Easton in considerable detail, with the new house built after the Restoration by Preston Hippisley at its centre, surrounded by an enclosed garden. A loop of roads surrounds the garden, with a large fishpond nearby. The house was enlarged into a Palladian-style mansion, probably in the time of John Hippesley Coxe, who took up residence in 1738. This rebuilding may have been contemplated for some years, since there is another undated plan showing the outline of a larger house with an elaborate garden design. The old fishpond was to be converted to an ornamental lake, with cascades and a robing house at one end and a dam at the other, concealed as a grotto with further cascades. There was to be a formal parterre south of the house, flanked by a grass esplanade and saloon on one side and by a stable block on the other;

a kitchen garden and orchard with hothouses were planned to the south-east, with an avenue continuing southwards through partly formal woodlands. However, several houses in the village stood in the way of the implementation of this plan, and it is doubtful whether it was ever completed in the form shown.[38]

FARMHOUSE GARDENS

Contemporary depictions of smaller farmhouse gardens are rare, but at Charity Farm, Lovington, a delightful naive painting of the front garden, probably dated to *circa* 1700, survives on a wooden panel over the fireplace. The east face of the house is shown with a railing and a row of clipped shrubs. In front of this are two geometric flower-beds, each divided by gravel walks into quarters, with their central islands each containing a large shrub. At the outer end of the grass walk between the two beds is a sundial on a pillar. On the north side of the garden is a stone wall with a row of bee boles containing skeps. This wall, with eleven bee boles, is the only feature of this garden to survive today.[39]

ORANGERIES

Citrus trees had become a popular feature of Italian renaissance gardens, but even in southern Europe they needed protection from winter frosts. This was achieved either by placing some sort of temporary shelter over trees planted in the ground, or by planting the trees in tubs which could be brought indoors during the cold season. The fashion had spread to northern France by the 1550s, and in 1562 we find the first records of orange and lemon trees being grown in south-east England.[40]

Initially protection was given by a mobile wooden-framed glass shelter which could be moved into position when required; this type of device is still used at Dunster Castle to protect the lemon tree growing against the south wall. By the 1620s, however, the first permanent orangeries were being constructed in England. The very attractive example at Redlynch is certainly older than the existing house, and may date back to the 1670s when the previous mansion was built.

KITCHEN GARDENS, HOP GARDENS and VINEYARDS

During the early eighteenth century, as the design of pleasure-gardens and parks increasingly revolved around aesthetic considerations, there was a move towards segregating the more mundane cultivation of fruit and vegetables into a walled kitchen garden, often out of sight of the great house. For example, new kitchen gardens were laid out south of Crowcombe Court by Thomas Carew in the 1730s.[41]

Small hopyards continued to feature on some Somerset estates through the later seventeenth century. The description of Montacute in 1667 listed a hop garden an acre and a half in extent, while another occupied part of the old royal park of North Petherton

Fig. 6.15
Farmhouse garden at
CHARITY FARM, LOVINGTON,
as shown on panel painting.

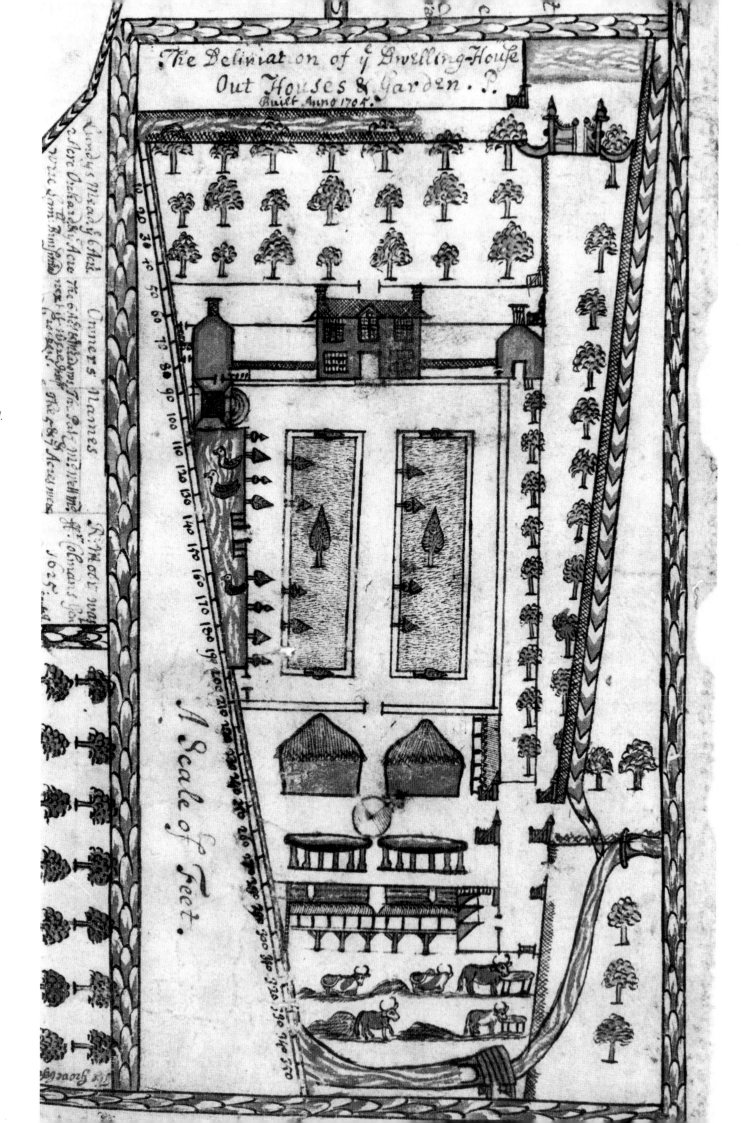

Fig. 6.16
ROUGHMOOR FARM,
BISHOPS HULL,
from a 1718 plan, showing the small
formal garden and orchard adjoining
the farmhouse, with the rickyard beyond.

in 1670.[42] However, hops never became a commercial crop in Somerset, and their cultivation declined during the eighteenth century.

Vine growing revived on a limited scale in the late seventeenth century. Sir William Bassett established a new vineyard on the slopes of a sheltered combe south of Claverton, which attracted John Aubrey's praise as the best in England. According to Stephen Switzer, Sir William produced several hogsheads of good-bodied, palatable wine every year. The depiction of the site on a map of 1805 suggests that vines were still cultivated there, and Canon Ellacombe describes the ancient three-sided vineyard wall and what may have been the winepress building, still visible in the late nineteenth century. Another vineyard at Walcot is said to have produced 66 hogsheads in 1718, but its cultivation had been abandoned by about 1730.[43]

PRIVATE GARDENS in TOWNS

Like smaller country gardens, town gardens of the late seventeenth and early eighteenth centuries have, as yet, received little study. Written records, particularly from parsonages, occasionally fill in some detail of what was grown. When Martin Strong was instituted as vicar of Yeovil in 1690, he found "*the Vicarage House and gardens miserably ruinous and out of all repair*", and forthwith began repairing the house and planting "*all the codling-hedges, artichokes, asparagus, gooseberries, cherries and hedges*"; he planted a new hedge of codlings, a small hard apple probably used for cider, in 1703.[44] Early large-scale maps such as those of Bath by James Gilmore (1694) and Charles Harcourt Masters (1787 and 1794/5) and William Simes's plan of

Wells (1735) suggest that formal layouts were general in town gardens, and continued well into the later eighteenth century.

A most informative painting of the 1680s depicts Ladymead House off Walcot Street in the northern suburbs of Bath. Between the house and the river a large walled garden is shown, divided into two unequal compartments by a canal. The rectangular southern part is the ornamental garden, with a cruciform pattern of paths beginning outside the rear door of the house with steps and topiary. A summerhouse stands at the south-eastern corner. The larger northern part is square, divided into quarters by grass walks and apparently used as a kitchen garden. From the summerhouse a wall and a double row of pollarded trees is shown running all along the river front below both parts of the garden.[45]

An opportunity to investigate the archaeology of another eighteenth-century Bath garden arose in 1984. A proposal had been put forward to recreate a Georgian garden in the grounds of no.4 The Circus, a house first built in 1757-60 to the design of John Wood I. The Bath Archaeological Trust undertook the complete excavation of the site to determine whether any of the original garden features remained. The entire plan of the original garden was found to have survived beneath over a foot of Victorian overburden. The original sloping ground surface had been levelled up with spoil dug during the construction of the cellars of the house. Topsoil was then brought in to create linear flower-beds along both side walls and towards the rear wall. Soakaways were cut along the inner edge of both side beds, and an area of gravel spread over the centre, extending in two curving arms to enclose the end bed. Post-holes in this end bed may represent some sort of pergola. Finally along the central axis three island beds were

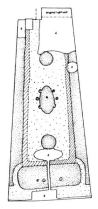

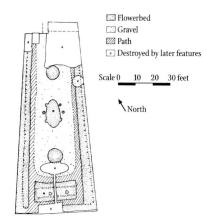

☐ Flowerbed
☐ Gravel
▨ Path
⊡ Destroyed by later features

Scale 0 10 20 30 feet

↘ North

Fig. 6.18
Plans of excavations carried out at
NO.4 THE CIRCUS, BATH.
top: Phase I, 1760-c.1775
above: Phase II, c.1775-c.1835.

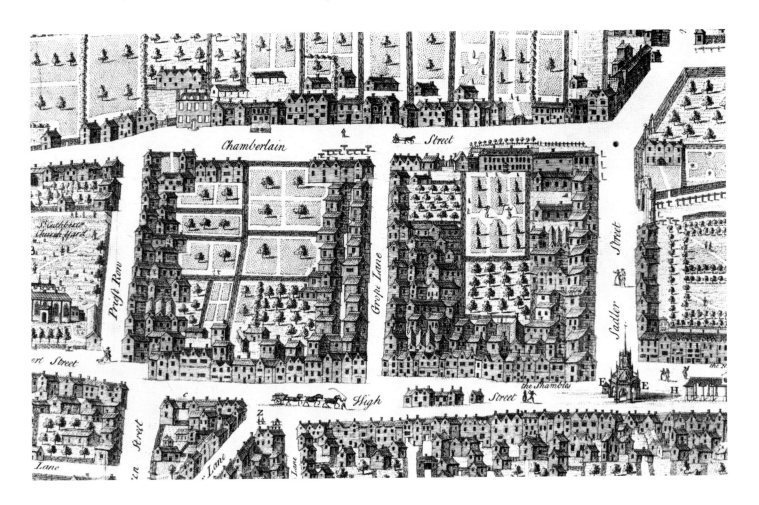

Fig. 6.17
An extract from
PLAN OF THE CITY OF WELLS
by William Simes of 1735
showing urban formal gardens.

created, two circular, the central one oval. Six small holes around the perimeter of the oval bed probably contained clipped dwarf evergreens . Traces of mortar and clinker bedding for flagstone paths survived all around the central gravel rectangle, separating it from the side and end beds. There had been minor alterations to the bottom end of the garden in the last quarter of the eighteenth century, but essentially the formal Georgian garden survived until about 1835, when it was buried beneath a further dump of clay produced by the extension of the basement area. Unfortunately soil samples from the Georgian levels failed to produce any traces of pollen or seeds. However, the garden has now been recreated along the lines of its original plan through the advice of John Harvey, using planting schemes appropriate to the period, and visitors can now gain an accurate impression of a formal town garden of the mid-eighteenth century.[46]

PUBLIC GARDENS and PROMENADES

The seventeenth century saw the first provision of gardens and parks for public recreation in towns. At first these were designed primarily for the enjoyment of the wealthy, not for all and sundry. Following the success of the Pantiles development in Tunbridge Wells, other spa towns like Bath quickly recognised the need for attractive public walks where visitors could meet and take exercise.

Bath's earliest fashionable promenades all lay near the abbey, where Celia Fiennes commended the pleasant greens, walks and rows of trees.[47] Gilmore's map of 1694 shows five separate areas of open space near the abbey church. About a hundred yards to the south was 'Abbey Green', then down to grass with a row of trees; it survives today as a small paved court. Next, the 'Abbey Garden', immediately south of the church, was laid out in formal style with geometrically-planned walks and standard trees; this is now largely built over. Immediately east of the Abbey Garden was the 'Old Bowling Green', laid out over the former Upper Abbey Orchard, extending eastwards to the city wall. This was reserved for 'Lords, Knights, Gallants and Gentlemen of the best rank and quality'. It was sacrificed in the late 1720s for the building of Terrace Walk and John Wood's Lower Assembly Rooms. Further north, and immediately east of the abbey church, the 'Gravel Walks' had been planted out in 1675 with eighty sycamores in parallel rows, kept pruned and tidy. The exclusive nature of these walks was emphasized by a railing along the north side and two gates on the west side. Finally, north-east of the abbey church, Gilmore shows an open area named 'Miter Green', originally part of the churchyard, which had come into the hands of the Corporation in 1572. The northern portion was built over soon afterwards, but the rest remained open space, used for shooting butts in 1597, then levelled before 1614 to make a public bowling green.

Between 1701 and 1708 a narrow strip of land along the southern boundary of the Gravel Walks, previously occupied by a row of stalls selling souvenirs to visitors, was built up on a piecemeal basis by members of the Corporation. A couple of lines of sycamores had to be sacrificed as cellars were excavated out in front of each property, but a broad parade, probably paved with stone flags, gave some unity to the row. The Gravel Walks were still being maintained by the

Corporation in the 1710s, but they no longer pruned the sycamores, and by the 1730s it was recorded that their branches and boughs shut out so much light from the new row of houses that *"many people were obliged to dine by candle-light at four o'clock in the afternoon in the month of May"*.

Parts of the ground north and north-east of the abbey church had also been lost to building developments during the 1720s and 1730s, and in 1732 the Corporation decided to regularise the remaining open space. Because of the piecemeal nature of the earlier developments the opportunity to create a town square of unified design had been lost; nevertheless, something attractive could still be achieved. The overgrown sycamores of the old Gravel Walks were all felled and sold for timber, and the gates and walls were removed. The Outer Green (Gilmore's 'Miter Green') was levelled up, several decrepit elms removed, and the whole replanted with seven or eight rows of elm saplings provided from Bathford by Thomas Robins. In 1735, following a suggestion of Beau Nash, an obelisk was built in the centre of the grove to commemorate the previous year's visit by the Prince of Orange to take the cure. The Orange Grove, as it came to be known, remained a focal point of fashion in Bath for some forty years; but as the town expanded northwards and eastwards it slowly lost its exclusive character, and butchers, coal merchants and other traders moved in.[48]

More ambitious schemes were in the wind as early as 1674, when Bath Corporation opened a subscription fund to pay for the transformation of part of the city walls into an attractive promenade to give views out over the surrounding countryside. Outside the walls to the east, centred on the low-lying space known as St James's Triangle between Terrace Walk, the Parades and the River Avon, further private walks and pleasure-grounds were laid out in 1708 by Thomas Harrison for the enjoyment of those *"People of Rank and Fortune"* who attended the Lower Assembly Rooms. The triangle was planted up with high beech hedges and groves surrounding an open circular glade, to which access was gained by three entrances in the midpoint of each side, shown on John Wood's plan (1740). The groves have gone, but elements of this layout still survive today in modified form, the circular glade having a bandstand in the centre. Outside the

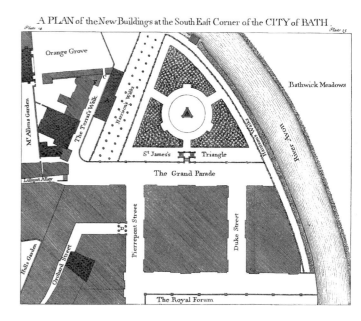

Fig. 6.19
John Wood's plan of 1740 showing the scheme for
ST JAMES'S TRIANGLE, BATH.

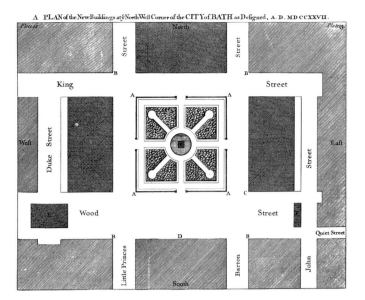

city walls to the west Celia Fiennes had enjoyed the meadow walks in Kingsmead. As building encroached into this area in the 1730s, two small squares, Beaufort Square and Kingsmead Square, were laid out by John Strahan. The first of these may never have been more than a strip of grass, but a plan of 1776 shows Beaufort Square laid out as a formal garden. Finally, to the north, John Wood's much more ambitious plan for Queen Square, begun in 1728, shows the centre as a formal parterre with a round pool and obelisk in the centre and a cruciform pattern of gravel walks. By contrast the open space in the centre of the Circus, begun in 1754, was never intended as a garden and was originally paved all over with stone setts.[49]

Outside the spa towns, public gardens often developed from ornamental grounds and bowling-greens attached to taverns. Bridgwater Corporation owned a bowling-green in the Eastover district of the town, and a map of c.1720-30 shows a bowling-green at East Quay on the north side of the bridge.[50]

The SURVIVAL of FORMAL GARDENS and LANDSCAPES

Despite the profound changes in fashion to be described in the following chapter, traditional geometrically-planned gardens did not all disappear overnight. Anthea Taigel and Tom Williamson have recently reminded us of the innate conservatism and pragmatism of the country squire: "*Art historians often give the impression that the eighteenth-century landowner was interested, above all, in poetry, painting and philosophy. In reality, most gentlemen were concerned with planting things and killing things*".[51] Even if the enclosed garden was increasingly old-fashioned, it was valued so long as it was enjoyed by the family and contributed towards the domestic economy. Sentimental reluctance to alter the achievements of earlier times, inertia or simple lack of resources could inhibit change late into the eighteenth century or even beyond.

When Edward Phelips inherited Montacute in 1750, the estate was in debt, and he was forced to sell some of the land. However, careful management, aided by two substantial inheritances, reversed the decline and allowed him to embark upon a new programme of improvement. Samuel Donne's map, made just before Edward Phelips's final alterations in about 1782, shows the square east forecourt with its corner pavilions, though the central gate lodges had by then disappeared. Beyond it the lime avenue leads eastwards over a field called Fore Leaze. The main north garden still retains its original terraced perimeter walk and includes a path leading from the house past a pond to the central prospect mound. The nearer part of the park is labelled as the bowling-green. The kitchen gardens lie immediately beyond the outbuildings south of the house, with another line of trees to the east. Despite the changes, much of the formal setting of the house survived.[52]

The fourth Sir Abraham Elton, inheriting Clevedon Court in 1761, made considerable changes to the gardens there, again without destroying their essential formality. He extended the original terraces further to the west, building an octagonal gazebo at the west end of the middle terrace and a simple summerhouse at the east. Both structures are shown in drawings made in 1788 by his son-in-law, Oldfield Bowles. Plantings of London plane took place behind the upper terrace, together with the evergreen holm oak, which soon became naturalised in this warm coastal situation, creating a Mediterranean air, while Scots pine, beech and sycamore began to clothe the bare hills above.[53]

Formal elements probably lingered longest in the more remote parts of south and west Somerset. As late as 1842, when John Claudius Loudon travelled the road from Bridgwater to Williton, he remarked upon "*several villas, one or two of which still retain clipped yew hedges and other vestiges of the geometric style*".[54]

Fig. 6.20
John Wood's plan for
QUEEN SQUARE, BATH, *1727.*

Figs. 6.21 & 6.22
The restored Georgian garden at
NO.4 THE CIRCUS, BATH.

REFERENCES. - Chapter 6

Fig. 6.23

The Manor of Montacute.
This map was probably drawn in 1782 by Samuel Donne. The original was missing from its place in the Phelips Papers when deposited in Somerset County Records Office. A photocopy of part of the lost original was used in this reconstruction. The map shows the surroundings of the house before Edward Phelips made his 'intended west front' and (from his own diary) "began forming a new road to the west front of Montacute House from the public road through Boys Court orchard by filling up millponds, levelling hedges etc." in 1785-6. This reconstruction is by Robert Pearce for J. H. C. Phelips.

1. See, for example, *The Anglo-Dutch Garden in the Age of William and Mary*, ed. John Dixon Hunt & Erik de Jong (Jnl.of Garden History nos.2-3, April-September 1988); D. Jacques & A.J. Van der Holst, *The Gardens of William and Mary* (1988); David Green, *Gardener to Queen Anne: Henry Wise (1655-1738) and the Formal Garden* (Oxford, 1956)

2. Worlidge's works included *Systema Horticulturae* (1667), describing the art of gardening, and *Vinetum Britannicum* (1678), describing the growing of cider apple trees and the making of cider. John Evelyn's most influential book was *Sylva, or a Discourse of Forest Trees*, first published in 1664.

3. Switzer's first major publication was *The Nobleman, Gentleman, and Gardener's Recreation* (1715), later extended into three volumes entitled *Ichnographia Rustica* (1718).

4. Batty Langley's many publications included *New Principles of Gardening* (1728) and *Pomona, or the Fruit Garden Illustrated* (1729).

5. *The Journeys of Celia Fiennes*, ed. Christopher Morris (1947), pp.20-21, 23, 240, 242; Daniel Defoe, *A Tour through the Whole Island of Great Britain* (1724-6).

6. Kilton: Somerset C.R.O. DD/L 2/6/33; Toomer: DD/MDL bx5 FT 2; East Quantoxhead: DD/X/LTR.1; Marshwood: DD/L 1/10/35A; Heyfield: DD/L 1/10/35A; Dunster: DD/L, now G2 ND 10.

7. John Harris, *The Artist and the Country House* (1979) traces the origins of this fashion from sixteenth-century Italy through to the later nineteenth century.

8. Kip's engravings were published in two great compilations, *Britannia Illustrata* (1715, 1740) and *Le Nouveau Theatre de la Grande Bretagne* (1716, 1724).

9. Alice M. Coats, *The Quest for Plants: a History of the Horticultural Explorers* (1968)

10. John Evelyn, *Pomona* (Appendix to 1729 edition of Silva), p.56; *The Journeys of Celia Fiennes*, p.13; Philippa Legg, *So Merry Let us Be: the Living Tradition of Somerset Cider* (Somerset County Council, 1986).

11. Evelyn, *Silva* (5th edn,1729), pp.135-8, 141-2, 150-2.

12. Colin G. Winn, *The Pouletts of Hinton St George* (1995), p.157.

13. E. Chisholm-Batten, 'The forest trees of Somerset', *P.S.A.N.H.S.* Vol.36 (1890), ii, pp.183, 185-6.

14. John Harvey, 'Parks, gardens and landscaping', in Michael Aston (ed.), *Aspects of the Medieval Landscape of Somerset* (Somerset County Council, 1988), p.102; Harvey, *Early Nurserymen* (Chichester, 1974), p.71.

15. T.W. Mayberry, *Orchard and the Portmans* (Winchester, 1986), pp.23-5.

16. Robert Dunning, *Some Somerset Country Houses* (Wimborne, 1991), pp.18-20.

17. Michael McGarvie, *Notes towards a History of Gardening at Marston House, 1660-1905* Frome Historical Research Group, Occasional Papers no.4 (1987), pp.3-4.

18. Harvey, 'Parks, gardens and landscaping', p.102; William Phelps, *The History and Antiquities of Somersetshire*, Vol.1 (1836), pp.247-55; Michael Havinden, *The Somerset Landscape* (1981), p.235.

19. Robin Atthill, *Old Mendip* (Newton Abbot, 2nd edn, 1971), pp.29-30; R.J.E. Bush, 'Crowcombe', *V.C.H.* Vol.5 (1985), p.57.

20. M.A. Aston, 'Gardens and earthworks at Hardington and Low Ham', *P.S.A.N.H.S.* Vol.122 (1978), esp.pp.17-26. I am grateful to Rob Wilson-North for discussion of the Royal Commission's recent work on the site.

21. *Country Life*, 9th February 1989, pp.82, 87; R.W. Dunning & M.C. Siraut, 'Goathurst', *V.C.H.* Vol.6 (1992), pp.45, 49.

22. R.J. Bush, 'Nettlecombe Court: 1: The Trevelyans and other residents of the Court'. *Field Studies* Vol.3 no.2 (1970), p.283.

23. Michael McGarvie, 'Marston House: a study of its history and architecture', *P.S.A.N.H.S.* Vol.118 (1974), pp.17-19; McGarvie, *Gardening at Marston House, 1660-1905*, pp.6-13.

24. Michael McGarvie, *Witham Friary* (Frome Historical Research Group, 1989), p.34; Robert Wilson-North, 'Witham: from Carthusian monastery to country house' *Current Archaeology* Vol.13 no.iv (1996), pp.151-8.

25. *Country Life*, Vol.4, 29th October 1898, pp.528-32; Vol.29, 24th June, 1911, pp.924-33; 1st September, 1983, p.552; Dunning, *Some Somerset Country Houses*, pp.148-153; Phelps, *History and Antiquities of Somersetshire*, Vol.1, p.297.

26. R.W. Dunning, 'Hinton St George', *V.C.H.* Vol.4 (1978), pp.38-40, 'Dinnington', *V.C.H.* Vol.4, p.147; Winn, *The Pouletts of Hinton St George*, pp.158-63.

27. Nicholas Pearson Associates, *Newton Park, Historic Survey and Restoration Plan* (Report to Duchy of Cornwall,1993); I am grateful to Mary Stacey for access to a copy of this report.

28. I am grateful to Jan Woudstra for this information.

29. Anon., *Dunster Castle* (National Trust, revised edn 1990).

30. R.W. Dunning, 'St Decumans, including Watchet and Williton', *V.C.H.* Vol.5 (1985), pp.149, 155.

31. Robin Atthill, *Old Mendip* (2nd edn, Newton Abbot, 1971), pp.35, 37-8.

32. Arthur & Margaret Ann Elton, *Clevedon Court* (9th edn,1986), pp.12-13; Margaret Elton, *Annals of the Elton Family: Bristol Merchants and Somerset Landowners* (Stroud, 1994), pp.35-6; Stewart Harding & David Lambert, *Parks and Gardens of Avon* (Bristol, 1994), p.37.

33. *Country Life* Vol.82, 28th August 1937, pp.220-25; J. Harris, *Gardens of Delight* (1978), pp.67-8; Harding & Lambert, *Parks and Gardens of Avon*, p.36.

34. R.W. Dunning & M.C. Siraut, 'North Petherton', *V.C.H.* Vol.6 (1992), pp.281, 296.

35. Dunning, *Some Somerset Country Houses*, p.59; Dunning & Siraut, 'Stogursey', *V.C.H.* Vol.6, pp.140-1.

36. R.J.E. Bush, 'Crowcombe', *V.C.H.* Vol.5 (1985), pp.57-8.

37. M.C. Siraut, 'Nether Stowey', *V.C.H.* Vol.5 (1985), p.194; the plan, in Somerset C.R.O., is conveniently reproduced in this volume, facing p.156.

38. Dunning, *Some Somerset Country Houses*, pp.142-3.

39. Ron Gilson & Commander E.H.D.Williams, 'Vernacular architecture', *P.S.A.N.H.S.* Vol.126 (1982), p.90; Eva Crane, *The Archaeology of Beekeeping* (1983), p.119, fig.138.

40. Citrus trees were being grown by William Cecil, Lord Burghley, at Theobalds, Hertfordshire, and by Sir Francis Carew at Beddington, Surrey, in 1562; May Woods & Arete Warren, *Glass Houses: a History of Greenhouses, Orangeries and Conservatories* (1988), pp.10-14.

41. R.J.E. Bush, 'Crowcombe', *V.C.H.* Vol.5 (1985), p.58.

42. For Montacute, see Chapter 5, reference 16; R.W. Dunning & M.C. Siraut, 'North Petherton', *V.C.H.* Vol.6 (1992), p.303.

43. Savage & Meyler, *Map of Five Miles around Bath* (1805); Canon H.E. Ellacombe, 'The vineyards of Somerset and Gloucestershire', *Proceedings of Bath Natural History & Antiquarian Field Club*, Vol.7 no.i (1890), p.35; Hugh Barty-King, *A Tradition of English Wine* (1977), p.105; Mike Chapman, *A Guide to the Estates of Ralph Allen around Bath* (Bath, 1996), pp.19-20.

44. John Goodchild, 'Martin Strong, vicar of Yeovil, 1690-1720', *P.S.A.N.H.S.* Vol.78 (1932), ii, pp.113, 116.

45. Christopher Pound, *Genius of Bath: the City and its Landscape* (Bath, 1986), pp.22-3

46. Robert D. Bell, 'The discovery of a buried Georgian garden in Bath', *Garden History* Vol.18 no.i (1990), pp.1-21.

47. *The Journeys of Celia Fiennes*, p.23.

48. Trevor Fawcett & Marta Inskip, 'The making of Orange Grove', *Bath History* Vol.5 (1994), pp.24-50.

49. *The Journeys of Celia Fiennes*, pp.20-21; Pound, *Genius of Bath*, pp. 39-45; Barry Cunliffe, *The City of Bath* (Gloucester, 1986), pp.120-27.

50. R.W. Dunning & M.C. Siraut, 'Bridgwater', *V.C.H.* Vol.6 (1992), p.204. The map is Somerset C.R.O. DD/SH c/202.

51. Anthea Taigel & Tom Williamson, *Parks and Gardens* (1993), p.64.

52. Dudley Dodd, *Montacute House, Somerset* (1978), pp.25-6, 49, where part of the map of *c*.1782, Somerset C.R.O. DD/PH/159, is reproduced.

53. Elton & Elton, *Clevedon Court*, p.14; Elton, *Annals of the Elton Family*, pp.68, 75.

54. John Claudius Loudon (ed. Priscilla Boniface), *In Search of English Gardens: the Travels of John Claudius Loudon and his wife Jane* (1990), p.226.

Chapter 7

LANDSCAPE PARKS of the EIGHTEENTH CENTURY

LAKES AND POOLS OF IRREGULAR SHAPE, SERPENTINE PATHS,
CLASSICAL TEMPLES AND STATUES, GROTTOES ...

INTRODUCTION

Formal parks and gardens remained popular in England well into the eighteenth century. However, the new political climate created in 1714 by the Hanoverian succession and the whig ascendancy was soon to be reflected by changes in landscaping fashions more fundamental than any that had gone before. With the autocratic rule of the Stuarts ended and a more democratic society emerging, huge expenditure upon conspicuous displays of continental-style waterworks and parterres seemed increasingly inappropriate. The Hanoverian court played less of a role as an arbiter of taste, and it was the English aristocracy which now set the pace, led by Richard Boyle, 3rd Earl of Burlington (1695-1753). Burlington was the patron of William Kent, whom Horace Walpole was to describe as the 'father of modern gardening'. The horizons of English gentlemen became broadened by the vogue for the continental 'Grand Tour'. They became inspired by the works of French and Italian artists such as Claude Lorraine (1600-82), Gaspard Poussin (1613-75) and Salvator Rosa (1615-73), who had recreated in their paintings idealised Arcadian landscapes with torrents, pools, wild crags and forests, often including ruined temples to give an appropriate touch of melancholy. Increasing familiarity with such scenes fostered a growing delight in 'natural' scenery, compared with which the constraints of the formal garden began to seem dull and stultifying. There was a new enthusiasm for genuinely classical art and sculpture (as opposed to the art of the renaissance), fostered by the first archaeological excavations at Herculaneum (1738) and Pompeii (1748). New ideas about art, architecture and garden design circulated within the Kit-Cat Club, an influential clique of prominent whig landowners, politicians and writers.[1]

A more focused reaction against formality and the recognition of 'Nature' as a new symbol of liberal, humanist principles came from the pens of English writers and philosophers such as the 3rd Earl of Shaftesbury, who wrote in 1710 of his preference for *"things of a NATURAL kind: where neither ART, nor the CONCEIT or CAPRICE of Man has spoil'd their genuine order ... Even the rude Rocks, the mossy CAVERNS, the irregular unwrought GROTTOS and broken FALLS of waters, with all the horrid graces of the WILDERNESS itself, as representing NATURE more, will be the more engaging, and appear with a magnificence beyond the mockery of the princely gardens"*.[2] At the same time Joseph Addison was promoting the works of nature as *"more delightful than artificial shows"*, depicting his own garden at Bilton near Rugby as *"a confusion of kitchen and parterre, orchard and flower-garden, which lie so mixt and interwoven with one another that it resembles a natural wilderness and one of the uncultivated parts of our country"*.[3] Alexander Pope, in an essay published in 1713, mocked the artificiality and symmetry of the traditional garden, urging a return to the *"amiable simplicity of unadorned nature"*. Later, he was to deride the formal parterre, where

> *"Grove nods at grove,*
> *Each alley has a brother,*
> *And half the platform*
> *Just reflects the other'"*

Pope expressed his fundamental philosophy of gardening in his exhortation, *"In all, let Nature never be forgot ... Consult the Genius of the Place"*: predetermined designs should not be imposed upon the landscape, instead the character of a garden should be allowed to evolve respecting the natural contours of the ground. He put his theories into practice in his own garden at Twickenham.[4]

The Palladian style of architecture, introduced by Inigo Jones a century earlier but stillborn through the strife of the Civil War, enjoyed a vigorous revival after Lord Burlington decided to model his own house at Chiswick upon one of Palladio's villas near Vicenza. Baroque, with its flamboyant scale and flagrant disregard for the rules of proportion, was now seen to epitomise extravagance and bad taste, whereas Palladianism reflected rationalism and restraint, qualities dear to the whig aristocracy. As many country houses and villas were built or remodelled in the new style, so careful thought was given to providing them with an appropriate romantic, pastoral setting; a setting in which the traditional formal garden played no part.

It is legitimate to question how much impact the experiments of these urbane men of letters really had upon the small provincial landowner. Certainly at first their ideas circulated mainly amongst the *cognoscenti*, raising few ripples in the remoter parts of Somerset. As the eighteenth century progressed, however, the enthusiasm for all aspects of 'improvement' gained momentum. Open-field landscapes were transformed through enclosure by agreement and large-scale drainage works were resumed in the Somerset Levels. The developing network of turnpike roads made it easier to enjoy exploring other parts of the country. Slowly but inexorably the climate of opinion became open to new ideas and ready to accept change. By the end of the third quarter of the century the lead given by a few men was eagerly being followed even by the lesser local gentry, the clergy and the emerging professional classes.

WILLIAM KENT and the ORIGINS of the LANDSCAPE GARDEN

The pioneer of informal landscape gardening in England was William Kent, who had met Burlington in Italy and worked for him at Chiswick. The essence of Kent's style, best exemplified at Rousham in Oxfordshire, involved the replacement of formal canals with lakes and pools of irregular shape, the replacement of straight avenues by serpentine paths, the provision of temples, statues and sham ruins to provide focal points within the garden, and the planting of conifers and evergreen oaks alongside the native trees to imitate the cypress and ilex groves of the Mediterranean. In addition to classical temples and statues, Kent also experimented with grottoes and garden buildings in gothick, rustic and rococo styles. His employment of the sunken wall or ha-ha provided the illusion of expansiveness towards the wider view, while still providing an effective barrier to farm livestock.

Kent's commissions were concentrated in south-east England, and he did little work in the west country, except for designing the magnificent Worcester Lodge at Badminton and drawing up plans for Oakley Wood on Lord Bathurst's Cirencester estate and Lord Clinton's Castle Hill in Devon.[5] However, others soon began to imitate his style, most notably Henry Hoare, owner of Stourhead in Wiltshire, who

Fig. 7.1
PRIOR PARK, BATH.
A view over the lakes and Palladian Bridge towards the city. Designers of early landscape gardens rarely achieved a completely natural effect with their lakes, the water ending in a sharply visible line against the dam. A generation later Capability Brown would have concealed the dam from the main viewpoints.

Fig. 7.2
LANDSCAPED PARKS of the 18TH CENTURY.
♣   *Parks with significant landscape features*

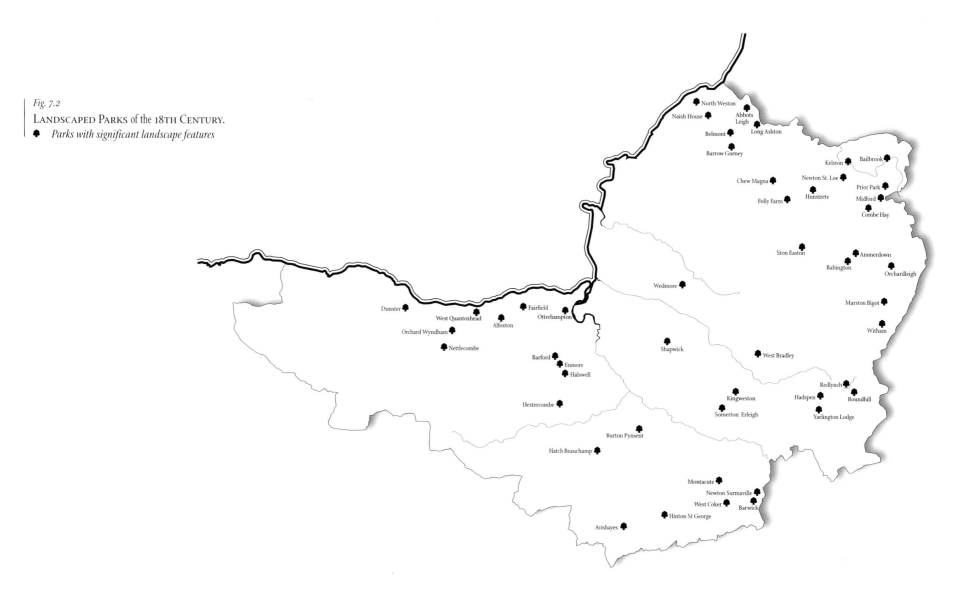

Fig. 7.3
ALFRED'S TOWER.

employed Henry Flitcroft, one of Kent's associates and another Burlington protégé, to design the various temples around the lake there. The outer circuit of the Stourhead ride briefly crossed the border into Somerset over Kingsettle Hill in Brewham, and here in 1762 Flitcroft built a triangular brick tower, 160ft high, with a crenellated parapet and round corner towers, commanding splendid views over Selwood Forest. A statue of King Alfred was set over the doorway, beneath a gothic canopy. Alfred's Tower commemorated the recent accession of George III, seen as a worthy successor to Alfred himself, and in typical contemporary style it incorporated an inscription stating that on that same summit in AD 879 King Alfred "*Erected his standard against the Danish Invaders: To Him we owe The origin of Juries, The Establishment of a Militia, the Creation of a Naval Force: Alfred, the light of a benighted age was a Philosopher and a Christian, The Father of his People, The Founder of the English Monarchy and Liberty*".[6] Flitcroft may also have been responsible for the gothic arch at Redlynch Park, since he is known to have worked at the house in the 1750s.[7]

Four outstanding examples of the early style of landscape gardening were created in Somerset between the 1730s and 1760s: Prior Park, Marston Bigot, Halswell and Hestercombe.

PRIOR PARK, BATH

Prior Park was not the seat of an ancient landed dynasty, but a new creation by a self-made businessman.[8] Ralph Allen, born in 1693, came from a Cornish family of modest means and status. He moved to the developing spa of Bath in 1710, soon becoming deputy postmaster there. During the Jacobite rising of 1715 he established his whig credentials by acting as an informer to General Wade (a statue of Wade in Roman dress, no longer extant, was later set up on the terrace south of the Prior Park mansion). By the 1720s his reorganisation of the postal system had brought him considerable wealth, but since his income depended ultimately upon Government favour, he made a point of cultivating the leading whig politicians. William Pitt the Elder, who suffered severely from gout, frequently visited Bath for the sake of the waters, and it was largely through Allen's influence that Pitt was elected MP for the city in July 1757. Like others of the select whig circle, Pitt was deeply interested in both architecture and gardens, and Allen soon realised how effectively the acquisition of a suitable house and grounds would enhance his own social position. Despite this, he had no overwhelming personal ambition to live in a great mansion, and when Prior Park was completed, he and his wife only occupied a modest apartment in one of the wings.

One of the problems which had inhibited the growth of Bath was its poor communication links, and in 1724 Allen became a leading promoter and shareholder of the Avon navigation. As the city began to grow there was a need for building stone, and in 1726 he purchased the old quarries between Combe Down and Widcombe and began expanding them with an eye to a much wider market. To carry the great blocks of stone he had an inclined tramway built, linking the Combe Down quarries with the Avon, whence the stone could be carried by barge down to Bristol and elsewhere. This tramway is a prominent feature in the foreground of Anthony Walker's engraving of about 1754, the earliest known illustration of Prior Park.

Allen's early attempts to sell Bath stone as far afield as London had not been successful, and it was perhaps partly to demonstrate his faith in its qualities that he decided to employ it for his own new house outside the city. Having already engaged the elder John Wood to alter his town house in Lilliput Avenue, he now invited Wood to prepare designs for a new Palladian mansion to be built on the slopes of Combe Down. Building commenced in 1734, but after some disagreement with Wood the eastern range of the house was completed by Allen's clerk of works, Richard Jones, in a modified form which destroyed the symmetry of the original design. The site chosen for the house occupied a splendid position at the head of a long combe within the derelict deer park of the medieval priors of Bath, and unlike most of the early landscape gardens, here house and grounds were interlinked from the start. Features of the view included the church and manor-house of Widcombe, lower down the combe, and the rising ground on the further side of the Avon valley beyond. Since the abandonment of the deer park the land had been turned over to farming, and Allen began planting on either flank of the valley to conceal the bare slopes and to frame the view down from the house.

Ralph Allen had met Alexander Pope in Bath in 1735, and in the following year visited both Pope's garden at Twickenham and Lord Burlington's garden at Chiswick. Pope stayed with Allen for three months over the winter of 1739-40, and almost certainly advised on the planting. His name is also associated with a small circular pool and sham bridge in the grove on the west side of the combe. In May 1740 he wrote to Allen enquiring about the "*Elmes we planted on each Side of the Lawn and of the Little Wood-work to join one wood to the other below*". After Pope's death in 1744 his gardener, John Searle, moved to Bath to take charge of the Prior Park grounds.

Interestingly, Thorp's map of Bath and five miles around, published in 1742, shows that geometric planting was even then not yet wholly abandoned. Avenues of trees converged on the south front of the house and upon the site of the Upper Lodge.

Elsewhere less formal belts and clumps were preferred. A mile and a half to the north of the house, the old rabbit warren on Bathampton Down was stocked with Scots firs and spruce in 1742, and Richard Jones later stated that 55,146 trees, mostly firs and pines, had been planted all round the estate. The use of conifers on the skyline, as ornament, as windbreak, and as a screen to conceal the stone quarries, was a remarkable innovation. Further accounts after

Fig. 7.4
Ralph Allen's house at PRIOR PARK.

Allen's death list plantations of oak, beech, larch, bay, laurel, yew, holly, cedar and Spanish chestnut. An article in the UNIVERSAL MAGAZINE in May 1754 gave praise to the way that Allen "*has pursued only what the natural situation has pointed out to him; and by that means rendered it one of the cheapest, and at the same time one of the most beautiful seats in England. He has levelled no hills, but enjoys the beauty of the prospects they afford; he has cut down no woods but struck through them with fine walkes*". Dr Richard Pococke in 1754 described how "*the great beauty of the place is the lawn and wood below, and prospect of Bath, and the villages round about down that valley, with rising ground on each side...*" Collinson, too, praised both the setting of the house, "*acknowledged to command perhaps the finest view in the kingdom*", and the extensive groves of fir trees which Allen had planted. Sadly their extent was later much reduced by the demand of local coal mines for pit-props.[9]

Ralph Allen's clerk of works, Richard Jones, developed a rococo woodland garden with serpentine walks north-west of the house between 1750 and 1760. Like the term 'baroque', 'rococo' is a concept borrowed from architecture, and in its application to gardens it is an entirely modern label, implying a garden stocked with an eclectic variety of rather frivolous ornaments.[10] At Prior Park these included a gothick summerhouse of Bath stone, a room ornamented with close-set perpendicular panelling fronted by a loggia of three ogee arches on clustered shafts; the design was adapted from two of the plates in Batty Langley's 1749 pattern book, GOTHIC ARCHITECTURE IMPROVED .... Early in the present century this building was removed to a new site three-quarters of a mile away, at Rainbow Wood House.[11] Stone-lined rills led through the woods, culverted beneath areas of open grass, originally feeding a cascade in the middle of the combe (shown on a sketch of 1758 by Thomas Robins). Other features included a small Gothic cottage east of the mansion built by Richard Jones for the gardener, Isaac Dodsley, one of the earliest essays in genuine gothic revival as opposed to the more playful gothick of the rococo designers; a grotto of tufa, its roof and sides studded with shells, fossils and minerals, its floor paved partly with bone and inlaid with fir-cones, of which only one arch remains; a statue of Moses with his hand striking the rock above a 20ft-waterfall; and a cold bath. Chinoiserie became fashionable as part of the rococo movement in the 1740s and 1750s, and a Chinese gate was made near Middle Lodge on the western boundary of the Prior Park estate.[12] The outward view was further enlivened by a new Doric pavilion built for Squire Bennett at

Fig. 7.5
A detail from a 'SURVEY OF THE CITY OF BATH AND OF 5 MILES AROUND' *by Thomas Thorp, 1742.*

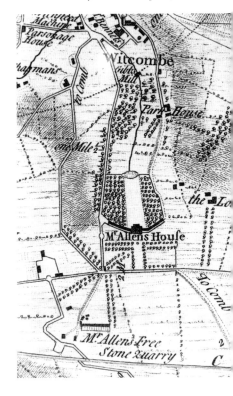

Fig. 7.6
The PALLADIAN BRIDGE
at Prior Park in 1966.

Widcombe Manor, at the southern end of the terraces; the lavish use of tufa in its construction suggests that, like the Prior Park grotto, it too was probably built by Jones.

The crowning glory of the Prior Park landscape was a Palladian bridge, spanning the lake below the house and disguising the cascade beyond. The span is rusticated, with a wide shallow central arch, and it carries a balustraded parapet and superstructure of Ionic columns with a single-bay open-arched pedimented pavilion at either end. This was copied with minor modifications from the Earl of Pembroke's bridge at Wilton, built twenty years earlier, and from Lord Cobham's bridge at Stowe, both of which in their turn were loosely derived from original designs by Palladio and by a drawing by Vincenzo Scammozi in Lord Burlington's collection. The architect is unknown. Richard Jones recorded towards the end of his life that he was the builder and that Allen laid the foundation stone on May 29th, 1755, but he never laid claim to any credit for its design. Tim Mowl puts up a good case for William Pitt's nephew Thomas, in his time highly respected as a gentleman architect, and it would have been a characteristic and appropriate piece of flattery for Allen to seek his advice. The bridge is first illustrated on a sketch by Thomas Robins in 1758.[13]

Beyond the park, Allen laid out an extensive network of drives over his estate, estimated by Dr Pococke to be ten or twelve miles in length, taking advantage of the spectacular views from the edge of the Downs. The Sham Castle on Bathampton Down, begun in 1762 on the site of the earlier warrener's lodge, was not part of the Prior Park landscaping, but was intended rather to be seen from Allen's town house. Pitt wrote to Sanderson Miller on October 30th 1755, inviting him to design a "*very considerable Gothic Object which is to stand in a very fine situation on the Hills near Bath*". Miller had considerable repute as a designer of castellated gothic ornaments, but it now seems unlikely that he had any part in the Sham Castle at Bathampton, and Richard Jones later claimed that the design and execution were his, grumbling at the same time that he wanted to build it bigger, "*but was hindered by my master and other gentlemen*".[14]

The undated estate survey made by Thomas Thorp and John Overton in about 1760 shows how 'natural' the Prior Park landscaping had become. The earlier kitchen garden had been removed, trees were scattered informally around the eastern side of the lawn, a clearing had appeared in the western grove, and there were lakes lower down the valley. The survey includes sketches of some of the park buildings, including the Palladian bridge, the Gothic Lodge and gardener's cottage, the Sham Bridge, the Sham Castle on the Warren, the Dairy House, the Thatched House, the Cold Bath and the Gothic Temple in the Woods. Not all of these features have survived, and even the precise site of some of them is unknown.[15]

MARSTON BIGOT

René Parr's illustration of 1739 displays the formal gardens at Marston Bigot at the end of their baroque phase, but they were still relatively small and lacked much in the way of ornamental garden buildings. John Boyle, 5th Earl of Cork & Orrery decided to embellish and enlarge the grounds. The new works were carried out in two stages under the direction of James Scott, with Stephen Switzer returning to advise. The first stage began in the autumn of 1738 and continued to 1746. One of the first jobs was the completion of a circular lawn, the location of which is unclear. Next the easternmost of the 1st Earl's two mounts alongside the Frome road was enlarged as the 'Temple of the Goddess Cloacina'; a further change of plan converted this to an icehouse in 1744. Statues were brought in, including one of Apollo. A grotto was constructed over a spring some distance west of the house, dedicated in 1742 to Orrery's friend, Dr King. It included a stone bench under an old oak tree, and was planted about with yews, firs, laurel, bays, roses, woodbine and jasmine. It is no longer extant, but can probably be identified with a grotto described as "*near the spring nearly opposite the [new] church at Marston*" on a sketch made by the Rev. John Skinner in 1835. In 1743 a second grotto was constructed at the north end of the old garden near the western prospect mount, and this survives. Lady Cork's Bath, the only other extant eighteenth-century garden building, was probably built at the same time. This was a miniature Roman temple with a pedimented front and Doric arch containing a spring-fed cold bath, all set within an imitation cemetery complete with counterfeit Roman tombstones. It stood out in the park some 330 yards east of the house, approached by a causewayed path. In 1744 further elms, oaks and ashes were planted and new terraces planned. Four cedars and twenty mulberry trees were ordered, and one of the cedars planted at this time may be that which still stands south-east of the house. In 1745 one of the coppices on the estate was divided up into walks and rides with open glades for the deer. Work was then temporarily suspended in 1746 while the family moved to one of their Irish estates.

The Orrerys returned to Marston in 1749 and work on the grounds was resumed, still under James Scott's direction. A monument was erected to a favourite dog called Hector. The garden was now extended to the north-west. In July 1752 a rustic cottage alongside the road in the corner of the new garden was restored, with its own cottage garden described by the local poet Samuel Bowden:

> "*... a garden, neat and clean*
> *With leeks, and box forever green,*
> *Where sage, rosemary, crimsons grow,*
> *And savory, pot-herbs in a row.*"

Scott died in 1753, and most of the work in hand was nearing completion by the following year when Dr Richard Pococke visited Marston and described its grounds. Pococke mentions "*a lawn with a statue of Minerva at the end of it*", perhaps on the line of the original broad walk between the house and the Frome road; to the east of this was "*another lawn*", presumably the former bowling green, "*with a plantation of wood adorned with busts, and an open temple with an altar in it, and ancient statues*". To the west of the first lawn a winding walk led to the rustic cottage. "*At the other end of the garden in a corner is a little Hermitage near finished for my Lord's youngest son; there is a deep way cut down to it with wood on each side, a seat or two in it - one is made in the hollow of a tree; it leads to a little irregular court, with a fence of horses' heads and bones. It is a cabin poorly thatched, and a bedstead covered with straw at one end, a chimney at the other, and some beginning made of very poor furniture. In one part of the garden a very fine horse of my Lord's is buried with a monument - a pedestal, with an urn, I think, on it*"

Fig. 7.7
The house at MARSTON BIGOT
viewed from the park.

(the horse, rather engagingly, was called Nobby). He also describes the cold bath, "*as in the enclosure of an ancient cemetery, with several old inscriptions made for it, and at the end is a small room very elegantly furnished, this I take to be Lady Orrery's place of retirement*". Apart from the remains of the cold bath none of these features survive, and Pocock's description gives us a valuable glimpse of an early landscape garden developed from a formal nucleus, with its numerous ephemeral buildings and ornaments.[16] Much of this was to be swept away later in the century, when the grounds were remodelled in the style of Capability Brown.

Halswell Park, Goathurst

The formal grounds at Halswell were converted to a 'natural' landscape by Sir Charles Kemeys-Tynte, who inherited the property in 1740. The park occupied only 30 acres at this time, but it was more than doubled in size during the 1750s and had reached 132 acres by the later part of the century. A series of plantations, including chestnuts and firs, was established within it. The old formal canal was converted to a small winding lake, with a rockwork grotto at the head,

built in 1753. The dam at the north end of the lake was crossed by a bridge faced on its upper side with an arched rusticated screen incorporating a large pedimented niche and a female herm. Below the dam the water cascaded into a circular pool. Behind the house was a stepped pyramid in Ham stone, capped by a gryphon bearing a shield, certainly predating the fashion for pyramids inspired by Napoleon's Egyptian campaign of 1798. On the further side of the lake, then on a smooth grassy rise, but now concealed by woods, a Doric rotunda was built in 1755, with an icehouse beneath. On the crest of the hill above the house, commanding wide views from the Quantock Hills to Mendip, a thatched building of rendered brick known as Robin Hood's House was erected in 1765. The rear of the building, the side from which it was probably intended to be approached, is of rustic style with appliqué bark to the eaves; two massive hollow tree trunks originally framed the door. The front has a central canted verandah of ogee arches on clustered columns, flanked by gothick windows, derived from Batty Langley's pattern-book. Behind the arches an octagonal room, over 20ft across, has a neo-classical plaster frieze of twisted vines and a fluted dome above; another small room was used as a kitchen. This has been attributed to Thomas Wright, but there is a plan and elevation of "*a Gothick Pavilion at Halswell House*" by Henry Keene which was perhaps an early draft of the design. A further building, now beyond the bounds of the much-contracted estate, is the Temple of Harmony, designed by Thomas Prowse of Axbridge and built in 1764. This is a small pseudo-peripteral temple built in fine ashlar, formerly containing a figure depicting Terpsichore, with a neo-classical tabernacle on the inner wall. A visitor in 1756 noted "*a Druid's Temple in a just style of Bark etc, the view quite gloomy and confined, nearby is a gushing fall which hurts not the moods raised by so sequestered a scene*". By 1756 avenues of trees led westwards from the house, and northwards towards Goathurst. The formal terrace near the house was reduced in size in 1769.[17]

HESTERCOMBE PARK

In 1750 Copleston Warre Bampfylde, a noted book illustrator and artist, succeeded to the Hestercombe estate. Bampfylde's friends included the younger Henry Hoare of Stourhead and Charles Kemeys-Tynte of Halswell, and he shared with them a delight in romantic, arcadian landscapes. His brother-in-law, Edward Knight, also introduced him to William Shenstone, poet and landscape designer of the Leasowes in Worcestershire, who had first defined "*landskip or picturesque gardening*" as "*pleasing the imagination by scenes of grandeur, beauty or variety*".[18] Hestercombe Park, covering some 55 acres, was developed over the following decades into a fine landscaped park with magnificent elms, a pair of serpentine fishponds and a curving carriage drive sweeping in from the western lodge gates. The most spectacular and picturesque features were concentrated in a 35-acre combe behind the house, centred upon a series of ponds. Here a high cascade fell through rocks, imitating Shenstone's waterfall at the Leasowes, fed by a sinuous 300-yard-long brick and stone contour leat. A painting of the Hestercombe cascade by John Inigo Richards hangs on the north wall of the saloon at Stourhead. Henry Hoare is known to have admired it and, probably with Bampfylde's help, designed something similar below the lake in his own grounds. On either side of the combe walks were laid out between lawns and newly-planted trees, with Chinese and gothic seats. There was a small grotto on the west and a root-house, hermitage or witch's cave on the east, the latter inspiring the vicar of Blagdon to write,

"*O'er Bamfylde's woods by various nature graced,
A witch presides, but then that witch is Taste.*"

A Doric temple was added in the late 1770s or early 1780s on the same slope, containing an urn commemorating Bampfylde's friendship with Hoare and Kemeys-Tynte. In 1787 Henry Temple, 2nd Viscount Palmerston, visited Hestercombe and declared the "*romantick and beautiful cascade*" to be "*one of the best things of the kind I have seen in the territory of any private person*".[19]

Other EARLY LANDSCAPE GARDENS

Dr Pococke noticed several other landscaped grounds during his travels through Somerset in 1754. At Redlynch "*the ground of the park is very fine, and there is a large piece of water before the house*". At Combe Hay "*Mr Smith has a very good house, and has made a fine*

serpentine river by stopping the water". On a smaller scale, at Batheaston Mrs Ravoe and her companion Mrs Riggs had built a new house and "*improved the side of a hill to the road in beautiful lawn, walks, garden, cascades, a piece of water and a stream running thro' the garden, and live there in a very agreable retirement*". The park at Redlynch praised by Pococke had been landscaped during the early eighteenth century by the creation of the existing lake and ornamental plantations for Henry Thomas Fox, Earl of Ilchester. By the time Collinson was writing the village had been reduced to eight houses, while the old chapel had been replaced in 1740 by a 'truly elegant' new building north of the great house. Current work by the Victoria County History will throw more light on this important site when it is published.[20]

The idea of opening up the house to the wider countryside soon proved attractive to many. In 1701 James Laurence Churchey had built a new brick house at Roundhill Grange north of Wincanton, a former property of Stavordale Priory. Phelps describes how originally "*the gardens and court were surrounded with brick walls, giving a gloomy and confined appearance to the whole*", but subsequently "*some of these were removed and the house laid more open*" to views bounded by the woods of the Stourhead estate.[21]

The new interest in the wider landscape also produced a fashion for gazebos on high points, even where there was relatively little attempt to integrate these within designed grounds. On the summit of the prominent hill west of Newton Surmaville in 1745 Swayne Harbin built a three-storey octagonal summerhouse with a pyramidal roof and two-storeyed flanking wings, commanding fine views all around the surrounding countryside.[22]

Any landowner with imagination, but only limited financial means, could experiment with an idea first promoted by Stephen Switzer in 1715. Switzer had suggested "*mixing the useful and profitable Parts of Gard'ning with the Pleasurable*", later introducing the French term 'ferme ornée' to describe the type of layout he had in mind. The idea was to develop an ornamental walk within the context of a working farm, integrating the two by laying paths and even planting

*Fig. 7.9
A watercolour of the Pear Pond,*
HESTERCOMBE GARDENS
by C. W. Bampfylde, c.1775.

flower-beds beside pre-existing hedgerows into which a range of ornamental shrubs and climbers had been introduced, and then protecting the paths and beds from farm livestock by means of fences or ditches. The walk could then be punctuated with seats and artificial ornaments as desired.[23] The most notable example of this practice was William Shenstone's small estate at the Leasowes near Halesowen, commenced in 1735. A few examples did appear in the west country, and Mark Angliss has suggested that vestiges of a ferme ornée may survive at Folly Farm, located in a splendid natural amphitheatre near Stowey, north of the Mendip Hills. Here Sir Henry Strachey of Sutton Court carried out improvements in the 1780s, planting clumps of firs, larches, oaks, beeches and lombardy poplars over the hills, damming the streams to make pools and cascades and laying out a walk with wooden bridges and seats around the combe above the farm to provide a succession of views.[24]

CAPABILITY BROWN

The dominant personality in landscape design throughout the third quarter of the eighteenth century was Lancelot Brown, nicknamed 'Capability' from his habit of declaring, when faced with a possible new commission, that the place had "*great capabilities for improvement*". Brown was the son of a yeoman farmer, born at

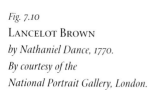

Fig. 7.10
LANCELOT BROWN
by Nathaniel Dance, 1770.
By courtesy of the
National Portrait Gallery, London.

Kirkharle in Northumberland in 1716. On leaving school he joined the staff of a local estate where he became actively involved in reclamation and planting, and this practical experience was to stand him in good stead for the remainder of his career. In 1741 he became head gardener on Viscount Cobham's estate at Stowe in Buckinghamshire, where he met William Kent, then approaching the end of his career, but still making occasional advisory visits. Brown soon earned a good

reputation for his honesty and integrity, and Lord Cobham gave him increasing responsibility for developing the grounds of Stowe, also loaning him out to friends and neighbours to help with their own improvements. After Cobham died in 1750, Brown decided to leave Stowe to set up his own independent practice.[25]

Brown worked on the grand scale wherever the size of the grounds permitted him to do so. His earliest designs were still influenced by the contrivances of Kent, depending on set vistas involving temples and other eyecatchers, but as he developed the confidence to create his own style, his aim was to create the appearance of a truly natural landscape. He was never given to theorising about his work, nor did he produce any manuals describing how he achieved the effects he sought. He would prepare plans and drawings to show to his clients, but he was not a particularly accomplished draftsman, and his drawings often do scant justice to the end result. Clearly he depended more upon his own reputation and the recommendations of his clients than upon any form of literary self-advertisement. It is, therefore, easy to underestimate the care and attention which went into producing such apparently effortlessly informal scenes. His obituary notice in Horace Walpole's notebook suggested that where he was most successful he would be least remembered; so effectively did he imitate nature that his very best works would be mistaken for those of nature herself.[26]

The typical Lancelot Brown landscape depended upon a combination of several elements. Firstly the basic contour of the ground would be altered where necessary to produce smooth, rounded slopes. Any terraces or parterres near the house would be removed, and grass brought right up to the walls of the house itself, with a ha-ha to keep livestock at a safe distance. Paths and drives were never exaggeratedly serpentine in the mode of Switzer, Bridgman or Kent, but wound their way unselfconsciously around the contours, affording the best views possible over the estate. Wherever there was sufficient water this would provide a sinuous river or lake. Earlier designers, like Hoare at Stourhead, had failed to make their lakes appear completely natural because of the obviously artificial line of the dam. Brown became adept at concealing the dam from all viewpoints on the main rides by hiding it around a bend in the valley, by constructing it obliquely to the line of the stream, and by screening it with trees. Perimeter screen-belts of trees gave privacy and shelter within the park, and rounded clumps gave variety. Brown used native trees almost exclusively, particularly beech, also ash and oak; Lebanon cedars were about the only exotic to find much favour. Hal Moggridge's investigations at Brown's masterpiece, Blenheim, have suggested that his groupings of trees were not just randomly scattered, but that the shape and location of each clump was based upon an intricate geometry of intersecting sight-lines from a string of viewpoints on the main drives and walks around the park.[27] If this view is correct, then Brown's landscapes represent an achievement far more complex and far more subtle than the contrived vistas of William Kent. Brown was less inclined than his predecessors to scatter his landscapes with temples and follies, particularly in his mature years; nevertheless, buildings sometimes played an important element in his designs, and he had a particular fondness for gothic crenellations.

Fig. 7.11
NEWTON PARK.
Brown's earliest undertaking in Somerset
was carried out for Joseph Langton at
Newton St Loe. Langton was the
grandson of the Joseph Langton who had
first created the park in the late 1660s
(Chapter 6), and he had just employed
the architect Stiff Leadbetter to replace
the fortified medieval house with a new
mansion sited a short distance to the
north-east. A letter of 1761 describes the
park as "laid out by Mr Brown", and
when Humphry Repton prepared his
own plans for the grounds 35 years later,
he commented "such are the natural
beauties of the situation and so neatly
are kept the grounds around the house
that to a common eye it would appear
presumptuous to suggest improvements
to a spot which Mr Brown is supposed to
have finished with great attention".
Brown's contribution seems to have
included the enlargement of a flight of
small fishponds in the valley into two
bigger lakes (there was also a third,
higher pond, now silted up, and perhaps
specifically designed as a silt trap); the
planting of trees to frame the approach
to the house and to hide the nearby coal
mines; the addition of exaggerated
battlements to the gatehouse and tower
of the medieval house (an alternative
attribution of the crenellations to
Repton's partner John Nash is
invalidated by their depiction in a
drawing by Samuel Hieronymus Grimm
dated 1790); and the completion of a
footpath circuit to link the various
elements. An estate plan of 1789 shows
the park planted with clumps and
groups of trees with individual trees in
key locations, but further away from the
new house Brown had allowed the earlier
formal avenues to remain. There is also
an interesting drawing made by Grimm
in 1789 depicting the informal planting
around the mansion.[28]

Brown has been credited with the remodelling of up to 170 different estates in all parts of the country. Conscientious and hard-working though he undoubtedly was, he can never have given all the projects associated with his name his full, undivided attention. Probably in some cases he merely paid one or two visits to inspect the site and offer advice, which the estate steward would then put into effect to the best of his ability. His several commissions in Somerset were all relatively small-scale jobs, and cannot be regarded as prime examples of his work, though they all have features of some interest.

In October 1764 Sir William Pynsent, a somewhat eccentric whig gentleman who Walpole tells us "*was said to have had not many scruples, living to her death with his only daughter in pretty notorious incest*", then approaching his 90th year, decided to draw up a new will. He left his only surviving relatives 1000 guineas each, while his estate at Burton Pynsent, overlooking Sedgemoor, went to William Pitt the Elder, in the hope that he "*will like my Burton estate ... well enough to make it his country seat*". He recorded no reason for this bequest; he and Pitt had never met, though he appears to have admired Pitt's work as Leader of the House of Commons during the Duke of Newcastle's premiership, and in particular approved of Pitt's opposition to the tax on cider proposed by the Earl of Bute's administration in 1763. Although Pitt quickly came down to Burton to examine the property, his responsibilities in London made it difficult for him to take up immediate permanent residence or to oversee the works in person. He had met Lancelot Brown amongst Lord Cobham's coterie at Stowe, and the two men had remained close friends ever since. It was natural, therefore, that Pitt should turn to Brown when he decided to set up a

monument on the estate to commemorate his gratitude for Pynsent's gift. Brown wrote to Pitt in terms which, though couched in the usual conventional compliments, leave little doubt of his own genuine respect: "*I have sent by your Steward a design for the Pillar which I hope will merit your approbation; if there are any parts you disapprove of, we can very easily correct them when I shall have the honour of seeing you. The figure I have put on the Pedestal is that of Gratitude, conveying to Posterity the name of Pynsent; which indeed he himself has distinguished and without flattery done in the most effectual manner by making you His Heir. On this topic I could say more, but may my silence convey my respect. And that your King and your Country may be long , very long, very long blessed with your unparallelled abilities will be the constant wish of Sir, your most obliged and most obedient, humble servant, Lancelot Brown*".

Stone suitable for the column was located at a depth of 17 feet beneath a nearby field by Philip Pear, a builder from Curry Rivel, and it was erected on the summit of Troy Hill facing the house. It took the form of a Tuscan pillar with an internal stairway, faced with Portland stone. Brown's letter to Pitt tells us that it was originally crowned with a statue representing Gratitude, but this figure had been replaced before the late nineteenth century by an urn. It was finished in the later part of 1767 at a cost of some £2000.

Although Pitt had become Prime Minister in 1766, being raised to the peerage as the 1st Earl of Chatham in the same year, he was already suffering severely from gout, and by 1767 was contemplating moving to Burton Pynsent as a permanent retreat from the cares of state. Brown often wrote, enquiring after his health: "*I wish above all things to know [how] my lordship does, and how the Pillar*

Fig. 7.12
The Pynsent Monument
at Burton Pynsent.

park for Ralph Allen in 1755. Some have taken this to refer to the Palladian Bridge though, as stated earlier, there are other more likely candidates for this job. The estate accounts include a bill for the fairly trifling sum of £60 for surveying and drawing up plans which were submitted by Brown after Ralph Allen's death in 1764. These plans appear not to have survived, and their precise object is unknown. Quite possibly Brown may have been recommended to Allen by his old friend William Pitt, but any 'capabilities' which Brown saw for improvement there were probably aborted by Allen's death. Although the planting which framed the valley between the house and the Palladian bridge has been described as typical of Brown's style, there is good evidence that this was already well-established long before the 1760s.[33]

Capability Brown's last known work in Somerset was undertaken at Kelston Park in 1767-8 for Caesar Hawkins, King George III's surgeon. Brown had been appointed Surveyor to His Majesty's Gardens at Hampton Court three years before, and enjoyed an easy relationship with the new monarch; it is, therefore, quite likely that his recommendation came from the King himself. Hawkins had demolished the Elizabethan house of Kelston Court and abandoned its old terraced gardens. To replace it he had the younger John Wood build a new house towards the top of the hill, on the site of the old summerhouse, enjoying fine views over the Avon valley. Brown was paid £500 for work which probably included planting up the wooded slope below the house.[34]

Lancelot Brown died in 1783. Few individuals can ever have had such a massive impact upon the course of landscape design in England. His prodigious energy took him into almost every corner of the country, and he developed a style which is instantly recognisable. Even in his own time, however, he was not without his critics. Brown aimed at serenity, but some found his landscapes merely dull and stereotyped. His ruthless obliteration of formal gardens around the house were seen by many as mere vandalism, though it is often forgotten how much of the earlier formal landscapes he did allow to remain further away from the house. By the end of the eighteenth century the exponents of the new Picturesque style were ridiculing and vilifying his works, and his reputation has only been restored to its rightful position in the last forty years. What he did achieve was the creation for the first time of a uniquely English style, based on rolling contours, sweeping curves and subtle contrasts of green, which owed nothing to French, Dutch or Italian influence.

pleases his lordship." The following year Pitt retired to Burton Pynsent, to enjoy most of his declining years redesigning the grounds. There is no evidence that Brown had any further involvement. Pitt had considerable experience in improving the surroundings of some of his previous homes, and was perfectly competent to handle the task in person.[29] Some formal gardens with a broad balustraded terrace (which Brown would surely have removed) were allowed to remain by the house, and Philip Pear provided seats and Chinese railings for them. Plantations were established around and below the surrounding lawns, with birch, ash, maple and buckthorn, together with black spruce (*Picea mariana*) sent from Nova Scotia by Captain Samuel Hood. An open ride between oaks and beeches gave a vista towards the column. Farm buildings on the estate were adorned with Tuscan columns. No expense was spared to disguise any features which spoiled the view. A public road was sunk into a hollow-way to hide it from the house. In one direction there was a bare, open hill, and Lord Macaulay records how Pitt here "*ordered a great extent of ground to be planted with cedars. Cedars enough for the purpose were not to be found in Somersetshire. They were therefore collected in London, and sent down by land carriage. Relays of labourers were hired; and the work went on all night by torchlight*".[30]

Lady Chatham lived on at Burton Pynsent after her husband's death in 1778 for another 25 years. After her death much of the estate fell into the hands of speculators, a large part of the house was pulled down in 1805, and the grounds fell into neglect. Brown's column became increasingly unsafe, despite repairs in 1905, and the entrance had to be blocked up after a cow managed to climb the spiral staircase and fell to its death from the parapet in 1948.[31] The cost of restoration may be five times the original cost of building.[32]

At Prior Park the main evidence for Brown's involvement comes from Repton's statement that he designed some addition to the

Other Landscaped Parks of the Later 18th Century

One of the attractions of Capability Brown's style was that it could be imitated relatively easily and relatively cheaply without massive disruption to the productive management of the estate. A great deal of landscaping was carried out during the later eighteenth century, not by professional designers, but by local landowners, or their stewards, working on their own account.

The park at Hinton St George was further enlarged during the 1760s by the 3rd Earl Poulett. Although the grounds were in process of transformation into a landscape park, some semi-formal elements were still being created. The statue of Diana was removed from its earlier site to a hill-top and set on a tall cylindrical pedestal of Ham stone within a double circle of limes. Some of the older formal elements were, however, removed. Collinson's engraving shows that the gates and railings shown on Prideaux's view of 1735 had been taken away so that the lawns now swept right up to the house. Although tree-planting and other works continued intermittently into the early part of the following century, not all of the park was intensively landscaped: the Old Park had been divided in order to lease the grazing in 1744, and for the rest of the century cattle continued to graze there. In the 1790s the amalgamation of two ponds into a larger lake and the planting of perimeter screens of trees were suggested, but never completed.[35]

Dr Pococke visited Witham Charterhouse in 1754 and was impressed with the park, but he records that Sir Charles Wyndham had recently abandoned his decaying mansion there and had removed all his furniture from it. In 1762 Wyndham sold the estate to William Beckford of Fonthill, Alderman and Lord Mayor of London. Beckford immediately commissioned Robert Adam to produce a design for a new mansion. Adam's plan and elevation is well known, but until recently it was uncertain whether the house portrayed had ever been built. However, the field south-west of the earlier gardens is named 'New Building Ground' on the sale map of 1812, and it has recently been realised that earthworks in this area, now levelled but visible on earlier aerial photographs, corresponded almost precisely with the Adam plan. Certainly, therefore, the house was begun, even if it was never completed. The two lakes in the Frome valley, which may have

been created fifty years earlier to adorn the approach to the Wyndhams' house, would certainly have played their part in a new landscape park. However, for Beckford's mansion the approach was altered, a new drive coming from the south-east, ending immediately south of the house in a large turning-circle for carriages. Interestingly, only the final 600 yards of this new drive pointed directly towards the new house, the previous mile being aligned upon its predecessor, where Adam may have had thoughts of stripping away the Wyndhams' additions to reveal the monastic remains as a gothic eyecatcher. After Alderman Beckford's death in 1770, however, the new house at Witham was abandoned, and the site was sold by his son William in 1810. The younger William Beckford was by then already sinking much of his fortune into the building of Fonthill Abbey.[36]

Witham was not the only scheme of this period to have a short life. During the 1770s Francis Popham began building a new mansion at Houndstreet (now Hunstrete) near Marksbury, and to provide it with an appropriate setting he began developing a landscaped park within a screen of tree plantations. A long, sweeping carriage drive between avenues led to the house. A chain of six lakes was laid out, though the general slope of the ground northwards did not permit a particularly natural alignment and necessitated lengthy dams along the contour. A summerhouse was built to give a view over the park, probably within the feature now called 'The Hawhaw', a low mound surrounded by a shallow ditch. However, this landscape was not maintained for very long. Francis Popham died in 1779 with the house uncompleted, and although his widow continued the work, they had no children. When she died in 1797 the property went to a more distant relative who lived in Wiltshire and was unable to maintain it.

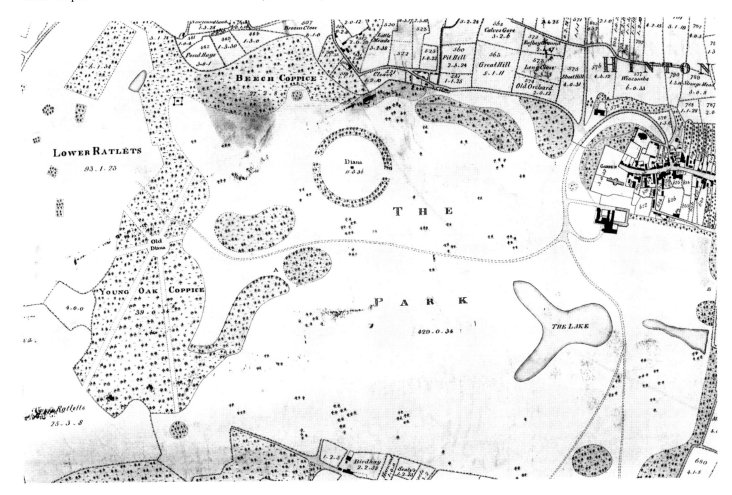

Fig. 7.13
HINTON ST GEORGE *Tithe Map.*

Fig. 7.14
The Statue of Diana at
HINTON ST GEORGE.

Fig. 7.15
A view towards the observation tower on St Michael's Hill, Montacute *from the Tuscan pillars near the summerhouse.*

century, but no documentary evidence for their precise date has yet been discovered. To the west of the park, on the further side of the town, the tall cylindrical observation tower on top of St Michael's Hill was also built by Edward Phelips V in 1760. It has a Greek inscription over the door, meaning 'Look Out', and the viewing gallery at the top, approached up a spiral stairway, gives a fine view back over the little town towards the house, gardens and park. The brick-lined icehouse below the north-west angle of the main garden, with its Latin inscription over the door meaning 'Freshness springs from the ice and snow', was probably built at about the same time.[38]

Some landscaped parks of the later eighteenth century had no older nucleus, being laid out entirely over farmland. The most important of the completely new parks was Ammerdown, made for Thomas Samuel Jolliffe. Jolliffe was the second son of the Member of Parliament for Petersfield, descended from a family of cloth-merchants. In 1778 he married Anne Twyford, heiress to the manor of Kilmersdon, and immediately began a programme of extensive agricultural improvements there.[39] By January 1788 he was sufficiently established to invite the fashionable London architect James Wyatt to design a new house, selecting a site on rising ground at Ammerdown, a mile east of Kilmersdon village. The house was built in Bath stone and as the original east front shows, it was relatively small, with Venetian windows and Tuscan pilasters. It was substantially completed by 1791, though it may have been another year or two before the Jolliffes finally moved in. The site commanded fine views of the surrounding country, and a landscaped park to complement the house was clearly intended from the outset, though no professional gardener or landscape architect had any part in its design. By 1790 Joliffe had enclosed some of his fields and sheepwalks to make the first substantial nucleus of parkland. To give the new park an appearance of antiquity, some of the larger pollarded hedgerow ashes and elms were retained as isolated specimens, though their true origins are still betrayed by the tell-tale low banks and ditches of the grubbed-out field boundaries. Many new groves and clumps of beeches were established, with some Turkey oaks. Subsequently silver fir plantations were added on the higher ground, and lime on the lower ground. Later additions extended the size of the park to about 500 acres, with further plantations and coverts being established in the late nineteenth century. The stone park wall was about four miles in circumference and up to eight feet high. The park at Dillington had a similar origin, although the house here has a much older core. The landscaped setting was created by George Speke, who had aquired the property in 1719 and proceeded to absorb three small freehold properties, demolishing one house and converting their fields to open grassland. A rectangular lake was laid out alongside the old Whitelackington road, surviving until the 1830s, when it was drained. By 1768 the setting of the old house within the park had been further enhanced by ornamental grounds including a wilderness, herb garden, walks, cherry orchard, nursery and a pond with an island. Further tree planting took place in the early nineteenth century.[40]

An alternative way of giving a new park a spurious air of antiquity was to take in an old wood-pasture common containing ancient pollard trees. Since the sixteenth century the manor of Nettlecombe, the ancient seat of the Trevelyans in west Somerset, had

John Skinner, rector of Camerton, who visited Hunstrete in 1822, described how, "*Although upwards of £30,000 were expended on the Mansion and grounds not many years since, the whole is fast going to decay... the noble piece of water is covered with weeds and long grass; thistles and nettles cover the walks...*" By 1831 the house was in poor condition and the decision was taken to demolish it, retaining only the stable block for conversion to a much smaller dwelling. Six pillars from the drawing-room windows of Popham's mansion were re-erected as an artifical ruin in a field visible from the new house.[37]

At Montacute much of the formal landscape still remained, but some fundamental alterations were made to the entrance. Visitors had originally approached the main eastern forecourt of the house along the lime avenue through the park, but in 1785 Edward Phelips V acquired some of the decorative stonework from the recently-demolished mansion of Clifton Maybank (five miles away on the further side of Yeovil), using it to provide Montacute's western facade with a new porch. A new drive up to this front was begun in December of that year, hedges being grubbed up and an old millpond filled in to accommodate it. The new approach, completed by the end of January, followed a gentle serpentine course southeastwards from a gate at the north end of Bishopston before turning eastwards to the house. The existing stables, and possibly the lodge at the southern entrance to the grounds, seem to have been added around the end of the eighteenth contained a park a quarter of a mile north-east of the manor-house. However, this was on low ground more suited to meadow than pasture, and by the early eighteenth century it had contracted from 80 acres to 20 acres. In the 1730s Sir John Trevelyan decided to create a new park on the higher ground south of the house, initially 97 acres in extent, enlarged by his successors to some 185 acres. The new park incorporated a large area of former common resembling a traditional deer park, and became noted for its magnificent oaks. Although surplus trees produced a steady income through sales of timber for shipbuilding and church roof repairs, many ancient oak standards and pollards still remain, clearly much older than the park itself. Some of the trees have girths of up to 23ft., and are also rich in epiphytic lichens, including species regarded as good indicators of ancient woodland. According to Shirley the new park was fenced with old ship's timbers purchased at the seaport of Watchet, 4 miles away, some of the posts still surviving in the 1860s. After Sir John's death in 1755 his son Sir George squandered the assets of the estate to pay his gambling debts, leasing much of the land and selling as much timber as he could. Sir John's old friend John St Albyn of Alfoxton deplored this behaviour, declaring that "*a man ought not to be trusted with any power whatsoever*" who would "*cut down such whole avenues of maiden trees, and such numbers of other stately, maiden, ornamental, as well as sheltring trees round the poor old mournful mansion house at Nettlecombe*". Fortunately Sir George's son, John, married the daughter of a wealthy London merchant, and when he inherited the estate in 1768 he was able to restore it to its former glory, gathering in the leases as they fell

vacant, and beginning an extensive programme of replanting. In 1792 Sir John Trevelyan did finally call in a professional, Thomas Veitch of Exeter, to landscape the grounds in the style of Capability Brown. Veitch made "*a sunk fence…in length 77 pole* (about 423 yards) *making the said sunk fence 7 feet deep on the side nearest Nettlecombe and 6 feet wide at the bottom, so as to make a proper fence for deer on one side and cattle on the other when a railing is put on the higher side of the sunk fence to be only 3 feet 6 inches high*". The ditch of this sunk fence can still be traced around the northern and western boundaries of the park. Plantings of elm, larch, acacia and black polar continued through the first half of the following century.[41]

The opportunities to combine minor landscaping works with the wide vistas offered by Somerset's natural topography benefited owners of many smaller estates. James Gordon, a Scot who had made his fortune in the Antigua sugar plantations, bought the manors of Portbury and Portishead, and in about 1785 selected Naish House on the Failand ridge to be his residence. His son, James Adam Gordon, who became private secretary to George Canning, enlarged the house with a gothick tower, and it was probably in his time that a small park was laid out before the house, with a zigzag drive up the steep slope from Clapton-in-Gordano planted with Scots pine.[42] During the 1790s Sand House in Wedmore was rebuilt by William White, a well-known local estate- and enclosure-map surveyor. White's nephew, who inherited the property after his death in 1816, describes in great detail the view which could be seen "*from a little mount on the premises*", extending as far as Alfred's Tower near Stourhead. The prospect

Fig. 7.16
Barrow Court, Barrow Gurney
*in its landscape setting; engraving from
Collinson's History and Antiquities of
the County of Somerset (1791).*

mound referred to still survives, on the brink of the slope down to the Brue valley, now topped by a chestnut tree. A variety of other trees were planted around the house.[43]

Somerset contains many other minor landscape parks laid out by owners and stewards during the late eighteenth or early nineteenth century, including Alfoxton and Barford House, both on the north-east slope of the Quantocks; Hill House at Otterhampton, overlooking the Parrett estuary; Barrow Court at Barrow Gurney, on the Backwell ridge in north Somerset; Hadspen, in the rolling hills near Castle Cary; and Somerton Erleigh lower down the Cary valley.[44] The antiquarian Phelps describes further examples, including Yarlington Lodge, ornamented with extensive plantations of fir and larch; Kingweston, near the east end of the Polden Hills, where the house was set in lawns studded with ancient elms below a wood; and the grounds of West Bradley manor-house, laid out by Colonel Pierce in the 1760s with a spacious lawn, fishponds, shrubberies and plantations.[45] The development of such grounds without professional involvement, often on a piecemeal basis, rarely produced much documentary record, and their history remains obscure.

The REVIVAL of the DEER PARK

Although most of the new parks were primarily aesthetic in purpose, the notion of the deer park as an aristocratic privilege still lingered on. This association particularly appealed to new landowners, who saw nothing incongruous in combining the most innovatory landscaping fashions with hints of a more ancient and prestigious past. Ralph Allen, for example, seems to have been well aware of the ancient unity of the medieval parks at Bath, which had been divided into agricultural parcels under multiple ownership in the seventeenth century. His purchases reunited them, and in the 1740s he reintroduced deer obtained from the Duchess of Marlborough into the higher, southern part of Prior Park. Alexander Pope advised him on their management and, despite the depredations of poachers, there were at least 60 head of deer when Allen died.[46]

In 1755 Henry Fownes, who took the name Luttrell on his marriage with Margaret, the heiress of Dunster, decided to create a new deer park, not where the medieval park had been, but on the high ground south of the castle. To achieve this, various plots of freehold land had to be purchased, and compensation paid to tenants for terminating their leases. The total area enclosed within the new park was 348 acres, much of it open, ferny heath, though a few hedges had to be removed from formerly cultivated portions. Where there was no adequate boundary a new paling fence some 6,390 feet in length had to be erected, for which detailed instructions survive. 710 posts, seven feet six inches long, were to be set two and a half feet into the ground, nine feet apart. The posts were to be morticed, one foot and four feet from the top. 1,420 rails, nine feet six inches long, were required, and the ends of the rails were to be driven through the mortices one over another so that they overlapped. Next, 4,260 pales six feet long and 7100 pales six inches shorter were required, to be nailed to alternate sides of the rails, two short ones to every long one, using no more than two nails to each pale. It was calculated that 22,720 nails would be required, "*if none be lost*". Once the enclosure was completed it was

stocked with deer brought in from Marshwood Park. A straight route, two miles long between the two parks, was created by making gaps in all the intervening hedges, and numerous local people were persuaded to turn out to drive the deer to their new home and prevent them from escaping into the neighbouring pastures.[47]

Halswell Park, greatly enlarged during the second half of the eighteenth century, had some 450 head of fallow deer by 1892, the largest herd in the county; in 1911 it also contained some red deer, by which time the park had been further enlarged to 220 acres. The will of Lancelot St Albyn, who died in 1878, records that Alfoxton Park should have been stocked with at least 50 head of deer, and in 1892 it contained 80 fallow deer on about 80 acres. In about 1834 Colonel John Twyford Jolliffe brought a few deer from Gloucestershire to Ammerdown Park; the herd had increased to 250 by 1892, and there were still about a hundred fallow deer there in 1911. Nettlecombe park had about 230 fallow deer in 1867, 180 in 1892. Even at the end of the nineteenth century, Whitaker was still able to list eleven Somerset parks, occupying over 2,570 acres, containing over 2,200 fallow deer between them, with small numbers of red deer also present in the parks of St Audrie's (West Quantoxhead) and Long Ashton.[48]

Despite this revival, however, ancient deer parks which had failed to attract an important residence could still fade into oblivion. The park at Staple Fitzpaine remained a recognisable land unit into the early nineteenth century, but the palings were sold off in 1761, and most of the land became pasture for bullocks; the deer had all been removed by 1826 and the remainder was enclosed as farmland very soon afterwards.[49]

FOLLIES and PARK ORNAMENTS in the LATER 18TH CENTURY

Despite the moves by Lancelot Brown to simplify landscape design and to purge it of unnecessary clutter, many of the local gentry continued to take delight in ornamenting their grounds with follies. The little park at Hatch Beauchamp was adorned with temples and seats after the rebuilding of the house in 1755.[50] One of the most bizarre collections is at Barwick Park near Yeovil, where an otherwise fairly dull park is enlivened by four follies on its boundary, at the cardinal points of the compass. Due north of the house is the Fish Tower, a slender round tower of rubble, about 50 feet high, resting upon a square plinth. At the top is a drum of Ham stone resembling a well-head, carved with rustic ogival arches, and capped by an iron cage which once carried a fish weather-vane. To the east is a rustic arch, the outer sides of which have two steps, carrying a large cylindrical tower with a spire on top, which in turn is capped by a ball finial and statue of Hermes. This figure is known locally as 'Jack the Treacle-Eater', being supposed to represent a footman of the Messiter family who used to run messages to and from London, reputedly training entirely on treacle. To the south is a thin obelisk of rubble, bent at the top. To the west is a tall, slender, hollow spire of rough stone, 75 feet high, pierced with seven tiers of rectangular holes. The top few feet are smooth, terminating in a ball finial, while the base is encircled with a square-section moulding. The whole spire rests upon a cylinder of

Fig. 7.17
'Jack the Treacle-Eater' at
BARWICK PARK.

Fig. 7.18
A drawing by Richard Phelps of a sham ruin on CONYGAR HILL, DUNSTER.

stone with pointed arches cut through three of its four segments, creating a curiously lop-sided effect. Behind the house a narrow path leads through a jagged stone arch into a stony gully, beneath yew trees, to a series of gloomy artificial caves. At one time this group of follies was attributed to George Messiter's attempts to relieve unemployment in the Yeovil glove trade in the early nineteenth century, but two of the follies appear in the background of family portraits of the 1770s-1780s.[51]

When Ralph Allen's niece Gertrude inherited Prior Park in 1764, one of her first acts was to pull down the Gothic Lodge which overlooked the main house, much to the distress of Allen's widow and the annoyance of Richard Jones. The materials were used to build a memorial to Allen higher up the hill. Another gothick folly probably dating from the 1760s is an octagonal battlemented gazebo at Ham Green, Easton-in-Gordano, rubble-built with ashlar dressings and ogee-arched windows, overlooking the river Avon.[53]

Henry Fownes Luttrell carried out much landscaping around Dunster in the 1760s and 1770s. Artificial ruins were made amongst the woods, and in 1775 a tall circular tower was built on the summit of Conygar Hill, clearly intended more as a landmark than a vantage-point, since it lacks a staircase. Within the castle grounds, he ordered the creation of a picturesque rocky cascade, a bridge and new planting with yews, cypress, conifers and flowering shrubs.[54]

Midford Castle is a castellated house, prominently sited to overlook the Midford valley south of Bath, built in the 1770s for H.W.D. Roebuck, son of a Nottinghamshire doctor. A small park was laid out on the slope, and several ornamental buildings erected within it over the next thirty years, including a gothic summerhouse, a hermitage, chapel, castellated gatehouse and stables.[55] Also during the 1770s William Turner laid out walks in the woods behind Belmont in Wraxall. One walk was planted with a yew avenue leading to a stone urn with an inscription dated 1778 commemorating Turner's friend Joseph Farrell. Selections from the poems of the writer and philanthropist Hannah More were painted on wooden tablets in the grounds.[56]

ROAD DIVERSIONS and SETTLEMENT CLEARANCES through EMPARKING

The creation of new parks and the enlargement of old ones continued to cause disruption to local roads and settlements throughout the eighteenth century. The enclosure of the new park at Avishays, perhaps in 1729, resulted in the diversion of the old road between Lydmarsh and Chaffcombe.[57] When the plans for the formal garden at Ston Easton (Chapter 6) were abandoned in the 1740s, a landscape park was created instead, with a broad vista south of the house. This required the diversion of a road and the removal of several cottages, though the old village church was allowed to remain as an eyecatcher.[58] The making of the new deer park at Dunster in the 1750s extinguished the old road between Gallox Cross and Carhampton.

The enlargement of the park at Hinton St George to its eventual maximum of 1,258 acres was achieved in stages by absorbing many smaller holdings, and although relatively few dwellings were

removed within the village, some reorganisation of the road system was necessary. In 1766 the 3rd Earl Poulett diverted the old coach road to Dinnington and Ilminster into a more northerly course over the brow of the hill to conceal it from the house, and those tenants who remained were required to agree not to plant trees or erect any buildings which might obstruct the view thereby gained. Around 1798 the 4th Earl closed off the nearer continuation of this road, in effect the west end of the main village street, to create an unimpeded walk between the mansion and the church, replacing it with a new route curving round the north side of the church. A new park entrance was then made at Brome's Lodge, with gate piers capped with stone pineapple finials. Part of the new park wall was built over the site of the former village horse pond, and subsidence over the unstable ground has caused it to lean ever since. The impact upon the ancient hamlet of Craft, south-west of Hinton, was more severe. Holdings here were gradually taken in hand from the 1740s, and by 1780 most of the settlement had been eliminated, though a few of its closes still survived within the park to the beginning of the nineteenth century. In 1765 a further new road was projected to replace the old route through Craft, running outside the eastern boundary of the park from Harford Lodge to Roundham Common. This was completed in 1795 and the old road closed. The last surviving dwelling at Craft became the nucleus of an estate farm within the park, now known as Oaklands Farm. Most of the inhabitants of the former hamlet were rehoused in new cottages within Hinton village itself.[59]

At Marston Bigot Edmund, 7th Earl of Cork, enlarged the house and remodelled the park in the style of Capability Brown: he would have been familiar with Brown's work at Longleat, just over the Wiltshire border. Lawns were brought up to the front of the mansion and a ha-ha made to separate it from the park, which was then enlarged to about 400 acres. This caused the final extinction of the old village, slight earthworks of which can still be seen in the pasture. The

below: Fig. 7.20
'St Audries. The Seat of
R. Everard Batch esq. ... drawn
and engraved by T. Bonner'
from John Collinson,
The History and Antiquities of the
County of Somerset (1791).
bottom: Fig. 7.21
West Quantoxhead, *1761.*
The map is annotated to show the new
road of 1770 and including houses
destroyed by the making of the park.

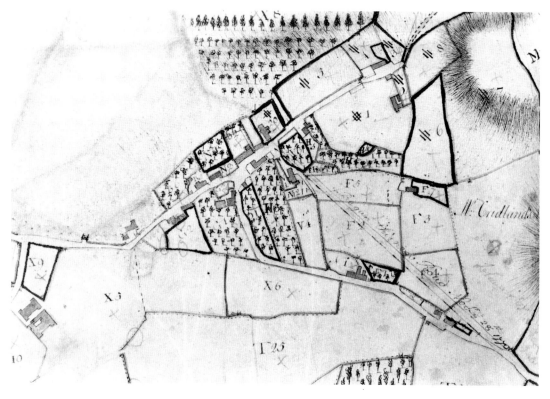

medieval church, which had stood within 100ft of the south front of the house was pulled down in 1786, though the ancient churchyard yew was allowed to remain. A new church was provided on the edge of the park, a quarter of a mile to the south-west. Alterations continued into the following century, with the making of a 20-acre lake in the 1830s and the rebuilding of the three park lodges.[60]

Samuel Donne's map of Montacute, made in about 1782, shows the line of the main street of the Borough continuing northwards towards the west front of the mansion, with several houses along its western side which have since disappeared. It is probable that at one time both sides of this street were lined with dwellings. The grounds of the mansion seem to have swallowed up the tenements in this part of the borough one by one, until by the end of the century the road was itself sealed off from the market square by the building of the existing extrance lodge.

The creation and enlargement of the new park at Nettlecombe led to the extinction of the small village there. The first step was taken in 1734, when Sir John Trevelyan obtained permission to enclose part of the highway to Nettlecombe church, provided that he created an alternative route. The Day & Masters map of 1782 still shows a number of dwellings along the valley at the south-east corner of the park. These were removed during the landscaping of 1792, their inhabitants being rehoused in new estate cottages built at Woodford. In 1838 the road through the park from the lodge to the church was closed, and the isolation of the church and manor-house was complete.[61]

The making of the park at Orchardleigh involved the damming of a tributary of the River Frome to create a large winding lake which flooded the site of the former village. Remarkably, the medieval church was marooned on a small island at the head of the water. The great house of the Champneys family, since demolished, lay immediately to the south. Although the park was further transformed in the following century, some of its eighteenth-century components survive, including a romantic boathouse at the east end of the lake and a rotunda above it.[62]

Even the creation of relatively small parks sometimes resulted in cottages being demolished and evictions taking place. The park attached to Enmore Castle was greatly extended during the 1760s by John Perceval, Earl of Egmont, when a small lake was created in the valley west of the castle. The village street stood in the way of expansion southwards; nevertheless, part of the churchyard was taken into the park in 1767, the rectory house and glebeland was bought up, and some houses were demolished shortly after 1790. However, the final step of removing all the houses and extending the park beyond the further side of the village street was never achieved.[63] At Babington the creation of the park by the Knatchbull family, probably in the 1740s, involved the removal of what remained of the village. The extension of the park of West Quantoxhead was also begun in the 1740s, initially limited to a small plantation and grounds near the house. An estate map of 1761 shows that there was still a substantial hamlet with at least ten dwellings between the manor-house and the church. An addition to that map records that the road to the church from Staple was straightened out, work beginning on November 28th 1770. This had the effect of moving traffic further away from the house, and opened the way for more substantial changes in the following century.[64] The development of a small park south of Shapwick House between the mid-1760s and 1790 resulted in the blocking of five lanes and the removal of 19 houses shown on estate maps of c.1764-5. Three of the lanes still show very clearly as cambered hollow-ways across the pasture. Some time between 1785 and 1791 Kent Lane, the original main approach to the village from the west, was diverted southwards around the edge of the park.[65]

There are many other instances where the course of roads was altered as a result of emparking in the late eighteenth century. Sir John Acland diverted the old Stogursey to Stringston road southwards away from the front of his house at Fairfield, building lodges at the two entrances, and planting many trees in the park. The creation of Kingweston Park blocked the road through the village to Butleigh. Today only the stub end survives of the old route westwards from Sampford Brett, obstructed by the making of Orchard Wyndham Park. At Chew Magna the diversion of the road to Stanton Drew around the grounds of Chew Court gave rise to a series of awkward bends on the eastern side of the village, and the original direct route between the Triangle and Bridge Farm can still be traced in part as a hollow way.

The blocking of rights of way not infrequently caused local dissent. In 1793 in the manorial court of North Weston near Portishead fourteen tenants accused George Wilkins of stopping up two footpaths, enclosing a quarter of an acre of North Weston Down with spring water and a pool common to eleven tenants, preventing a tenant from cutting fern, cutting down 20 pollard oaks in Highwood and carrying the trunks to his house, and rooting up and destroying the hedges of ten pastures *"to throw the same into his park"*.[66]

New Plant Introductions

The declining interest in flower gardens on the big estates meant that relatively few new species came into widespread cultivation, although plant collectors continued to send back species from distant parts of the world to botanical gardens. Early introductions to England from the far east included the common camellia (*C. japonica*) in 1739, the pink China rose (*R. chinensis*) by 1759, the yellow-flowered chrysanthemum (*C. indicum*) by 1764, the oriental clematis (*C. florida*) in 1776 and the Chinese peony (*Paeonia lactiflora*) in 1784. Fuchsias, introduced from South America in 1788, were already being sold commercially by 1793. Some of the new introductions came into their own as bedding plants in the following century. Others, after brief popularity, fell out of fashion, surviving only in a few cottage gardens.

Similarly few new vegetables were introduced in the eighteenth century. The main exception was the swede, first cultivated in England in the 1770s. The period saw the demise of the skirret, a once-popular vegetable almost lost to cultivation by the early nineteenth century.

The Turkey oak (*Quercus cerris*) was introduced from southern Europe by 1735, and became a popular parkland tree throughout southern England. Loudon recorded that a specimen planted at Nettlecombe Court around 1754 had achieved a height of 59ft and a girth of nine feet; by 1890 the girth of this tree had increased to 15ft and its spread to 120ft. Another Turkey oak planted a century later in a more sheltered position near Thornfalcon church had achieved a height of 65ft within forty years.[67]

Kitchen Gardens and Orchards

The specialised walled kitchen garden came into its own in the early 1700s, and remained an important feature of great estates, and smaller properties too, for the next two centuries. This may reflect a change in the food preferences of the gentry, from a diet based primarily on meat and grain to one in which fruit and vegetables played a much more important role. Eating raw fruit was finally acknowledged by medical opinion to be safe. At the same time a growing understanding of the mechanics of plant reproduction was beginning to make possible the scientific improvement of many varieties through selection and hybridization. Kitchen gardens could occupy anything from an acre to ten acres or more, depending on the wealth and status of the owner.[68] The desire for more extensive kitchen gardens was one reason for the enlargement of the park near the great house at Hinton St George in the 1760s and 1790s. However, as vegetable and fruit production became more efficient, it was also perceived as less attractive aesthetically, and there was an increasing tendency to relegate the kitchen gardens to concealed or remote locations within the grounds. At Marston Bigot the 7th Earl of Cork removed the old kitchen gardens from the south-western side of the house, probably in the 1770s, replacing them with a new enclosure further into the park, a quarter of a mile east of the house.[69] Fairfield House has a fine walled garden with an inscribed date of 1784. At Ammerdown in 1793 James Wyatt provided an attractive orangery on the edge of the new kitchen garden. Other examples survive at Kelston, Hazlegrove, and Naish House above Clapton-in-Gordano.

A refinement introduced from the Low Countries in the mid-eighteenth century was the crinkle-crankle or ribbon wall, which followed a tight, regular serpentine course rather than a straight one. Such walls were cheaper to build, since their inherent stability allowed them to be constructed using headers only without the use of buttresses. They were aesthetically pleasing. Above all, however, their concave recesses gave more shelter from the wind and retained and reflected the heat of the sun more effectively than a flat wall. Crinkle-crankles have an overwhelmingly eastern distribution in England, the greatest concentrations being in Norfolk and Suffolk; but Somerset has at least one example, visible from the M5 motorway, standing on its own in a field below Crook Peak near Webbington.

Flue-heated fruit-walls and glasshouses became increasingly popular. Prior Park had heated greenhouses capable of growing pineapples. Records of Halswell under the occupancy of Sir Charles Kemeys-Tynte's widow between 1785 and 1798 document the successful production of oranges, lemons, citrons, coffee trees, pepper trees and prickly figs, as well as a hotbed for melon. Goathurst manor also had hothouses by the later eighteenth century, noted for their variety of exotic fruit. There was also a nursery garden.[70]

By the end of the eighteenth century the rising profitability of both arable and livestock farming and the increasing availability of imported wines were beginning to lead to a significant decline in cider orchards in the west country, particularly in Herefordshire and Gloucestershire. However, this decline was less marked in Somerset, where apple trees were more frequently grown in hedgerows around small arable and pasture closes. The Court of Wick Pippin remained the favourite table and cider apple in north Somerset. Apples grown in central Somerset listed by Billingsley include the Royal Wilding, White-Styre, Pounset or Cadbury, Flood-Hatch, Black Pit Crab, Buckland, Mediate or Southam, Royal-Jersey, Woodcock, Red-hedge Pip, Old Jersey and Redstreak, all grafted onto crab stocks in the nursery. New cider varieties achieved considerable local popularity,

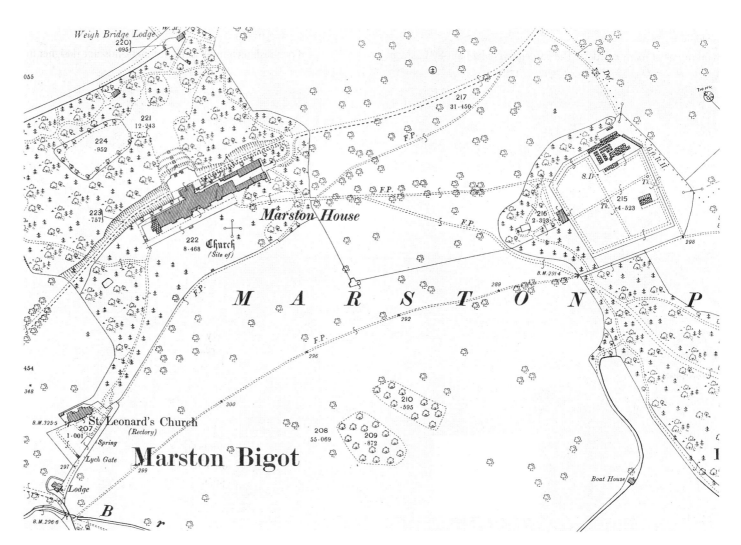

Fig. 7.22
An Ordnance Survey map of
MARSTON PARK *showing the*
kitchen gardens resited to the
east of the house.

such as the Kingston Black, first raised at Kingston near Taunton in the later eighteenth century. West Quantoxhead had a fruit tree nursery in 1748.[71]

PUBLIC PLEASURE GROUNDS

Many of the urban pleasure grounds of the eighteenth century differed from the later concept of public parks in that they were intended primarily as settings for open-air entertainments. Following the example of London's famous New Spring Gardens at Vauxhall, they were run as commercial operations, their maintenance costs being covered by admission charges, sales of refreshments and charges for special evening events like outdoor concerts, banquets and firework displays.

Locally, Bath continued to lead the way. Across the Avon from St James's Triangle, Thorpe's plan of 1742 shows that the development of Bath's own Spring Gardens had begun. Refreshments, balls and concerts on the Vauxhall model were advertised, and a visitor in 1753 described "*the fair Elysium of this place where sweet variety tempts every sense to rapture*". Not the least of its attractions in the early years was that the principal approach was by boat. A plan of 1772 shows Spring Gardens occupying a rectangular area roughly on the site of the present rugby ground. The layout was then asymmetrically formal, with two canals, geometrical walks and round and rectangular beds. Sadly, however, the completion of Pulteney Bridge in 1774 opened up the Bathwick estate on the east bank of the River Avon for

development, and the secluded setting of the gardens was spoiled. In 1795 they were abandoned and the site was then used by John Eveleigh as a builder's yard.

Another short-lived pleasure garden was developed after 1777 adjacent to James Ferry's Bathwick Villa. By April 1782 its grounds were said to comprise "*about an acre and a quarter, laid out in modern taste with serpentine gravel walks, valuable shrubbery, evergreens, fishponds, bridges, fruit trees in the highest perfection*", and were commended for their fine views over the city and the surrounding countryside. This site too succumbed to development pressures on the Bathwick estate, and the gardens were closed in 1790. The gothic villa (which stood near the intersection of the modern Forester Road and Forester Avenue) survived until 1897, but the site is now entirely built over.[72]

Although the expansion of building onto the east bank of the Avon had spelled doom for both Spring Gardens and the Bathwick Villa site, the development of the Bathwick estate included a new commercial pleasure garden to replace them, officially entitled Sydney Gardens Vauxhall. The principal axis of the Bathwick development was Great Pulteney Street, laid out by Thomas Baldwin in 1788-93. The vista along Great Pulteney Street from the end of Pulteney Bridge was closed by the Sydney Hotel, which was set in a large pleasure ground in the shape of a flattened hexagon. The original intention had been to erect neo-classical terraces around all six sides of the garden, then to continue the turnpike road in a straight line to Westbury, but this was aborted by the financial crisis in the wake of the French

Revolution, which caused the failure of several local banks and the bankruptcy of many builders. The gardens were laid out by Baldwin and Harcourt Masters between 1793 and 1795, and covered some 16 acres. They were divided into compartments by an irregular screen of trees and shrubs, and included serpentine walks, two bowling greens, a labyrinth twice the size of the maze at Hampton Court, an 'Ancient Dilapidated Castle' complete with cannon, a 'Cosmorama' depicting Vesuvius in eruption, a hermit's cave with a waxen hermit, grottoes and aviaries, swing boats, a Chinese bridge, a lake, waterfalls, stone and thatched pavilions, refreshment kiosks, dining boxes, orchestras and many other attractions. A carriage drive ran around the perimeter of the garden. John Kew, writing in 1825, described how "*The gardens are beautifully illuminated by upwards of fifteen thousand variegated lamps*". Sydney Gardens were bisected first by the Kennet & Avon Canal and then by the Great Western Railway, but both companies were permitted to traverse the ground only on condition that they provided suitably ornamental walls and bridges. Sydney Gardens were finally taken over by the City Council after the Great War as a public park.[73]

The last important venture of this type in Bath was Grosvenor Gardens Vauxhall, a mile upstream from the city centre on the north bank of the Avon, planned and partly executed by the builder John Eveleigh after 1791. The plan envisaged two streets of terraced houses between the London Road and the river, with gardens laid out on the meadow between them which would be accessible by boat from the city centre. A hotel, now Grosvenor House, was built on the London Road looking down over the centre of the pleasure-ground. A plan of 1808 shows a mix of straight gravel walks, formal avenues and circuses alongside informal serpentine walks, bowling greens and shrubberies, with a labyrinth in the north-east corner. Eveleigh was amongst those bankrupted by the collapse of the Bath Bank two years later, and although the gardens themselves struggled on for some years, the housing projects on either side were never completed.[74]

HUMPHRY REPTON

The last of the great national figures in Georgian landscape gardening was Humphry Repton. Repton was born in Bury St Edmunds in 1752, the son of a tax collector. After several unhappy years in the textile business he invested his limited capital in the purchase of a small estate in Norfolk. The life of a country gentleman was much more to his taste, and he gained valuable practical experience in farming and land management which was to stand him in good stead in years to come. He built up a wide circle of friends among the local landowners and gentry, who allowed him free access to their libraries and botanical collections, where he extended his knowledge of planting and the theory of landscape design. However, his waning financial reserves caused him grave concern, until it dawned upon him in a flash of inspiration that there had been no outstanding landscape gardener in England since the death of Capability Brown in 1783. Here was a potentially lucrative profession which could provide a suitable outlet for his talents; so, at the comparatively advanced age of 36 he began to solicit commissions for the design of parks and gardens amongst his Norfolk neighbours.

Soon he was working further afield, and by 1790 had achieved his ambition of establishing himself as the leading landscape designer in England.[75]

Much of Repton's rapid success was due to his method of presenting his ideas to his clients. He had a natural talent for water-colour, and he provided paintings with movable flaps to depict scenes before and after the proposed improvements, accompanying these with a hand-written text, all bound together within sumptuous red morocco leather covers. Repton's 'Red Books' became his trademark, and he claimed to have prepared over 400 of them, about half of which are known to survive. Undoubtedly the Red Books were a splendid advertisement, and probably prompted many further commissions. On the other hand, they took much time to prepare and gave the landowner the opportunity to have the works carried out more cheaply by his own estate staff without involving Repton further.

Repton was a great admirer of Brown's work, but his style, though still informal, was very different. He wrote prolifically on his own theories, publishing four illustrated books on landscape gardening between 1795 and 1816.[76] Here he set out his philsophy in terms of four basic rules: garden design must display the natural beauties and conceal the natural defects of every situation; it should give the illusion of extent by concealing the boundary; it should disguise every element of human interference in order to make the whole appear the production of nature only; and all necessary objects of convenience such as the kitchen garden, if incapable of being made ornamental or appearing part of the general scenery, should be concealed or removed. Repton's general theme has often been summed up as charm rather than grandeur. Unlike Brown, he rarely went in for resculpting the landscape through massive earth-moving, preferring to work on a more intimate human scale. His screens of parkland trees were more densely planted, mainly with deciduous hardwoods, often with a thorn understorey to protect the trees from livestock and to eliminate the effect of a horizontal browsing line with bare trunks beneath. Often the trees were irregularly thinned at the margins to produce a broken edge. More variety of trees, including evergreens, was permitted in the pleasure grounds around the house. Later in his career Repton began to restore some formal elements, such as balustraded terraces, fountains, pergolas and trellised enclosures for flower gardens, to the vicinity of the house. He felt that it was essential for the designer to have an adequate knowledge of architecture in order to provide the appropriate types of gate lodges, estate cottages and conservatories. His own leanings were to the gothic and to rustic styles involving thatch and timber, but he was equally willing to accommodate classical elements where he felt them to be correct. He entered into a partnership with the architect John Nash which lasted, not always happily, through the last decade of the century; in the later part of his career architectural designs were often provided by two of his sons, both of whom had been trained in Nash's office.

Although much of Repton's work took place in the home counties and in East Anglia, he carried out a significant number of commissions in the west of England, notably a spectacular example undertaken with John Nash at Blaise Castle on the outskirts of Bristol.

Potentially Repton's most impressive design was prepared for

Fig. 7.23
HUMPHRY REPTON
by Samuel Shelley, c.1800.
By courtesy of the
National Portrait Gallery, London.

Ston Easton Park. *This was Repton's first Somerset commission, undertaken for Henry Hippesley Coxe. A Red Book was presented in March 1793, and the works are further described in his 1795 publication. His main contribution here was the creation of an artificial river north and east of the house by damming a stream with two weirs with shutters to regulate the flow. Recognising the irregular régime of the natural stream, he recommended paving the bed of the new course with flat pieces of rock to create a much broader, shallow watercourse, "that the water in the driest summer will always be visible". The north end of the water was spanned by a curious bridge carrying part of a castellated wall, with the kitchen garden beyond.*[77]

William Gore Langton at Newton St Loe. Joseph Langton, Newton's previous owner, who had employed Capability Brown there, had died in 1779. His only daughter and heiress, Bridget, was brought up under the guardianship of Lord Methuen of Corsham Court in Wiltshire, where Repton was commissioned to improve the grounds in 1785. Two years before, Bridget had married William Gore of Kiddington in Oxfordshire, who immediately took the surname Gore Langton in token of his marital inheritance. Probably through Lord Methuen's recommendation, Gore Langton invited Repton to inspect Newton Park in November 1796, and a Red Book was presented in May of the following year.

Although Repton was appreciative of Capability Brown's earlier contribution there, he concluded: "*there are, however, many circumstances which would increase and heighten the interest both of the character and situation of Newton Park which shall be obvious when pointed out and described*". In addition to further selective thinning and new planting to screen or to open up new views, Repton recommended seven major improvements:

Firstly, where Brown had left the house in the midst of a "*bare lawn ... too often attended with want of comfort and baldness of effect*", Repton suggested planting "*flowering shrubs under the windows, as may hide part of the basement storey and spread perfume through the apartments in summer when the windows are thrown open*". Next, the watercourses and lakes required modification. According to Brown's scheme, "*the road to the [old] House came along the Avenue and therefore the ground below the water was never shown; but since the approach has been altered we are admitted...behind the scenes, and our surprise and*

pleasure at viewing the expanse of water is lessened by seeing the riverlet [below the lakes] and the manner in which that has been dammed up to form the several pools which we might otherwise have supposed to be an ample river". Even allowing for the change of access to the new house, Repton declared himself "*at a loss to conceive how Mr Brown could be satisfied to have made three pools without any attempt to disguise the end of any one, or to aim at an apparent union of the waters*". He suggested extending the area of water down-valley by the addition of two further lakes in order to remove the anomaly of the Corston Brook which "*has unfortunately been made more conspicuous and more unnatural by a number of little stops or weirs which alternatively produce small canals and trifling cascades*", while extra channels, islands and screening were to be added to the existing lakes "*to disguise those effects of Art by which five distinct pieces of water on different levels may be made to seem a continuation of the same river flowing through the Park*".

Repton's third suggestion was that the fir trees on Brown's lowest dam should be felled, since they robbed the water surface of much of its reflective brilliance while revealing the obviously artifical drop beyond through their bare trunks. In their place he recommended "*a few brushy alders and thorn judiciously disposed on the head and an opening left near one side*". Next, the two entrance lodges should be replaced with a single lodge, the new entrance to be made "*with a round Gatehouse on the right, a low iron fence with two low gateposts and ... a wooden gate just to the left hand side of the main entrance*". Fifthly, the approach drive from Wells should be realigned across the valley to cross between the two new lakes, where the dam should be disguised by the facade of a bridge, while the approach from

Bath should be realigned around the hill "*in such a direction as not to show the water till it is seen to the greatest advantage*", with a plantation to "*conceal all the ground below it*". Since the formal avenues did not focus upon the new house, they added little to its grandeur, and veiled the views of the park from the main approach. Repton's sixth recommendation was that the northern avenue should be thinned out further to admit more views, and he produced a sketch identifying specifically which of 23 trees should remain and which should be removed. Finally, a domed temple should be constructed on the lawn above the house to provide a focal point to the outward view.

Evidence from the early Ordnance Survey maps and from Greenwood's 1822 survey show that few of the Newton Park recommendations were ever carried out. The realignment of Brown's original drive to Corston has been attributed to Repton, but in fact it was clearly altered shortly before his first visit, between 1789 and 1797. The drive towards Bath via Newton St Loe was altered later, some time between 1840 and 1888, by which time the extensive ha-ha had also come into being.[78]

A scheme was prepared in 1802 for Sir Hugh Smyth of Ashton Court, Long Ashton. Here Repton was much impressed with the setting of the house within the medieval deer park, and he proposed a gothic extension to give the building a more picturesque profile. He also recommended that a new lake should be made to the south of the house, and marked out some of the land for plantations. He wrote to Sir Hugh in October of that year expressing the hope that the land had been prepared ready for planting that season, though there is no evidence that he was ever asked to continue the commission himself; and a draft reply from Smyth states that work had been abandoned for the time being. In the event the proposed lake was never made, but plantations were commenced in the following winter with some 10,000 trees, including Lebanon cedars, red and black American spruces, balsam poplars, maples, laburnums and acacias, purchased from Miller & Sweet's nursery in Bristol. The sweeping drives are also characteristic of Repton's style and may have been made with his advice, though other works were carried out contrary to his recommendations.[79]

Repton's book *Observations on the Theory and Practice of Landscape Gardening*, published in 1803, describes some of the plans for Newton St Loe and Ashton Court. It also mentions another commission for alterations to the house and grounds at West Coker, for which no Red Book is known to survive. Repton's advice was also sought by Valentine Jones, owner of Bailbrook House, a villa on the north side of the Avon valley a couple of miles above Bath. Drawings of a new colonnade around the house were made by Humphry and his eldest son John Adey Repton in 1803, and an engraving of another Repton picture of this site was published in William Peacock's *Polite Repository* in August 1806; but again no Red Book survives and it is not known whether any landscaping works were actually carried out.[80]

Towards the end of his career, in 1814, Repton worked for Philip John Miles at Abbots Leigh. Miles had made his fortune as a banker, and Repton somewhat disapproved of his nouveau-riche airs. The old house of Leigh Court had been replaced without Repton's advice by a new Greek Revival mansion in 1811, and in his Red Book he was harshly critical of its situation and of the views from it. His watercolour of the garden shows a prominent three-storey house which he describes as "*an obtrusive yellow mass of Ugliness*". However there were some compensating picturesque elements elsewhere in the grounds, and Repton's recommendations for a path down to a rock seat in Paradise Bottom, the valley leading to the river, were carried out. From this viewpoint some of his own works at the Royal Fort in Bristol and on the Blaise Castle estate were visible, as well as the natural scenery of the Avon Gorge and the Severn estuary. Some formal elements were also included, typical of Repton's later style, particularly a series of Italian-style terraced kitchen gardens and flower beds. A new approach to the house was also laid out within a couple of years of Repton's visit and, although this is nowhere mentioned in the Red Book, its similarity to the Blaise Castle drive strongly suggests that it was made on his advice.[81]

Apart from his work on country estates, Repton was also invited by Charles Meadows Pierrepont, Lord Newark, to prepare a scheme for the development of the Ham outside Bath, the area of low-lying market gardens south of John Wood the Elder's Parades. Repton's water-colour of a scheme which he proably designed in collaboration with John Nash, made shortly before 1799, survives at Thoresby Hall, the Pierrepont family seat in Nottinghamshire. It shows the existing South Parade facing an exact replica of itself, the two linked on the west side by a long colonnaded crescent of 36 bays and open to the river on the east, with a circular carriage drive around parkland in the centre. Two alternative schemes were put forward at the same time, James Lewis of London proposing a massive square open to the river, while William Wilkins of Norwich proposed a group of seven new streets with a much smaller central square. Resistance on the part of Bath Corporation to the employment of outsiders eventually resulted in the abandonment of all three projects.[82]

Repton's career bridges the eighteenth and nineteenth centuries. During the later part of his career he more than once expressed concern about the changes in the fabric of landed society, and he found himself drawn into public controversy about the very nature of landscape gardening. The cosy world of the Georgian landowner was soon to be turned upside down, and parks and gardens were to experience a series of even more drastic transformations.

Fig. 7.25
Ashton Court. *The south front of the house and parterre from J. Rutter's Delineations of the North Western Division of Somerset (1829). Deer still graze in the park in the foreground.*

REFERENCES - Chapter 7

1. There is a considerable literature on eighteenth-century landscape gardens. For a general introduction see Edward Hyams, *The English Garden* (1964), Chapter 2; Edward Malins, *English Landscaping and Literature*, 1660-1840 (1966); David C. Stuart, *Georgian Gardens* (1979); Miles Hadfield, *The English Landscape Garden* (2nd edn, Princes Risborough, 1988; Tom Williamson, *Polite Landscapes: Gardens and Society in Eighteenth-Century England* (Stroud, 1995).

2. Anthony Ashley Cooper, 3rd Earl of Shaftesbury, *The Moralists* (1709), quoted in John Dixon Hunt & Peter Willis (eds), *The Genius of the Place: the English Landscape Garden, 1620-1820* (1975), p.124. This compilation provides an invaluable mine of contemporary opinion and comment.

3. Joseph Addison, letter to *The Spectator*, no.477, 6th September 1712, quoted in full in Hunt & Willis, *The Genius of the Place*, pp.145-7. In fact a contemporary plan of the Bilton garden suggests that it was of a more traditional form and less revolutionary than Addison would have his readers believe.

4. Alexander Pope, Essay in *The Guardian* (1713), Epistle to Lord Burlington (1731), both quoted in full in Hunt & Willis, *The Genius of the Place*, pp.204-8, 211-14.

5. John Dixon Hunt, *William Kent: Landscape Garden Designer* (1987).

6. Kenneth Woodbridge, *The Stourhead Landscape* (1989), p.60.

7. Roger White (ed.), *Georgian Arcadia: Architecture for the Park and Garden* (Georgian Group,1987), p.20, no.10.

8. The following account is based largely upon Gillian Clarke, *Prior Park: a Compleat Landscape* (Bath, 1987); see also Christopher Pound, *Genius of Bath: the City and its Landscape* (Bath, 1986), pp.25-35.

9. *The Travels through England of Dr Richard Pococke*, ed.James Joel Cartwright, Vol.2 (Camden Soc., 1889, p.36; John Collinson, *The History and Antiquities of the County of Somerset* (Bath,1791), Vol.1, pp.150, 169-70; Mike Chapman, *A Guide to the Estates of Ralph Allen around Bath* (Bath,1996), p.12.

10. Michael Symes, *The English Rococo Garden* (Princes Risborough, 1991)

11. Pound, *Genius of Bath*, pp.33-4; Clarke, Prior Park, pp.55-6; White, *Georgian Arcadia*, p.49, no.239.

12. *The Travels through England of Dr Richard Pococke*, Vol.2, pp.36, 153; Clarke, Prior Park, p.57.

13. Clarke, *Prior Park*, pp.52-5; Tim Mowl, *Palladian Bridges: Prior Park and the Whig Connection* (Bath, 1993).

14. Barabara Jones, *Follies and Grottoes* (2nd edn, 1974), pp.58-9; Pound, *Genius of Bath*, p.61; Clarke, *Prior Park*, p.58; Mowl, *Palladian Bridges*, p.34.

15. Pound, *Genius of Bath*, pp.33-4; Clarke, *Prior Park*, pp.50-58.

16. *The Travels through England of Dr Richard Pococke*, Vol.2, pp.40-41; Michael McGarvie, *Notes towards a History of Gardening at Marston House, 1660-1908* Frome Historical Research Group, Occasional Papers no.4 (1987), pp.13-22.

17. John Collinson, *The History and Antiquities of the County of Somerset* (Bath, 1791), Vol.1, pp.81-3; *Country Life* Vol.24 (1908), pp.702-10; Jones, *Follies and Grottoes* (1974 edn), pp.18, 128, 384-5; White, *Georgian Arcadia*, p.23 no 39; p.40, no.151; p.46, no.208; p.54, nos.272, 275; R.W. Dunning & M.C. Siraut, 'Goathurst', *V.C.H.* Vol.6 (1992), pp.45-6, 49.

18. William Shenstone, *Unconnected Thoughts on Gardening* (1764), quoted in Hunt & Willis, *The Genius of the Place*, pp.289-97.

19. John Collinson, *The History and Antiquities of the County of Somerset*, Vol.3 (Bath, 1791), p.258; John Sales, *West Country Gardens* (Gloucester, 1980), pp.156-8; Philip White, 'Hestercombe', *Avon Gardens Trust Newsletter* no.16 and *Garden History Soc. Newsletter* no.48 (1996), pp.11-12; For Palmerston's visit see Hampshire C.R.O. 27 m 60.

20. *The Travels through England of Dr Richard Pococke*, Vol.2, pp.150, 32, 33; Collinson, *The History and Antiquities of the County of Somerset*, Vol.1, p.225; William Phelps, *The History and Antiquities of Somersetshire*, Vol.1 (1836), pp.247-55.

21. William Phelps, *The History and Antiquities of Somersetshire*, Vol.1 (1836), p.156.

22. White, *Georgian Arcadia*, p.48, no.231.

23. Stephen Switzer, *The Nobleman, Gentleman, and Gardener's Recreation* (1715); *Ichnographia Rustica*, Vol.3 (1742 edn), Appendix. The latter is quoted in part in Hunt & Willis, *The Genius of the Place*, pp.162-3.

24. I am grateful to Mark Angliss for discussion of this matter, which is further examined by Mike Chapman, *An Historic Landscape Survey of the Manors of Stowey and Knighton Sutton* (Avon County Planning Dept., 1992).

25. The standard work on Brown's career is Dorothy Stroud, *Capability Brown* (2nd edn, 1975); see also Edward Hyams, *Capability Brown and Humphry Repton* (1971) and Thomas Hinde, *Capability Brown: the Story of a Master Gardener* (1986).

26. Quoted in full in Stroud, *Capability Brown* (1975 edn), p.202.

27. Hal Moggridge, '"Capability" Brown at Blenheim', in James Bond & Kate Tiller (eds), *Blenheim: Landscape for a Palace* (Gloucester, 1987), pp.90-114.

28. Stroud, *Capability Brown*, 1975 edn., p.234; Nicholas Pearson Associates, *Newton Park, Historic Survey and Restoration Plan* (Report to Duchy of Cornwall, 1993).

29. Michael Symes, 'William Pitt the Elder: the Gran Mago of landscape gardening', *Garden History* Vol.24 no.i (1996), pp.126-36.

30. Stroud, *Capability Brown* (1975 edn), pp.135-6; Hinde, *Capability Brown*, pp.176-7; Robert Dunning, *Some Somerset Country Houses* (1991), pp.22-26; Lord Macaulay, *Essays* (1902 edn), p.781.

31. Jones, *Follies and Grottoes* (1979 edn), p.383.

32. Dunning, *Some Somerset Country Houses*, p.26.

33. Stroud, *Capability Brown*, (1975 edn), p.236; Clarke, *Prior Park*, pp.54, 58-9.

34. Stroud, *Capability Brown* (1975 edn), p.230.

35. R.W. Dunning, 'Hinton St George', *V.C.H.* Vol.4 (1978), pp. 40, 46; Colin G. Winn, *The Pouletts of Hinton St George* (Stroud, 1995), p.162.

36. *The Travels through England of Dr Richard Pococke*, p.42; Robert Wilson-North, 'Witham: from Carthusian monastery to country house', *Current Archaeology* Vol.13 no.iv (1996), pp.151-6. For a biography of the younger Beckford see Brian Fothergill, *Beckford of Fonthill* (1979)

37. J.H.Bettey, *Estates and the English Countryside* (1993), p.146. Skinner's journals are in the British Library, Add.MSS.

38. R.W. Dunning, 'Montacute', *V.C.H.* Vol.3 (1974), pp.212, 215; Dudley Dodd, *Montacute House* (1978), pp.38-41.

39. B. Little & A. Aldrich, *Ammerdown* (Unpublished MS, 1977) refer to an 1817 edition of J. Billingsley's *General View of the Agriculture of the County of Somerset* which I have been unable to trace.

40. J.C. Cox & W.H.P. Greswell, 'Forestry', *V.C.H.* Vol.2 (1911), p.569; B. Little & A. Aldrich, *Ammerdown* (Unpublished MS, 1977, at Ammerdown Study Centre Library); Harvey Sheppard, *Historical Notes on Dillington House* (Dillington, updated); Dunning, *Some Somerset Houses*, pp.37-42.

41. E.P. Shirley, *Some Account of English Deer Parks, with Notes on the Management of Deer* (1867), p.97; R.J. Bush, 'Nettlecombe Court, 1: The Trevelyans and other residents of the Court', *Field Studies* Vol.3 no.2 (1970), pp.283-5; Francis Rose & Pat Wolseley, Nettlecombe Park: its history and its epiphytic lichens: an attempt at correlation, *Field Studies* Vol.6 (1984), pp.125-7; M.C. Siraut, 'Nettlecombe', *V.C.H.* Vol.5 (1985), p.111.

42. George S. Master, *Collections for a Parochial History of Wraxall* (Bristol, 1900), p.42; Eve Wigan, *The Tale of Gordano* (Taunton, undated), pp.117-8.

43. I owe this information to Hazel Hudson and Frances Neale.

44. R.W. Dunning & M.C. Siraut, 'Stringston', *V.C.H.* Vol.6 (1992), p.172; Dunning & Siraut, 'Otterhampton', *V.C.H.* Vol.6, p.105; R.W. Dunning, 'Somerton', *V.C.H.* Vol.3 (1974), p.130.

45. Phelps, *History and Antiquities of Somersetshire*, Vol.1, p.278, 477, 594.

46. Chapman, *A Guide to the Estates of Ralph Allen*, pp.13-14.

47. Sir H.C. Maxwell Lyte, *A History of Dunster and of the Families of Mohun and Luttrell* (1909), ii, pp.345-6.

48. Shirley, *Some Account of English Deer Parks*, p.97; Joseph Whitaker, *A Descriptive List of Deer Parks and Paddocks of England* (1892); Cox & Greswell, 'Forestry', pp.569-570; Dunning & Siraut, 'Stringston', *V.C.H.* Vol.6, p.172.

49. R.A. Sixsmith, *Staple Fitzpaine and the Forest of Neroche* (Taunton, 1958), pp.32, 59.

50. Collinson, *History and Antiquities of the County of Somerset*, Vol.1, p.44.

51. Jones, *Follies and Grottoes* (1974 edn), pp.226-30.

52. Clarke, *Prior Park*, pp.61, 64; White, *Georgian Arcadia*, p.56, no.289; Chapman, *A Guide to the Estates of Ralph Allen*, p.15.

53. White, *Georgian Arcadia*, p.31, no.92, where it is compared with work at Arno's Court, Bristol, by the American-born architect James Bridges.

54. Lyte, *History of Dunster*, i, p.229.

55. *Country Life* Vol.95 (March 1944), pp.376-9; Jones, *Follies and Grottoes*, p.285.

56. Master, *Collections for a Parochial History of Wraxall*, p.75.

57. R.J.E. Bush, 'Chaffcombe', *V.C.H.* Vol.4 (1978), pp.121-2, 126.

58. Dunning, *Some Somerset Country Houses*, p.143.

59. Dunning, 'Hinton St George', *V.C.H.* Vol.4 (1978), pp.39-40, 46; Winn, *The Pouletts of Hinton St George*, p.159.

60. McGarvie, *Gardening at Marston House, 1660-1905*, pp.23-4.

61. Rose & Wolseley, 'Nettlecombe Park: its history and its epiphytic lichens', p.126; Siraut, 'Nettlecombe', *V.C.H.* Vol.5, p.111.

62. *Country Life*, Vol.10 (21st December, 1901), pp.808-15; John Sales, *West Country Gardens* (Gloucester, 1980), pp.173-4.

63. R.W. Dunning & M.C. Siraut, 'Enmore', *V.C.H.* Vol.6 (1992), pp.36-7.

64. M. Aston (ed.), 'Somerset Archaeology, 1976', *P.S.A.N.H.S.* Vol.121 (1977), pp.119-120; R.W. Dunning, 'West Quantoxhead', *V.C.H.* Vol.5 (1985), pp.129-3, 134.

65. James Bond, 'Earthwork surveys around Shapwick House', in *The Shapwick Report: an Archaeological, Historical and Topographical Survey*, 7th Report (in press, 1997); see also 'The Shapwick Project', *Current Archaeology* Vol.13, no.7 (1997), pp.248-9.

66. Wigan, *The Tale of Gordano*, pp.116-7.

67. E. Chisholm-Batten, 'The forest trees of Somerset', *P.S.A.N.H.S.* Vol.36 (1890), ii, p.183.

68. David C. Stuart, *The Kitchen Garden: an Historical Guide to Traditional Crops* (1984); Charles Lyte, *The Kitchen Garden* (Yeovil, 1984); see also Susan Campbell, 'A few guidelines for the conservation of old kitchen gardens', *Garden History* Vol.13 no.1 (1985), pp.68-74

69. McGarvie, *Gardening at Marston House, 1660-1905*, p.23.

70. Dunning, *Some Somerset Country Houses*, p.70; Dunning & Siraut, 'Goathurst', *V.C.H.* Vol.6 (1992), p.50, quoting Somerset C.R.O. DD/S/WH 267.

71. F.A. Roach, *Cultivated Fruits of Britain* (Oxford, 1985), pp.108-9; J. Billingsley, *General View of the Agriculture of the County of Somerset* (Bath, 1797 edition), pp.124, 221; Dunning, 'West Quantoxhead', *V.C.H.* Vol.5, p.134.

72. Pound, *Genius of Bath*, pp.52-4.

73. Stuart, *Georgian Gardens*, pp.184-6; Pound, *Genius of Bath*, pp.55-7; Harding & Lambert, *Parks and Gardens of Avon*, p.67.

74. Pound, *Genius of Bath*, pp.54-5.

75. The standard work on Repton's career is Dorothy Stroud, *Humphry Repton* (1962); see also Edward Hyams, *Capability Brown and Humphry Repton* (1971); and George Carter, Patrick Goode & Kedrun Laurie, *Humphry Repton, Landscape Gardener, 1752-1818* (1982)

76. Humphry Repton's principal general works were *Sketches and Hints on Landscape Gardening* (1795); *Observations on the Theory and Practice of Landscape Gardening* (1803); *An Inquiry into the Changes of Taste in Landscape Gardening* (1806); and *Fragments on the Theory and Practice of Landscape Gardening* (1816)

77. Repton, *Sketches and Hints on Landscape Gardening* (1795); *Country Life* Vol.97 (23rd March, 1945), pp.508-11; Stroud, *Humphry Repton*, p.68; Carter, Goode & Laurie, *Humphry Repton, Landscape Gardener*, pp.52-3, 161.

78. Stroud, *Humphry Repton*, p.97; Hyams, *Capability Brown & Humphry Repton*, pp.175-6, 235; Graham Davis, *The Langtons of Newton Park, Bath* (Bath, undated); Nicholas Pearson Associates, *Newton Park: Historic Survey and Restoration Plan*.

79. Stroud, *Humphry Repton*, pp.122-3; Hyams, *Capability Brown & Humphry Repton*, p.180.

80. *Peacock's Polite Repository, or Pocket Companion*, 1806; H.M. Colvin, *A Biographical Dictionary of English Architects, 1660-1840* (1954), p.491; Sir John Summerson, 'A Repton Portfolio', *Journal of Royal Institute of British Architects* (February 25th, 1933), pp.313-24; Carter, Goode & Laurie, *Humphry Repton, Landscape Gardener*, p.161.

81. *Notes on some general maxims of taste in Gardens from Mr Repton's Report*, Bristol University Library; Harding & Lambert, *Parks and Gardens of Avon*, pp.60, 65-6.

82. Tim Mowl, 'A trial-run for Regent's Park: Repton and Nash at Bath, 1796', *Bath History* Vol.3 (1990), pp.76-89.

Fig. 7.26
A drawing of 1770 of the gateway
to Redlynch Park.

Chapter 8

PARKS and GARDENS of the NINETEENTH CENTURY

A NEW INTEREST IN
PARKS AND GARDENS
NOW PERMEATED
EVERY LEVEL OF
SOCIETY.
GARDEN DESIGNERS
FELT FREE TO
BORROW FROM ANY
PERIOD AND ANY
PART OF THE WORLD,
PRODUCING AN
ECLECTIC RANGE
OF FASHIONS.
PLANT COLLECTORS
OPERATING IN MANY
REGIONS PREVIOUSLY
UNEXPLORED
EXCEEDED ALL
PREVIOUS
ACHIEVEMENTS ...

INTRODUCTION

The accelerating pace of social and technological change in the wake of the industrial revolution and the expansion of the Empire had a profound effect upon the cultivation of the land in all its aspects. In Somerset the first half of the nineteenth century saw the onslaught of reclamation achieving its most ambitious aims, when over 10,000 acres of the bleak uplands of Exmoor were converted to farmland and 2,300 acres of waste in the Forest of Neroche were enclosed, while drainage works continued in the Levels, and Parliamentary enclosure mopped up the remaining open-field lands.[1]

A new interest in parks and gardens now permeated every level of society. Great country estates were changing hands, and parks were no longer the exclusive preserve of the old landed aristocracy. Lawyers and bankers had entered the market for country properties in the eighteenth century, and they were now joined by new industrial dynasties who had made their fortunes from mining or manufacturing. Lower down the social scale the emerging middle class also aspired towards more gracious living, and gardens played an important part in their ambitions. Even the rapidly-expanding industrial workforce, lacking garden space in their own homes, could still enjoy the new public parks and might be able to cultivate an allotment. There were new employment opportunities for professional gardeners: even on a small estate, a head gardener could earn three or four times the wages of an agricultural labourer.

As the social order changed, garden designers were no longer inhibited by any straightjackets of 'correctness' or 'good taste'. They were now free to experiment, to borrow from any period and any part of the world, and this produced an eclectic range of fashions. Despite this licence, many theorists held strong opinions on the course that garden design should be taking, and the period was marked by sometimes acrimonious journalistic controversy. As always, there tended to be a lapse of time between the promotion of new fashions and their widespread adoption, so the variety of designs was increased still further by localised survivals of 'outdated' ideas.[2]

The rapid growth of interest in gardening at all levels of society produced an enormous new market for goods and services. Nurseries supplying plants and seeds proliferated. The industrial revolution had made possible the mass production of garden tools and furniture, and firms like Fussells of Mells were producing cast-iron garden seats, hothouse stoves, melon and cucumber frames and plant-containers as well as a wide range of spades, forks, hoes, scythes, rakes and trowels.[3] New types of machinery were developed, perhaps the greatest technological innovation being the cylinder lawn mower, invented by the textile engineer Edwin Beard Budding. Budding realised that the cylinder of angled blades used to trim the nap of cloth could be adapted for grass cutting, and in 1830 he went into partnership with John Ferrabee to manufacture lawn mowers at the Phoenix Ironworks at Thrupp Mill near Stroud.[4]

Experiments were carried out with a wide range of manures. The fortune of one great Somerset family was largely founded upon the import of guano from South America: William Gibbs had been born in Madrid to a merchant family with South American connections, and by 1844 this trade had brought him sufficient prosperity to enable him to purchase the Tyntesfield estate in Wraxall.

There was an upsurge of new books and magazines dealing with plants and their cultivation. The early journals, such as the Transactions of the Horticultural Society of London, which commenced publication in 1807, were beautifully designed but expensive, still catering for an exclusive market. Some of the leading garden theorists and designers were soon involved in the promotion of cheaper periodicals aimed more at the middle classes. In 1826 John Claudius Loudon launched the Gardener's Magazine, intended 'to disseminate new and improved information on all topics connected with horticulture and to raise the intellect and character of those engaged in this art'. Joseph Paxton was associated with both the Horticultural Register and General Magazine founded in 1831 and the weekly Gardener's Chronicle, founded in 1841. Cheaper paper and printing costs widened the range of publications still further after the middle of the century, though not all of the new ventures stood the test of time. William Robinson launched The Garden in 1871 and The Garden Illustrated in 1879. Though not specifically a gardening journal, the foundation of Country Life in 1897 was a significant landmark in the presentation of private gardens to a wider public.[5]

Horticultural societies also provided a forum for the exchange of ideas. The Bath and West of England Horticultural Society was founded in 1800, with the Bristol nurseryman Nehemiah Bartley as its first secretary. In 1873 the Royal Horticultural Society held the first of its great provincial shows in the Royal Victoria Park at Bath.

The Taunton & West Somerset Horticultural Society was founded in 1831 with the encouragement of John Young, another nurseryman whose grounds lay east of Staplegrove Road. Revived in 1866 as the Vale of Taunton Deane Horticultural and Floricultural Society, it has held regular shows in Vivary Park in Taunton ever since.[6]

PLANT COLLECTORS and NEW INTRODUCTIONS

New plant introductions had been entering Britain since Tudor times, but the sheer scale of the influx of new species during the nineteenth century greatly exceeded all previous achievements. Professional botanists and plant collectors were now operating all over the world, and in many regions previously unexplored. Joseph Banks, who had accompanied James Cook's voyage around the world in 1768-71, was elected President of the Royal Society in 1778 and was in all but name director of the Royal Gardens at Kew. Banks did much to encourage and support further scientific botanical expeditions.[7] Other explorations were sponsored by commercial nurseries, such as those of the Veitch family of Exeter and Chelsea.[8]

LAWN AND GARDEN CHAIRS
In all the newest and most comfortable designs, with Pitch Pine Seats, either varnished or painted.
THE NEW LAWN TENNIS OR CROQUET CHAIR,
So much in request during the past season.
MELON & CUCUMBER FRAMES.
Garden Hand Lights, from 12 to 24 inches square, or 24 inches wide to 6 feet long.
IMPROVED PORTABLE STEPS.
Somersetshire Hay Collectors, &c.
ALSO
FUSSELL'S NEW MINIATURE
Hothouse, or Propagating Stove
The simplest, cheapest, and best ever introduced for raising seeds and striking cuttings.

This handy little apparatus is designed expressly to meet a want long felt by possessors of gardens not containing the expensive appliances of Stoves, Hothouses, &c., for raising all kinds of half-hardy and tender annuals, biennials, cucumbers, vegetable marrows, melons, ornamental gourd; striking cuttings of choice plants; and in fact for any purpose requiring a steady heat.
Full particulars, with directions; also Illustrated Catalogue of Garden Chairs to be obtained on application to

WILLIAM A. FUSSELL,
MELLS, FROME.

Fig. 8.2
Advertisement for garden furniture by FUSSELLS *of Mells from Harvey's* FROME ALMANACK *for 1881.*

Fig. 8.3
Green's patent LAWN-MOWING MACHINE *of 1862. "By the use of these machines lawns can be brought to a state of perfection, unequalled by any other means; they are simple, durable, and effective, and are made in sizes suitable for the smallest plots, or lawns of the greatest extent."*

left: Fig. 8.1
BRYMORE, CANNINGTON *c.1875. A typical Victorian country house garden.*

New techniques of storage in transit ensured that the species collected by travellers now stood a much better chance of reaching England unharmed. Previously seeds had been carried in containers of honey or wax or in sealed barrels of soil, but few survived a long journey. It was then found that a much higher success rate could be achieved simply by carrying dried seeds in packets of brown paper. Live plants carried in the holds of ships had been even more vulnerable to rats, sea-water, changes of temperature and lack of care on the voyage; but in the 1830s a London doctor named Nathaniel Bagshaw Ward realised that live plants could be carried in a sealed glass case which formed in effect a self-sustaining environment, since water transpired by the plants condensed on the inner side of the glass. The Wardian Case, first used on an extensive scale by Robert Fortune's 1843-6 expedition to China, made possible the carriage of live plants with a much higher expectation of success.

There was often some delay between the discovery of a plant in the wild and its successful despatch to England, and a further delay between the safe arrival of seeds, bulbs or roots and the successful raising and sale of the plant by commercial nurseries. However, as new species became available they found a ready market. For many reasons gardeners were eager to grow as wide a range as they could. There was a simple delight in variety for its own sake. There was a particular pride in raising tender exotics, since success with temperamental tropical plants advertised the gardener's skill. There were new opportunities to extend the flowering season through more and more of the year, even into the depths of winter. The broadening of the colour range was also welcomed, especially the brighter hues favoured in bedding schemes.

Scientific experimentation was leading to a better understanding of the principles of selection and cross-breeding, both for fruit and flowering plants. To take one example, by 1830 no less than 70 cultivars of chrysanthemum were known in England, and within twelve years the number had increased to 110. Often the resulting hybrids displayed more vigour and a better range of colour, and the ancestral species disappeared from cultivation.[9]

The first big influx of new species came from the Americas. Some botanical collections were made during Lewis and Clark's first overland crossing of the North American continent in 1804-6. The west coast of North America was explored in the 1820s, and David Douglas was responsible for bringing into cultivation hundreds of new hardy plants from this region, including eighteen species of penstemon, several evening primroses (*Oenothera sp.*), the California poppy (*Eschscholtzia californica*), the poached-egg flower (*Limnanthes douglasii*), the red-flowering currant (*Ribes sanguineum*), the monkey-musk (*Mimulus moschatus*), the clarkia *C. elegans*, the ancestor of the modern lupin, *Lupinus polyphyllus*, and the only peony known from North America, the purple and yellow *Paeonia brownii*.[10]

Central and South America also yielded a rich haul. From the single red Mexican dahlia, *D.coccinea*, first grown successfully in England in 1802, a huge range of varieties was developed, much valued for autumn colour. Other introductions from Mexico included the zinnias and the bright red penstemon *P. hartwegii*, a parent of many garden hybrids, which arrived in 1835. In the 1840s William Lobb, a Cornishman employed by the Veitch nurseries, undertook two

expeditions to Brazil and Chile. Tender and half-hardy plants from South and Central America, such as salvias, verbenas, petunias and calceolarias, which could be grown from seed or cuttings in greenhouses and used in bedding, became popular in the 1840s and 1850s. The first begonias were introduced by another west countryman, Richard Pearce from Devonport, who worked for the Veitch firm in Bolivia and Peru through the 1860s and 1870s.

Although China ultimately provided some of the most popular new garden plants, travel there was especially difficult and dangerous for foreigners, and for long the country's rich botanical resources remained little known to Europeans. William Kerr, who collected there between 1803 and 1811, brought back to England the Jew's mallow (*Kerria japonica*), Japanese honeysuckle (*Lonicera japonica*), the white Banks's rose (*Rosa banksiae*) and the tiger lily (*Lilium lancifolium*). Other introductions from China included the scarlet Indian azalea *Rhododendron simsii* in 1808, the primula *P. sinensis* in 1820 and the pink camellia *C. reticulata* in 1822. The opium wars then made further exploration impossible until the 1842 Treaty of Nanking once more opened up the country. Robert Fortune's expedition in 1843-6 discovered many more Chinese plants which ultimately found their way into English gardens, including the white wisteria, the forsythia, the yellow winter jasmine (*J. nudiflorum*), the Japanese anemone (*A. hupehensis*), the bleeding heart (*Dicentra spectabilis*) and the miniature Chusan Daisy chrysanthemum (*C. rubellum*). The establishment of a French Jesuit mission in Peking provided the base from which Fr Armand David in 1869 discovered the striking pocket-handkerchief tree (*Davidia involucrata*), so eagerly sought by later collectors. The popular butterfly bush, *Buddleia davidii*, was another of Fr David's discoveries. The Veitch nurseries sponsored further expeditions to China led by Charles Maries in 1877-80 and by Ernest Henry Wilson in 1898. Wilson, a native of Chipping Campden, was sent out with the particular objective of bringing back more specimens of *Davidia involucrata*, since only one of the plants sent to Paris by Fr David had survived. Examples of this rare but spectacular tree can be seen in Somerset at Dunster Castle, at Wayford Manor, at Milton Lodge near Wells and at Walton-in-Gordano Manor. He made several further expeditions to China, and introduced over 1000 species to cultivation in the west, including over 60 rhododendrons, 20 viburnums, 18 roses, 14 flowering cherries, seven magnolias, the yellow poppywort *Meconopsis integrifolia* and the regal lily *L.regale*.[11]

Northern India, Nepal and neighbouring regions were explored in the 1840s and 1850s. Joseph Dalton Hooker's book on the rhododendrons of the Himalayas, based upon his own travels, did much to popularise them as a garden plant in Britain.[12] In Somerset rhododendrons became a particular feature of the gardens on the more acid soils in the west, but also provide fine shows at Dunster Castle, Wayford Manor and the Brackenwood Nurseries. In the same period Thomas Lobb, younger brother of William, was collecting for the Veitch nurseries in Burma, Malaya, Java and Borneo.

South Africa provided the first montbretias (*Crocosmia aurea*) in 1846, and was also the source of many heaths which would flower all year round. These became very popular during the later nineteenth century, though many have been lost from cultivation since. Japan had remained the most inaccessible of all countries before the middle of the nineteenth century, but the Veitch nurseries began collecting there in the 1870s.

The later nineteenth century saw an increasing interest in spring bulbs. Experiments with breeding new varieties of narcissus, jonquil and daffodil had begun in the 1820s, but it took another sixty years before an energetic campaign by the bulb merchant Peter Barr brought them into general cultivation. William Robinson was particularly fond of daffodils, planting them extensively in his own garden. Tulips enjoyed another vogue as the self-coloured Darwin varieties became available in the 1880s. Hyacinths, biennial wall-flowers, anemones and pansies added to the spring show.

Some of the newly-introduced trees did particularly well in Somerset. Fine male and female specimens of the Chinese maidenhair tree (*Ginkgo biloba*) stand near the entrance gate of the Botanic Garden in Bath, and examples also flourish at Nynehead Court, and in Yeovil.

The cabbage palm (*Cordyline australis*), introduced from New Zealand in 1823, became a distinctive feature of public and private gardens in the coastal resorts of Clevedon, Weston-super-Mare and Burnham-on-Sea. The Himalayan cypress (*Cupressus torulosa*), introduced to England in 1824, remained relatively rare, though Nettlecombe Park contains an outstanding specimen 100ft high with a girth of nearly 15ft. The monkey-puzzle tree (*Araucaria araucana*), coming from South America in 1795, was widely grown in the west of England; there is a fine example in the manor garden at Walton-in-Gordano, and others at Newton Park. Of the introductions from North America, Bath Botanic Garden contains fine examples of the sweet buck-eye chestnut (*Aesculus flava*) and the golden catalpa (*C. bignonoides 'aurea'*). The Monterey cypress (*Cupressus macrocarpa*) was introduced from California in 1838, and one near the south entry to Montacute is claimed as the largest in Britain, with a height of 115ft and a girth of over 24ft; Orchardleigh Park has other fine specimens. Seeds of the Californian coast redwood (*Sequoia sempervirens*) planted at Ashton Court by Sir Greville Smyth in 1866 have now grown to trees so large as to become an embarrassment. The Wellingtonia (*Sequoiadendron giganteum*) was first discovered in the Sierra Nevada of California in 1841 by William Lobb, and the Veitch nurseries were advertising its satisfactory propagation by 1854. Within two years specimens had been planted in the Botanic Garden at Bath. Several Wellingtonias at Wilton near Taunton, including one formerly by the church, are said

to have been planted from seedlings sold at the International Exhibition of 1862. The tree grew too big for small gardens, but by the end of the decade Wellingtonias were widely sold for planting on country estates. Bath Botanic Garden also contains a splendid silver pendent lime (*Tilia petiolaris*) introduced probably from the Caucasus, and there is another, even bigger example (108ft high, nearly 14ft girth) at Orchardleigh.[13]

Local collectors included the Reverend John Augustus Yatman, who began a plantsman's garden at Winscombe Hall in 1858. Although this contained a Tudor summerhouse and various architectural features, its main interest was the range of exotics which Yatman collected on his travels through Europe, with additional contributions sent from Australia by his brother-in-law and from New Zealand by his eldest son.[14] Canon Henry Nicholson Ellacombe of Bitton, just across the Gloucestershire border, was another noted plant collector and gardener, travelling through the Alps well into his eighties. Through the 1870s he was sending and receiving plants from botanical gardens in many parts of Britain, France, Belgium and Germany, and trying them out in different habitats within the vicarage garden. Between 1890 and 1893 he submitted a series of influential articles to the *Guardian* describing his garden through the year. He lamented the loss of so many old garden plants to the bedding craze, and was enthusiastic about rare native plants such as the Cheddar pink. Growing only in Cheddar Gorge in the wild, roots could be bought in Cheddar village at that time, and he mentions a garden near Bath where the pink had spread down over a stone wall to form a beautiful mat, five feet long and three feet across.[15]

NURSERY GARDENS

By the late eighteenth century a considerable concentration of nursery gardens had developed around the suburban fringes of London, providing fruit trees and ornamental shrubs and flowers for the new villas and pleasure-grounds of the rapidly expanding city. Similar developments occurred on a smaller scale around provincial towns.

In the west of England the most famous nurseries were in Exeter. Messrs Lucombe and Pince, who specialised in fuchsias and bedding plants and also introduced the semi-evergreen Lucombe Oak (*Quercus x hispanica*) as a popular garden tree, were prominent in the first half of the nineteenth century (a fine Lucombe oak grows at Nynehead Court). However, Lucombe & Pince were soon eclipsed by a rival firm. In the 1790s John Veitch, a native of Jedburgh, had come south to undertake several garden design commissions in Devon, also advising on the landscaping of Nettlecombe Park in Somerset, and in 1808 he established his own nursery at Budlake near Killerton. In 1832, in partnership with his son James, he moved to Mount Radford, and subsequent generations maintained the family business on various sites around Exeter until 1969. Many Somerset grounds were stocked by the Veitch nurseries. James Veitch was carrying out some planting at Petherton Park in 1815, and the remains of the garden there are probably represented by the earthworks east of the present Park Farm and Manor House Farm; he also supplied fruit trees and 25 vines to Nynehead Court in 1838, and a range of native and

Fig. 8.4
The CABBAGE PALM *(Cordyline australis). A native of New Zealand which has made itself at home in Somerset seaside resorts such as Clevedon.*

Fig. 8.5
The MONKEY PUZZLE TREE *(Araucaria araucana) at Walton-in-Gordano.*

ornamental trees for the grounds of Maunsel House near North Petherton in 1839.[16] The founder's elder grandson, also named James, moved to Chelsea in 1853 and developed there an international business, experimenting with hybrids and sponsoring plant-collecting expeditions all over the world.[17]

There were several important nurseries in Bristol. James Sweet, former head gardener at Ham Green, founded a nursery at the bottom of St Michael's Hill in 1785. He went into partnership with John Miller, who specialised in hothouse plants, and by 1822 the firm had established a flourishing nursery on Durdham Down, supplying plants all over the south-west. Sweet & Miller went bankrupt in 1837, but was resurrected by one of its former employees, James Garaway. William Maule & Co. were established on the Stapleton Road in 1815, and specialised in conifers, orchids and American bog plants. The latter firm also introduced from Japan, and propagated at great expense, a variety of quince, Maule's Quince (*Pyrus* or *Cydonia maulei*, now known as *Chaenomeles japonica*); sadly, although this plant is still grown today, it never achieved the mass popularity which the firm had

hoped for, and the investment proved misguided. Acoording to Canon Ellacombe disappointment over the limited sales of the quince probably hastened Maule's death. Other Bristol nurseries, including Peter Lauder at Lawrence Hill and Edward Spiring of Upper Easton, also supplied Somerset.[18]

The nursery trade was slower to develop in Bath, possibly because aristocratic residence in the city remained somewhat seasonal, and because those who were attracted to settle permanently within reach of the spa tended to be in poor health. Nursery gardens in Bath included those of Salter & Scammell (later Salter & Wheeler, first established in 1809 on Lyncombe Hill, later moving to the London Road and to the Victoria Nursery next to the Royal Victoria Park), and Edward Titley.[19]

The village of Merriott near Crewkerne had been noted for its nurseries and market gardens since the eighteenth century. Around 1850 the largest Merriott nursery, that of W.W. Webber, was bought out by John Scott, who went on to open a second nursery and shop in Yeovil. The fruit tree nursery at Merriott covered about 30 acres. Scott effectively publicised his goods by an extensive catalogue, the *ORCHARDIST*. In 1872 this was advertising for sale 1000 different varieties of apple, 1546 varieties of pear, 239 plums, 130 cherries, 97 grapes, 49 apricots, 43 nectarines, 43 figs and 25 currants. The apples not only included many local varieties such as Tom Putt, Royal Somerset, White Quarrendon, Early Pomeroy, Merchant, Fair Maid of Taunton and Court of Wick, but also many of Scott's own introductions from the continent and from America. Later on the business got into financial difficulties, but was revived in the 1920s and still continues today.[20]

At least two nurseries were operating in Taunton in the early nineteenth century. John Harris had acquired land at Mill Lane and North Town and was working a small nursery by 1800. Part of the business was continued by his son, the remainder of the land being sold to James and William Poole. In 1827 the Pooles' nursery was bought up by John Young, a Quaker who had established a seedsman's business in North Street two years before. Young acquired more land, increasing the extent of the nursery to about 15 acres, and by 1843 was attracting the praise of John Claudius Loudon. A second nursery, that of Hammond & Stephens at South Road, covered about four acres by 1840 and specialised in calceolarias, while also raising many other trees, shrubs and flowering plants.[21]

Nursery gardens also existed in several other Somerset towns. John Tucker had a nursery in Wells by 1798, and in the 1820s there were two nurseries in the city, Robert Giddings in New Street and Robert Holloway in Queen Street. James Kelway, who set up a business in Langport in 1850, was a pioneer in hybridising gladioli from South Africa, and by 1861 was able to market the first of the modern florists' gladioli; he also specialised in delphiniums and peonies.[22]

Villages on the warm southern slopes of the Failand ridge and the Mendip hills also developed horticultural specialities with crops like strawberries in the later nineteenth century. George Lee, who established a flower shop in Clevedon in 1852, acquired land at Highgrove in Tickenham as a market garden, and here he began specialising in the cultivation of violets, raising and hybridising many new varieties.[23]

Fig. 8.6
Extract from a map of Taunton (1840)
by John Wood, the prolific Scottish
cartographer, showing
JOHN YOUNG'S NURSERIES.

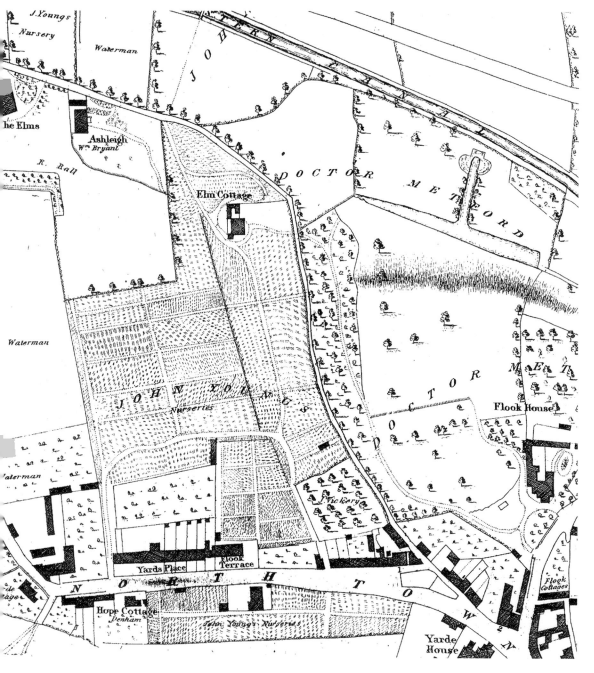

NEW STYLES: REGENCY PICTURESQUE

During the last decade of the eighteenth century the style of landscaping developed by Capability Brown had come under fire from two Herefordshire landowners, Richard Payne Knight and Uvedale Price. These men were keen protagonists of the 'picturesque' ideal, reviving the older concept of designing landscapes in the manner of pictures, and they deplored what they viewed as the impoverishment and disfigurement of the landscape by Brown and his followers.[24] In 1794 Payne Knight set down his view of how the landscape should reflect 'the true ingredients of the painter's grace', an ideal all too easily destroyed when

> ..... *"yon fantastic band*
> *With charts, pedometers and rules in hand*
> *Advance triumphant, and alike lay waste*
> *The forms of nature and the works of taste !*
> *T'improve, adorn and polish they profess;*
> *But shave the goddess whom they come to dress;*
> *Level each broken bank and shaggy mound,*
> *And fasten all to one unvaried round;*
> *One even round that ever gently flows,*
> *Nor forms abrupt, nor broken colours knows;*
> *But, wrapt' all o'er in everlasting green*
> *Makes one dull, vapid, smooth and tranquil scene....*
>
> *... Hence, hence ! thou haggard fiend, however call'd,*
> *Thin, meagre genius of the bare and bald;*
> *Thy spade and mattock here at length lay down,*
> *And follow to the tomb thy fav'rite Brown:*
> *Thy fav'rite Brown, whose innovating hand*
> *First dealt thy curses o'er this fertile land ..."* [25]

Humphry Repton was drawn into a lively public controversy with Price and Knight, who rather unfairly tarred him with the same brush as Brown. In fact Repton's later work was moving much closer to the 'picturesque' ideal, making full use of rustic structures, rocky cliffs and ancient trees to provide more points of interest in the view. However, it was left to William Sawrey Gilpin, nephew of the artist William Gilpin, to achieve the most complete expression of the 'picturesque' style through his writing and practical landscaping in the three decades after 1806.[26]

'Picturesque' principles were employed by many local designers during the early nineteenth century . Harptree Court at East Harptree was built for the Waldegrave family soon after 1800 on the site of an older house and garden. Sixteen fields were amalgamated to make a new 30-acre park, containing pasture dotted with specimen trees, a lime and sweet chestnut avenue, two small lakes linked by a serpentine river, and a grotto, all surrounded by a perimeter screen of woodland. A plan of these pleasure-grounds attributes their design to Charles Harcourt Masters of Bath, who may also have been responsible for the new house.[27] The present layout is somewhat different.

At Clevedon Court the mixed formal and informal landscape of the previous century had now matured, and during the 1820s and 1830s Sir Abraham Elton V, who was familiar with the writings of Repton and Price, and his wife, Mary Stewart Elton, herself a talented topographical artist, began laying out a series of romantic walks over Court Hill and Nortons Wood, extending all the way to the coast at Wains Hill and including the picturesque Swiss Valley. The woods were extended and interplanted with exotic trees. Twists in the paths were designed to reveal sudden unexpected views, to the prominent tower of Rickman's new church on Chapel Hill, and over the medieval Court to the moors beyond.[28]

In 1822 the eccentric William Beckford (son of Alderman Beckford for whom Adam had designed the abortive mansion at Witham Charterhouse described in Chapter 7) sold up his extravagant Wiltshire seat at Fonthill Abbey and arrived in Bath to take up residence at nos.19-20 Lansdown Crescent. Almost immediately he indulged himself in planning a picturesque private walk extending between his house and the top of Lansdown itself, a little over a mile to the north-west. Some 10-12 acres of grounds along the way were laid out by his gardener Vincent, who accompanied him from Fonthill. The terminus of the walk was a study-retreat housed in a two-storey pavilion with an extraordinary Italianate tower (two earlier gothic designs were rejected), designed by his architect Henry Edmund Goodridge. The walk was described in some detail by the topographical artist Henry Venn Lansdown, one of the few visitors whom Beckford admitted. Behind the dwelling a small 'pleasaunce' contained a 'Turkish tea-house'. Massively buttressed retaining walls enclosed a sheltered fruit and vegetable garden, converted from an old quarry, covering some 4 acres. Behind this the ground rose steeply, and two terraces were made, with a raised lane over vaulted stables and storage rooms leading to the machicolated and battlemented neo-Norman gateway which was the entrance to the walk. The path climbed uphill across open pasture, newly planted with clumps and thorn thickets, with rough-hewn seats at suitable vantage points, towards an old quarry. To compensate for his appropriation of a right of way, Beckford provided a new public road lined with a 300-yard avenue of lime trees, which still survives. Beckford's path then passed by a cottage, winding through woodlands adorned with flowering shrubs, and through a low door into a sunken walled garden some 400ft x 80ft in extent. Ancient apple trees were transplanted to this spot so that their blossom could be enjoyed in spring. At the far end the path left through an Italianate arch past a pond into a grotto tunnel 70ft long, passing under the track to Chelscombe Farm. Climbing up a flight of rustic steps into the open once more, the walk continued over the open down into woodland and shrubbery and past ornamental pools and a rockery to the tower. Here Beckford had planted exotic conifers from many parts of the world, along with American maples and Chinese roses. An account of 1830 describes the gardens around the tower as "*of Alpine character, replete with almost every plant and shrub appertaining to such a scheme*". The tower, built in 1825-6, is square with an octagonal lantern, 154ft high, the upper parts of timber, with cast-iron columns. After Beckford's death in 1844 his estate was broken up, and although some elements of the ride survive, its course has been disrupted by later building. Beckford was buried near his tower, and the garden around it was converted to a cemetery four years later.[29]

The walled and moated surrounds of the medieval episcopal palace at Wells were landscaped in romantic style for Bishop George Henry Law in 1824-5. The roofless shell of Bishop Burnell's monumental thirteenth-century great hall was partly dismantled to create an authentic gothic ruin. Ornamental trees and shrubs were informally dotted about the lawns, including a black walnut, Lebanon cedar, catalpa and ginkgo. A raised rampart walk was created around the inside of the wall, with access through one of the towers to the moat side. A bridge then led past a small waterfall to further ornamental trees and borders planted around the springs which supplied the town with water in the Middle Ages. From this viewpoint the cathedral reflected in the pools provides one of the finest scenes in Somerset.[30]

below left: Fig. 8.7
WELLS CATHEDRAL *from the Bishop's Palace gardens; the romantic landscaping of Bishop Law.*

below right: Fig. 8.8
The remains of the thirteenth century Great Hall of the BISHOP'S PALACE, WELLS, *incorporated into the romantic landscape.*

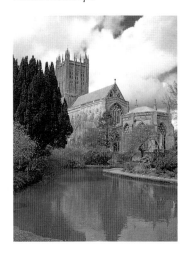

In contrast to the ancient Bishop's Palace, the Chantry near Whatley was built for the ironfounder James Fussell in about 1825, and some remains of the picturesque landscape laid out on the slopes below the house survive. A long ornamental lake in the narrow steep-sided valley to the south-east doubled up as a source of power for the Chantry ironworks below. In the hillside above the lake there are remains of two grottoes, the larger one a complex two-storey affair with caves, alcoves and rock seats.[31]

Another notable early nineteenth-century picturesque garden was made at Brockley Hall, which still has elaborate gates, the remains of a grotto tunnel with an entrance flanked by stone sphinxes, and ornate planting extending eastwards into the gorge of Brockley Combe. Further examples were at Cleeve Court and at Kingwell Hall in Farmborough.[32]

REGENCY ROCOCO

The early nineteenth century saw a brief re-emergence of the rococo fashion, which fitted quite comfortably into the picturesque ideal. The house at Jordans, near Ilminster, was built for the Speke family in 1795. An attractive circular grotto was built in its grounds, now surrounded by meadow, but originally standing on a small promontory or island in a lake. Its roof was thatched and crowned by a lantern, its walls and ceiling encrusted with sea-urchins, ammonites and other fossils and shells arranged in floral patterns. In the centre was a table, with seating all round the inside wall. The floor was made of sheeps' knucklebones laid in intricate patterns, with the date '1828'

Fig. 8.9
JORDANS GROTTO.

near the doorway, and included a small fountain. Two side chambers containing stained glass windows portraying the Speke arms were designed to house singing canaries for the delight of parties taking tea there. The birds were fed from outside, and three of the lead seed containers still remain.[33] At Chew Magna a mock gothick castle was surrounded by rockeries, a pool and specimen trees. Rococo lingered on into the middle of the century. The gardens at West Quantoxhead included a decorated shell grotto on the formal terrace, and a sea grotto made in 1858 near the cascade on the cliffs.[34]

Somerset's most notable garden in this style was at Banwell. During the eighteenth century miners prospecting the hill above the village for lead, ochre and calamine had discovered a stalactite cave, but this was subsequently almost forgotten. In the 1820s Dr Francis Randolph, vicar of Banwell, a man of antiquarian leanings, seems to have instituted a search for this lost cavern. William Beard, a farmer from Wint Hill, claimed the credit for its rediscovery, but he was probably shown the shaft by a local miner, John Webb. Since the land belonged to the see of Bath & Wells, Dr Randolph contacted the new Bishop, George Law, and the two men conceived the idea of opening the cave as an attraction for visitors, thereby raising money for local charitable purposes. The original entrance required ladders for access, and Randolph, unable to resist the opportunity for a sermon, had the following inscription placed over it:

> "*Thou, who, trembling, view'st this cavern's gloom,*
> *Pause and reflect on thy eternal doom,*
> *Think what the punishment of sin will be*
> *In the abyss of endless misery.*"

Concerned about the difficulty of access, Randolph paid Webb and another miner £1 in September 1824 to clear out a fissure in an old quarry which he thought might provide an easier entry into the stalactite cavern. However, they unexpectedly broke into a second cave, 30 feet in length and breadth and 18 feet high, which was found to contain the bones of many prehistoric animals, including bison, woolly rhinocerous, mammoth, lion, bear, reindeer, arctic fox and hyena. In the previous year William Buckland, Reader in Geology at the University of Oxford, had published his *RELIQUAE DILUVIANAE*, describing the bones of extinct animals found in such caves as indicative of the world's fauna before the Flood, so this new discovery aroused considerable interest. The self-styled 'Professor' William Beard was now engaged as guide and custodian, and supervised Webb and others in the removal of the most interesting specimens for safekeeping, stacking the remainder within the cave itself, where some of them still remain. A new entrance to the bone cave was opened up in 1826, with another inscription over its entrance:

> "*Here let the scoffer of God's holy word*
> *Behold the traces of a deluged world.*
> *Here let him learn in Banwell Cave to adore*
> *The Lord of Heaven, then go and scoff no more.*"

In 1827 Bishop Law had a small cottage ornée erected in order to afford his guests rest and shelter when visiting the caves. A second floor, balcony and rustic verandah were added in 1833. Over the next twelve years a series of structures were built in the grounds, linked by walks. Some were of typically rococo flimsiness, and not all have survived. There are today only slight ruins of the 'Osteoicon', a thatched building with bowed sides and a facade lavishly decorated with minerals, built in 1836-7 to serve as a museum for the bones from the cave. The druids were still a subject of great curiosity at this time, and it was felt that the site could not be complete without a Druid's Temple and Cromlech, so these were duly provided near the bone cave entrance. Accounts for the building of the cromlech are dated 1829-32, but this succumbed to army lorries during the Second World War. However, the Druid's Temple survives, built in 1834-5. On a marble tablet over its entrance the following rhyme can still be read:

> "*Here, where once Druids trod in times of yore*
> *And stain'd their altars with a victim's gore,*
> *Here now the Christian, ransomed from above,*
> *Adores a God of Mercy and of Love.*"

Early in 1835 work began on a classical Tuscan-style temple just west of the original stalactite cave entrance. This too has since been removed, though something of its appearance is known from two sketches by John Buckler. Further up the hill was a rock-cut alcove seat and an adjoining rustic summerhouse which replaced an earlier thatched building shown on a Buckler sketch made in late June 1828. The summerhouse was paved and faced with pebbles collected from the beach at Weston-super-Mare; payments are recorded in 1833 to Samuel Rodway for fixing the pebbles in the floor. It still survives in part, though now lacking the bishop's coat of arms which was originally set over the front and lacking also the figures of a lion and camel which stood on the corner piers.

Further east still the ruins of yet another building survive. In 1834 Bishop Law re-erected in his own grounds a gothick hermitage or gazebo which Dr Randolph had originally set up on Banwell Camp. This too had a floor of patterned pebbles, pointed windows and a ceiling set with iron spar and stones. The summit of the hill was at first ornamented with an obelisk, shown on Buckler's 1839 drawing; but in that year it was replaced with a tall three-storey octagonal prospect tower with a small belfry on top. The walk up to the tower was marked at intervals with pairs of 'druidical' standing stones, and extensively planted with ornamental shrubs and trees, most of which have since been swamped by invasive sycamore.

In 1842 the finding of a skeleton was reported during alterations to the bishop's cottage. It is not entirely certain whether this was a genuine discovery or a stunt concocted by Mr Beard to gain further publicity for the caves and gardens. However, a brick grave was made at the east end of the hill for its reinterment, with suitably funereal shrubs planted round, and an inscription carved upon a rough boulder set up to mark the spot:

> "*Beard with his kindness brought me to this spot*
> *As one unknown and long forgot*
> *He made my grave and buried me here*
> *When there was no kind friend to shed a tear.*
> *My bones are here but my spirit is fled*
> *And for years unknown, numbered with the dead.*
> *Reader, as I am now, so shall you be.*
> *Prepare for death and follow me.*"

The Banwell caves and gardens remained open to visitors for a while after Bishop Law's death, but entries in the visitors' book cease in June 1865.[35]

BANWELL BONE CAVES.
Fig. 8.10
A lithograph showing the Ornamental Cottage.
Fig. 8.11
The Druid's Temple, fronted by a pediment and two gothic arches.
Fig. 8.12
The Interior of the Druid's Temple, which has five seats in a rusticated niched wall.
Fig. 8.13
The octagonal Prospect Tower drawn by John Buckler.

background: Fig. 8.14
The pebble Summerhouse.

MID-19TH CENTURY FASHIONS: the GARDENESQUE, the REVIVAL of FORMALITY and the BEDDING SYSTEM

The picturesque style promoted by Knight, Price and Gilpin was passing out of favour by the 1830s, and some designers urged a return to formality. As early as 1828 Joseph Jopling, the Northumbrian architect called in by Colonel John Twyford Jolliffe to redesign the house at Ammerdown, proposed that a formal garden would provide a more appropriate setting for his new classical design, though nothing immediately came of this.[36]

The most influential figure of the second quarter of the nineteenth century was John Claudius Loudon, son of a small farmer in Lanarkshire. Loudon moved to London in 1803, initially advertising himself as a landscape gardener espousing the principles of Uvedale Price. However, he made his reputation as a prolific writer rather than as a practitioner, and the 1822 edition of his famous ENYCLOPAEDIA OF GARDENING shows that his early enthusiasm for irregular gardens was waning: "*to say that landscape gardening is an improvement on geometric gardening is a misapplication of language, like saying that a lawn is an improvement on a cornfield... It is absurd...to despise the ancient style because it has not the same beauties as the modern, to which it never aspired*". In 1832 he devised a new style, unhelpfully naming it 'gardenesque'. Deliberately rejecting the picturesque ethic which took delight in gnarled and twisted trees and dense thickets, he proposed that every individual plant should be grown to develop its natural character as perfectly as possible, trees developing their full spread without pollarding or trimming by livestock. To show that the scheme was not natural but a work of art, exotic plants were to be preferred to native species, and even the turf ought to be recognisably different from the pasture of neighbouring fields. The result would have resembled a museum of specimen plants rather than a coherently organised landscape. This concept was not widely understood, and never became popular, though the term 'gardenesque' was used again later in a much looser sense. Loudon toured through parts of Somerset in 1842 and left some interesting descriptions of the parks and gardens he saw along the way.[37]

Many writers had begun to express regret over the destruction of the old formal gardens, and this could only be remedied by the creation of new ones. The revival of formality gained rapid momentum during the 1830s. When John Vivian, a Cornish barrister, acquired the manor of Claverton, he decided to replace the Elizabethan house near the church, and employed Sir Jeffry Wyatville to build him a new classical mansion on the hill above. The old house was demolished in 1823 and its ancient terraced gardens abandoned. The new house had the advantage of a parkland setting and extensive views over the Avon valley, but Vivian was sufficiently influenced by the current shift of opinion to have new formal gardens made around it, including a high balustraded upper terrace with urns and climbing roses, turfed lower terraces, lawns planted with cedars and Irish yews, a fountain and a grotto. Beeches, limes and holm oak were planted along the drive.[38] Clavelshay in North Petherton, one of the minor properties of the Portman family, also had a terraced garden on the west side by the 1840s.[39]

Some designers, notably Charles Barry, drew inspiration directly from Italian renaissance gardens. Others, like William Andrews Nesfield, preferred the model of Louis XIV's parterres. Later commentators, such as Inigo Triggs, were somewhat scathing about the Victorian recreations, preferring to look back at surviving Tudor and Stuart fragments for their models; yet they were striking achievements on their own terms. Barry's Italianate style, with its loggias, balustrades, staircases, urns and fountains, was especially influential between the 1840s and 1860s.

Neither Barry nor Nesfield is known to have worked in Somerset, though Nesfield was the brother-in-law of Anthony Salvin, the architect who numbered Dunster Castle among his many medieval reconstruction essays. However, an example of a layout resembling Barry's style can be seen at St Catherine's Court near Bath. Here the outline of the Jacobean terraces was retained, but the plan was altered and extended, first by Colonel J.H. Strutt in the 1840s and then by his daughter, the Hon.Mrs Charlotte Olivia Drummond, who made a new bowling-green. A paved court with an octagonal pool was made below the north front of the house. To the west the principal terrace was fitted out with new Jacobean-style balustrades with alternate ball finials and flower urns, the central steps flanked by pillars with urn finials. A massive clipped yew hedge separated this from further enclosed gardens and a pool higher up the slope. A painting by Thomas Hunn shows the terrace above the flower border, with its steps and topiary in all its Victorian splendour. Despite the strongly formal framework, much of the planting was freely arranged, without any very precise order, with some of the trees and shrubs allowed to take their natural shape alongside the clipped cones of yew and more ornate topiary.[40]

Another very influential figure of the mid-nineteenth century was Joseph Paxton, who made his name working for the 6th Duke of Devonshire as head gardener and forester at Chatsworth between 1826 and 1858. He designed the Crystal Palace for the Great Exhibition of 1851, and the elaborate gardens at Sydenham where the great glasshouse was subsequently rebuilt. The Crystal Palace gardens were designed for the enjoyment of the general public, and made an enormous impact, but their scale was too grand for widespread imitation. However, one of Paxton's assistants, Edward Kemp, became interested in adapting his style and methods to suit smaller properties. Kemp recognised three styles, the 'old formal or geometrical style', the 'picturesque', and the 'mixed, middle or irregular style which Mr Loudon called the gardenesque'.[41] In fact, whereas Loudon had conceived of the 'gardenesque' as a particular planting convention, Kemp used the term in a much wider sense, to mean a free and eclectic combination of formal and informal elements. Kemp's 'gardenesque' became the prevailing fashion, in so far as there was one, throughout the mid to late nineteenth century.

The 1830s and 1840s had witnessed a huge increase in the range of successful imports of exotics. The new tender and half-hardy flowering plants - calceolarias, heliotropes, lobelias, pelargoniums, petunias, salvias, verbenas - offered a dazzling range of summer colours, and gardeners began to experiment with massing them in formal beds where the design could be changed every year. Donald Beaton of Shrubland Park, one of the pioneers of the bedding system, was also a well-known garden journalist, and his advice helped to popularise this new idea. By the 1860s the bedding season was being extended through the year by the use of tulips and hyacinths in spring, chrysanthemums in autumn, and even dwarf conifers and evergreens in winter. There was also something of a reaction against the garish colour schemes of the 1830s and 1840s. Between the 1860s and 1880s gardeners experimented with subtropical foliage plants offering more subtle ranges of colour - rex begonias from Assam, crotons from Malaya, dieffenbachias and philodendrons from Brazil and Colombia, pampas grasses and even bamboos. The style known as 'carpet bedding', using dwarf or creeping foliage plants which could be trained into a flat uniform surface, such as the iresines and alternatheras from South America and dwarf succulents such as echeverias and sempervivums, was also developed at this time. At first simple geometric designs were employed, later more elaborate zoomorphic and emblematic patterns.

Gardens in Somerset accommodated these new fashions to varying degrees, dependent upon the adaptability of the sites and the resources of their owners. Loudon visited Dunster in 1842, 25 years before Salvin began the reconstruction of the castle, and described the recent transformation of its garden terraces: *against the walls are some fine exotics, among which are a large lemon tree protected by glass during winter, a large pomegranate, large myrtles, passion flowers, wistarias, coronillas, and an immense hydrangea with both blue and pink flowers as a finale*. The oval bowling green on the summit of the hill commanded a panoramic view of the surrounding country, and the park beyond was a mix of verdant meadows, wooded slopes and thickets of fern, holly and thorn.[42] The impact of new plants here was obvious, but the strong natural topography inhibited any major restructuring of the garden.

The more subdued relief of Montacute offered greater possibilities, yet here there was another constraint, the strong architectural framework of the Elizabethan gardens. Indeed, several early garden historians regarded Montacute as a fine example of a surviving Elizabethan layout, without appreciating quite how much the detail had been changed in the nineteenth century.[43] When William Phelips in 1845 married Ellen Helyar, the wealthy heiress of Coker Court, her gardener, Mr Pridham, came with her to help redesign the Montacute grounds. The internal layout of the main north garden was completely remodelled, only the earthen terrace around the perimeter and the central prospect mound surviving from the Elizabethan plan. Tall yew hedges were established to shield the garden to north-west and north-east. Forty-four clipped Irish yews, with American hollies on the bank behind, were planted around the former plat, which was now converted to a sunken lawn divided into quarters by gravel paths. Reginald Blomfield visited Montacute in 1889 collecting material for his book on formal gardens, and made measured plans of the north and east gardens and sketches of the urns, balustrades and topiary. Further drawings by R. Shekleton Balfour made in 1894 had been assumed to date the removal of the Elizabethan prospect mound from the centre of the north garden and its replacement by the present balustraded lily pond and fountain, but Blomfield's sketches show that this had taken place some years earlier. The plans by Balfour and Inigo Triggs both show raised oval flower

beds within each of the four quarters of the main north garden, which have since been grassed over. Triggs also describes the east court as converted to lawns, with a fountain pond in its centre, and clipped yews within the line of the flower borders. This pond has gone, but traces of it can be seen in the lawn in dry summers.[44]

A new 'Upper Garden', now known as the 'Cedar Lawn', replaced the early nineteenth-century bowling green. The lawn is about 325ft long, its northern end dominated by two massive sweet chestnuts (*Castanea sativa*). A tall yew hedge was planted along its western side to screen it from the gardeners' and servants' path beyond. The eastern side has a gravel path now flanked with two rows of Irish yews. At the south-western end of the lawn a summer-house was erected, behind which are three tall specimens of the rough-barked Arizona cypress (*Cupressus arizonica*), first introduced to Britain in 1882.

Both entries to Montacute were altered during the nineteenth century. Some time after 1838 the north end of Bishopston was diverted westwards, away from the gate made by Edward Phelips sixty-odd years before. As a result of this change the curved late eighteenth-century western approach was realigned in 1851-2 as a straight avenue and a new entry made with iron gates, flanked by two square stone pillars crowned by the Phelips family crest of a basket of flames. Clipped Irish yews were planted along it against a background

Fig. 8.15
MONTACUTE HOUSE.
The balustraded Victorian lily pond in the main North Garden showing the summerhouse at the south west end of the lawn.

Fig. 8.16
The West Drive to
MONTACUTE HOUSE
as realigned in the early 1850s.

of beech, lime, Lebanon cedar and exotic evergreens, with an outer avenue of Wellingtonias. The alignment of the southern approach from the Borough was not altered, but its character was transformed by the planting of a variety of exotic trees, many of which were recent introductions to England: a pair of golden yews by the stables, a fine fern-leaved beech near the laundry court, and what is believed to be the largest Monterey cypress now existing in England. A fine avenue of giant Californian coast redwood (*Sequoia sempervirens*) along the drive was cut down in the Second World War, but new bushes have regenerated from their stumps.[45]

The Orchardleigh estate, following the bankruptcy of Sir Thomas Champneys in 1854, was bought by William Duckworth, who came from a long line of Lancashire lawyers. He immediately pulled down the low-lying Champneys mansion south of the church, and invited a Mr Page to design a new house to be built on top of the ridge north of the lake. Page's plans for "*a grand terrace before a mean*

and uncomfortable house" were rejected and Thomas Henry Wyatt's alternative design was adopted instead. However, Page was retained to work on the balustraded garden terraces outside the south front, where many eighteenth-century urns and statues salvaged from the old house were set up. Work progressed rapidly, and by August 1858, Duckworth's son's diary described the terraces as already "*brilliant with flowers*". West of the house the main pleasure-garden was laid out with a central broad grass walk, gravel paths winding between groves of specimen exotic trees and shrubs, and a rockery, fernery, pool and watercourse, terminating in a vista through a yew hedge into the park. A brick walled enclosure contemporary with the old house provided a site for a formal Italian-style garden of radiating beds with a rose pergola.[46]

At Clevedon Court a great parterre was laid out immediately behind the house in 1857. Early photographs show this as a sloping lawn cut by a D-shaped arrangement of gravel paths enclosing a small

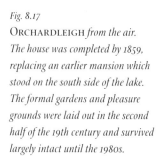

Fig. 8.17
ORCHARDLEIGH *from the air. The house was completed by 1859, replacing an earlier mansion which stood on the south side of the lake. The formal gardens and pleasure grounds were laid out in the second half of the 19th century and survived largely intact until the 1980s.*

fountain with a radiating pattern of flower beds, with further island beds and evergreen trees and shrubs in the outer sectors. The terraces above it were remodelled in the 1880s by Dame Agnes Elton, with hedges, lawns, potted plants and rather fussy square beds. The results were lavishly praised in 1899: "*a place that has received bold and effective treatment; radiant colour, applied with a bold character and yet with a palette not too garish, finds its counterpoise in the magnificent hill of foliage ... we may go far indeed before we find terraces so beautiful as these... Arches of roses perfume the air as we walk along, vases of fragrant flowers flank the pathway, and tall yews cast their shadows over the greenest of turf... Clevedon Court, in the general character of its gardens, is scarcely excelled in England*". Only a few years later, however, Gertrude Jekyll was criticising the "*poverty*" of the middle terrace with its "*succession of small square beds that break forward in each bay between the piers, and that seem to be planted without any general design or distinct intention*". She went on to condemn the scheme below the lowest wall as "*quite indefensible. The foot of one of the noblest ranges of terrace walls in England is too good to be given over to the most commonplace forms of bedding*".[47]

The gardens of Brympton d'Evercy were reconstructed by Lady Georgiana Fane, who ran the estate from 1857 up to her death in 1874. She rebuilt the terrace in front of the south facade of the house, made a lake on the site of the old parterre, and carried out extensive planting, including thousands of oaks.[48]

New formal gardens continued to be made throughout the second half of the nineteenth century, though not all of them can be firmly dated. One of the most striking examples is at Nynehead Court, where a terrace with two large urns south of the house overlooked an elaborate square parterre of bedding plants between clipped low evergreens, bounded on the outer three sides by box-edged beds in guilloche-pattern. West of the parterre is a lawn, with a smaller square enclosed garden by the south-west corner of the house. Another enclosed garden lies beyond the greenhouses, with a central path flanked by long herbaceous borders. A curved tunnel of clipped yew links the south-east corner of the house with the adjoining churchyard, while from the front of the parterre a grass avenue leads into the park.[49]

Orchard Portman had become increasingly neglected during the eighteenth century as the family spent more time in their London house in Portman Square and at their new country mansion at Bryanston in Dorset. The old house was finally demolished in 1843. However, within thirty years the family had acquired another Somerset home. Hestercombe House was purchased in 1872 as a secondary summer residence by Edward Berkeley, 1st Viscount Portman, who engaged James Baker Green of Blandford to rebuild it. Green's design produced a clumsy edifice of pink sandstone in debased Italian renaissance style, redeemed only by its setting. The garden front faces south, commanding superb views over the Vale of Taunton Deane towards the Blackdown Hills. Viscount Portman began remodelling the grounds, adding what is now the top terrace by the house, and planting it out with lawns, gravel paths and rectangular borders with elaborate patterns of bedding plants and a small single-jet fountain in the centre; he also increased the shrubberies and evergreen planting elsewhere in the grounds.[50]

Some garden works had been undertaken at Tyntesfield in 1863-6 when John Norton enlarged the house, and a Gothic seat in the grounds may date from that time. More extensive works were carried out in the 1880s by Dr W. Cave, including three formal terraces linked by broad flights of steps, plantations of Irish yews, Portugese laurels and hollies, and woodland walks extending out into the park. Photographs of the house at the turn of the century show the terrace below the south front with gravel paths, urns and a geometrical bedding scheme.[51]

Formal gardens covering nearly 4 acres were also created at Ashton Court in the late nineteenth century, incorporating some older features. Low walls on the south in the form of curved ornamental gables bounded an elaborate terraced flower garden, since converted to lawn. A walk and flight of steps led to a 'wilderness' with a basin fountain at its centre. There was a rose garden. A lime avenue led to a rustic summerhouse. A winter garden with tropical plants, water and a grotto was also made in about 1885.[52]

GARDEN DESIGN in the LATE 19TH CENTURY: WILLIAM ROBINSON and REGINALD BLOMFIELD

Eventually the increasing complexity of exotic bedding displays began to provoke a reaction in favour of a return to simpler ideas, and the last quarter of the century saw a revival of interest in historical authenticity in formal gardens and a renewed popularity of the sort of flowers grown before the eighteenth century.

During the final decade of the nineteenth century opinions on garden design once more became polarised between two very different schools of thought, one favouring a 'natural' style, the other a more formal architectural approach. The chief protagonist of the informal school was William Robinson, who had worked with native English herbaceous plants at the London Botanic Garden and had become a great lover of the English countryside and of the cottage garden. He was a man of extreme views, vigorously expressed. He felt that the garden should appear part of the natural scene, embellished by selection. He accepted that the effects of nature could be assisted by the introduction of some hardy exotics such as the new rhododendrons and magnolias then coming in from China, but he strongly resisted the straightjacket of Victorian formal planting. Indeed, he condemned all forms of geometric bedding as "*pastry-work gardening*" and formal terraces as "*railway-embankment gardening*", also scorning all topiary and architectural embellishments. Robinson was perhaps more successful as a garden writer than as a practitioner, though his own garden at Gravetye in Sussex and his design for Shrubland Park were notable. His style was well-suited to the smaller garden, and had the advantage that, at a time of sharply-rising labour costs, it could be achieved without employing too many gardeners. His ideas gained widespread support in the home counties, where the new middle classes were developing large suburban gardens.[53]

During the 1890s, however, the formal garden began to make a significant comeback. In 1892 Reginald Blomfield published a counterblast to Robinson entitled *THE FORMAL GARDEN IN ENGLAND*, in which he argued that garden design should be primarily an architectural skill, with the horticulturalist simply filling in the detail. Blomfield's grasp of garden history, on which he based his case, was in some ways weak, but the impact of his book in reviving interest in formalism was enormous, and he gained many followers. Blomfield's illustrator was F. Inigo Thomas, whose own designs include one notable garden in north Somerset.

INIGO THOMAS and BARROW COURT

In 1880 the Barrow Gurney estate was acquired by Henry Martin Gibbs, son of William Gibbs of Tyntesfield, and he immediately began a major reconstruction programme, rebuilding the medieval church and replacing many of the dilapidated cottages in the village with new estate housing. The Jacobean house, which had been restored and extended only five years before Gibbs acquired it, lay on the edge of an eighteenth-century park. He decided to develop new formal gardens around it, engaging the 26-year-old Inigo Thomas for the project in 1892. Thomas had begun designing country house gardens in his youth and enjoyed rapid success through his family connections. He supported Blomfield in his advocacy of the architectural approach to garden design, modelling his plans upon the enclosed gardens of the Elizabethan period, and perhaps more upon the grander gardens of the Restoration; but he added his own very distinctive personal stamp. His best-known and best-preserved garden, Athelhampton in Dorset, was begun the year before his first invitation to Barrow Gurney.

BARROW COURT.
right: Fig. 8.18
The Exedra Screen and the
Daughters of the Year.
below right: Fig. 8.19
The small eastern lawn, view to the
Venetian Summerhouse; the ornate apse
on the right contains a large winged
statue.

At Barrow Court he developed a spectacular series of compartmented formal gardens on different levels occupying nearly 15 acres on the north side of the house. At the top a broad terrace leads westwards from the house towards a distant view beyond an avenue of trees. Steps descend from this level to a parterre with a central formal goldfish pond flanked by yews, originally clipped to resemble battlemented walls with doors and windows. On either side of the pond the parterre is grassed with formal squares of L-shaped beds, originally planted with a mixture of dwarf conifers and annuals with a bay tree in the middle of each bed, but now given over to herbs and roses. Urns on pillars provide focal points. At either end of this parterre were two small walled and paved courts containing sheltered seats, ornamented at each corner with stone obelisks. From the western court steps led down to an extensive rectangular lawn, divided from the park on the north side by a long balustraded wall punctuated by square pillars with ball finials. The lawn was terminated at its western end by a striking semicircular exedra screen with a central gate, giving views out over the park and along the Failand ridge towards Tyntesfield. The heavy wrought-iron gates were carried on gigantic high piers, crowned by baroque urns and flanked by lions carved by the sculptor Alfred Drury. The twelve stone pillars carrying the wrought-iron screen were crowned with allegorical sculptures also by Drury representing the Daughters of the Year - January, represented by a young girl, at the north end, December, represented by an aged matriarch at the south, each figure sculpted with flowers appropriate to the month. At the east end of the lawn the axis runs through a small shrubbery or arboretum of exotics, which was originally planted formally with avenues of limes alternating with holly clipped into spheres. The arboretum leads to a smaller, more intimate walled rectangular lawn with a hipped-roofed open-fronted summerhouse at the upper end, its forecourt fronted by concave balustrades and giving a view down to a Venetian gazebo at the park end. In the centre of its high east wall, closing the vista at the end of the arboretum walk, is an ornate apse flanked with Corinthian pillars and urn finials containing a large aluminium statue of a winged figure, presumably Mercury.[54]

The success of Inigo Thomas's design depends upon subtle changes of level, a careful balance of colours and textures between high evergreen hedges, open lawns and flowering plants, the setting of formal beds within a framework of walls and hedges, and the well-judged use of pavilions, obelisks, statues and other architectural and sculptural details to provide focal points in vistas. His style was at its most popular in the 1890s, but it was a short-lived fashion. His last commissions were for two sites in west Dorset in 1910, and he undertook no further garden designs for the remaining forty years of his life.

ROCK GARDENS

During the nineteenth century more and more English tourists were drawn to the Alps, combining mountain-climbing with plant collecting, and there was a vogue for alpine gardens and rockeries. Orchardleigh and Ashton Court both had fine rock gardens. The 1880s also saw the first appearance of the garden gnome, invented by Sir Charles Isham for the rockery of Lamport Hall in Northamptonshire, though mercifully it was some time before they became generally popular.[55]

As natural stone for rockeries became increasingly expensive, there were experiments with artificial materials. In the 1840s James Pulham, son of one of the pioneers of Portland cement manufacture, succeeded in producing a very convincing type of imitation stone, which was widely used throughout the later nineteenth century and on into the 1920s. Two adjoining late examples of Pulhamite rockwork gardens were constructed in the woods on the Somerset side of the Avon Gorge. In 1896 the tobacco baron Melville Wills built a new house at Bracken Hill, his property extending northwards across the road where he added an estate office, a curious timbered and thatched cottage resembling a Swiss chalet (now known as Rayne Thatch). The Pulham firm probably began landscaping the steep north-facing slope below the office in about 1907, including a Pulhamite pumphouse in gothic style housing a pump which circulating water through a series of five linked pools and cascades, all overhung with rockwork arches and grottoes. The garden was illuminated at night by coloured glass bulbs suspended from the trees. Work was resumed after the Great War in the two acres of grounds around Bracken Hill House itself, using alternate layers of Pulhamite and natural limestone from Cheddar Gorge built into archways, with two further pools and alpine flower-beds. Much of this work survives today.[56]

Landscape Parks
of the Mid-19th Century

Although the focus of interest had swung towards smaller, more intimate gardens, numerous parks still remained. Christopher Greenwood's county map of 1822 shows about 150 parks in Somerset. Some of these still functioned as deer parks, and a few had continued this use unbroken since the Middle Ages. Although their overall numbers had declined, as late as 1892 Joseph Whitaker was still able to list 11 deer parks in Somerset, ranging from the 1000 acres of Ashton Court with 400 fallow and 25 red deer down to the 13 acres of Combe Sydenham and 8.5 acres of Hatch Beauchamp, with 17 and 40 fallow deer respectively.[57] Not all the deer parks were ancient. Even in the late nineteenth century a few new examples were still being created. On Exmoor some time after 1820 John Knight enclosed a new deer park north of Simonsbath within a massive stone wall, originally up to nine feet high in places; but this still could not confine the fallow deer he installed there, and they caused so much damage to the crops of neighbouring farmers that they were all killed off twenty years later. A ruined round stone tower near Prayway Head may have been built as a shooting-box.[58] On the Quantocks Alfoxton Park had been created around an older house before 1839 for Langley St Albyn, containing 80 fallow deer by 1892. Deer parks still covered over 2,570 acres of the county in that year, feeding over 2,200 fallow deer.[59]

Deer coursing, whereby deer were released from a pen and chased along a defined course to a finishing point a mile or so away by two greyhounds racing against each other had been introduced to England in the sixteenth century, and remained a popular pastime. A

number of parks were modified to accommodate such courses, by the provision of deer pens, dog kennels, course boundaries and viewing stands for spectators. At Mells Park in the nineteenth century arrangements were made for the deer to be chased across the park in a south-westerly direction. However, deer coursing had fallen out of repute by the end of the century, and in 1905 Greswell was describing it as "*hardly worth the name of sport*".[60]

Nettlecombe Park was estimated at 97 acres by Whitaker, and it then contained 180 fallow deer; but like many others, it had for some time served an important ornamental function also. In 1792 John Veitch had made a ha-ha between the deer park and the meadows and a new carriage road to the front of the house, levelled up disturbed ground and sown it with grass seed, and planted laburnums in the grove by the stables.[61] Between August 29th and September 5th 1842 John Claudius Loudon, his wife and daughter, stayed with Sir John Trevelyan at Nettlecombe Court. He was enchanted with the romantic setting of the court, and with the immense elms nearby: "*We were astonished and delighted with the view from the windows of the house, looking up the steep sides of the rounded hills that rose on every side, and which were mostly crowned with old oak woods ... The great novelty and charm of Nettlecombe are, that, the house being situated in a bottom, the scenery on every side is looked up to, instead of being looked over; the effect of which, united with the immense mass of wood, is romantic in a very high degree. Some of the valleys are so deep, that the sun does not shine into them, for between two and three months every winter. In consequence of the bold undulations and deep valleys, the shadows produced by the varying positions of the sun are continually changing... so as to form a perpetual variety.*" The drives through the estate were "*varied and beautiful, and exhibit fine combinations of pasture and woodland, comfortable cottages and most substantial farmhouses*".[62]

At Hinton St George a new deer enclosure had been made by 1802, and further extensive ornamental planting continued between 1812 and 1817, including the 'American clumps' near the house and the improvement of drives. Here, however, expansion had reached its limits, and by 1839 the park had been reduced to 184 acres of ornamental grounds, less than a quarter of its former size, the remainder being broken up into farm holdings.[63] The grounds of Maunsel House near North Petherton were extended by the creation of a new park north of the house for Sir John Slade between 1823 and 1838, and in 1839 James Veitch was supplying oaks, chestnuts, filberts, walnuts, maples, beeches, willows, hornbeams, limes, conifers, acacias and mountain ash for planting along the new north drive, around the earlier canal, and east of the house.[64]

Plantings of both native and exotic trees enriched the appearance of several older parks during the 1860s. Orchardleigh, which had become choked with overgrown timber, was partly cleared and then replanted with beeches, hornbeams, oaks, sycamores and horse chestnuts, with a few grey poplars to provide a lighter summer foliage, creating a succession of vistas across open spaces between dense woods. The lake was dredged, its sluicegates repaired, and the trees on the dam which were causing it to leak were cut down. New drives were made across the park, though an older avenue over the top of the hill in the southern part of the park was retained.[65] The Ashton Court estate in Long Ashton was inherited by Sir Greville Smyth, who

BRACKEN HILL.
top: Fig. 8.20
A Pulhamite arch.
above: Fig. 8.21
A rock pool surrounded by
Pulhamite beside the house.

Fig. 8.22
ALFOXTON PARK.
Feeding of the deer from the park c.1890.

planted new avenues of sequoias and cedars and many other single specimin conifers in the park. At Newton St Loe cedars, sequoias, monkey puzzle trees and other conifers were supplied by local nurserymen, Maule & Son and Joseph Dublin. Native woodland in the grounds of Cleeve Court and Clevedon Court were similarly interplanted with Monterey pine, Arizona cypress and other exotic tress and shrubs. This process continued into the present century, with plantations of larch, Japanese larch and Douglas fir in the park at Halswell between 1906 and 1910.[66]

New country landowners also continued to demand a landscaped park to enhance the setting of their house. John Hubert Hunt had an extravagant gothick castle built at Compton Pauncefoot between 1821 and 1830, surrounded by extensive grounds with woodland plantations, a lake held back by a dam which also carried the entry drive, a succession of cascades, and an enormous mass of artificial rockwork.[67] The park of Tyntesfield in Wraxall, made in the 1840s for William Gibbs, occupied some 320 undulating acres on the south face of the Failand ridge, with scattered trees and clumps backed by more extensive woodland covering 150 acres on the steeper slopes above. There was also a small lake.[68] Only the presence from the outset of new exotic trees within the plantations distinguishes these new parks from their Georgian models.

On a smaller scale, the manor house at Dinder had been rebuilt by William Somerville shortly before his death in 1803, and his widow, who lived on in the house for another 27 years, made extensive ornamental plantations in the grounds and converted the stream to a fine stretch of water spanned by a handsome bridge carrying the drive from the turnpike road, making effective use of the church and village as a picturesque backdrop.[69] John Paget had a boating lake made and stocked with brown trout at Merehead in Norwood in East Cranmore in 1821, surrounded by a woodland garden with rock steps, seats and a boathouse. Paget had hundreds of daffodils and ornamental trees planted to beautify the surrounds, and his son continued tree planting through the 1840s and 1850s, mainly beeches, oaks, ashes, elms and chestnuts, with some walnut. The lake and much of the woodland has since been destroyed by stone quarrying.[70] Knowle Hall at Bawdrip was surrounded by a new park and plantations by the early 1840s, while Bridge Park at South Petherton was laid out around a new house built in 1859. At Stockland Bristol the vicar, Henry Daniel, resigned the living in 1884, and in order to stay on in his home, which had been extensively rebuilt only twenty years earlier, he provided a new vicarage house. He renamed the old vicarage 'Stockland Manor', and then created a small park out of the former glebe land south of the house.[71]

Follies and Park Ornaments of the Later 19th Century

Relatively few isolated follies or park ornaments were built after the 1820s. One exception is the column in the park at Ammerdown. In 1849, at the age of 70, Col.John Twyford Jolliffe conceived the idea of building a memorial to his father, Thomas Samuel Jolliffe, who had died 25 years earlier. He called back Joseph Jopling, who had earlier prepared plans for the house and gardens, to design a suitable column. Jopling was a civil engineer as well as an architect, and he had a particular interest in the application of mathematical theory to design. In accordance with his ideas, both the column and its base display remarkable curvatures. The base was formerly ornamented with Coade stone statues and had inscriptions in Latin, French and English taken from Thomas Jolliffe's obituary, while the top consisted of an iron-framed glazed dome which gave it the appearance of a lighthouse. Col. Jolliffe died after a fall from his horse in 1854 and did not see the column completed, but it was finished in the following year by his brother who succeeded to the estate.[72] A curiously spindly Italianate tower with a pyramidal cap and two external iron balconies was built on a hill a mile north of Cranmore Hall for John Moore Paget to the design of Thomas Wyatt. The progress of building is well documented in Paget's diaries from July 1863 through to December 1865.[73] At Knowle Hall a large sham castle was built for Benjamin Greenhill in 1870, consisting of two circular towers, only one of which was finished, linked by a battlemented curtain wall two storeys high, with footings of two more towers surrounding an oval bailey which was laid out as a croquet lawn.[74]

Road Diversions and Settlement Clearances

The creation of new parks and the enlargement of old ones continued to disrupt the pattern of communications as it had done in earlier centuries. At Fairfield Sir John Acland extended the park southwards between 1806 and 1822, diverting the old road to Stringston. In the parish of Elworthy the building of Willett House in about 1816 was followed by amalgamation of surrounding closes to make a new park of 40 acres, and in 1820 the old road from Plash to Willett was closed. At East Cranmore an estate map of 1814 shows a lane called Mead Lane, and another crossing it from north to south, passing between a series of closes south and east of the hall, all of which have been absorbed into the park. The estate map made for Ralph Allen in the eighteenth century shows the road from Claverton Down descending to the Avon valley just south of Claverton Church. George Vivian diverted this road further south into a new course between stone pillars in the 1830s to gain more privacy for his new mansion.[75]

Even in the nineteenth century emparkment could still occasionally cause the complete extinction of a village. Admiral Alexander Hood, 1st Viscount Bridport, began the removal of the decayed settlement of Cricket St Thomas in the 1830s, closing off roads and footpaths till only a single house remained, and expanding the park until it occupied virtually the entire parish.[76] Similarly at West Quantoxhead the park of St Audries was expanded on a piecemeal basis, resulting in the progressive destruction of the village. The tenants were gradually rehoused in new estate cottages at Staple. The old coast road was initially diverted to the north in 1815 in order to run further away from the house. Then in 1828 it was entirely superseded by a new route, adopted by the Minehead Turnpike Trust, which was cut into the steep hill east of the house, turning south to pass between church and rectory before heading westwards round the head of the combe to link up with the Staple - Watchet road. Two of the ten houses in West Quantoxhead village shown on the 1761 map had been removed by 1835. The old road running north-westwards from the manor-house was closed in 1839, so that the village street then led only to the house. By 1840 only five houses were left, and another had gone by 1853. During the 1850s the southern boundary of the ornamental grounds was pushed up to the line of the new turnpike road, taking in part of the new road made to the church in 1770. The church was itself taken down in 1854, to be replaced two years later by a new church built a short distance away on the edge of the park. Four new entrance lodges were built during the 1850s, and the whole park surrounded by ornamental iron fencing. The turnpike road was spanned by a bridge, which survived until the late 1940s, linking the ornamental grounds with the deer park. The latter was itself a nineteenth-century creation, formed from a nucleus of woodland east of the church. By 1817 it had incorporated the site of the medieval rabbit warren to the north, and by 1835 it amounted to 66 acres. Subsequently it was extended southwards over Stowborrow Hill to an eventual area of 350 acres. In 1911 it contained 120 fallow and 25 red deer.[77]

Fig. 8.23
Ammerdown Column.

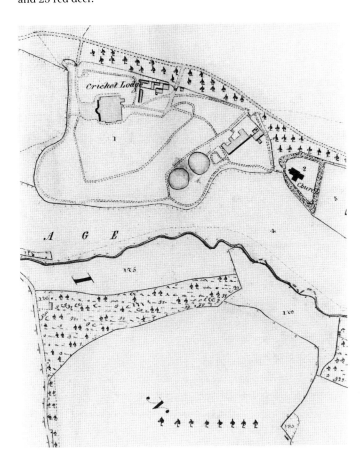

Fig. 8.24
Cricket St Thomas *c. 1831.*
The church, now isolated within the park, is all that remains of the ancient village.

PARK GATE LODGES

Park entrance lodges played an important role in proclaiming the importance of the grander residence that lay within, while discouraging access to those who had no business there; yet they have only recently attracted the attention they they deserve.[78] Some existing park lodges date back to the eighteenth century. The Lower Lodge of Prior Park in Bath, a three-storey Palladian house with rusticated quoins and Venetian and bull's-eye windows, was designed by John Wood. Richard Jenkins's gothick house of Chewton Mendip

Fig. 8.25
A vignette from a map of
ORCHARDLEIGH *of 1818-19*
illustrating the lodge and towers
at the entrance to the park.

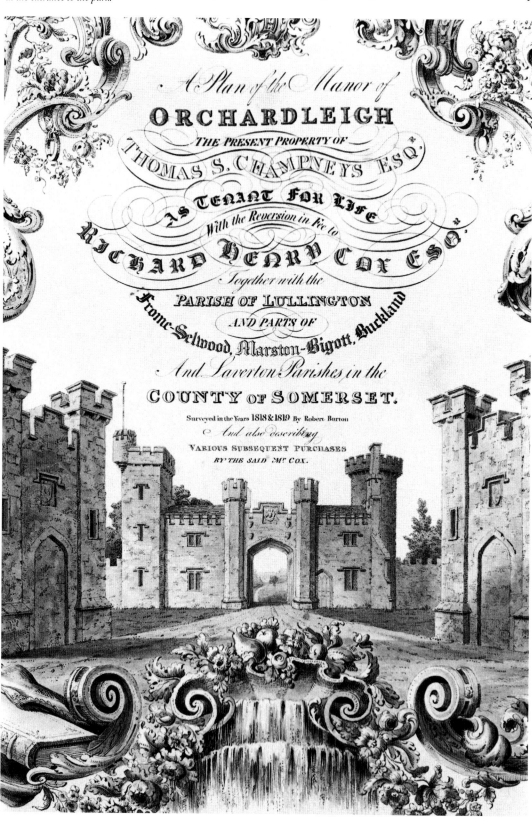

Priory has been outlived by the late Georgian lodge, built in the same style, with a tree-trunk verandah. The majority, however, belong to the nineteenth century.

New lodges were a feature both of newly-created parks and of older ones which had been redesigned or extended. Their architectural style may or may not reflect that of the main house. Lodges of the early nineteenth century tended to imitate medieval castle gatehouses, with varying degrees of seriousness. In 1802 Henry Wood designed the Lower Lodge on the Bristol side of Ashton Court. Farleigh House at Farleigh Hungerford acquired a large castellated gatehouse some time between 1806 and 1813. The lodge of Midford Castle, built in 1810, is a playful gothick fantasy, a central pointed carriage arch with blind quatrefoils and battlements, flanked by battlemented octagonal turrets. By contrast, while the Combe Lodge of Ashton Court, built in the same year, also employs battlements and octagonal turrets on either side of a central carriage arch, it is a much more substantial structure in correct gothic style. A few years later, in about 1816, Sir Thomas Champneys had the Lullington gate built at Orchardleigh Park. This is a remarkable design, the park boundary being interrupted by two modest battlemented towers opening into a walled grassed courtyard, beyond which is the lodge itself, a battlemented two-storey range with machicolated octagonal stair-turrets flanking the central carriage arch, with taller square and round towers on either flank. This creates the momentary illusion that the lodge, only seen when the visitor has passed through the outer towers into the courtyard, must be the house, followed then by the anticipation that there must surely be yet greater glories beyond. Tudor-style lodges were added further south in the later 1820s.

Thatched gate lodges in cottage ornée style also enjoyed a brief vogue in the early nineteenth century, probably owing much to the inspiration of Nash and Repton's Blaise Castle Hamlet, north of Bristol. Lodges at Halswell and at Combe Hay follow this pattern. The thatched roof of the lodge at Halswell is projected forward over rustic poles to form a verandah with a floor of patterned pebblework.

Classical forms, particularly Greek Revival, then became more popular. The gate to Leigh Court on the Bristol-Portishead road, dating from the second decade of the nineteenth century, rises high above the single-storey flanking lodges, with giant Ionic columns. Although Cothelstone House, designed by Charles Harcourt Masters in 1818, has gone, its entrance lodge survives, square in plan with apsidal bays to each side and a bowed classical pediment over the door. Ammerdown Park had a pair of Greek-style lodges built probably in the 1830s, with a pediment supported by Ionic columns. The east and south lodges at Fairfield were rebuilt in the later 1830s, and three new entries to Cricket St Thomas park, the London, Grosvenor and West Port lodges, were built in the same period.

The Italianate style became particularly popular in Bath and the surrounding area, due mainly to the influence of Henry Edmund Goodridge, who had himself toured Italy in 1829. The lodge of Montebello, Goodridge's own villa on Bathwick Hill, provided the prototype for others nearby, including that of Bathwick Hill House. Ashley Lodge in Widcombe, Henley Lodge on the Weston Road, the lodges of Kelston Park, and the lodge to Merfield House at Rode follow in this tradition.

High Victorian lodges continued to vary in style, though gothic forms were generally favoured. In 1857 Henry Clutton designed the gatehouse for Quantock Lodge on the Aisholt road at Over Stowey to resemble a great embattled gatehouse with a wide round arch. In 1877 John Foster and Joseph Wood designed a new castellated main entrance for Ashton Court facing Leigh Woods, with an oriel window and the Smyth arms over the carriageway, flanked by two grand machicolated towers. The gates of Tyntesfield Park at Wraxall were worked by windlasses inside the lodges, and there were further lodges within the park for domestic servants.[79]

ORCHARDS and HOPYARDS

From the Board of Agriculture reports it can be estimated that in 1877 Somerset still contained some 21,000 acres of apple orchards, mostly cider varieties. The nineteenth century saw the development of many new strains of fruit, including eating and cooking apples. Successful local varieties included the 'Beauty of Bath' apple, raised at Bailbrook, north-east of Bath, and first marketed by Cooling of Bath in 1864. The Merchant apple was grown around Ilminster.[80]

As farming and horticulture became increasingly scientific, the somewhat hit-or-miss techniques of traditional farm cider production began to cause concern, and in 1893 experiments were commenced by Neville Grenville of Butleigh Court, supported by the Bath and West Agricultural Society and by the Board of Agriculture. This work led directly to the establishment of the National Fruit and Cider Institute in 1903, with its Research Station at Long Ashton.[81]

Hop cultivation was now in terminal decline locally, and the abandonment of the 20-acre hop garden at Orchard Portman in about 1845 marked the end of any serious attempt to grow this crop in Somerset.[82]

KITCHEN GARDENS

The nineteenth century was the heyday of the great walled kitchen gardens.[83] Some vegetables and fruits introduced earlier, like potato, celery, marrow and tomato, had not found immediate popularity, and only now became widely cultivated. The Brussels sprout was introduced into Britain for the first time in the early nineteenth century. Celeriac was also a newcomer to the kitchen garden.

At Montacute the two walled kitchen gardens beyond the laundry range south of the house were highly productive in the nineteenth century. The nearer garden was largely given over to green vegetables, potatoes and asparagus, with strawberry beds and raspberry canes. Along its west wall were beds of onions and shallots and a herb border with mint, thyme, sage, rosemary, fennel and garlic. Inside the east wall was a herbaceous border with roses. Nectarines, plums, pears and apples were grown in espalier fashion around the walls. Against the south-facing laundry wall there was a fig tree near the fruit house. The further garden included the potting shed, tool shed and store with vineries, peach houses, cucumber and melon frames, a soft fruits cage, bee skeps, further vegetable plots and strawberry beds, plum, nectarine and peach trees, rose borders and a path lined with box hedging and pink carnations.[84]

John Claudius Loudon was a great admirer of efficiently-managed kitchen gardens, and he commended those at Nettlecombe Court, which he visited in 1842: "*There is an admirable kitchen garden here, with the walls covered with the very best kinds of peaches, nectarines and pears, all in fine order, while the fig ripens as a standard. We observed a very excellent kind of cabbage, which we were informed by the gardener, Mr Elworthy, was raised between the Paignton and Cornish cabbages, and which is called the Nettlecombe cabbage.*" He goes on to mention the planting of capers in a sheltered site in an old quarry near the house, and lemon trees growing against the garden walls.[85]

Further new walled kitchen gardens were created in the early nineteenth century at Newton Surmaville and in the later nineteenth century at Ashton Court, Tyntesfield and Barrow Court. The kitchen gardens of Hinton St George contained over a dozen different varieties of grape in 1895, all healthy and producing large crops, for which the head gardener had won many prizes.[86]

GREENHOUSES and CONSERVATORIES

Orangeries had been used for sheltering citrus trees through the winter for a couple of hundred years. As further exotic fruits were introduced, their cultivation under glass now reached its highest levels of achievement. In 1837 the nurserymen Dodds of Salisbury supplied fifteen pineapple plants in three different varieties to the gardens of Nynehead Court at 5 shillings each.[87]

Fig. 8.26
The park lodge at
BARROW GURNEY.

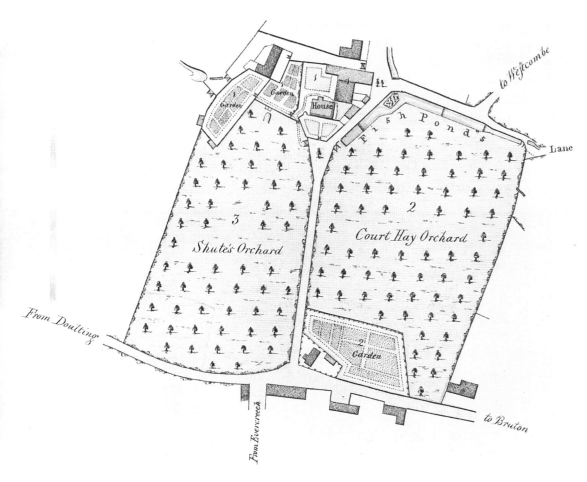

Fig. 8.27
STRATTON HOUSE, EVERCREECH.
A map of 1821 showing its kitchen gardens and orchards.

Fig. 8.28
WOODLANDS, HOLFORD, *c.1890.*
A typical Victorian country house with greenhouse.

conservatory at Dunster Castle dates from the 1870s. Thomas Henry Wyatt's conservatory at Orchardleigh, built in the later 1850s, is now roofless, but the interior has been converted into a rose arbour.[88]

Except where a wish to conform with the style of the house dictated it, relatively few orangeries or conservatories were built of stone after the middle of the century. The technological breakthrough of coke smelting in the 1760s had permitted the moulding of more complex patterns in iron, and so iron-framed glasshouses became available in a wide variety of attractive ornamental patterns. Cast-iron conservatories gave extra light to plants, even if they were more expensive and more subject to condensation and loss of heat. Cast-iron pipes conveying hot water or steam could now provide a more efficient means of winter heating than under-floor and wall flues conveying warm air, so heat loss through the glass became less of a drawback. The firm of Henry Ormison of Chelsea supplied a new iron conservatory for East Cranmore Hall in 1868, which still survives, though in much altered form. A new conservatory supplied to Newton St Loe by the ironfounders Masters, Stothert & Pitt of Bath in 1877 cost £24 3s 8d. At about the same time a new conservatory was added beyond the east range of Newton Surmaville by George Harbin. Panes were small at first because crown- or plate-glass was taxed by size. Sheet glass was introduced in 1833, though it proved less suitable for glasshouse use because its very transparency rendered plants more vulnerable to scorching in the summer sun. The abolition of the tax on glass in 1845 reduced the price and brought the conservatory and greenhouse within reach of the middle-class gardener, and they soon became a common feature of detached suburban villas.[89]

More functional wooden-framed greenhouses were widely used as an adjunct to both the flower garden and vegetable garden for raising new plants from seed and potting on. An early greenhouse survives at Linden in Weston near Bath, while there are extensive late Victorian kitchen garden glasshouses at Ashton Court, Ammerdown and Nynehead Court.

Some estates had a considerable range of glasshouse facilities. William Gibbs added to the west end of the house at Tyntesfield a conservatory with gothick ironwork and a large onion-shaped dome (since demolished), while the extensive kitchen gardens south of the house included a handsome stone-built orangery, spacious greenhouses and residences for the gardeners. In addition to the stone conservatory at Dillington, an inventory made in 1882 on the death of

Humphry Repton had become interested in the application of a variety of architectural styles to glasshouses. Partly through his influence, the garden conservatory became increasingly popular through the early nineteenth century, either linked directly with the house or standing near it. Its purpose was no longer merely winter storage, but the permanent cultivation of tender and exotic plants to provide a year-round attraction.

Regency and early Victorian conservatories were normally built around a solid architectural framework in some sort of traditional style. An early nineteenth-century example at Cricket St Thomas has Doric pilasters between the glazing. At Dillington a Tudor-style stone conservatory with a glass ridge roof was added to the south end of the house in 1831 by James Pennethorne, adopted son of Repton's partner John Nash and pupil of Pugin. At Ven House near Milborne Port Decimus Burton (who was later to design the great Palm House and Temperate House at Kew Gardens) added a seven-bay classical conservatory as a western extension to the south front of the house in 1836. A smaller detached stone orangery of seven bays with a low hipped roof and obelisks along the eaves line, designed to blend in with the Elizabethan detail of the garden walls, was added to the west end of the terrace walk north of Montacute House in 1848. At East Cranmore Hall John Moore Paget had a Jacobean-style arcaded orangery with a strapwork parapet built in the early 1860s, immediately after the completion of the house. A delightful Strawberry Hill gothick conservatory, of three bays with crocketed pinnacles, buttresses and cusped arched lights was added to the south end of Lympsham Manor in 1867. Anthony Salvin's three-bay

the then owner, Vaughan Hanning Vaughan-Lee, lists the potting house, fruit house and four hothouses in the walled garden. A description of Hinton St George in 1895 mentions a conservatory with a fernery at either end containing ornamental ponds and fountains, hothouses providing roses and cucumbers all year round, and a tomato house. At Marston Bigot a conservatory was built on the site of the old laundry in 1872, and when the estate was sold in 1905 the walled garden contained a long lean-to peach house with store-room and shed, three extensive ranges of hot frames, four double-space hot-houses, a double-span palm house, a lean-to double vinery and a lean-to hot-house, as well as a tile-roofed stone potting shed and store.[90]

Private Gardens in Towns and Suburbs

The confined spaces of town gardens lent themselves less readily to experimentation with radical new designs, but even so there is some evidence that traditional formal layouts were finally falling out of favour. At No.4 the Circus in Bath the formal Georgian garden survived until the 1830s, when it was buried beneath a spread of clay excavated from the basement extension, allowing the creation of a completely new asymmetrical layout with a central lawn and irregular plantings of trees and shrubs.[91] The shelter provided by small enclosed gardens permitted the cultivation of tender plants which sometimes surprised visitors from further north. Sir John Thomas Stanley, later 1st Baron Stanley of Alderley, had been much impressed with the Mediterranean myrtles which had once covered the front of the Old Manor House at the west end of Axbridge. When he revisited Somerset in 1804, he was disappointed to find that they had been cut down, though a few branches still grew from the old stumps. In their place, however, there grew a profusion of grapes and a specimen of *Buddleia globosa*, a South American shrub with clusters of round yellow flowers which he had regarded as a hothouse plant only.[92]

As the town centres of Bristol and Bath became increasingly busy and overcrowded, so the prosperous middle classes began to look for quieter, more secluded accommodation. Large detached villas in their own grounds became a feature of the outer suburbs and the nearby countryside of north Somerset. A sort of informal picturesque layout involving sinuous walks between shrubberies and irregular lawns became popular. Evergreen shrubs like privet and yew were particularly valued for the seclusion and privacy they afforded. The rolling hills around Bath provided special challenges and opportunities, with formal elements often reasserting themselves on the flatter ground near the house, combined with informal picturesque details on the steeper slopes beyond. By the time that Granville published his description of Bath in 1841, detached villas with large gardens had spread widely over the hills overlooking the city.[93]

Classical villas began to appear up the slopes of Bathwick Hill in the 1810s. A particularly interesting group was developed there in the 1820s and 1830s. Their architect, Henry Edmund Goodridge, as we have seen, was a protégé of William Beckford, and he adopted an irregular Italianate style for the houses, giving them towers, loggias

and balconies. Smallcombe Grove, now called Oakwood, was built for the landscape painter Benjamin Barker, known as the 'English Poussin'. On the west side of the house there was a formal flower garden. Terraces to the south, with a walk along a shrub border, gave striking views across a steeply-sloping lawn to a picturesque series of pools and cascades spanned by a balustraded stone bridge, with woodland forming a backdrop to the scene. Sadly the cedars which once overhung the lawn were wrecked in the storm of 1990. Goodridge's own villa of Montebello (now Bathwick Grange), built in 1828, also still has some remains of the original paths, steps and pond.

A contrast in style was provided by another Bathwick villa, Vellore, later used as a college, nurses' home and finally the Bath Spa Hotel. This was built for a retired Indian army general, Augustus Andrews, in 1836. He spent twenty years developing an elaborate walled garden on six acres of sloping ground with 'consummable taste and judgement'. Packed into the enclosed space were terraces and parterre flower beds, long flights of balustraded steps, a Doric temple, a formal pond, a tufa grotto, shrubberies with serpentine paths, another pool, a rustic summerhouse and statues. A conservatory, now gone, is said to have included 2000 exotic plants. The sale catalogue of 1858 claims that the gardens included nearly 200 varieties of roses, and there were many other fine trees and shrubs.

Cranwells, built for Sir Jerom Murch in the north-western suburb of New Weston in about 1850, had more extensive grounds amounting to 35 acres, sufficient to contain deer as well as a large collection of conifers; but this property was soon fragmented and infilled with smaller houses.

Slightly later in date, Crowe Hall, on the eastern side of Bath, occupies a spectacular site above Widcombe looking across towards Prior Park. Here the owner Henry Tugwell and his head gardener

Fig. 8.29
The Conservatory at DILLINGTON HOUSE *added by James Pennethorne in 1831.*

Fig. 8.30
An 1846 plan of houses and gardens on the north side of EAST STREET, CREWKERNE, *showing the survival of a formal plan in a town garden.*

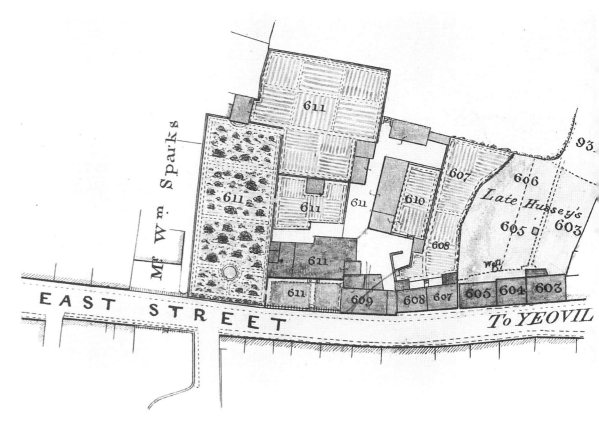

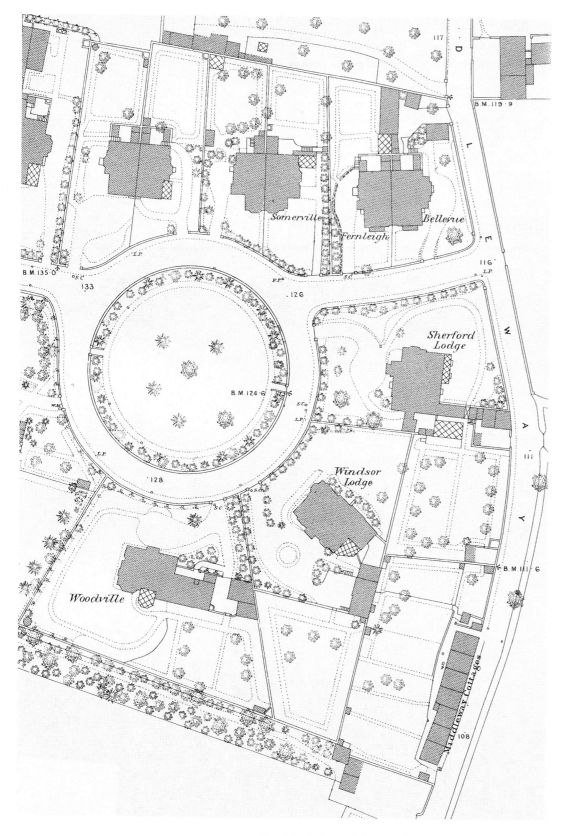

Alfred Wills, another member of the tobacco dynasty, purchased the spectacularly-sited house of Burwalls, immediately above the suspension bridge, there developing a terraced garden within more extensive grounds which incorporated the remains of the prehistoric hill-fort from which the site was named. The house, built seventeen years earlier, was itself set within ancient lime and oak woodland which had previously been part of the Ashton Court estate, and the giant Wellingtonia east of the house dates from Sir Greville Smyth's planting in the 1850s. A cave in the gorge below was lit up for tea parties and evening entertainments. The view over the bridge with the docks and tobacco bond warehouses beyond may not have suited a Georgian aristocrat, but it was entirely in keeping with the late Victorian admiration of trade and technological achievement.[95]

Seaside resorts also attracted many new settlers. Clevedon developed rapidly after the 1840s, with many detached Italianate, gothic and Jacobean-style villas. The grounds of Clevedon Hall (recently St Brandon's School), built for Conrad Finzel, a German-born Bristol sugar merchant, contained formal flower beds, evergreen shrubberies, statues, a fountain and a fishpond with three tiny islands. The vicarage garden at The Knoll is another good example of late Victorian style. At Weston-super-Mare, which enjoyed more lasting success as a popular resort, pressure upon space soon caused the subdivision of the large gardens of many of the early villas: for example, the gardens of the Villa Rosa, built in 1847, lasted barely twelve years before being sacrificed to new building.[96]

In the more remote parts of south and west Somerset more conservative formal elements seem to have lingered on. When John Claudius Loudon passed through the region in late August and early September 1842 he noted on the road from Bridgwater to Williton "*several villas, one or two of which still retain clipped yew hedges and other vestiges of the geometric style*".[97]

COTTAGE GARDENS

As always, it is the smaller gardens of country artisans and labourers which are least well documented. Nevertheless, contemporary writers give us occasional glimpses of them. During Loudon's journey through Somerset in the autumn of 1842, he admired the local whitewashed cottages, and noticed one on the road from Williton to Nettlecombe Court, "*the walls of which were covered with the broad and narrow-leaved myrtle both 12 feet high and overspread with bloom*". He also commented on the many large blue-flowered hydrangeas which he saw growing widely in both Somerset and Devon.[98]

Topiary had survived on a small scale in cottage gardens long after it had fallen out of favour amongst the aristocracy and gentry. Its general popularity revived in the 1860s, which saw a vogue for hedges clipped in architectural forms, such as walls and battlements, while in the 1880s sculpted birds and other shapes also became popular.

Cottage gardens also often provided a refuge for varieties of plants which had gone out of fashion in the greater gardens. They were to provide an inspiration for some of the famous garden designers of the present century, notably Gertrude Jekyll, Vita Sackville-West and Margery Fish.

William Carmichael (formerly head gardener to the Prince of Wales at Sandringham) developed a splendid Italianate villa garden during the 1870s and 1880s, with a terrace, formal beds, pond and lawn lined with balustrades and urns, connected by yew-shaded paths through rockwork and a grotto to a wilderness below.[94]

The dramatic and picturesque wooded scenery of the west bank of the Avon gorge attracted many wealthy merchants and industrialists from Bristol, once the opening of the Clifton Suspension Bridge in 1865 had made it accessible. Bracken Hill in Leigh Woods, built for Melville Wills, has already been mentioned. In 1894 George

PUBLIC PARKS IN TOWNS

Concern about overcrowding in the rapidly expanding towns in the early nineteenth century led to a movement to provide free public parks and gardens for the enjoyment of the urban population as a whole. This was a rather different idea from the commercial pleasure-grounds of the eighteenth century, where the gardens were merely settings for entertainments, although the two concepts were not incompatible and could be combined. One of the earliest advocates of public urban parks was John Claudius Loudon, who first proposed their creation in 1822. Loudon went on himself to design public gardens in Gravesend and Derby, and his lead was followed elsewhere by other eminent designers such as Joseph Paxton. Public parks and gardens were seen as an especially important amenity in spas and seaside resort towns, which were now competing with each other to attract visitors.[100]

Urban parks could be created in several different ways. Sometimes a local philanthropist would provide land by private gift or lease. Sometimes former grazing commons were acquired by a town corporation to prevent building encroachments and to preserve them as public open space (Clifton and Durdham Downs were preserved in this way by Bristol City Council and the Merchant Venturers under a special Act of Parliament in 1862). Sometimes public subscriptions were organised to purchase land for a new park and to lay it out and maintain it. Both formal and informal designs were used. The earliest examples were often planned in Loudon's 'gardenesque' mode, with an underlying philosophy of informal education, providing a wide range of specimen trees and shrubs to resemble a living museum; some even included a complete botanical garden. From the middle of the nineteenth century there was more emphasis on display, with the introduction of bedding employing brightly-coloured annuals of uniform height planted out in increasingly elaborate patterns. Annual bedding was developed to a fine art in public parks, and survived there long after it had gone out of fashion in private gardens.

The first true public park in Somerset was the Royal Victoria Park in Bath. The heyday of the fashionable spa was nearly over, and the town's tradesmen now wished to attract new permanent residents as well as visitors. In the autumn of 1829 a group of prominent citizens and businessmen led by J Davies and T B Coward met to consider proposals for the formation of "*Ornamental plantations, Walks and Rides*" intended to provide "*health and recreation to all classes*". The site selected lay west of the city on Bath High Common, where there had been a history of conflict between the Corporation, who wished to keep the land open for public enjoyment, and the city's Freemen, who wished to break up the commons for building development to increase their own income. Initially only the Crescent Fields south of the Royal Crescent were considered, but this area was considered too small and further land was acquired on lease from the Freemen around the perimeter of the Middle Common to the west. A plan for the new park drawn up in 1829 by Edward Davis, a local architect, shows a ride and promenade laid out around the perimeter of the Middle Common, the central part of which was initially excluded from the lease and remained open. The drives were constructed by William, son of John Macadam, who some years earlier had been appointed Surveyor to the Bath Turnpike Trust. The Royal Avenue was laid out as an approach over Crescent Fields, on land leased from Lady Rivers. There were two gateways, Rivers Gate at the entrance to the approach drive near Queens Parade, and Spry's Gate or Victoria Gate at the park entrance itself, neoclassical designs for both gates being drawn up by Davis in 1830. There was to be a picturesque 'Gothic farmhouse' near the Victoria Gate and a 'Cottage ornée' towards the west end of the park near the site of the later Botanic Garden. The 1829 plan also shows a proposal to carry the Weston Road on a viaduct over a passage linking the Middle Common with the High Common to the north, with serpentine drives on the High Common, but these were never constructed.[101]

The creation of the park here was financed largely by public subscription with a grant from the city council, and it was run by an independent committee. It was formally opened on October 23rd 1830 in the presence of the eleven-year-old Princess Victoria. The early years were not without the problems of vandalism all too familiar today: railings had to be erected, the gates closed at night, a park keeper appointed and night patrols instituted, despite which one contemporary report describes the park as neglected and dirty and a "*reproach both to our morality and decency*".

An old stone quarry on the north-western corner of the Middle Common was planted up with conifers and converted to an ornamental ground known as the Great Dell in 1836 by Jerom Murch, Unitarian minister and Mayor of Bath, with the advice of William Beckford. By the 1850s the initial concept of purely ornamental plantations was giving way to a more serious educational purpose, with the whole park gradually being developed into a fine arboretum, following the model of Loudon's arboretum at Derby. Some of the surviving Californian coast redwood and Wellingtonias, new introductions of the 1840s and 1850s, may have been planted at this time. In 1871 22 more Wellingtonias were planted along the north

opposite: Fig. 8.31
HAINES HILL, TAUNTON.
Ordnance Survey map of 1888 showing part of the 'garden suburb' laid out by Richard Carver (1792-1862). Described in the Taunton Courier as providing space for a further "... 16 beautiful Suburban Villa Houses... handsomely planted. The site commands extensive, varied and highly picturesque views being one hundred and forty feet above the Town Parade, the air pure, dry and healthy..." Carver designed a range of houses, each with access to a central circular pleasure garden, on payment of £1 per annum. According to the property deeds the area was to be enclosed with a "... handsome lias stone wall of a height of 3 feet having a battering exterior face and to be coped with the like stone... a neat pair of folding gates of 9 feet in width to be painted Green... The inside of the wall to be planted with a hedge of Thorn or Privet... The whole to be dug over and laid out with a stoned and gravelled walk around it the surface of earth to be seeded down for Grass and the borders and surface to be planted with evergreen and other shrubs and trees...."

below: Fig. 8.32
In the front garden of a modest cottage in the hamlet of CROSS near Compton Bishop four Topiary Spires were established in the late 1840s; these have been added to by four generations of the family, and are now a remarkable 20 feet in height.[99]

walks. Almost from the start there had been plans to include a botanical garden, although another half-century elapsed before this was achieved.

Public parks were often used as places for the celebration of patriotic pride, for the commemoration of great events, and for cultural allusions. The Royal Victoria Park is particularly well stocked with commemorative monuments. In 1831-2 Mr C. Geary presented two lions of Coade stone, originally bronzed, for the piers of the Rivers Gate. In 1837 an obelisk with crouching lions at its base was designed by G.P. Manners to stand just inside the Victoria Gate to commemorate the majority of Princess Victoria, and it was officially unveiled on Victoria's coronation day on 28th June 1838. In 1839 a giant stone head seven feet high was set up in the Great Dell. Crowds flocked to admire this remarkable monument, and Granville compared it favourably with Giambologna's famous sculpture at Pratolino in Tuscany. The sculptor, John Osborne, was portrayed by Granville as "*an untutored genius ... born in penury...a mere shepherd's boy*", who had settled in Bath and purchased the six-ton block of stone from his life's savings; the scale of the project taxed his strength to the

limit, and he died from exhaustion soon after its completion.[102] Posterity has identified the statue with Jupiter, although Osborne always denied that this was his intention. In September 1857 two Russian cannon from the Crimean War were placed on either side of the obelisk on the second anniversary of the fall of Sebastopol. Elsewhere in the Great Dell another memorial taking the form of a votive altar was erected in 1864 to commemorate the tercentenary of William Shakespeare's birth. In 1874 two vases of Carrara marble which had once been given by Napoleon Buonaparte to the Empress Josephine, brought to England after the Peninsular War, were bequeathed to the park authorities by Joseph Fuller, a resident of Lansdown Crescent, and were set on the lawn by the bandstand. In 1880 the 'Victoria Vase' was placed by the lake to mark the fiftieth anniversary of the park's opening. A fourth vase, the so-called 'Miller' or 'Batheaston Vase', was set up under a canopy at the end of the Lower Drive. This is said to have been found near Cicero's villa at Frascati in 1769, subsequently being brought to Batheaston, where it was used for the deposition of verse by Lady Miller's weekly literary salon; however, there is some doubt about this attribution. Vandalism caused its removal from its original site, and it was re-erected without its canopy in 1924 near the Royal Avenue, facing the approach from Upper Church Street. Yet another vase was brought from Italy to be placed by the Rivers Gate in 1914. A bandstand was provided in the late 1880s, and by 1891 was in use six times a week. Other schemes for a Winter Garden and Pavilion were not pursued to fruition. Commemorative trees were also used. On March 10th 1863 an oak was planted near the obelisk to commemorate the marriage of Princess Alexandra of Denmark to Edward, Prince of Wales, while in 1887 another oak was planted for Queen Victoria's jubilee.[103]

The elliptical pond in the southern part of the park shown on Davis's plan of 1829 was enlarged fifty years later by Edward Milner, a former pupil of Paxton. It was given a very irregular shape with an island and promontories which prevented the whole from being seen from any one viewpoint, thereby making it seem larger than it really was, a technique which Paxton himself had perfected at Birkenhead Park. A rustic footbridge carried a path over the eastern arm of the lake.[104]

Elsewhere in Bath, the stone setts of the Circus had been replaced with grass and trees by 1801. One of the city's oldest open spaces, the Orange Grove, was surrounded by railings and laid out with bedding in 1820. By the time of Granville's visit the rows of elms in the Orange Grove had been replaced by a circle of sycamores.[105] Beechen Cliff was purchased by Bath City Council in 1860 to preserve it as a wooded open space giving views over the city from the south, and Magdalen gardens and Alexandra Park were laid out above it around the end of the century. Alexandra Park was opened to commemorate Edward VII's coronation in 1902. Hedgemead Park was formed on unstable ground below Camden Crescent which had initially been built over by speculators. A series of landslips, one of which destroyed 135 houses in 1881, demonstrated that the land was unsafe for building. The city council acquired it, built a massive turreted and battlemented revetment wall to stabilise the slope and made rockeries and plantings above, opening it as a public park in 1889. Henrietta Park in Bathwick was acquired by the city in 1897. A scheme for potentially the most spectacular Victorian garden in Bath, published in 1850, would have laid out the fields below the Royal Crescent with a pair of gigantic fountains, a wide stepped gravel walk between, and geometric flower beds. Perhaps fortunately, this was never put into effect.[106]

The rapid growth of seaside towns was now usurping some of the resort functions of the older spas, and there too public gardens were laid out as an amenity to attract visitors. At Weston-super-Mare the first generation of parks - Eastfield Park, Ellenborough Park and The Shrubbery - was provided mainly in association with private housing schemes. In 1888 the widow of Henry Davies, a prominent Weston builder, gave 16 acres for the creation of Clarence Park. At first the sea front itself remained largely undeveloped, apart from a low sea wall and gravelled promenade at the north end of the bay between Knightstone and Regent Street. The long beach and dunes behind had been the main attraction for picnickers and day trippers. However, the rank and number of visitors declined through the 1870s as they were tempted away by more fashionable resorts such as Torquay. To restore Weston's fortunes, Edwin Knight in 1879 proposed large-scale

improvements to the sea front, including a new sea wall and the creation of lawns and gardens, a carriage drive and promenade over the dune belt. Despite some opposition from those who feared the social impact of increasing numbers of trippers, the scheme was carried through and largely completed by 1885. During the period of prosperity which followed, further amenities were added through private investment: the Winter Gardens in 1882 (redesigned in the 1920s), and a fifteen-acre recreation ground in 1885. Other public gardens followed: Prince Consort Gardens on Flagstaff Hill; Grove Park, formed out of the private garden of the former manor house in 1891; and Ashcombe Park, opened in 1902. Elaborate pictorial carpet-bedding depicting coats of arms and floral clocks remained a feature of Weston-super-Mare's parks well into the present century.[107]

Fig. 8.34
GROVE PARK,
WESTON-SUPER-MARE.
Carpet bedding, c.1910-15.

At Clevedon three small plots of ground in the higher part of the town were given in the 1860s by Sir Arthur Hallam Elton, lord of the manor, for the creation of Alexandra Gardens, Herbert Gardens and Pier Copse. Overlooked by buildings and over-densely planted, these have become somewhat gloomy as their trees have grown to maturity. Green Beach and Walton Gardens, laid out by the council later in the century, have a more open aspect on the coast, and Green Beach has an attractive bandstand erected in 1887. The garden of Sun Hill, an Edwardian private house, became a public park when the dwelling was converted to use as the Community Centre.

Other Somerset towns had to wait until the end of the century before public gardens were developed. The best example is Vivary

Fig. 8.35
GREEN BEACH, CLEVEDON.
Seaside gardens and bandstand.

GARDEN CEMETERIES

The need for new burial grounds in towns was becoming urgent by the early nineteenth century, as rapid population growth filled the ancient churchyards to overflowing, and concern grew about the threat to public health. The idea of the 'garden cemetery', where burials took place in pleasant ornamental grounds, was introduced to England from France in 1824, and it found an enthusiastic supporter in John Claudius Loudon. A new Act of Parliament enabled city parishes to purchase land outside their boundaries for this purpose. In Bath in 1843 the Abbey parish of SS Peter and Paul bought some land in Widcombe not far from Prior Park, and this was planted out to Loudon's own design only a few months before his death. A neo-Norman mortuary chapel designed by G.P. Manners was added in the following year.[109]

BOTANICAL GARDENS

The enlargement of the role of the medieval physic gardens into museums of living plants and centres of botanical research had begun in the universities of renaissance Italy during the sixteenth century. In England the first University botanic garden was established in 1621 at Oxford, where the first curator, Jacob Bobart, built up a collection of over 2000 plants. The Royal Botanical Garden at Kew had dominated the scientific study of plants in England since the 1770s, when its horticultural adviser, Joseph Banks, began organising collecting expeditions to many different parts of the world, a policy resumed by Kew's first professional director, Sir William Jackson Hooker (1841-1865) and his son and successor Joseph Dalton Hooker (1865-1885). Scientific botanical explorations promoted a widespread popular interest in horticulture, which demanded more accessible collections to admire and to study.

Botanical gardens began to be established in provincial cities from the end of the eighteenth century, and by the 1830s were to be found in most larger towns. Most of the earliest examples were private collections which their owners decided to make accessible to the public, either out of philanthropy or from commercial motives. The first botanic garden in Bath was opened in 1793 by John Jelly, a local builder, in the garden of his own house, Elm Bank off Camden Road. It occupied about three quarters of an acre, and admission was by annual subscription. Half a guinea gave access to walk in the garden and to make use of a small library, while a guinea entitled subscribers to roots and seeds of plants when available. Unfortunately Jelly went bankrupt in 1795 and his house and garden with all the glass frames and plants were sold.[110]

In 1837 a notice in Loudon's *GARDENER'S MAGAZINE* announced the formation of a new botanical garden at Bath by one Mr Forrest, probably Richard Forrest of Miller's Durdham Down Nurseries, designer of the Botanical Gardens in Bristol. Other writers credit this to W.H. Baxter (later curator of the Oxford Botanic Garden) in 1840.[111] It was later recorded that Loudon himself selected the trees, though there seems no contemporary evidence for his involvement.

Although some specimens may have survived, this garden in the north-west corner of the Royal Victoria Park did not last long as an

Park in Taunton, laid out on land purchased by the borough council in 1894. It took its name from two medieval fishponds (*vivaria*) which had formerly belonged to the Bishop of Winchester. The splendid iron gates and bandstand were made the following year. The fountain, set up in 1907 as a memorial to Queen Victoria, was cast by Walter Macfarlane & Co. of the Saracen Foundry, Glasgow, and is identical with a fountain on the sea front at Torquay. It was financed by cash left over from the local celebrations of Edward VII's coronation. Blake Gardens in Bridgwater were opened in 1902 (with a bandstand added in 1908), followed by Eastover Recreation Ground in 1905 and Victoria Park in the late 1920s.[108]

entity, and nothing further was done until 1886, when an eminent local botanist, Christopher Edmund Broome died. Broome was a Fellow of the Linnaean Society, an expert on fungi, and had developed a magnificent private garden at his home at Elmhurst in Batheaston. Following his death, his widow offered his entire collection of 2000 rare and exotic plants to the park's management committee. Supported by the Mayor, Sir Jerom Murch, who had his own collection of conifers in his garden at Cranwells, and by Canon Ellacombe of Bitton, already noted as an authority on plants, the committee successfully applied to the city council for a grant towards the costs of transplanting and maintaining the collection. Canon Ellacombe had agreed to supervise the planting himself, but in the end the work was undertaken by his friend J.W. Morris, also a Fellow of the Linnaean Society, who became the garden's curator. John Milburn was brought from Kew as superintendent, and further plants were donated by Canon Ellacombe and by Lady Lushington, who gave her entire collection of plants from her garden at Great Bedwyn (Wiltshire). The new planting covered some three acres, and provided the nucleus of the fine gardens we see today. The only loss was the Park Cottage, one of Edward Davis's original buildings, demolished to create the necessary space.[112]

REFERENCES - Chapter 8

1. C.S. Orwin, *The Reclamation of Exmoor Forest*, 2nd edn, revised by R.J. Sellick (Newton Abbot, 1970); Michael Williams, *The Draining of the Somerset Levels* (Cambridge, 1970); W.E. Tate, *Somerset Enclosure Acts and Awards* (Somerset Archaeological & Natural History Society, 1948).

2. For a general introduction to gardens of the period see Tom Carter, *The Victorian Garden* (1984); Brent Elliott, *Victorian Gardens* (1986); David Stuart, *The Garden Triumphant: a Victorian Legacy* (1988); and Joan Morgan and Alison Richards, *A Paradise out of a Common Field: the Pleasures and Plenty of the Victorian Garden* (1990).

3. Robin Atthill, *Old Mendip* (2nd edn, Newton Abbot, 1971), pp.68-94.

4. Roger D.C. Evans, 'One man went to mow: the invention of the lawn mower', *Historic Garden* no.5 (Spring, 1993), pp.24-5.

5. A fuller list of periodicals is provided by Ray Desmond, 'Victorian garden magazines', *Garden History* Vol.5 no.iii (1977), pp.47-66, and 'Garden journalism' in *The Oxford Companion to Gardens*, ed. Geoffrey & Susan Jellicoe, Patrick Goode & Michael Lancaster (Oxford, 1991), pp.212-3.

6. Stewart Harding & David Lambert, *Parks and Gardens of Avon* (Bristol, 1994), pp.91-2; Robin Whalley, 'The Royal Victoria Park', *Bath History* Vol.5 (1994), p.163;. R. Bush, *The Book of Taunton* (Chesham, 1977), p.104.

7. Patrick O'Brian, *Joseph Banks*, (1987).

8. Alice M. Coates, *The Quest for Plants: a History of the Horticultural Explorers* (1968); Sandra Raphael, 'Plant collecting', in *The Oxford Companion to Gardens*, pp.435-8. This invaluable compilation also includes brief biographies of many of the great collectors.

9. Richard Gorer, *The Development of Garden Flowers* (1970), pp.71-74.

10. William Morwood, *Traveller in a Vanished Landscape: the Life and Times of David Douglas* (1973).

11. Roy W.Briggs, *'Chinese' Wilson: a Life of Ernest H. Wilson, 1876-1930* (1993)

12. Joseph Dalton Hooker, *Rhododendrons of the Sikkim-Himalaya* (1849-51)

13. John Sales, *West Country Gardens* (Gloucester, 1980) provides a valuable introduction to the botanical content of some local gardens. Other information has come from A. Mitchell, *Trees of Britain and Northern Europe* (1994 reprint); S.D. Hitt, *Bath Botanical Gardens* (Bath, 1994); H. St George Gray, 'Notes on Wilton', *P.S.A.N.H.S.* Vol.88 part i (1942), p.14n.

14. Harding & Lambert, *Parks and Gardens of Avon*, p.88.

15. Canon Ellacombe, *In a Gloucestershire Garden* (1895, reprinted 1986), p.134.

16. R.W. Dunning & M.C. Siraut, 'North Petherton', *V.C.H.* Vol.6, p.287; Shirley Heriz-Smith, 'The Veitch nurseries of Killerton and Exeter, c.1780 to 1863: part 1', *Garden History* Vol.16 no.i (Spring 1988), p.47; the bill for the Nynehead planting is Somerset C.R.O. DD/SF 4249. The list of trees supplied to Maunsel House, discovered by Tony Baggs, is summarised in an addendum to part 2 of Shirley Heriz-Smith's article, in *Garden History* Vol.16 no.ii (Autumn 1988), p.187.

17. The fullest account of the Veitch nurseries is Heriz-Smith, 'The Veitch nurseries of Killerton and Exeter, c.1780 to 1863: part 1', *Garden History* Vol.16 no.i (Spring 1988), pp.41-57; part 2, *Garden Hist.* Vol.16 no.ii (Autumn, 1988), pp.174-188; and 'James Veitch & Sons of Exeter and Chelsea, 1853-1870', *Garden Hist.* Vol.17 no.ii (Autumn 1989), pp.135-153; See also Audrey Le Lievre, ' "To the Nobility and Gentry about to Plant": nurseries and nurserymen', in Steven Pugsley (ed.), *Devon Gardens: an Historical Survey* (Stroud, 1994), pp.91-105.

18. Harding & Lambert, *Parks and Gardens of Avon*, pp.68, 95.

19. Harding & Lambert, *Parks and Gardens of Avon*, p.68.

20. Scott's Orchardist, or Catalogue of Fruits cultivated at Merriott, Somerset (2nd edn., 1872); John Harvey, *Early Nurserymen* (Chichester, 1974), p.71; R.W. Dunning, 'Merriott', *V.C.H.* Vol.4 (1978), p.57.

21. Harvey, *Early Nurserymen*, pp.103-4.

22. Harvey, *Early Nurserymen*, pp.xiii, 104; Alice M. Coats, *Flowers and their Histories* (1956), p.69; Richard Bisgrove, *The National Trust Book of the English Garden* (1990), p.160.

23. J.D. Hanwell, Some Aspects of Horticulture in the Cheddar Valley, Somerset, with special reference to the Strawberry Crop (Unpubl. B.Sc. thesis, Dept. of Geography, University of Hull (1957); J. Burrows, 'George Lee and his Clevedon Violets', in *The Annals of Clevedon* (Clevedon Civic Society, 1988), pp.1-5.

24. Uvedale Price, *Essay on the Picturesque (1794-1801)*; Richard Payne Knight, *An Analytical Inquiry into the Principles of Taste* (1805).

25. These lines are from Richard Payne Knight, *The Landscape: a Didactic Poem* (1794).

26. William Sawrey Gilpin, in *Practical Hints upon Landscape Gardening* (1832) defines various aesthetic categories, the 'Beautiful', the 'Romantic', the 'Rural' and the 'Grand' as well as the 'Picturesque'.

27. Atthill, *Old Mendip*, pp.39-40; Harding & Lambert, *Parks and Gardens of Avon* pp.72-3.

28. Margaret Elton, *Annals of the Elton Family* (Stroud, 1994), pp.121-2; Harding & Lambert, *Parks & Gardens of Avon*, pp.82-3.

29. Brian Fothergill, Beckford of Fonthill (1979), pp.327-8; Christopher Pound, *Genius of Bath: the City and its Landscape* (Bath, 1986), pp.82-3, 86; Philippa Bishop, 'Beckford in Bath', *Bath History* Vol.2 (1988), pp.85-112; Harding & Lambert, *Parks and Gardens of Avon*, pp.70-71.

30. Anon. guidebook, *The Bishop's Palace at Wells* (1991)

31. *Country Life* Vol.129 (1st June 1961), pp.1266-7.

32. Harding & Lambert, *Parks & Gardens of Avon*, pp.72-4.

33. Roger White (ed.), *Georgian Arcadia: Architecture for the Park and Garden* (Georgian Group, 1987), p.34, no.110.

34. Harding & Lambert, *Parks and Gardens of Avon*, p.72; R.W. Dunning, 'West Quantoxhead', *V.C.H.* Vol.5 (1985), pp.131-2.

35. Michael Cousins, 'The caves at Banwell, Avon', *Follies* no.9 (Spring 1991), pp.7-11.

36. B. Little & A. Aldrich, Ammerdown (Unpublished MS, 1977, at Ammerdown Study Centre Library), p. 11.

37. Loudon's career is admirably described by Melanie Louise Simo, *Loudon and the Landscape: from Country Seat to Metropolis* (New Haven, 1988). His own account of his travels between 1829 and 1842 has been published under the title *In Search of English Gardens*, edited by Priscilla Boniface (1990).

38. *Gardeners Chronicle*, Vol.2 (1903), p.34; *Country Life* Vol.147 (19th March 1970), p.682; Sales, *West Country Gardens*, pp.139-40.

39. R.W. Dunning, 'North Petherton', *V.C.H.* Vol.6, (1992), p.288.

40. *Country Life*, Vol.4 (24th December 1898), pp.792-96; Vol.13 (1903), pp.494-6; Vol.20 (24th November), pp.738-47, (1st December 1906), pp.774-79; H. Inigo Triggs, *Formal Gardens in England and Scotland* (1902), pp.13-14; Gertrude Jekyll, *Garden Ornament* (1918), pp.52, 55, 72, 75, 282; Robert Cooke, *West Country Houses* (Bristol, 1957), pp.42-5; A. Clayton-Payne & B. Elliott, *Victorian Flower Gardens* (1988), pp.130-1.

41. Edward Kemp, *How to Lay Out a Small Garden* (1850, 3rd edn 1864).

42. Loudon, *In Search of English Gardens* (ed. Boniface), p.233.

43. Triggs, *Formal Gardens in England and Scotland*, pp.11-12; H. Avray Tipping, *Gardens Old and New* (1909), pp.89-100.

44. The plans and sketches by Blomfield and Balfour in the collections of the Royal Institute of British Architects have been published and discussed by Jane Brown, *The Art and Architecture of English Gardens* (New York, 1989), pp.124-5, 128-9.

45. Dudley Dodd, *Montacute House* (1990), pp.25-6; Sales, *West Country Gardens*, pp.166-71.

46. *Country Life* Vol.10 (21st December 1901), pp.808-15; Sales, *West Country Gardens*, pp.173-4; Michael McGarvie, 'The Duckworths and the building of Orchardleigh House', *Transactions of the Ancient Monuments Society* Vol.27 (1983), pp.119-145.

47. *Country Life* Vol.6 (2nd December 1899), pp.692-8; Gertrude Jekyll, *Wall and Water Gardens* (1901).

48. The balustraded terrace and stairway were praised by Gertrude Jekyll, *Garden Ornament* (1918), p.58; see also Jane Fearnley-Whittingstall, *Historic Gardens* (1990), p.63; Robert Dunning, *Some Somerset Country Houses* (1991), p.20.

49. Marcus Binney & Anne Hills, *Elysian Gardens* (1979), includes an aerial photograph of the Nynehead Court gardens, p.22

50. T.W. Mayberry, *Orchard and the Portmans* (1986), pp.36-44.

51. George S Master, *Collections for a Parochial History of Wraxall* (Bristol 1900), f.p.73; *Country Life* Vol.11 (17th May 1902), pp.624-30.

52. Harding & Lambert, *Parks and Gardens of Avon*, pp.81-2.

53. Robinson's books include *The Wild Garden* (1870), *Alpine Flowers for Gardens* (1870), *The English Flower Garden* (1883), *Garden Design and Architects' Gardens* (1892) and *Gravetye Manor, or Twenty Years' Work...* (1911).

54. *Country Life*, Vol.11 (18th January 1902), pp.80-87; Jekyll, *Garden Ornament*, p.228; Harding & Lambert, *Parks and Gardens of Avon*, pp.85-6.

55. Sir Charles Isham, *Remarks on Rock Gardens*, also *Notes on Gnomes* (c.1890)

56. Sally Festing, "Pulham has done his work well", *Garden History* Vol.12 no.ii (Autumn 1984), esp.pp.152-6.

57. C. & I. Greenwood, *Map of the County of Somerset* (1822), which has conveniently been republished as part of *S.R.S.* Vol.76 (1981); Joseph Whitaker, *A Descriptive List of Deer Parks and Paddocks of England* (1892)

58. Roger A. Burton, *Simonsbath* (Barnstaple, 1994), pp.28-33.

59. Whitaker, *Descriptive List of Deer Parks*; Cox & Greswell, 'Forestry', *V.C.H.* Vol.2 (1911), p.570.

60. W. Greswell, *The Forests and Deer Parks of Somerset* (1908); Cf. Katie Fretwell, 'Lodge Park, Gloucestershire: a rare surviving deer course...', *Garden History* Vol.23 no.ii (Winter 1995), pp.133-44. I owe the information on Mells to Jan Woudstra.

61. The contract for work carried out by Veitch is quoted by S. Heriz-Smith in *Garden History* Vol.16 no.2 (Autumn 1988), p.187.

62. Loudon, *In Search of English Gardens* (1990 edn), pp.226-233.

63. R.W. Dunning, 'Hinton St George', *V.C.H.* Vol.4, (1978), p.40.

64. R.W. Dunning & M.C. Siraut, 'North Petherton', *V.C.H.* Vol.6 (1992), pp.281, 296, 315; the list of trees supplied is quoted by Heriz-Smith, *Garden History* Vol.16 no.ii (Autumn 1988), p.187.

65. McGarvie, *'The Duckworths and the building of Orchardleigh House'*, pp.134, 137; Sales, *West Country Gardens*, pp.173-4.

66. Harding & Lambert, *Parks and Gardens of Avon*, pp.81-4, 89; J.C.Cox & W.H.P. Greswell, 'Forestry', *V.C.H.* Vol.2 (1911), p.570.

67. William Phelps, *The History and Antiquities of Somersetshire*, Vol.1 (1839), pp.407-8; Robert Dunning, Somerset Castles (Tiverton, 1995), pp.73-5

68. *Country Life* Vol.11 (17th May 1902), pp.624-30; Harding & Lambert, *Parks and Gardens of Avon*, p.79.

69. Phelps, *History and Antiquities of Somersetshire*, Vol.2, p.192.

70. Mary de Viggiani, *Two Estates: the Story of an East Mendip Village* (Cranmore, 1988), 27, 32, 41.

71. R.W. Dunning & M.C. Siraut, 'Bawdrip', *V.C.H.* Vol.6 (1992), p.184; Dunning, 'South Petherton' *V.C.H.* Vol.4, p.183; Dunning & Siraut, 'Stockland Bristol', *V.C.H.* Vol.6, p.126-7.

72. Little & Aldrich, *Ammerdown*, unpubl.MS., pp.12-14.

73. de Viggiani, *Two Estates*, pp.62-4.

74. Dunning, *Somerset Castles*, p.75.

75. Dunning & Siraut, 'Stogursey', *V.C.H.* Vol.6, p.134; Siraut, 'Elworthy', *V.C.H.* Vol.5 (1985), p.70; de Viggiani, *Two Estates*, p.42; Mike Chapman, *A Guide to the Estates of Ralph Allen around Bath* (Bath, 1996), p.19.

76. R. Bush, 'Cricket St Thomas', *V.C.H.* Vol.4, pp.133-41.

77. M. Aston (ed.), 'Somerset Archaeology, 1976', *P.S.A.N.H.S.* Vol.121 (1977), pp.119-20; Dunning, 'West Quantoxhead', *V.C.H.* Vol.5, pp.129-30; Cox & Greswell, 'Forestry', *V.C.H.* Vol.2, p.569.

78. Tim Mowl & Brian Earnshaw, *Trumpet at a Distant Gate: the Lodge as Prelude to the Country House* (1985).

79. Tim Mowl, *Bristol: Last Age of the Merchant Princes* (Bath, 1991), pl.52; George S. Master, *Collections for a Parochial History of Wraxall* (Bristol, 1900), p.75.

80. See also Ethel M. Hewitt, 'Cider and Wine', *V. C. H.* Vol.2, pp.403-5; F. A. Roach, *Cultivated Fruits of Britain* (1985), pp.93-7; Philippa Legg, *So Merry Let Us Be: the Living Tradition of Somerset Cider* (Taunton, 1986), pp.7-14.

81. Long Ashton Research Station Jubilee Volume, *Science and Fruit* (1953); R. W. Marsh, 'The National Fruit and Cider Institute, 1903-1983', Long Ashton Research Station, *Annual Report* (1983).

82. Mayberry, *Orchard and the Portmans*, p.40.

83. William Cobbett, *The English Gardener, or, a Treatise on the ... Laying-Out of Kitchen Gardens, on the Making and Managing of Hot-beds and Green-Houses, and on the Propagation and Cultivation of all sorts of Kitchen-Garden Plants, and of Fruit-Trees...* (1833) provides an indication of the range of contemporary kitchen garden crops and methods of cultivation.

84. National Trust, *The Gardens of Montacute House* (guide leaflet, 1985).

85. Loudon, *In Search of English Gardens*, p. 228.

86. Quoted in Colin G. Winn, *The Pouletts of Hinton St George* (Stroud, 1995), pp.157-8.

87. Harvey, *Early Nurserymen*, p.101. For a general discussion of conservatories and glasshouses see May Woods & Arete Warren, *Glass Houses* (1988); and Morgan & Richards, *A Paradise out of a Common Field*, esp.pp.70-80.

88. Nikolaus Pevsner, The Buildings of England: South and West Somerset (1958), p.140; Woods & Warren, Glass Houses, pp.103, 127; Dodd, Montacute House (1978), p.26; Mary de Viggiani, A Cranmore Chronicle (East Cranmore, 1985), p.1; Dunning, Some Somerset Country Houses, pp.79-80; Dudley Dodd, Dunster Castle (revised edn.,1990), pp.28,57; Sales, *West Country Gardens*, p.174.

89. de Viggiani, *Two Estates*, p.88; Harding & Lambert, *Parks and Gardens of Avon*, p.84; Dunning, *Some Somerset Country Houses*, p.114.

90. George S Master, *Collections for a Parochial History of Wraxall* (Bristol, 1900), p.75; Robert Cooke, *West Country Houses* (Bristol, 1957), p.170; Dunning, *Some Somerset Country Houses*, p.42; Winn, *The Pouletts of Hinton St George*, pp.157-8; McGarvie, *Gardening at Marston House, 1660-1905*, pp.25-6.

91. Robert D. Bell, 'The discovery of a buried Georgian garden in Bath', *Garden History* Vol.18 no.i (1990), esp.pp.14-16.

92. Todd Gray, 'A Compton Bishop garden, 1804', *S.D.N.Q.* Vol.34 (March 1997), p.123.

93. A.B. Granville, *Spas of England*, Vol.2 (1841), pp.365, 368-9, 371, 439.

94. The paragraphs on the Bath villas are drawn largely from Harding & Lambert, *Parks and Gardens of Avon*, pp.74-5, 87, 89, 93; see also Pound, *Genius of Bath*, pp.73-7, 80-82.

95. Jane Jerrard, 'The view from near the bridge', *Nonesuch* (University of Bristol Magazine, Autumn 1995), pp.45-6.

96. Winn, *The Pouletts of Hinton St George*, pp.157-8.

97. Loudon, *In Search of English Gardens*, p.226.

98. Loudon, *In Search of English Gardens*, p.226.

99. Ethne Clarke & George Wright, *English Topiary Gardens* (1988), pp.120-1.

100. Loudon, *Encyclopaedia of Gardening* (1822), p.1,186-8. For a general background on public parks elsewhere see Hazel Conway, *People's Parks: the Design and Development of Victorian Parks in Britain* (1991); Susan Lasdun, *The English Park* (1991), pp.119-66; Harriet Jordan, 'Public parks, 1885-1914', *Garden History* Vol.22 no.i (Summer 1994), pp.85-113; Hilary A. Taylor, 'Urban public parks, 1840-1900: design and meaning', *Garden History* Vol.23 no.ii (Winter 1995), pp.201-21.

101. Robin Whalley, 'The Royal Victoria Park', *Bath History* Vol.5 (1994), pp.147-169.

102. Granville, *Spas of England*, Vol.2, pp.423-5.

103. Whalley, *'Royal Victoria Park'*, pp.158-9.

104. Whalley, *'Royal Victoria Park'*, pp.164-5.

105. Granville, *Spas of England*, Vol.2, pp.398-9.

106. Whalley, *'Royal Victoria Park'*, p.148; Pound, *Genius of Bath*, pp.82-3.

107. Bryan J.H. Brown & John Loosley, *The Book of Weston-super-Mare* (Buckingham, 1983), pp.85-7, 128; C. Young, 'The acquisition of Weston-super-Mare's Victorian parks', *The Local Historian* Vol.20.iv (November 1990), pp.158-65.

108. R.Bush, *Somerset: the Complete Guide* (Wimborne, 1994), p.204; Derrick Warren (ed.), *Somerset's Industrial Heritage: a Guide and Gazetteer* (Somerset Industrial Archaeology Society, 1996), p.48; Philip J. Squibbs, *History of Bridgwater* (ed. J.F. Lawrence, Chichester, 1982), pp.106, 111, 113, 125.

109. James Stevens Curl, 'John Claudius Loudon and the Garden Cemetery movement', *Garden History* Vol.11 no.ii (Autumn 1983), pp.133-56; Pound, *Genius of Bath*, pp.85-6.

110. Harding & Lambert, *Parks and Gardens of Avon*, pp.67-8.

111. F.Hanham, *A Manual for the Park* (1857), p.vi, quoted by Whalley, *'Royal Victoria Park'*, p.163; Hitt, *Bath Botanical Gardens*, p.3.

112. Whalley, *'Royal Victoria Park'* pp.163-4; Hitt, *Bath Botanical Gardens*, pp.3-4.

Chapter 9

Parks and Gardens in the Twentieth Century

A century of massive social upheavals, dominated by the decline of the great landed estates and the rise of an increasingly numerous and demanding urban population ... Parks and gardens can now be enjoyed by far more people than ever before.

INTRODUCTION

No previous century has witnessed such massive social upheavals as the present one: a century of great wars and mass unemployment, but a century also of improving living standards, better education, more leisure and greatly increased mobility. Two themes have dominated the evolution of parks and gardens since 1900. Many of the old landowning families have vanished from the scene, their great houses taken over by institutions of one sort or another; while the expectations of an increasingly numerous and demanding urban population have placed unprecedented pressures upon the countryside.

The decline of the hereditary private estates had begun in the 1870s, when a series of bad harvests disrupted the capacity of English farmers to continue supplying the rapidly expanding towns with plentiful cheap food. The opening up of the great prairies of Alberta and Saskatchewan by the Canadian Pacific Railway permitted massive imports of cheap grain, imported wheat exceeding home production for the first time in 1872. In 1885 the first refrigerated ships began bringing meat and dairy products from Argentina and New Zealand. British farming entered the great depression. Political reforms between 1832 and 1918 had progressively extended voting rights to the town-dwelling middle and working classes, thereby ensuring that Parliament could erect no further protective barriers against imported foodstuffs. For centuries landownership had been the only truly sound investment and the only mark of social respectability. Now that no longer applied; and it was the old landed aristocracy and gentry, those most dependent upon agricultural rents, who were hit hardest. The introduction in 1894 of estate duty, payable upon the property of all deceased persons, added to the pressures; and in a new age which increasingly rejected all forms of privilege and élitism there was precious little sympathy for the difficulties faced by the landowners.

All over England mansions and parks were leased out or sold up. Perhaps Somerset suffered less disruption than other parts of the country where great estates were a more dominant feature of the landscape. Nevertheless, a number of local families were left with no alternative but to sunder connections with lands and houses that had been in their possession for three or four centuries. At Montacute William Robert Phelips was forced in 1895 to sell the family portraits and valuables, and then to break up the farms; in 1911 he leased out the house, which his son eventually sold in 1931. Marston Bigot was sold by the tenth Earl of Cork in 1905. The Medlycotts had moved out of Ven House by 1906, finally selling it in 1957. The eighth Earl Poulett disposed of most of his Hinton St George estate in 1942 and the remainder, including the house, in 1968. In 1946 the Smyths left Ashton Court, which fell into dereliction, being saved only by its acquisition by Bristol Corporation a dozen years later. The great house itself did not always survive the estate's dismemberment. The early Victorian Butleigh Court was abandoned and partly demolished in 1952, the Waldegraves' late Georgian gothic house at Chewton Mendip was dismantled in the mid-1950s, and the regency classical house of Cothelstone Park was demolished in 1964.[1]

Even where the house remained a family home, the old régime could not survive unchanged. The old walled kitchen gardens could no longer compete against cheap imported fruit, rapidly transported by rail. Owners who could still afford it were spending more of their winters abroad, and no longer wanted fruit, flowers and vegetables forced in glasshouses through the darkest and coldest months. Between the wars widespread unemployment meant that outdoor garden staff were readily available at low wages; but legislation to improve the lot of the working man after the Second World War resulted in rising wage bills which could no longer be afforded. Slowly the neat rectangles of fruit and vegetables gave way to weeds and the glasshouses became empty and melancholy skeletons.

Public urban parks came under pressures of a different kind. The development of organised games in the later nineteenth century had produced a new demand for sports pitches. Tennis courts, bowling greens and a cricket ground spread over parts of Vivary Park in Taunton, where the corporation also opened a golf putting course in 1926.[2] Inexorably the Victorian aspirations of spectacular display allied with informal education waned. Labour-intensive practices such as annual bedding displays were reduced as financial demands upon local authorities mounted.

At the time when traditional values of the countryside were most under siege, two influential initiatives were taken by those who were concerned about the blight of industrialism and urban sprawl. In 1895 the National Trust was founded as a charitable body dedicated to the preservation of landscapes and buildings of historic importance. Barrington Court was the first large house and garden to come into the care of the Trust in 1907, followed, nearly a quarter of a century later, by Montacute. Since then the Trust has built up a special expertise in conserving and managing historic parks and gardens, not just for a single family's benefit, but for the enjoyment of hundreds of thousands of visitors every year.[3] The second initiative was the launching of the influential journal COUNTRY LIFE by Edward Hudson in 1897. From the outset this publication lauded the country house as a sort of ideal life-style, and its well-illustrated accounts of gardens and country estates have become important records in their own right.[4]

One positive advance was the emancipation of women, which allowed some great talents to come to the fore in garden design which undoubtedly would have been stifled in earlier generations. Another remarkably successful venture was the initiation of the National Gardens Scheme as part of a charitable fund set up in memory of Queen Alexandra in 1927. It was suggested that one way of raising money might be for owners of private gardens to open them to visitors one day a year. Response from both owners and visitors exceeded all expectations, and it was decided to extend the scheme on an annual basis. In 1996 over 3,500 gardens were opened under the scheme, raising well over £1 million. In Somerset alone over 130 individual gardens were opened on one or more days in the year, ranging from cottage gardens occupying fractions of an acre up to estates of considerable size.

Since the last war shorter working hours, better wages and improvements in transport have made it possible for many more people to visit the numerous gardens now open to the public; also to work in the town while dwelling in the suburbs or the country, thereby giving them more opportunity to cultivate gardens of their own. Radio and television gardening programmes have brought inspiration and

Fig. 9.1
HESTERCOMBE GARDENS.
The Rotunda from the East Rill.

instruction to a vast audience. Commercial garden centres catering like supermarkets for a mass clientele have proliferated. All these things have widened and deepened the appeal of gardens to an extent that even a great populariser like Loudon could never have anticipated.

PLANT COLLECTORS and NEW INTRODUCTIONS

The heroic years of plant collecting, which began in the nineteenth century, continued almost up to the Second World War. The far east, which had generally become more accessible despite intermittent political troubles, remained the most prolific source of new introductions. Ernest Wilson returned to China and Japan on several occasions in the 1900s and 1910s. Reginald Farrer sent back the scented winter-flowering *Viburnum farreri*, along with varieties of rhododendron, buddleia, jasmine and gentian from China and Burma. George Forrest worked on in China, Burma and Tibet up to his death in 1922, adding over 300 new rhododendrons, over 50 new primulas and several camellias to the available stock. Frank Kingdon-Ward discovered the giant cowslip *Primula florindae* in Tibet, and from the same region sent back the first seeds of the blue Himalayan poppy (*Meconopsis betonicifolia*) to be grown successfully in cultivation. Some of the new oriental species did particularly well in the west of England, where high humidity and rainfall and infrequent frosts resembled the climate of their natural habitats.

However, by the middle of the present century the law of diminishing returns had begun to set in. The Royal Botanic Gardens at Kew continue to sponsor fieldwork in remote regions, but few parts of the world remain wholly unexplored, while the costs of full-scale scientific expeditions have spiralled. Slowly the emphasis has shifted towards the breeding and conservation of plant stocks, just in time as so many wild plants have come to be threatened with extinction through man's exploitation of their natural habitats.

BOTANICAL COLLECTIONS

From its foundation the Bath Botanical Garden was designed to be attractive and enjoyable as well as to provide botanical instruction. It has been enlarged on several occasions, and now occupies some nine acres. During the 1920s it was extended eastwards with a small waterfall and serpentine pool. Immediately north-west of the pool stands the Temple of Minerva, a small rectangular pavilion of Bath stone with three arches in the facade, and the name AQVAE SULIS worked into the parapet with the city's arms. This was originally exhibited by the city of Bath at the British Empire Exhibition at Wembley in 1924, and moved to its present site two years later.[5] To commemorate the centenary of the gardens in 1987 two acres of the Great Dell were incorporated from the neighbouring park.

The layout of the garden remains informal. Its various components, including herbaceous borders, a rock garden, a heather garden with many lime-tolerant winter-flowering species, a stream-side garden with exotic shade- and moisture-loving plants, a magnolia lawn, a berberis plantation containing some 35 species, a section given over to plants which attract butterflies, and borders of scented plants and shrub roses, are linked by a winding path. A range of Himalayan conifers grow in the Great Dell to the north, where the spring bulb displays include the Tenby daffodil and the white form of snakeshead fritillary. Other notable specimens in the grounds include a fine example of the corkscrew hazel, *Corylus avellana 'Contorta'*, first discovered in a hedge in Tortworth (Gloucestershire) in about 1863; a young dawn redwood (*Metasequoia glyptostroboides*), a deciduous conifer which was unknown until 1941 when the first living specimens were found growing in China; and one of the tallest examples in Britain of the Chinese necklace tree (*Populus lasiocarpa*).[6]

The Somerset College of Agriculture and Horticulture was founded at Cannington within the old walled gardens of the Priory in 1921, and has since built up there one of the largest collections of ornamental plants in the south-west of England. The shelter of the sandstone walls and the mild coastal climate permit a considerable range of half-hardy species to survive in the open, and there are collections of ceanothus, eucalyptus, fremontia, iris, mahonia, pittosporum, phormium and wisteria. Ten massive aluminium-framed heated greenhouses shelter tender varieties of abutilon, bougainvillea, brugmansia (angels' trumpets) and passiflora (passion flowers). New teaching gardens have all been effectively landscaped, and include a large formal bedding area, a rose garden, ground cover plantings, tree and shrub collections, and experimental plots for lawn grass and sports turf mixtures. Within the new buildings is a striking courtyard garden dominated by silver and glaucous foliage plants.[7]

The University of Bristol Botanic Garden, founded in 1882, had its first site off what is now University Road, but the subsequent expansion of the University buildings twice caused its removal to other sites nearby. Finally, in 1959, it was able to take refuge on the Somerset side of the Avon. Douglas, son of Melville Wills, gave a little over 5 acres of ground at Bracken Hill in Leigh Woods to serve the University as a horticultural centre. The botanic garden there now contains over 4,500 species, including special collections of cistus, campanula, hebe, ferns, salvia and sempervivum along with many native species, and much more under glass. Wills's Pulhamite rock garden survives as a feature in the grounds.

GARDEN STYLES of the EARLY 20TH CENTURY

The extraordinary cornucopia of new plant species imported from all over the world during the nineteenth century threatened severe indigestion, as rival theorists strove to find the most effective ways of making the fullest possible use of them in the garden. During the Edwardian period the tension between the formalists, preferring their gardens to be developed around a firm architectural framework, and the Robinsonian school, using native and imported plants to imitate nature, was largely resolved by merging the best features of both. There was renewed interest in cottage gardens as a source of inspiration for planting schemes in large as well as small spaces. Roses came into particular favour as experiments with hybridisation now offered larger, more brightly-coloured, repeat-flowering varieties. Rose-gardens sometimes filled the niche left by the abandonment of carpet-bedding. Even before the end of the nineteenth century notable rose-gardens had been laid out at both Marston Bigot and Hinton St George, consisting of enclosed circular lawns with geometrically-arranged beds and canopies or arches carrying climbers or ramblers. Another new rose garden was developed at Tyntesfield in about 1910, backed by trees, with balustraded retaining walls, steps flanked with sculptured animals, and two summerhouses.[8]

WAYFORD MANOR and the DESIGNS of HAROLD PETO

The style of architectural garden pioneered by Blomfield and Thomas in the late nineteenth century was developed further by Harold Ainsworth Peto, an antiquarian collector and architectural partner of Sir Ernest George. Peto knew Italy well and had become deeply influenced by the formal Italian garden. For much of his career he was experimenting with ways of adapting that style to the English climate and landscape. In 1899 he purchased Iford Manor, on the Wiltshire bank of the River Frome between Hinton Charterhouse and Westwood, and lived there until his death in 1933, developing on the steep valley side a spectacular series of terraced gardens which included a loggia and patio, a cloistered enclosure and a classical colonnade. Springs fed a series of pools, and the gardens provided a setting for an assortment of classical and medieval sculptural fragments collected on Peto's travels. Italian cypresses were prominent in the planting, but a wide variety of flowering plants was also used to soften the formal framework.

Peto's principal Somerset commission was at Wayford Manor near Crewkerne. This seventeenth-century house had been purchased in 1899 by his brother-in-law, L. Ingham Baker, who employed Sir Ernest George to add a north wing to balance up the asymmetrical front of the house. Baker's son, Humphrey, then called in Peto to redesign the gardens. Like Iford, the site was on a steep slope, occupying a little over three acres, and commanding fine views towards the hills of Dorset. The paved front court contains terracotta pots and a large magnolia, enclosed within clipped yew hedges. A yew alcove contains a replica of a Byzantine font from Ravenna. Along the south front of the house and extending westwards beyond it Peto reconstructed a series of three terraces. The upper terrace was paved, the middle one grassed, the two separated by a rocky bank. The top terrace has a small arbour against its west wall, shaded by two enormous horse chestnuts, and a lily pool surrounded by paving and topiary with an angel and dolphin fountain. A conservatory and three-arched loggia was built at the east end of the middle terrace. Along the front of the grass terrace is a balustrade, from which a stone staircase leads down to a third level, partly lawn and partly flower-beds, one of

the features of which is a great magnolia. From this level a gate leads through to a sheltered secret garden, with two Japanese maples shading lilies and irises, a concealed seat in a niche, and a large rectangular lily pool with a cherub fountain. Lower down the hill another path crosses at right-angles leading to the kitchen garden. Below this point formality was abandoned, and there are a series of less regulated areas, each with its own special character: a rock garden with conifers, a pool with Japanese maples and a stone Buddha, an orchard of cider apples with daffodils and crocuses surrounded by borders of rhododendrons, cherries and maples, a woodland area with rhododendrons and Japanese maples, and right at the bottom a water-garden with water-lilies and marsh plants.[9]

The eighteenth-century gardens of Widcombe Manor near Bath were altered in Italianate style in the 1930s, with a bronze Venetian fountain installed in the southern forecourt and two lower terraces added on the western side, divided down the centre by an elaborate double staircase. Beneath the lower terrace a square stone-edged garden with a sunken octagonal centre was laid out. This design has also been attributed to Harold Peto. Considerable alterations were carried out around 1970, with a rectangular pool added on the central axis enclosed within yew hedges and a semicircular beech hedge below. Something of Peto's distinctive style can also be detected in the yew-hedged terraced gardens of Barley Wood in Wrington, though it is not known whether had any personal involvement in this design.[10]

SIR EDWIN LUTYENS and GERTRUDE JEKYLL

When Ammerdown was completed in the later eighteenth century the house was surrounded by its park, and the deer are said to have come up to the windows to feed. There were no gardens, apart from the walled kitchen garden and orangery some distance away. In 1901 Hylton George Jolliffe, 3rd Baron Hylton, called in Edwin Landseer Lutyens to alter its setting. Lutyens was then in his early thirties, already an experienced architect, versatile in a variety of styles, but particularly interested in the relationship between house and garden. At Ammerdown it was the gardens which were to be his main concern, and he produced a formal scheme appropriate to the setting of a classical mansion. The main problem he faced was that Wyatt's orangery and the walled kitchen garden were differently orientated to the house, and some original geometry was needed to link the two effectively. His solution was to create a circular Italian garden centred on the point where the axes from the house and orangery met, balancing the obtuse angle of the vista to the orangery with a crossing path which led to a circular rose garden. The focal point of the three axes was surrounded by an intricate pattern of beds edged in box with statues at the corners, all enclosed within a massive sculpted yew hedge of square outline. A pergola was erected west of the rose garden. The main axis of the garden was then continued into the park by an avenue of limes.[11]

In the year that Lutyens undertook his Ammerdown commission, he was also requested to design a new wing for Redlynch

WAYFORD MANOR.
left: Fig. 9.2
A gate ornament.
top: Fig. 9.3
The formal garden terraces.
above: Fig. 9.4
The informal garden at the bottom of the hill.

135

House and to advise on the gardens. Here the formal layout east of the house, including the paved terrace, steps and summerhouse, are his design. Lutyens also worked at Mells Park, where he rebuilt the house in 1923 for Reginald McKenna, Chairman of the Midland Bank, but in this case the three-acre gardens which he designed around the south and east fronts of the house have not survived.[12]

While Lutyens was working on his first architectural commission he had been introduced to Gertrude Jekyll. Miss Jekyll

had studied at Kensington School of Art and had commenced a career as a painter, but, increasingly hampered by failing eyesight, had turned to garden design instead. Though she was 26 years his senior, the two struck up an immediate rapport, and they embarked upon a very successful professional partnership, with Jekyll contributing the planting plans to accompany Lutyens's buildings. She became a prolific writer on gardening. Like Robinson before her, she reacted against the regimented bedding schemes of many contemporary large gardens, deriving inspiration instead from cottage gardens, with their traditional mix of useful and ornamental plants. Her interest in colour was one of the hallmarks of her work, an understanding of harmony and contrast within the spectrum arising out of her artistic training. Perhaps because of her poor sight, she preferred strong groupings of plants all flowering at the same time rather than sporadic dots of bloom. Her fondness for highly scented varieties of roses, honeysuckle and mignonette probably arose from the same cause. Foliage was equally important to her, and she had a particular liking for grey-leaved plants.

One of the finest surviving products of the Lutyens-Jekyll partnership is at Hestercombe. In 1892 this property had passed to the grandson of the first Viscount Portman, the Hon. E.W.B. Portman, and it was he who commissioned Lutyens and Jekyll eleven years later to redesign the grounds. The house was not the family's main seat and was only occupied in high summer so the brief was to provide a garden which would be at its best around June, when the family was in residence.

Lutyens planned the architectural framework of the garden to take advantage of the south-facing slope below the house, forming a series of terraces and vistas covering some 3.75 acres. His design effectively combined the sense of shelter and security reminiscent of an enclosed Tudor garden with the expansiveness of a magnificent outward view over the countryside from the surrounding raised walks. The orangery and the stone gateposts and alcoves follow more closely the style of the later seventeenth century. A particular feature of the design is the use of carefully-selected and contrasting building materials: the rough-split pinkish-grey Devonian shale quarried from

the hills above the house, used in the rubble walling and paving, and the fine orange-buff Ham Hill stone for dressings and balustrades. The formal foundation of the garden was perfectly complemented by Gertrude Jekyll's plantings, with drifts and clumps of perennials carefully chosen for their colouring and texture, softening the edges and spilling over the terraces and walks.

Viscount Portman's Victorian upper terrace was left untouched by the new scheme. From the west end of this top terrace steps lead down to a small enclosed formal rose garden shaded by an alcoved arbour of wych elms. An elaborate stone tank in front of the arbour fed water into a central rill. French bur millstones appear in the paving of the walk, an idea used by Jekyll in her own garden at Munstead Wood in Surrey. From the rose garden further steps lead down to the the lower terrace, with a long lawn running from east to west below the revetment wall. This is known as the Grey Walk because of the predominance of silver foliage and pastel shades, with cascades of yucca, catmint, cotton lavender, pinks, Jerusalem sage, rosemary and soapwort, and boxes of myrtle and choisya framing the doorways.

At either end of the Grey Walk doorways lead to two raised terraces aligned at right-angles to it, the three elements framing and overlooking the sunk garden in the centre. At the head of both terraces is a circular pool with a dished stone bed, the rear half of which is overshadowed by a quarter-spherical alcove cut into the revetment of the balustraded terrace above. From the retaining wall a single jet of water spouts from a mask at the top of the arch into the pool, creating ripples from which reflected sunlight dapples the concave alcove above. Beyond either side of the round-arched pool, bull's-eye recesses are set into the revetment wall below the balustrade, echoing the spherical motif. Below each pool the water is then led along a straight stone-lined rill, punctuated by two small round pools, running the whole length of both terraces. Architecturally the two rill terraces are identical, but the pattern of planting is quite different. The eastern terrace has gypsophila, scarlet poppies, asters, lavender and echinops, red-hot pokers and large clumps of iris all along the borders, while the rill itself was planted with forget-me-not, water plantain, arum lily and arrowhead. The west rill terrace has white and orange lilies, old roses, delphiniums, campanulas and foxgloves, with edgings of London pride, pinks, saxifrage, hostas and bergenia.

The centrepiece of the whole scheme was the large sunk garden known as the Plat, 125 feet square, entered by quadrant stone steps from each corner. The position of the entries necessitated a diagonal division of the square, with broad grass panels intersecting at a central sundial. The lawns and the triangular beds between them are bordered by rough stone sets laid out in geometrical patterns. Gertrude Jekyll's original planting scheme envisaged cannas, gladioli and phlox here, but early on this seems to have been rejected in favour of llies, roses, peonies and delphiniums, edged with evergreen bergenia. The surrounding borders echo the themes of the terraces above, with roses and pinks; there was also much planting within the terrace retaining walls.

From the end of the rill terraces the water drains into two rectangular pools with steps leading down to them. The floor of each pool is made of pitched stone paving, to create an interesting texture visible through the water. The terrace around each pool is enclosed on its outer side by stone walls containing almond-shaped openings to give a peephole glimpse into the neighbouring fields; enormous scented purple wisterias frame the gateways giving entry to the steps down to the Plat. Between the two pools and closing the whole of the southern side of the Plat is a long pergola, with alternate square and round stone piers spanned by arched oak beams, carrying climbing roses, clematis, vines and forsythias, underplanted with English and cotton lavender and Jerusalem sage. Gaps in the pergola at either end command a sweeping view over the Vale of Taunton Deane to the Blackdown Hills. The sheer drop to the south provides a strong boundary between garden and park.

Another arm of the garden takes off to the north-east to include the orangery terrace. This axis is aligned at an angle of 110 degrees to the main garden, and the junction is achieved by a rotunda above the head of the eastern rill terrace, acting as a pivot. A circular pool surrounded by stone paving occupies the centre of the rotunda, which is enclosed by high stone walls over which wintersweet climbs prolifically, with clipped orange trees in tubs around the perimeter,

flanking the doorways. Round niches in the walls contain stone baskets of fruit and flowers, and the entrance piers are adorned with small figures of winged cupids.

From the rotunda a double flight of steps set with millstones and overhung with lilac and acanthus leads down the north-eastern axis to Lutyens's orangery. This is a fine classically symmetrical rectangular building of seven bays, with three tall fanlight-headed lights separated by two lower square-headed windows with circular recesses above, and a blank segmental-arched niche in each end bay flanked by rusticated pilasters. The mixture of local rubble and Ham stone dressings is used to good effect. In front of the orangery a paved terrace adorned with clumps of rosemary, lavender and choisya looks down across a sloping lawn with informally-grouped trees towards the orchard.

Finally, beyond the east end of the orangery, a further broad flight of balustraded steps leads up to the Dutch garden, a raised square platform created by Lutyens over an old rubbish dump, with beds of roses, catmint, lavenders, yuccas and hostas interspersed with complex paving patterns. Four massive terracotta urns gave a vertical

Fig. 9.6
The Plat, HESTERCOMBE GARDENS.

emphasis to this garden (the originals have been smashed, but copies have been made to replace them). A Chinese gateway looks out to the pond of the old sawmill, whose long tiled roof closes off the further end of the garden.[13]

After the Great War Gertrude Jekyll continued to design gardens up to her death in 1932. At Barrington Court she became involved only after considerable works had already been undertaken. The house had been occupied by a succession of tenants and was in semi-derelict condition until 1907, when it was acquired by the National Trust. Twelve years later, the Trust itself leased out the estate to Col. Abraham Lyle, who embarked upon a programme of re-creation and enhancement, purchasing neighbouring land and erecting model estate buildings in the style of the Arts and Crafts movement. During the early 1920s he employed the architects Forbes and Tate to convert the seventeenth-century stable block to domestic quarters, with a new terrace on the west front; this was then named Strode House, after William Strode, who first built it in 1674. The architects were also to provide a new set of traditional-style farm buildings and tenants' cottages to the north-east, north and north-west, linked to the house by a cruciform arrangement of horse chestnut avenues. A large walled kitchen garden was laid out behind the estate buildings north-west of the house. Within it gravel paths outline a square, crossing at the centre, where there is a small round fountain basin. Espalier fruit trees and perennial flowers border the paths, with further fruit trees trained over the walls, and extensive beds of vegetables and soft fruits between. South of the main vegetable garden a second walled enclosure contains greenhouses, and in the south-east corner of the kitchen-garden complex is a stone building with a hipped and gabletted tile roof: despite its appearance, carefully contrived to resemble some rustic farm building, this was built as a squash court.

The walled ornamental gardens to the west of Barrington Court and Strode House were laid out between 1920 and 1925. The original scheme conceived by the architect Forbes was for a more extensive and elaborate design occupying ten acres, with yew hedges covering the south front of the court and an Elizabethan-style garden in what is now the orchard. A broad herbaceous border facing south across the orchard was planted and still remains. The west and north sides of the gardens were bordered by a moat outside the wall, formed by canalising an existing stream. However, the Forbes scheme was, on the whole, felt to be too complicated, and both the National Trust and the tenant were in agreement that there should be no visual distraction from the architecture of the house.

Col. Lyle then called in Gertrude Jekyll, who adapted and simplified Forbes's scheme, leaving the orchard as it was, and reducing the overall area. She acquired soil samples from various parts of the garden before drawing up her planting scheme. Some of the herbaceous plants she supplied herself, the hedging plants came from Scotts of Merriot, and most of the remaining plants came from nurserymen as far afield as Chiddingfold, Colchester and Woodbridge.

The basic layout of Gertrude Jekyll's gardens survives at Barrington, though the planting is now somewhat altered. The modern entrance is from the direction of the kitchen garden, by a bridge over the east arm of the moat. This gives access to a series of separate walled enclosures. The first is the square iris garden, with its right-angled beds and central fountain; this formerly also contained pink roses, now replaced by lavenders and purple clematis. Next came the rose garden or white garden, made in 1925, with beds forming segments of a circle, partly enclosed within box hedges. To the north the white garden backs onto a range of Victorian cattle-stalls, one of the few older structures to be retained. A box hedge and brick path separates the iris garden from a border west of the cowhouse, which was originally intended to provide cut flowers for the house. This was replanted by Mrs Lyle in 1960 in the Jekyll style, with colours graded from yellow through orange and red to mauve and blue. To the south

of these compartments, abutting upon the west front of Strode House, is the lily garden, with a central oblong pool, lawns, narrow paths of bricks laid in basket-weave pattern and flower borders against the walls. In its present form this is a simplified version of the Jekyll plan, with raised beds of azaleas flanking the pool instead of the hydrangeas and crinums she had intended. The raised corner beds, where Miss Jekyll had intended to plant yuccas, now contain crinums. From a doorway in the mid-point of the south wall of the lily garden access is gained to the large south lawn, which extends across the south front of the Court itself and terminates in a ha-ha overlooking the park. East of the Court is a small arboretum and lime walk. The front of the forecourt north of the house is also defined by a moat with a central bridge carrying the main drive.[14]

Edwin Lutyens and Gertrude Jekyll were frequent visitors to Sir John and Lady Horner at Mells Manor in the early 1900s and, although no plans are known, it is likely that they advised on the gardens there. The loggia of Tuscan columns on the terrace overlooking the flower garden to the south looks like the work of Lutyens. Miss Jekyll also provided designs for Marksdanes, a house on the north-east side of Bruton, in 1919, and for Stowell Hall near Templecombe in 1925, but it is not known whether her schemes were ever carried through on either site.[15]

GARDENS between the WARS

Two great gardens of the 1920s and 1930s, Lawrence Johnston's Hidcote in Gloucestershire and Vita Sackville-West's Sissinghurst in Kent, dominated the development of garden design between the wars. Both were created by owners who maintained a deep personal commitment over a prolonged period, and who combined a scientific interest in plants with the vision to group them in effective settings. Their use of separate garden 'rooms' and their experiments with single-colour plantings became enormously influential.

In Somerset intermittent works continued after the Great War on a number of other large gardens. At Newton Surmaville a start had been made on remodelling the grounds around the main pond east of the house in 1909, but this was interrupted by the war and only resumed in the 1920s. A rose garden and herbaceous borders were then laid out to the east of the pond, while on the opposite bank a stone path was backed by a rockery and small shrubs, with espaliered apple trees behind.[16] Further works were carried out at Montacute by Lord Curzon, tenant of the house from 1915 to 1925, a former Viceroy of India who became Foreign Secretary in 1919. Curzon was responsible for the Elizabethan-style facade of the summerhouse overlooking the cedar lawn, adding a balustraded parapet carrying a curvilinear pediment with the Strode arms supported on three rusticated arches. Garden seats from a Lutyens design were also

brought in during his time.[17] At St Catherine's Court Mackay Hugh Baillie Scott designed further Italian-style gardens with two pergola walks south of the house in the 1920s for the Hon. Richard Strutt.[18]

The three most influential Somerset gardens of the inter-war period were all in the Ham stone belt in the south-east of the county. They were developed by three quite remarkable women, who came to know each other well, and shared many plant-hunting expeditions together among the local cottage gardens.

PHYLLIS REISS at TINTINHULL

In about 1900 Tintinhull's owner, Dr S.J.M. Price, had begun redesigning its grounds, which then occupied less than an acre of fairly flat ground, in formal style. In 1933 the property was purchased by Captain F.E. Reiss, whose wife, Phyllis, had once lived near Hidcote and was clearly influenced by Johnston's work there. Over the following 28 years she transformed the Tintinhull gardens, experimenting with a variety of planting schemes. The grounds have been developed further since 1980 by the well-known garden designer and writer Penelope Hobhouse.

The basic framework of the Tintinhull grounds has been a formal one throughout, but as in other great gardens of the first half of the twentieth century, the detailed planting within that framework is soft-edged and free-flowing. Within the mix of trees, shrubs, perennials, biennials and bulbs, unity of design is achieved by compatiblity of form and colour rather than by regimentation. An ancient Lebanon cedar, two tall yews and two evergreen oaks provide pools of shade. Like Hidcote and Sissinghurst, Tintinhull also consists of separate garden 'rooms', each with their own special character.

From the west front of the house a path of triangular and diamond-shaped York stone flags, laid down by Dr Price during the First World War, and flanked by domes of box first planted in the 1920s, leads through two more or less square compartments. First comes the Eagle Court, so named from the stone eagles on piers which flank the further exit. This was for two centuries no more than an entrance courtyard, until Mrs Reiss converted it to a square lawn with perimeter flower borders; here the crab apple, flowering cherry and mahonia japonica still survive from her time. Next comes the Middle Garden, on the same level, which is more shaded (particularly by the two evergreen oaks at its south-western corner) and less formal, with curved flower beds around a central lawn. In the middle of the south border a replica eighteenth-century urn provides both a viewpoint and the terminus of a north-south vista along the rectangular pool to the north. The path continues down four steps into the Fountain Garden in the south-west corner, where it encircles a round lily pool forming the centre of a cruciform plot laid out as a white garden on the Sissinghurst model. The east side, originally planted by Phyllis Reiss with the yellow azalea pontica, has been re-established by Penelope Hobhouse with a wider variety of golden and yellow plants. The west side was replanted by Paul Miles, National Trust gardens adviser in the 1970s, with foliage plants. At the west end of the axial path a white seat beneath an arbour of bay laurel gives a view back through all three compartments to the early-eighteenth-century west front of the house.

Fig. 9.10
Pear cordons at
BARRINGTON COURT.

Fig. 9.11
A drawing by Lutyens of
GERTRUDE JEKYLL,
made about 1896.

TINTINHULL HOUSE.
above: Fig. 9.12
The west front and Eagle Court.
right: Fig. 9.13
The Pool Garden.

Northwards from the Fountain Garden beyond a yew hedge lies the rectangular kitchen garden, again with a cruciform pattern of paths lined with catmint and spurges. Honeysuckles and other ornamental climbers on frames give colour, height and variety to the more utilitarian vegetables and fruit. In front of the yew hedge Mrs Reiss planted a carpet of *Rosa gallica* var. *officinalis*, the ancient red rose of Lancaster or apothecary's rose. North of the middle garden is the Pool Garden, a former tennis court converted by Mrs Reiss in 1947 in memory of her nephew, a pilot killed near the end of the Second World War. The centrepiece is a long rectangular lily pool aligned north-south, with lawns on either side and a loggia beyond its northern end. The lawns are flanked by two colour-graded borders, one with glowing reds, oranges and yellows, the other with softer pastel pinks, mauves and pale blues. The final compartment, north of the house, is known as the Cedar Court, from the large multi-trunked cedar against its north wall. It consists of a central lawn surrounded by borders, with several magnolias. The western border, dominated by purple and gold foliage plants, is perhaps Mrs Reiss's best-known contribution, and has been widely imitated.[19]

VIOLET CLIVE at BRYMPTON d'EVERCY

The Brympton d'Evercy estate had passed from Lady Georgiana Fane to her nephew, Spencer Ponsonby. His grand-daughter, Violet Ponsonby-Fane, who had married Captain Edward Clive, spent thirty years as a widow at Brympton. She travelled widely, collecting rare plants in a spongebag, and brought many of them successfully into cultivation. She replaced the formal Victorian bedding just after the end of the First World War, developing a garden which anticipated Sissinghurst in many of its details - the careful use of cottage garden plants in situations which best showed off their form and foliage, the mix of shrubs and herbaceous plants in wide borders in drifts of subtle colouring, and the use of foliage to complement architectural features. In later years the American garden designer Lanning Roper vividly recalled the grey-and-pink, grey-and-orange and grey-and-yellow gardens at Brympton.[20] Mrs Clive salvaged sufficient material from the demolition of the fire-damaged old town hall at Yeovil in 1935 to build a classical temple with pillars at the east end of the south terrace, while a spare stone pier serves as the base for a dovecote in front of the stables. Other stone fragments and urns salvaged from the estate itself were used to make steps from the north side of the forecourt up to a vineyard newly-established on the upper terrace. Violet Clive's brother, Richard Ponsonby-Fane, spent much of his life in Japan, and the area south of the lake contains a stone lantern from his garden in Kyoto (one of several in the garden) along with many Japanese camellias, azaleas, junipers and peonies.[21]

MARGERY FISH at EAST LAMBROOK

In 1937 Walter and Margery Fish, who both had careers in journalism in the capital, bought the Manor House at East Lambrook as a wartime country retreat. At that time the house had only two small lawns and a farmyard to the rear and the only notable feature was a large variegated sycamore (*Acer pseudoplatanus 'Leopoldii'*). Walter Fish had some practical knowledge of gardening, and had traditionalist views about the desirability of colourful summer-flowering plants such as dahlias, lupins and delphiniums, with neat lawns, paths and hedges as a backdrop. Margery, who had reached the age of 46 with no interest or experience in gardening whatsoever, developed a different philosophy which she came to describe as 'jungle gardening', preferring combinations of smaller, less showy plants, including spring- and autumn-blooming species, in less regimented contexts. She began collecting botanical and horticultural books and visiting other gardens, and was particularly influenced by William Robinson's philosophy of natural gardening, but her ultimate success owed more to instinct, trial and error and sheer hard work than to any preconceived theory. It was not surprising that the Fishes were not always in accord as the garden developed, and Margery writes humorously of their widely divergent views on planting, watering and manuring.

The style of East Lambrook is unpretentious. Since the garden was developed piecemeal without any overall master-plan, it lacked the strong architectural framework of Tintinhull. The effects were achieved more through careful attention to the particular qualities of individual plants. The planting was mixed, with shrubs, bulbous plants and foliage plants punctuated by evergreens. Nevertheless, different parts of the garden developed a very distinct character of their own as work progressed.

The first task was to improve the east boundary wall, and Mrs Fish used aubrieta, alyssum, valerian, arabis and a variety of rock plants planted in crevices to soften its outline. The barton yard in front of the farm buildings was then cleared of rubbish, and laid out as a gravel drive. Some of the debris was used as the base of a banked rockery on the north side of the barton gate. One of the charms of Margery Fish's account is her cheerful admission of early errors, such as sloping the slabs of the rockery outwards so that soil was washed out by the rain, and her unorthodox experiments, such as planting the rockery with a joyous mix of annuals including antirrhinum, mignonette, zinnias, clarkia, godetia and candytuft. 'Dresden China' daisies were planted between the flat slabs fronting the rockery.

A small functional herb garden was made immediately outside the back door, with mint, parsley, tarragon, pennyroyal, marjoram, winter savory, chives, and caraway, while more decorative herbs such as rue, sage, hyssop, angelica, fennel, bergamot and rosemary slowly came to feature in other areas. The tiny front garden of the house was repaved with slabs set in concrete under Walter Fish's supervision, but Margery describes how she surreptitiously created cracks and holes with a crowbar and hammer to provide a home for a multitude of thymes, saxifrages and other creeping plants. The bare walls of the house and farm buildings were slowly mantled with the blue Clematis jackmanii, ceanothus, roses, pyracantha and cotoneaster.

The Fishes were agreed on the virtues of a spacious lawn, and the ground between the barton and the north front of the house was laid down to grass, partly shaded by the pre-existing sycamore. Mrs Fish built a low wall between the lawn and drive, planting it initially with alpines. Next, in the winter of 1938, she turned her attention to the slopes west of the house, there constructing a series of informal terraces with stone steps and low stone revetments. For immediate effect spreading plants which had a long season and needed no staking were employed here - the pink *Geranium endressii*, white candytuft, pulmonarias, shamrock and catmint in the beds, gypsophila, aubretia and Cheddar pink spilling over the walls and London pride, white rock cress, stonecrops and rock campanulas filling the cracks. A curving path was made up the slope between two rows of conically-

pruned cypresses (*Chamaecyparis lawsoniana 'Fletcheri'*), planted in the summer of 1940 to replace the pole-trained roses initially established by Walter Fish. The orchard at the top was underplanted with daffodils, but mowing proved a problem, and in due course it was tidied up and hedged with the shrub honeysuckle Lonicera nitida.

A neighbouring strip of orchard was acquired with the intervening boundary ditch in order to make a water garden, but the water unexpectedly dried up, so the banks were planted with alpine strawberries, violets, London pride, primroses and primulas. Subsequently snowdrops and polyanthus were added. In the early 1950s one of the banks was scooped out to accommodate a peat garden. Part of the ditch, known as the 'Lido', was densely planted with a jungle of skunk cabbage, ornamental rhubarbs and rodgersias. The old orchard verge alongside was underplanted with a range of hellebores, which have since hybridized.

Walter Fish died suddenly in 1947. His widow visited the United States several times over the next few years, where she came to know the work of Beatrix Farrand, becoming especially enthused with Mrs Farrand's use of ground-cover plants. She then returned to Lambrook permanently and continued to develop the garden until her own death in 1969. She rescued many unfashionable and almost-forgotten plants from obscurity, such as lambs' ears (*Stachys byzantina*), an eighteenth-century introduction from the Caucasus, which she found lingering on in some local cottage garden. Even well into her 70s she was still experimenting: a small 'silver garden' was developed on the southern fringe of the terraces, and in 1966 she began a 'green garden' not far from the rockery, using euphorbias, hellebores, alchemillas, bergenias and periwinkles beneath a blue cedar and a Chusan palm. She also embarked upon a new career in garden writing, submitting her first article to *The Field* in 1951, and five years later publishing her first book, *We Made a Garden*, which describes the evolution of Lambrook.

Through her writing and through her practical example Margery Fish was very influential in popularising the 'cottage garden' style. The less demanding qualities of an informal layout, where knowledgeable owners could do the greater part of the work themselves, well suited the post-war climate of high labour costs. However, as the garden at East Lambrook became ever more complex, as writing and lecturing demanded more of her time, and as her own health began to weaken, she too was forced to take on help, and compromises were made for easier maintentance, such as the resurfacing of the gravel drive in the barton with bitumen and the replacement of the gravel paths with stone paving. The task of upkeep proved increasingly difficult after Margery Fish's death, and her nephew who had inherited the property decided reluctantly to sell in 1984. Fortunately the new owners, Mr and Mrs A. Norton, have dedicated themselves to the continuation and restoration of the garden, and it is now re-emerging in its full glory.[22]

Fig. 9.14
The north front of East Lambrook.

Modernist Designs

The stirrings of a reaction against the Edwardian Arts and Crafts tradition can be detected in the late 1920s and 1930s, as a few designers, influenced by contemporary European developments in art and architecture, began experimenting with new geometric forms using concrete paving, steps and walls and minimalist planting. Sir Geoffrey Jellicoe, one of the best-known landscape architects of recent years, began designing in traditional style, but became interested in the modern movement early on in his career. In 1934, in partnership with Russell Page, he submitted a design for a restaurant and visitor centre in Cheddar Gorge, completed four years later. This was one of the pioneer modernist buildings, and was accompanied by appropriate roof-garden planting incorporating a glass-bottomed pool. However, the austere lines of modernism failed to find immediate favour, and the outbreak of the Second World War temporarily put up a barrier to continental influences. Jellicoe's Cheddar essay was altered almost beyond recognition in the 1960s.[23]

The American garden designer Lanning Roper had first met Walter and Margery Fish at East Lambrook while he was still a lieutenant in the United States Naval Reserve in 1943, and Mrs Fish subsequently introduced him to Tintinhull, Montacute, Brympton d'Evercy, Barrington and other Somerset gardens. This experience did much to set him upon his future career. He was enthusiastic about the cottage garden style at Lambrook, but became even more impressed by the self-contained vistas of Tintinhull, and the way in which the arrangement of the garden there complemented the house.[24] He assisted in the planning of the gardens of the American Museum at Claverton, to be discussed below. In 1969 he advised General McCreery on a design for Stowell Hall near Templecombe, and some of the plants he recommended, such as the Frau Dagmar Hastrup roses, still grow there;[25] but this was his only other Somerset commission. Elsewhere Roper developed considerable expertise in devising garden settings for modern buildings which were easy to maintain and interesting throughout the seasons; but he never forgot his delight in the more traditional gardens he had seen in Somerset.

Professional landscape architects have continued to experiment with modernist forms in some new housing developments, shopping centres, industrial estates, and motorway service stations; but such adventures have generally had little influence upon the design of private gardens, where conservatism verging upon nostalgia has tended to reign supreme.

GARDENS from the SECOND WORLD WAR to the MILLENNIUM

The 'Dig for Victory' campaign during the Second World War did something to revive old kitchen-garden skills, but little else was possible during the period of post-war austerity. So far as style is concerned, the recovery since the 1960s has itself been marked more by revivalism than new invention, with the reappearance and fusion of many garden elements and cultures of centuries past.

One feature that has returned to widespread favour is the herb garden. Sometimes this has been deliberately designed as a museum display. At Claverton Manor in 1964 a formal herb garden with cobble-edged flagstone walks and box-edged beds with a beehive at the centre was created by Ian Mylles on behalf of the Southampton (New York) Garden Club for the American Museum in Britain. This contains examples of the culinary, medicinal and aromatic herbs taken by the early settlers to America or brought into cultivation there, also a range of dye plants, including indigo, woad, alkanet and pokeroot. At Lytes Cary the National Trust have reintroduced herbs of Henry Lyte's day - mints, rue, artemisia, lavender and lilies. Elsewhere re-creations of herb gardens have been seen simply as a fitting complement to an ancient house. At Gaulden Manor the herb garden is laid out in the form of a cross, with flagstone paths meeting at a central sundial. Another herb garden was created as part of the programme of restoration at Combe Sydenham in the 1970s.[26]

Combe Sydenham and Gaulden Manor both also have collections of old roses, and the revival of interest in varieties which at one time seemed doomed to extinction can be seen as part of a wider movement in plant conservation to which we will return in the final chapter. A particularly interesting venture has been the opening of the Time Trail of Roses in Wells, a private collection of over 1500 varieties planted out over half an acre of ground in date order of their introduction.

Another feature of medieval cultivation which has been revived on a much more extensive scale is the growing of the grape vine. Since 1964 Mr and Mrs Nigel Godden have very successfully re-established over four acres of vineyards at Pilton Manor, with a modern winery. By the 1970s the renewed interest in viticulture had expanded sufficiently for the Long Ashton Research Station to respond with an advisory publication.[27] Today at least eighteen commercial vineyards operate in Somerset, particularly around Bath and Glastonbury.

Although this book has been concerned with the evolution of gardens and parks from ancient times, the vast majority of private gardens we see today are themselves of quite recent origin. Let us conclude by selecting three examples begun since the 1950s.

One of the more notable gardens to have been developed in recent times is that at Clapton Court near Crewkerne. Like Harold Peto's Wayford Manor, not far away, this has both formal and informal planting, but here the two components are of different dates. The formal terraces, borders, lawns and rose garden, covering eight acres beside the house, were first laid out by Louis Martineau in the early 1950s. The basic framework of his garden remains in use, though the planting pattern has been modified, the rose garden being redesigned by Penelope Hobhouse. The property was taken over in 1978 by Captain and Mrs Simon J. Loder. An earlier member of the family, Col. G.H. Loder, had been much influenced by the principles of William Robinson, which he applied at his house at Handcross in Sussex in 1903. In the same tradition, the Loders have converted a belt of derelict woodland covering the steep slopes flanking a small streamlet on the further side of Clapton Court into a woodland garden covering some 2.5 acres. The native woodland has been underplanted with rhododendrons, azaleas and other exotic and rare trees and shrubs, while the stream has been dammed up to make small ponds as a habitat for waterside species. The woodland area includes a fine example of the much sought-after pocket-handkerchief tree, *Davidia involucrata*. On the edge of the garden is a massive ash-tree, claimed to be the oldest in Britain.[28]

The herb and rose gardens of Gaulden Manor have already

CLAPTON COURT.
Below: Fig. 9.15
The Formal Garden.
Bottom: Fig. 9.16
The Woodland Garden.

been mentioned. Here, on the eastern foothills of the Brendons, Mr and Mrs J. le Gendre Starkie have created three acres of new gardens out of a wasteland since 1967, designed to be in keeping with the Tudor house, including a fishpond with an island, a bog garden and a butterfly garden. Primulas are a special feature of the planting.[29]

The gardens around the manor-house at Walton-in-Gordano were begun by Mr and Mrs Simon Wills in 1976. The fastigiate oaks along the drive were underplanted with daffodils and crocuses. Mediterranean plants were established along the sheltered, south-facing entrance front. Behind the house an area of sloping lawns was converted into a series of long informal island beds with a mix of small trees, shrubs, herbaceous plants and bulbs, designed to be walked round and seen from all sides. To the west an old tennis court has been enclosed within yew hedges and converted to a small formal garden with four square pools and stone-flagged paths between fragrant plants of predominantly pastel pink, blue and white colouring. Raised beds along either side contain unusual alpines. Beyond this to the west again the ground rises through an area of informally-planted trees, which includes specimens of Dawyck beech and the pocket-handkerchief tree.[30]

In earlier centuries gardens were conceived as an oasis of order within the wilderness, a place from which the unruly forces of nature could be excluded, where plants could be brought under control and regulated for both consumption and ornament. During the nineteenth century, with increasing industrialisation and urbanisation, the broader countryside itself became a place of renewal and refreshment, where man could regain some contact with nature. In the more recent past, as ever more land disappears beneath the relentless advance of buildings and tarmac and as traditional farming practices give way to heavily-mechanised, chemically-supported monocultures, much of the man-made environment has itself come to seem increasingly hostile. Parks and gardens have become oases of a different sort, green refuges and havens for wildlife.

It is perhaps fair to conclude that the contribution of the present century to garden design has for the most part been unadventurous, and more influenced by nostalgia than by any contemporary movements in art and architecture. Whether or not that is itself a good thing only future generations can judge; but the wholly justified modern concern for conservation has made it inevitable. On the positive side, however, there is no doubt whatsoever that parks and gardens are now enjoyed by far more people than ever before; and a proper understanding of their history can add immeasurably to that enjoyment. Today, thanks to the generosity of owners who have been prepared to open their grounds to the public, we can all enjoy the rewards of the vision and labours of those who have created and maintained them in the past.

REFERENCES - Chapter 9

1. Roy Strong, Marcus Binney & John Harris, *The Destruction of the Country House, 1875-1975* (1974).

2. R. Bush, *The Book of Taunton* (Chesham, 1977), p.105.

3. John Gaze, *Figures in a Landscape: a History of the National Trust* (1988)

4. A selection of articles from *Country Life*, first published as *Country Gardens Old and New*, has been reprinted as a facsimile edition under the title *Gardens in Edwardian England* (Woodbridge, 1985). Ray Desmond's invaluable *Bibliography of British Gardens* (Winchester, 1984) provides a comprehensive site-by-site list of entries in the journal.

5. Robin Whalley, 'The Royal Victoria Park', *Bath History* Vol.5 (1994), p.164.

6. S.D. Hitt, *Bath Botanical Gardens* (Bath, 1994).

7. John Sales, *West Country Gardens* (Gloucester, 1980), p.177.

8. Michael McGarvie, *Notes towards a History of Gardening at Marston House, 1660-1905* (Frome, 1987), pp.24-5; Colin G. Winn, *The Pouletts of Hinton St George*, (Stroud, 1995), p.158; *Country Life* Vol.11 (17th May, 1902), pp.624-30.

9. *Country Life* Vol.76 (29th September 1934), pp.336-41; Vol.177 (7th March 1985), p.560; Sales, *West Country Gardens*, pp.184-6.

10. *Country Life* Vol.82 (28th August 1937), pp.220-25; Stewart Harding & David Lambert, *Parks and Gardens of Avon* (Bristol, 1994) p.87.

11. *Country Life* Vol.65 (16th February 1929), pp.216-23; (2nd March, 1929), pp.292-98; (9th March, 1929), pp.330-35; A.S.G. Butler & George Stewart, *The Architecture of Sir Edwin Lutyens, Vol.2: Gardens* (1950), p.12; Jane Brown, *Gardens of a Golden Afternoon* (1982), pp.79-81, 166).

12. Redlynch: *Country Life* Vol.172 (23rd September 1982), p.940; Sales, *West Country Gardens*, p.176. Mells Park: Brown, *Gardens of a Golden Afternoon*, p.174.

13. Butler & Stewart, *The Architecture of Sir Edwin Lutyens, Vol.2*, p.12; Sales, *West Country Gardens*, pp.156-9; Brown, *Gardens of a Golden Afternoon*, pp.83-5; Richard Bisgrove, *The Gardens of Gertrude Jekyll* (1992), pp.90-93, 159-65.

14. Gertrude Jekyll's original plans for Barrington are now in the Reef Point Gardens Collection in the University of Berkeley, California; Sales, *West Country Gardens*, pp.133-7.

15. Mells Manor: *Country Life* Vol.131 (24th May 1962), p.1254; Brown, *Gardens of a Golden Afternoon*, p.166. The original drawings for Marksdanes and Stowell Hall are in the Reef Point Gardens Collection, University of Berkeley, California, quoted by Brown, *Gardens of a Golden Afternoon*, pp.190-1.

16. *Country Life* Vol.112 (5th September 1952), p.676-9.

17. Dudley Dodd, *Montacute House* (1990), p.26.

18. C.G. Holme & Shirley Wainwright (eds.), Modern Gardens, British and Foreign (special winter edition of *The Studio*, 1926-7), p.53.

19. *Country Life* Vol.119 (1956), pp.736-9, 798-801; Sylvia Crowe, *Garden Design* (1958), pp.181-4; Graham Stuart Thomas, *Gardens of the National Trust* (1979), pp.226-7; Sales, *West Country Gardens*, pp.180-83; Penelope Hobhouse, *On Gardening* (1994).

20. Quoted by Jane Brown, *Sissinghurst: Portrait of a Garden* (1990), p.126.

21. Jane Fearnley-Whittingstall, *Historic Gardens* (1990), pp.63-4.

22. Margery Fish, *We Made a Garden* (1956); Sales, *West Country Gardens*, pp.149-51; Susan Chivers & Suzanne Woloszynski, *The Cottage Garden: Margery Fish at East Lambrook Manor* (1990).

23. Illustrated in Michael Spens, *Jellicoe at Shute* (1993), p.9.

24. Lanning Roper, 'Superb planning at Tintinhull', *Gardening Illustrated* (January 1951).

25. Jane Brown, *Lanning Roper and his Gardens* (1953), p.24; Sales, *West Country Gardens*, pp.178-9.

26. E. & R. Peplow, *Herbs and Herb Gardens of Great Britain* (Exeter, 1984); Guy Cooper, Gordon Taylor & Clive Boursnell, *English Herb Gardens* (1986); Kay N. Sanecki, *History of the English Herb Garden* (1992), esp.pp.109-22.

27. F W Beech, E. Catlow & E.G. Gilbert, *Growing Vines in the Open in Great Britain* (Long Ashton Research Station, 1974).

28. Sales, *West Country Gardens*, p.138; George Plumptre, *The Latest Country Gardens* (1988), p.156; Fearnley-Whittingstall, *Historic Gardens*, p.115.

29. Sales, *West Country Gardens*, p.152-3; Fearnley-Whittingstall, *Historic Gardens*, pp.118-9.

30. Plumptre, *The Latest Country Gardens*, p.164; *Country Life*, Vol.183 (October 5th 1989), pp.118-21.

Fig. 9.17
Walton-in-Gordano.
Walk in the Manor House garden.

Fig. 9.18
Garden tools at East Lambrook.

Chapter 10

Garden Conservation and Restoration

IN MANY WAYS THE REQUIREMENTS OF CONSERVATION AND OF PUBLIC ACCESS ARE IN DIRECT CONFLICT; THE
CHALLENGE IS TO RECONCILE THEM IN THE BEST INTERESTS OF ALL.

INTRODUCTION

The juggernaut of progress inevitably brings destruction in its wake, followed, usually belatedly, by awakening concerns about what is being lost. One reaction has been a spate of legislation aimed at protecting ancient monuments, historic buildings, areas of outstanding natural beauty and sites of special scientific interest. Parks and gardens, however, have been left largely uncovered by any consolidated form of protection. Indeed, it has been only in the last couple of decades that there has been any real recognition of the threats they face, or any moves to compensate for this by selective restoration.

For the conservation ethic to have any validity, it is vital that it should be underpinned by sound knowledge based upon solid research. The Garden History Society, founded in 1965, has had a crucial role in initiating and encouraging scholarly investigations into the historical evolution of gardens. It has created a forum for debate through its meetings, it has provided an outlet for the publication of research in its journal, and it has campaigned vigorously for the protection of sites throughout the country. However, for protection measures to be effective it is also essential that the right information and advice is available when planning policies are being formulated and when decisions on planning applications are taken, and here the County Sites and Monuments Records have a vital role to play.[1]

The legislative framework still remains notoriously weak. Some official recognition was granted under the 1983 National Heritage Act, which resulted in English Heritage compiling the first National Register of Parks and Gardens of Special Historic Interest. The local lists from this register were circulated in 1985, the modern county of Somerset including 38 examples, and what was then the county of Avon a further 29 examples.[2] However, as yet many important gardens remain unlisted, while none of them enjoy any statutory protection.

Continuing concern over this problem resulted in the creation of the Avon Gardens Trust and the Somerset Gardens Trust later in the 1980s. These were educational charities designed to encourage public interest in local historic gardens and to promote their conservation and enhancement. The Avon Gardens Trust in 1991 compiled and published a revised list of 289 gardens of interest which had been brought to the notice of the planning authorities in that county, a tenfold increase over the English Heritage register which underlined the limitations of the latter.

It is not only the plans and design features of parks and gardens that are under threat through development or neglect. Plants themselves are a vital element of most gardens, yet there has been a growing perception that market forces threaten to impoverish the range, since most commercial garden centres naturally enough stock only those varieties which sell best. In response to this concern, the National Council for the Conservation of Plants and Gardens was established in 1978 with the aim of safeguarding all varieties of cultivated plants by creating national collections of species, hybrids and cultivars within a particular genus. Somerset holds a number of national collections, including asters at Quarry Farm, Wraxall; dodecatheon at Walton-in-Gordano Manor; passiflora at Greenholm

Nurseries in Congresbury; taxus at the University of Bath; rodgersia at Hadspen House; hedychiums at Hooper's Holding in Hinton St George; caltha at Cannington Mill; thymes at Quantock Herbs in Cothelstone; and polystichum, erythronium, vaccinium and gaultheria at Greencombe near Porlock. Similarly, E.E.C. regulations designed to serve the interests of large-scale commercial growers have prohibited the sale of numerous old vegetable varieties, but since 1975 the Henry Doubleday Research Association, now based at Ryton-on-Dunsmore in Warwickshire, has established a seed library to preserve the hundreds of varieties thereby threatened with oblivion.

PROBLEMS of CONSERVATION and RESTORATION

Great estates have always needed to pay their way, but in the recent past this has often had regrettable consequences for park landscapes, as old pasture has come under intensive cereal cultivation or been resown for paddock grazing, and too many mature trees have been felled in order to realise the value of their timber. However, even where conservation is accorded a high priority, parks and gardens cannot be preserved in aspic. Garden plants and trees are living things, with their own cycle of growth, decay and death. The visual impact of the end of this cycle can be particularly severe in the case of the largest and longest-lived species, whose demise leaves a gap which cannot easily be filled. Many of the trees planted for landscaping in the eighteenth century are now approaching the end of their natural life-span, and even when they are replaced by new planting, this takes decades to approach maturity. The problems of maintaining an adequate tree cover have been exacerbated by the devastation caused by Dutch Elm Disease in 1970s, the effects of several recent severe summer droughts, and the gales of 1990. Any plan for the restoration of parkland has to find some means of perpetuating an illusion of appropriate tree cover which will not suffer cyclical spells of baldness. Planting any sort of tree randomly wherever there is a convenient space is not the answer. New plantations of species which are out of keeping with an established landscape, and trees planted in situations where they may block rather than frame significant vistas, aesthetically do more harm than good.

There is a delicate distinction between conservation, which implies sensitive management in order to secure the protection and continuation of something which is already there, and restoration, the reconstruction of something which is in an advanced state of decay, or which has been lost from view entirely. Conservation can be seen as a policy which is generally desirable in the long-term interest as a matter of principle; restoration is more actively geared towards presentation for public display and enjoyment. The two aims are not always necessarily in harmony with each other. Both can also be in conflict with other areas of conservation. For example, the continued presence of exotic species and the more intensive forms of management necessary to maintain some types of parkland and most forms of garden may militate against the use of sites as nature reserves. A further distinction must be made between restoration, which can be defined as the precise repair and replanting of an original

Fig. 10.1
CLAVERTON MANOR.
*Ageing trees are a problem
in many parks today.*

arrangement on the original site, and re-creation, which is the imaginative remaking from scratch of a period garden without any direct evidence for the previous existence of a garden of that particular form on that particular site. A sound scholarly basis is as important for re-creation as for restoration; but where the purpose is simply to create a generally correct impression, some compromises may be acceptable on the grounds of economy and long-term maintenance.

Even if the desirability of restoration is accepted in specific cases and the practical problems of finance and future management can be overcome, there are still ethical dilemmas to be faced. Many landscapes and gardens are characterised by an especially dominant contribution from one particular period, and there is understandably a strong temptation to take that period as the base-line for any restoration plan - all the more so if this can be linked with a 'big name' such as Brown, Repton or Jekyll. However, all parks and gardens are in truth multi-period landscapes and, whatever the dominant period, there are likely to be some relics of what was there before and some additions which have been made since. Georgian parkland not infrequently includes the slight earthwork remains of medieval settlements and fields which occupied the ground before their creation, sites which owe their preservation to the very fact that they were imparked; yet they can easily be overlooked and destroyed by misguided conservation or restoration measures. Fine specimen trees, plantations, attractive new species or buildings can be added at a later date which may block an original view, or may conflict in some other way with the intentions of the original designer - should these then be removed, irrespective of their own merit? In both conservation and restoration very difficult decisions sometimes have to be made.[4]

PROBLEMS of VISITOR MANAGEMENT

Few garden restoration projects will be contemplated today without the intent of opening the grounds to a wider public. Yet this in itself brings many problems of management. The tranquility which is surely one of the essential characteristics of most gardens, is a fragile thing, easily shattered by shrill voices. A small and intimate garden space designed for private family use does not readily accommodate coachloads of tourists. People themselves can be a gross visual intrusion. How many of us have waited, seemingly for hours, to photograph some perfect garden vista while an endless procession of visitors, all wearing unsuitable gaudy clothing, dawdle across the foreground at a snail's pace, only to find that we are ourselves causing some other would-be photographer to fume by standing directly in his line of sight? Visitors want 'value for money', and tend to have high expectations of finding everything in perfect order all the time. Many gardeners must be tempted to fall back upon showy repeat-flowering blooms which can be counted on for a long season, and surfaces which can be kept clear of all weeds at little cost; yet that way lies blandness and uniformity. There are safety aspects to be considered. Every custodian dreads the arrival of the kamikaze family whose children climb trees only to fall out of them, drop over terrace parapets onto paved surfaces, fall into fishponds and pick and eat poisonous berries. Lawns, paths and even steps can be eroded out of existence by sheer numbers. Demands for car and coach parking space, lavatories and

refreshments all have to be accommodated somehow. In many ways the requirements of conservation and of public access are in direct conflict; the challenge is to reconcile them in the best interests of all.

GARDENS in CARE of the NATIONAL TRUST

The deliberate reconstruction of historical garden designs is essentially a modern phenomenon, and it has been carried out with a variety of different motives and with varying degrees of scholarly rigour. The National Trust was the first organisation to realise the desirability of displaying houses within a fitting garden context; but on their properties the creation of an attractive appearance was generally given precedence over absolute historical authenticity. At Barrington Court nothing was known of the original Elizabethan garden layout, and it was left to the tenant, Col. Lyle, to commission an appropriate new formal design, as described in Chapter 9. The Lyle family continued to develop the gardens in subsequent years. Sir Ian Lyle made further informal plantings of trees and shrubs on the eastern side of the grounds, and some restoration was carried out after his death in 1978. As the gardens stand today they are certainly not a recreation of an Elizabethan garden, nor are they even quite as Gertrude Jekyll had envisaged them; but they retain many details and ideas from her concept.

Montacute House came into possession of the National Trust in 1931, when it was saved from demolition by the Society for the Protection of Ancient Buildings through a donation by Mr E. E. Cook. Here too the Trust took steps to develop the grounds in accordance with the expectations of visitors at the time; there was no attempt at an accurate reconstruction of the Elizabethan layout, but rather a progressive development of gardens intended to provide year-round interest. The former walled kitchen gardens south of the house were adapted to provide car parking, with Norway maples planted to provide shade. Below the southern raised walk of the main garden a rose border was planted in the late 1940s by Vita Sackville West and Graham Thomas, using old varieties such as the Rosa Mundi (*Rosa gallica 'versicolor'*), the red rose of Lancaster (*R. gallica 'officinalis'*), and the double white form of Jacobite rose (*R x alba 'maxima'*). In the east court mixed herbaceous and shrub borders were planted along the lines suggested by Vita Sackville-West by Mrs Phyllis Reiss of Tintinhull, who supervised the Montacute gardens in the 1950s. Initially only subdued colours were used, but within a year it was decided to employ a more lively palette. Vines and clematis were trained over the walls, and red and orange roses, yellow dahlias and lupins, blue delphiniums, plume poppies, yuccas and purple-leaved barberries provided the main components of borders now intended to provide bright colours and a range of foliage throughout the growing season. These borders were replanted in the 1970s , reintroducing the species employed by Mrs Reiss.

Elsewhere in the grounds of Montacute, the hybrid American thorn *Crataegus x lavallei* was planted around the raised walks of the main north garden in 1964 to replace the worn-out cypresses. South of the cedar lawn a new small semicircular garden was made in the late

Fig. 10.2
LYTES CARY.
*Herbaceous borders within the
walls of the Tudor Gardens.*

1960s, with a seat set in a yew hedge and a row of stone columns lining the path alongside a small semicircular lawn containing two beds of Yucca recurvifolia and a small round stone pond. The west avenue was reinforced by a new planting of limes behind the evergreens in 1976, to ensure a succession.

Lytes Cary was bequeathed to the National Trust by Sir Walter Jenner in 1948. The garden had been much altered since Henry Lyte compiled his herbal there in the sixteenth century, and the layout inherited by the Trust, with its pattern of 'rooms' and 'corridors' separated by yew hedges, was largely the work of Sir Walter, who had acquired the house in 1907 and saved it from ruin. The Trust and its tenants have maintained the gardens to this plan since. While again there has been no attempt to re-create the style of the Tudor gardens, one of the borders against the house has been planted up with species in cultivation in Henry Lyte's time. There are pleached limes on the drive up to the house. On the east front, where there was originally a small forecourt, a flagstone path now leads from the east porch straight across the lawn between clipped domes of yew to a gate on a ha-ha. In line with the path, in the paddock beyond the gate-piers, the vista is closed by what looks like a medieval round stone dovecote: in fact this is a carefully-disguised water tower. Box and yew hedges enclose this part of the garden against the wall, while the border against the house includes the purple *Clematis viticella* and *Hydrangea villosa*. A door through a wall on the north side of the front lawn leads to another long flagstone-paved walk. The wide border between the wall and the path was planted by the National Trust's horticultural adviser, Graham Stuart Thomas, in the style of Gertrude Jekyll, using colourful herbaceous perenniels, roses, shrubs and clematises, contrasting with the varied greens of the strip on the south side of the path, where the grass was backed by a yew hedge with buttresses framing stone bowls on columns. At the far end from the house is a small enclosed white garden, made up of the usual white-flowering and silver-leaved plants. This gives access to a raised walk along the eastern side of the orchard, flanked on the outer side by another tall yew hedge and edged on the inner side by Rose of Sharon and regularly-spaced pillars of Irish yew. The orchard itself is planted with a variety of fruit trees in diagonal rows with weeping ash and black walnut in the corners. At the southern end of the raised terrace walk is a stone seat giving a view along a further grass walk along the south side of the orchard, framed by a pair of yew hedges, leading to a circular pool. The three statues in this part of the garden, one in the centre of the pool, along with the figures of Flora and Diana in the angles of the southernmost yew hedge, are positioned to be seen from the great chamber of the house. At the western end the walk leads through an alley of pleached hornbeam into a small shaded secret garden.

Clevedon Court came to the National Trust in 1961 with an endowment from Sir Arthur Elton. Here too there has been no attempt to devise an historically accurate recreation of the garden to any particular period of its past, but rather to develop it in a way which will appeal to visitors while respecting its major historic components. The prim and fussy Victorian parterre behind the house was removed and replaced with a more varied planting with hollies, cypress, magnolias and old roses, with ceanothus, white crinums, arum lilies and pomegranates below the wall. The square beds on the terrace above, which so offended Gertrude Jekyll, have been replaced by informal arrangements of shrubs and plants with interesting foliage and subtle colouring which she would surely have approved of. The top terrace is of more Mediterranean character, predominantly evergreens, with Judas trees, yuccas and dwarf palms, and the strawberry tree and laurustinus naturalising into the adjoining woodland. New trees have been planted in the old orchard. The garden fountains were restored in 1982.

Elsewhere the National Trust has carried out some notable authentic garden restorations based upon sound research. So far as their Somerset properties are concerned, however, their basic philosophy has been merely to enhance their attractiveness by providing garden displays which visitors can enjoy throughout the open season. This is a perfectly legitimate and laudable aim in its own right, even if it fails to provide any accurate sense of the setting of the houses when they were first occupied. All those gardens described above have many supporters who love them in their present form, and who would be horrified at the thought of any purge to return to the more limited flora and more formal design of earlier times.[5]

Garden Restorations by Local Authorities

A number of historic parks and gardens have come into local authority care and, despite the financial constraints imposed by central government since the 1980s, there have been some remarkable achievements. Outstanding among them was the restoration of the gardens at Hestercombe, which had fallen into decay after the Second World War. The lawns had become unkempt and many of the beds submerged beneath amorphous shrubberies. After the death of the Hon. E.W.B. Portman's widow in 1951, the property was leased to Somerset County Council, who acquired the freehold outright in 1975. A restoration programme was begun in 1973. Some of Gertrude Jekyll's original plans were found at Hestercombe itself, others were located amongst the papers salvaged from her home at Munstead Wood which had found their way to the University of Berkeley, California. The aim has been to follow the original scheme so far as is practical, with minor simplifications of the planting in order to reduce the burden of maintenance. Viscount Portman's top terrace, untouched by Miss Jekyll, was redesigned to bring it into greater harmony with the rest of the garden. The rose garden was replanted with old-fashioned gallica roses in 1976-7. In 1975 the County Council

fittingly received a European Architectural Heritage Year award in recognition of its success in restoring the Hestercombe gardens to their former splendour.

In 1984 Bath City Council decided to sponsor a project to re-create the Georgian garden of no.4 The Circus, and here for the first time archaeological excavation was used to explore the original layout before replanting began. This project has been described in Chapter 6. Since completion of the excavation the garden has been reconstructed on the same site along the lines of its original plan through the advice of John Harvey, using planting schemes appropriate to the period, and visitors can now experience an accurate impression of a formal town garden of the mid-eighteenth century.

More recently attention has been turned to parkland restoration. Bath City Council has prepared plans to restore Royal Victoria Park and Sydney Gardens to something like their original designs. Bristol City Council has commissioned a restoration plan for Ashton Court, and clearance work has begun to remove scrub from the wood margins, to eliminate the invasive sycamore and ash which had shaded out so many of the ancient pollard oaks, and to reinstate the old wood pasture with its more open vistas.

Garden Restorations by Other Institutions and Private Owners

In 1959 Claverton Manor was acquired for the American Museum in Britain, which opened to the public in 1961. It now includes a replica of George Washington's garden at Mount Vernon on the Potomac River in Virginia. This has two compartments, one of curved parallel beds and the other with a curvilinear saltire pattern of gravel paths, planted out with appropriate varieties of flowers within box hedging, all enclosed within a white picket fence, with an

Fig. 10.3
CLAVERTON MANOR.
Formal terraces and gravel walks around the new mansion.

octagonal summerhouse in the corner. There is also a fern collection and an arboretum of American trees planted in the 1960s. New borders were designed by Lanning Roper. Although this is a transplantation rather than a restoration in situ, there is an historical connection with Somerset. When Washington was enlarging the Mount Vernon garden in 1785 plants and seeds were sent to him by the Fairfaxes of Writhlington near Radstock, and a local farmer went over to help with the planting.

There have also been some notable restoration enterprises carried out by private owners. Brympton D'Evercy was occupied as a school for twenty years after the Second World War. Charles and Judy Clive-Ponsonby-Fane returned to the house in 1974, and began restoring the gardens to something of their former glory within the necessary constraints of a low-maintenance régime, using dense planting and ground-cover plants to suppress weeds and foliage. Since the 1970s the Combe Sydenham estate have also embarked upon a long-term plan to reinstate some two acres of Elizabethan-style gardens around the house.[6]

REGISTER of PARKS and GARDENS of SPECIAL HISTORIC INTEREST

The National Heritage Act, 1983, enabled English Heritage to compile a *REGISTER* of nationally important parks and gardens of special historic interest which were conceived and started over 30 years ago. The main purpose of the *REGISTER* is to identify and draw attention to the best historic parks and gardens and in doing so encourage and help local authorities to provide adequate protection for these sites in their planning and development control. It is also intended to encourage owners and others to appreciate, maintain and enhance these sites.

The *REGISTER* does not provide statutory protection, nor does it imply any additional power to control development or work to such sites, beyond the normal planning controls. However, the historic interest of a park or garden is established as a material planning consideration. Accordingly, before a local planning authority can grant planning permission for development which is likely to affect any park or garden on the *REGISTER* they are required to consult the Garden History Society. In the case of a Grade I or Grade II* site English Heritage must also be consulted.

GRADING

While all sites on the *REGISTER* are considered to be of special historic interest, their individual importance varies. As with registering, grading is a comparative assessment, dependent on a knowledge of garden history. Sites of *exceptional* historic interest are assessed as Grade I, those of *great* historic interest as Grade II*, and those of *special* historic interest as Grade II.

The grading of a site reflects the importance of the most significant features of the site and there is scope for parts to differ in importance within the historic boundary. Of the 49 sites on the current *REGISTER* for Somerset, 6 are classed as Grade I, 12 Grade II*,

and the remaining 31 Grade II. The grading of these sites is independent of the grading of any listed building which falls within the area.

CRITERIA FOR SELECTION

1. Parks and gardens formed before 1750 where the original layout is still in evidence.

2. Most parks and gardens laid out between 1750 and 1820 if they still reflect the intentions of the original layout.

3. The best parks and gardens laid out between 1820 and 1880 which are in good or fair condition and of aesthetic merit.

4. The best parks and gardens laid out between 1880 and 30 years ago which are in good condition and of aesthetic merit.

When a more detailed assessment of a site is possible particular attention can also be paid to:

5. Parks and gardens which are influential in development of taste, whether through reputation or reference in literature.

6. Parks and gardens which are early or representative examples of a genre of layout or of the work of a designer of national stature.

7. Parks and gardens having an association with significant historical events or persons.

8. Parks and gardens with group value, especially as an integral part of the layout surrounding a major house or as part of a town planning scheme.

The following list for Somerset gives the registered name for each park or garden, the civil parish in which it is sited, its grade and a brief description. Inclusion of a park or garden on the *REGISTER* does not imply that the property is open to the public.

For more detailed information the *REGISTER* can be inspected at the local authorities offices and copies can be obtained from English Heritage.

Fig. 10.4
WELLINGTON PARK.

REFERENCES - Chapter 10

1. For a wider perspective see Kenneth Brown, Robert Croft & Russell Lillford, 'Conserving the Historic Landscape', in Michael Aston (ed.), *ASPECTS OF THE MEDIEVAL LANDSCAPE OF SOMERSET* (Somerset County Council, 1988), pp.108-127.

2. English Heritage, *REGISTER OF PARKS AND GARDENS OF SPECIAL HISTORIC INTEREST IN ENGLAND* (1985).

3. Stewart Harding & David Lambert, *GAZETTEER OF HISTORIC PARKS AND GARDENS IN AVON* (Avon Gardens Trust / Avon County Council, 2nd edn, 1991).

4. See David Jacques, 'Restoring Historic Gardens and Parks', *JNL. OF HISTORIC HOUSES ASSOCIATION* (1978); Graham Stuart Thomas, *RECREATING THE PERIOD GARDEN* (1984); Garden History Society & Ancient Monuments Society, *THE CONSERVATION OF HISTORIC GARDENS* (1984); John Harvey, *RESTORING PERIOD GARDENS* (Princes Risborough, 1988); John Sales, 'Garden restoration, past and present', *GARDEN HISTORY* Vol.23 no.1 (Summer 1995), pp.1-9.

5. For a brief history of the National Trust's role in garden management see John Gaze, *FIGURES IN A LANDSCAPE: A HISTORY OF THE NATIONAL TRUST* (1988), pp.165-173. See also Graham Stuart Thomas, *THE GARDENS OF THE NATIONAL TRUST* (1979) and John Sales, *WEST COUNTRY GARDENS* (Gloucester, 1980), pp.133-7, 140-43, 160-62, 166-71.

6. Jane Fearnley-Whittingstall, *HISTORIC GARDENS* (1990), pp.61-7, 115-16.

Fig. 10.5
REGISTER of PARKS and GARDENS of SPECIAL HISTORIC INTEREST.

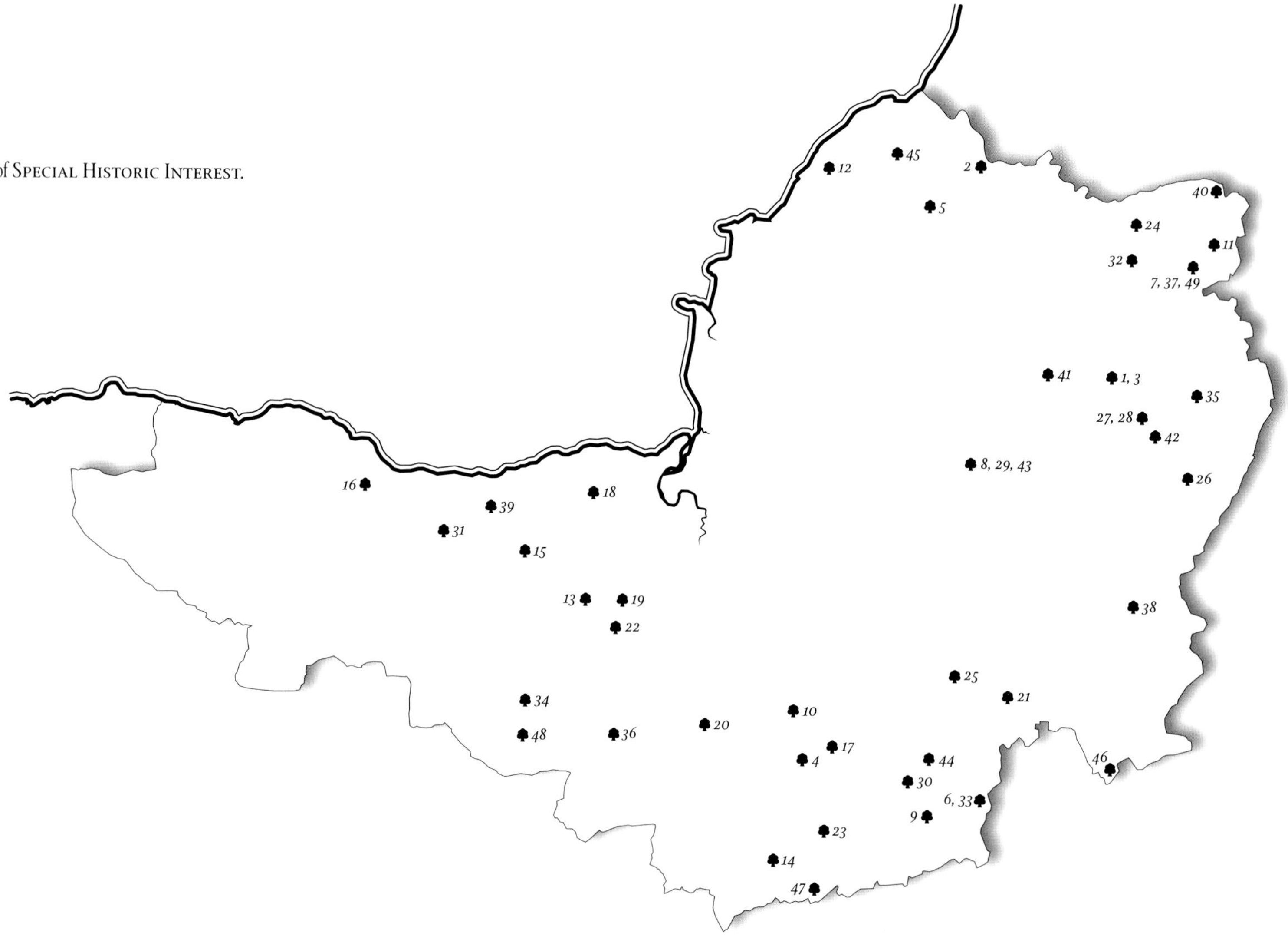

1. AMMERDOWN HOUSE, Kilmersdon, Grade II*.
    Italianate formal garden layout, 1901-3 by Sir Edwin Lutyens;
    park of late 18th Century to early 19th Century by Thomas
    Jolliffe.

2. ASHTON COURT, Long Ashton, Grade II*.
    Landscape park circa 1801 after design by Humphry Repton;
    formal gardens of late 19th Century.

3. BABINGTON HOUSE, Kilmersdon, Grade II.
    Gardens and park mid 18th Century onwards.

4. BARRINGTON COURT, Barrington, Grade II*.
    Mainly formal garden enclosures and layout, 1920-25, partly
    to designs by Gertrude Jekyll. Restored late 1970s-80s.
    National Trust.

5. BARROW COURT, Barrow Gurney, Grade II.
    Remains of 18th Century park and enclosed formal garden
    layout designed by Inigo Thomas in 1890.

6. BARWICK PARK, Barwick, Grade II*.
    Landscape park, with follies, probably late 18th Century.

7. BECKFORD'S RIDE, Bath, Grade II.
    Irregular but continuous areas of garden and woodland,
    developed in 1822-44 by William Beckford.

8. BISHOP'S PALACE, Wells, Grade II.
    Walled and moated precincts of bishop's palace, medieval,
    but landscaped 1824-45. Remains of deer park.

9. Brympton d'Evercy, Brympton, Grade II*.
    Early formal gardens and pleasure grounds, late 17th
    Century, altered and added to circa 1723, 1860 and 1910.

10. BURTON PYNSENT, Curry Rivel, Grade II.
    Landscaped pleasure grounds and park, mainly circa 1765 by
    Capability Brown with William Pitt.

11. CLAVERTON MANOR, Claverton, Grade II.
    Remains of terraced gardens of circa 1580, gardens and
    pleasure grounds of early 19th Century with American
    garden layout of 1960s. Park-like landscape, 18th Century to
    early 19th Century.

12. CLEVEDON COURT, Clevedon, Grade II*.
    Terraced gardens of circa 1700 extended circa 1775 with
    planting of 18th Century to 1840. National Trust.

13. COTHELSTONE MANOR, Cothelstone, Grade II.
    Formal drive, forecourt and remains of formal gardens.

14. CRICKET HOUSE, Cricket St Thomas, Grade II*
    Terraced gardens, late 17th Century to early 18th Century.
    Pleasure grounds and park, late 18th Century to early 19th
    Century. Now forms part of wildlife park.

15. CROWCOMBE COURT, Crowcombe, Grade II.
    Walled gardens and landscape park, circa 1723 onwards.

16. DUNSTER CASTLE, Dunster, Grade I.
    Gardens and woodland on castle hill. Early and late 18th Century, mid 19th Century, on medieval site. National Trust.

17. EAST LAMBROOK MANOR, Kingsbury Episcopi, Grade I.
    Plantsman's garden created by Margery Fish from 1937.

18. FAIRFIELD, Stogursey, Grade II.
    Enclosed gardens and park.

19. HALSWELL PARK, Goathurst, Grade II.
    Landscaped pleasure grounds and park mainly mid to late 18th Century by Sir Charles Kemeys Tynte.

20. HATCH COURT, Hatch Beauchamp, Grade II.
    Gardens, landscaped pleasure grounds and deer park, mid 18th Century.

21. HAZELGROVE HOUSE, Queen Camel, Grade II.
    18th Century landscape park with formal garden in front of house.

22. HESTERCOMBE, Cheddon Fitzpaine, Grade I.
    Formal layout 1904-10 by Sir Edwin Lutyens and Gertrude Jekyll, restored 1973-8; remains of parkland; landscaped combe of circa 1750-90 by Coplestone Warre Bampfylde.

23. HINTON HOUSE, Hinton St George, Grade II.
    Gardens and pleasure grounds, landscape park, late 17th Century and mid 18th Century onwards.

24. KELSTON PARK, Kelston, Grade II.
    Landscape park 1767-68 by Capability Brown. Terraced garden.

25. LYTES CARY, Charlton Mackrell, Grade II.
    Garden enclosures, in Elizabethan manner created in 1907-20 by Sir Walter Jenner, restored 1960s in the Jekyll tradition. National Trust.

26. MARSTON HOUSE, Trudoxhill, Grade II.
    Remains of pleasure grounds and landscape park, 1724-45 by Stephen Switzer, 1819-22 by Sir Jeffry Wyatville, and late 19th Century.

27. MELLS MANOR HOUSE, Mells, Grade I.
    Gardens circa 1520 and circa 1900 with advice from Sir Edwin Lutyens and Gertrude Jekyll.

28. MELLS PARK, Mells, Grade II.
    Gardens by Sir Edwin Lutyens of circa 1924, altered; landscape park, late 18th Century.

29. MILTON LODGE and THE COMBE, Wells, Grade II.
    Early 20th Century terraced gardens and parkland; detached early 19th Century walled pleasure ground.

30. MONTACUTE HOUSE, Montacute, Grade I.
    Formal garden enclosures and remains of parkland. Late 16th Century through to mid 19th Century. National Trust.

31. NETTLECOMBE Court, Nettlecombe, Grade II.
    Pleasure grounds and landscape park, mid to late 18th Century.

32. NEWTON PARK, Newton St Loe, Grade II.
    Landscaped pleasure grounds and park, circa 1760 by Capability Brown, 1796-97 by Humphry Repton.

33. NEWTON SURMAVILLE, Barwick, Grade II.
    Gardens and pleasure grounds, mid 18th Century, later 19th Century.

34. NYNEHEAD COURT, Nynehead, Grade II*.
    Ornamental 19th Century parterre with extensive 18th Century landscape park.

35. ORCHARDLEIGH, Lullington, Grade II*.
    Formal gardens and pleasure grounds, mainly 19th Century, 1856 by Mr Page; landscaped deer park, medieval onwards.

36. POUNDISFORD PARK, Pitminster, Grade II.
    Enclosed garden, 17th Century; deer park, medieval onwards.

37. PRIOR PARK, Bath, Grade I.
    Landscaped pleasure grounds and park, 1734 onwards by Ralph Allen with advice from Alexander Pope, 1762-65 by Capability Brown. National Trust.

38. REDLYNCH PARK, Bruton, Grade II.
    Gardens circa 1901 by Sir Edwin Lutyens, pleasure grounds, park from 17th Century.

39. ST AUDRIES, West Quantoxhead, Grade II.
    Gardens and pleasure grounds, mid 19th Century on earlier site; landscaped deer park, mid to late 18th Century.

40. ST CATHERINE'S COURT, St Catherine, Grade II*.
    Terraced gardens, late medieval, early 17th Century, with 19th Century planting.

41. STON EASTON PARK, Ston Easton, Grade II.
    Landscaped pleasure grounds, remains of park, circa 1793 by Humphry Repton; gardens circa 1814 by Lady Hippisley.

42. THE CHANTRY, Whatley, Grade II*.
    Remains of landscape with lakes and grottoes, circa 1825.

43. THE DEANERY, Wells, Grade II.
    Gardens enclosed by medieval and later walling, the garden of Dean William Turner, 16th Century.

44. TINTINHULL HOUSE, Tintinhull, Grade II.
    Formal garden layout circa 1904 by Dr J.S.M. Price, 1933 onwards by Phyllis Reiss. National Trust.

45. TYNTESFIELD, Wraxall, Grade II*.
    Formal terraced gardens, pleasure grounds, in landscape park. Kitchen gardens, late 19th Century, garden buildings and ornaments 1885 by Sir Walter Cave.

46. VEN HOUSE, Milborne Port, Grade II.
    Early formal garden layout; late 17th Century to early 18th Century; landscaped pleasure grounds, late 18th Century to early 19th Century, a modification of early formal layout; remains of formal park layout; kitchen gardens.

47. WAYFORD MANOR, Wayford, Grade II.
    Terraced gardens, in formal woodland garden, 1900-19 by Harold Peto and Humphrey Baker; partly on site of Elizabethan garden.

48. WELLINGTON PARK, Wellington, Grade II.
    Edwardian public gardens laid out by F.W. Meyer, landscape gardener.

49. WIDCOMBE MANOR, Widcombe, Grade II.
    Garden terrace and landscape, 18th Century, extensively developed in 1930s.

Case Study 1

HALSWELL PARK

by Russell Lillford

Fig. 10.6

HALSWELL HOUSE, *showing the 1689 north range in front of the earlier 16th century buildings.*

Halswell Park is located near the village of Goathurst, about three miles south-west of Bridgwater. The old manor house at Halswell (pronounced Haswell) was built more or less on the spring line, just below the 100-metre contour, and two streams in particular shape the lie of the land. One rises only fifty yards or so to the east of the house and falls in a chain of ponds to the village of Goathurst. The other runs in a deeper valley or combe to the west, long known as Mill Wood.

The ruined and decaying garden buildings which stand in farmland around Halswell House are the remnant of what was among the finest eighteenth-century landscapes and which, according to the National Trust book *FOLLIES*, "*lacks only a good prospect tower to make it one of the finest folly groups in southern England.... enough remains to satisfy nearly every taste.*" In the laying out of the park and pleasure grounds, in the exploitation of the topography of the site, and in the variety of the buildings and structures which adorned it, Halswell was an exemplar of mid-Georgian landscape design.

A receipt of money for "*building of the manor of Halswell*" in 1536 suggests a date for the Tudor great hall (later turned into the kitchen) on the east front, and might also imply an improvement in the fortunes of the Halswell family who had lived on the site since before 1280.

In the mid-seventeenth century, Jane Halswell, the last of her line, married John Tynte of Chelvey, near Weston-super-Mare, and their son, Sir Halswell Tynte, created a baronet in 1674, rebuilt the north range, now the principal wing of the house, by 1689. Nikolaus Pevsner described it as "*the most important house of its date in the country*", and Gervase Jackson-Stops praises it as "*a remarkably assured essay in the Wren style, with features derived from contemporary French pattern-books*".

A fascinating picture by an unknown artist of circa 1710, illustrating the original formal gardens at Halswell, shows a substantial parterre with terraces, and a square brick and stone pavilion. It is difficult to say whether Sir Halswell, who died in 1702, or his son John, who died prematurely in 1710, was responsible for this formal garden. But few changes are likely to have been made to it during the minority of the third baronet, who also died prematurely in 1730, or his brother, the Rev. Sir John, who never married. Their youngest brother Charles, who became fifth baronet in 1740, also inherited the Kemeys estate of Cefn Mably (Glamorgan) on his mother's death in 1747. Although never rich by the standards of the great whig aristocracy of the day, he could nevertheless afford to make substantial improvements to both houses, and to sit as Tory MP for the county until 1774. The transformation of the landscape at Halswell was carried out during Sir Charles's 44-year reign as squire.

The deer park, probably created in the late seventeenth century, measured 30 acres in 1744, more than doubled in the next ten years, and later in the century was 132 acres. A hundred years later, in 1892, the park extended to 193 acres, reaching its peak in the early twentieth century at 220 acres. In its heyday in the 1750s and 1760s the landscaped parkland was surrounded by a home park of another 1500 acres and supported by satellite farms, in both Somerset and South Wales, covering at least a further 2000 acres.

During his ownership of the Halswell estate, Sir Charles transformed the garden and park, renovating the earlier formal garden in front of the house, naturalising the landscape and adorning it with ornamental structures. In doing so he was entirely in the spirit of the times. His landscape at Halswell reflected the various central preoccupations of mid-eighteenth century landscape designers: the relations between Nature and Art in the laying out of gardens and the arrangement of buildings and other ornaments to make sentimental, mythological or other allusions.

Sir Charles's work at Halswell can be summarised as affecting three discrete aspects of the gardens and park: first, the immediate setting of the house, where the formal garden was removed and the ground naturalised; second, the Pleasure Grounds in Mill Wood, which were planted and embellished with new structures; and third, the wider park, which was extended and planted.

Fortunately, the progress of most of these works can be followed with the invaluable help of a long memorandum written by the steward of Halswell, Richard Escott, on his retirement in 1781. Escott's year-by-year summary of work on the estate begins with his appointment in 1753, but obviously a start had been made on 'naturalising' the formal garden before then. A painting of about 1750 shows the old red pavilion still surviving, near the site of the present Rotunda, but the terraces below have been smoothed away, forming an undulating lawn with a lake, probably based on an earlier straight-sided canal, and ultimately deriving from the round pond of the formal parterre. The removal of the unfashionable formal garden was thus the first priority; but the avenues to the west of the house were retained and shown on the 1756 survey, and indeed, are also present on the Ordnance Survey map of 1809, although they are now lost.

Near the south-west corner of the house is a curious stepped pyramid crowned by a griffin holding the family coat of arms. Built above the main well serving the house, it has an open tank with water gushing into it on one side and an inscription on another face, now sadly too weathered to decipher, but thought to have been dedicated to 'a pure nymph', a possible reference to one of Sir Charles's nieces who died prematurely in 1744. The pyramid may well date from before 1753, as there is no reference to it in Escott's papers, and it predates the later Egyptian taste. The first addition listed by Escott was the *"Rock Work"* at the head of the canal on the lawn, made in 1754. This impressive rockwork screen or grotto survives at the lower end of the lake and originally it formed a dam, with a large round pond below.

The next two years were equally active. Three important structures followed: in 1755 the ornamental Bath stone bridge in the wood, Mrs Busby's Temple on the lawn - the Rotunda - and in 1756 the Druid's Temple in the wood, possibly by John de Wilstar. John de Wilstar was the surveyor responsible for the 1756 estate map, but he is also recorded as an architect and builder working in Bristol in the 1740s, and may have been the author of these buildings. On the other hand, they all have close affinities with the designs of Thomas Wright, and it is significant that Sir Charles Kemeys Tynte and his amateur architect friend Thomas Prowse were both among the subscribers to Wright's *Book of Arbours*, which appeared at this very moment, in 1755. The thatched Druid's Temple, at the upper end of Mill Wood, was virtually identical to the engraving on the front piece of Wright's book, while the bridge and the rockwork screen correspond closely with drawings for a *"River Head"* and a *"Break Water"* on adjoining pages of an album on Wright's drawing. Mrs Busby's Temple, apparently named after Lady Tynte's sister, is also comparable with Thomas Wright's rotundas at Stoke Gifford (Gloucestershire) and Culford (Suffolk).

Interestingly, the Bath stone bridge, which is actually a dam with a cascade between two of the ponds in Mill Wood, can be seen under construction - complete with workmen and scaffolding - in the background of a portrait of Sir Charles.

Escott's writings offer glimpses of the work going on in Mill Wood: the ponds being stocked with goldfish, trout and gudgeon, the Druid's Temple being erected, and a constant stream of visitors to see the gardens. At the southern end of Mill Wood the stream sprang from three large apsidal rockwork niches. Here a tablet celebrates Nature's gifts in pastoral verse:

> *"Ye happy swains for whom these waters flow,*
> *Oh may your hearts with grateful ardours glow,"*

going on to celebrate the surrounding countryside:

> *"Lo! Here a fountain streams at his command,*
> *Not o'er a barren but fruitful land,*
> *Where Nature's choicest gifts the valleys fill,*
> *And smiling plenty gladdens every hill!"*

Below the spring were five small lakes, the first terminating with the bridge, the second with a huge rockwork arch, beneath which originally stood a large stature of Neptune, all ending in rockwork cascades. Sequences of informal rockwork cascades were also a feature of Bampfylde's garden at Hestercombe.

After 1756 there seems to have been something of a gap in Sir Charles's activities. Then, in 1761 the park was greatly extended to the east and in 1764-5 he embarked on a new spate of building, beginning with the Temple of Harmony at the bottom end of Mill Wood. The Temple is the most distinguished of all the garden buildings at Halswell and has been attributed to Robert Adam, on the basis of his three drawings for the interior dated 1767, now in the Soane Museum in London. However, a letter written to Sir Charles the same year proves that it was actually designed by Thomas Prowse of Axbridge, in memory of their mutual friend Peregrine Palmer of nearby Fairfield, MP for the University of Oxford, who died in November 1762. Prowse was also an MP for 27 years and was a member of that circle which included Sanderson Miller, the Gothic revivalist.

The design of the Temple of Harmony is derived from the drawings of the Temple of Fortuna Virilis in Rome (built in the first century BC) given in Palladio's *Four Books of Architecture*, the English editions of which were the authoritative texts for the Palladian movement which dominated English classical architecture at that time. Robert Adam's designs for the interior were only partially executed. His neo-Classical aedicule, supported by Palmyra columns, still exists, though with an antique sarcophagus panel below the niches in place of his suggested decorative panel. The plasterwork in the manner of Joseph Rose, indicated by Adam, was never carried out. Instead the plasterwork can be attributed to the Bristol plasterer Thomas Stocking, to whom Prowse sent a drawing in August 1766, with instructions to attend Sir Charles at Halswell. In the central niche stood the statue of Terpsichore, the muse of song and dance, dedicated to Prowse after his death in 1767. It was carved by the London statuary John Walsh, and is signed and dated 1771.

The construction of the Temple of Harmony was the final architectural embellishment of the pleasure grounds in Mill Wood, although planting appears to have continued. Arthur Young's very full description of Halswell in his *Tour Through the West of England* (1771) shows that the walk through Mill Wood was intended to arouse a whole range of emotions, evoked by scenery ranging from the silent waters and *"gloomy and confined"* views under the Druid's Temple to the more cheerful vale round the Temple of Harmony, where *"every part is riant, and bears the stamp of pleasure"*.

Robin Hood's Hut was built a year after the Temple of Harmony. The approach to the banqueting house high on the brow of the hill south of the house was conceived for maximum dramatic effect: a serpentine drive through dark woodland brought the visitor to the back of the building, covered in bark and knotted tree trunks, and only then was a door opened by the hermit to reveal the view from the central loggia (or umbrello), a breathtaking panorama over the vale to the Bristol Channel and the island of Steep Holm, and beyond these the mountains of Wales.

The Temple of Harmony was a reconstruction of an ancient temple dedicated to an antique virtue and to friendship. Robin Hood's Hut, on the other hand, was gothic and commemorated a national legend who may have been seen as a hero of English liberty. The

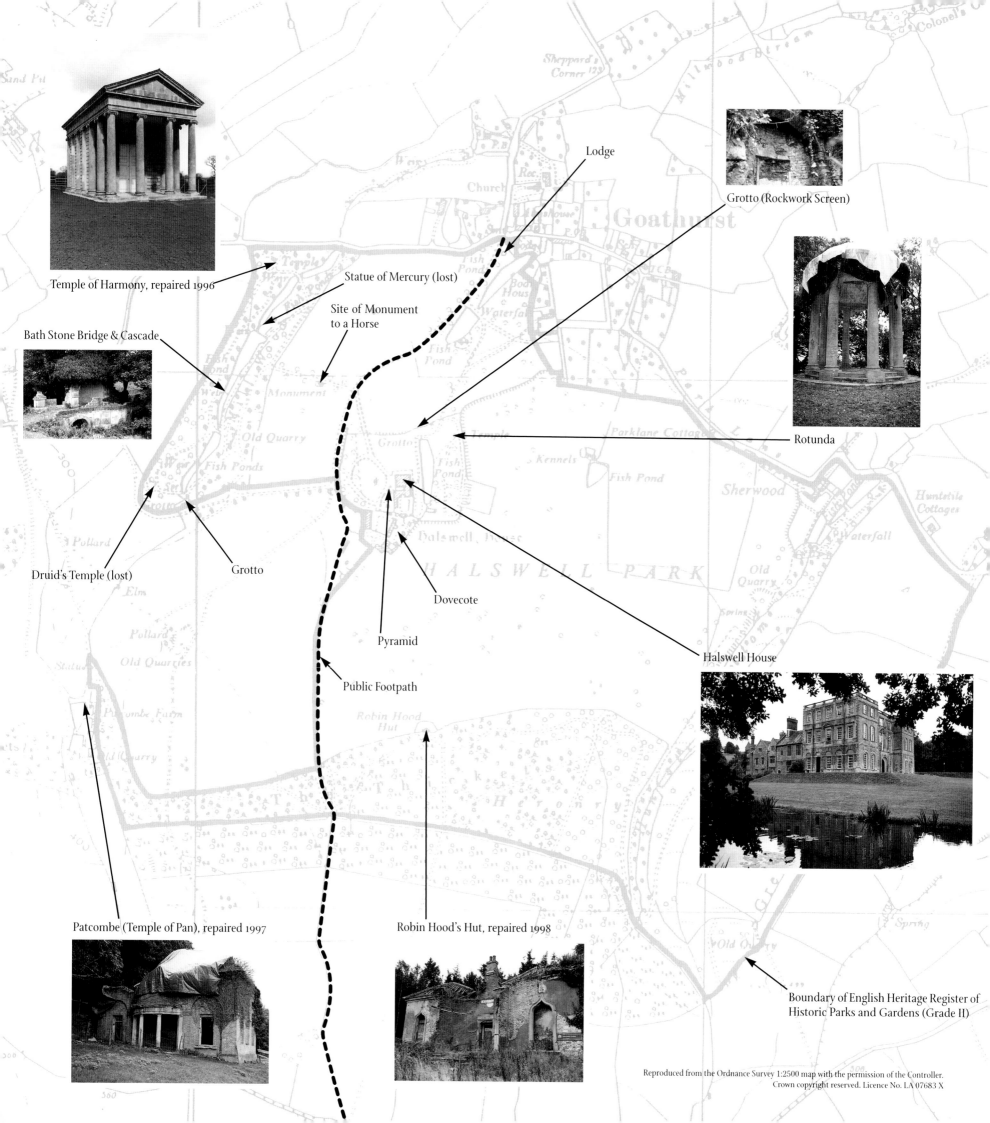

Temple of Harmony, repaired 1996

Lodge

Grotto (Rockwork Screen)

Statue of Mercury (lost)

Site of Monument
to a Horse

Bath Stone Bridge & Cascade

Rotunda

Druid's Temple (lost)

Grotto

Dovecote

Pyramid

Halswell House

Public Footpath

Patcombe (Temple of Pan), repaired 1997

Robin Hood's Hut, repaired 1998

Boundary of English Heritage Register of
Historic Parks and Gardens (Grade II)

Reproduced from the Ordnance Survey 1:2500 map with the permission of the Controller.
Crown copyright reserved. Licence No. LA 07683 X

agent's house on the eastern edge of the park, called Sherwood, may explain the building's name.

The architect for Robin Hood's Hut was almost certainly Henry Keene (1726-1776), Surveyor of the Fabric at Westminster Abbey. An alternative proposal for a gothic pavilion inscribed for Sir Charles Kemeys Tynte survives among a set of designs by Henry Keene at the Victoria and Albert Museum. According to Richard Escott, the Robin Hood house was built in 1765 at a cost of £300 but, if so, it was still being fitted up in 1767 when Sir Charles wrote: "*as for the Building on the Hill in the Park, the first room, which I call the hermit's room, must have an earthen floor, the kitchen on the left, a brick, and the little room for China, must be board'd.*"

In 1765 he also constructed, halfway down the avenue leading from the house to Mill Wood, a strange monument to the memory of a favourite horse. Apart from the icehouse, built below the Rotunda in 1767, the most important of the later building listed by Escott is the so-called Temple of Pan at Patcombe in the south-west corner of the park, dating from 1771. This brick house was for his bailiff and has a pedimented front (oddly facing almost into the hill) and a simple convex Doric portico behind which the wall is concave so as to form an oval loggia. In plan the loggia repeats that of Robin Hood's Hut. A life-size bronze statue of Pan formerly stood on the axis of the house at a distance of about 50 yards from the front. The Temple may well be by the architect John Johnson (1732-1814), who exhibited a Temple of Pan in the gardens of Sir Charles Kemeys Tynte at Halswell at the Society of Artists in 1778.

A letter from Bampfylde throws light on the last years of Sir Charles's long reign at Halswell. After praising the newly altered "*lower piece of water*" - evidently a 'naturalised' version of the large round pond below the surviving rockwork grotto - he calls the upper pond on the lawn "*in every respect an Eye Sore*" for its artificiality. Evidently the rockwork at its southern end was to be removed in any case, for he continues: "*if you differ in opinion, I shall with pleasure make any design for decorating the Head that my poor fancy can furnish.*"

The estate remained in the Kemeys-Tynte family until after the Second World War. In 1950 it was sold and split into a number of ownerships, the coach house and stables were converted into freehold residences and the house only avoided demolition through conversion into flats. The 'lawn' on the east became a wilderness, with the Rotunda and grotto buried deep in saplings and undergrowth, while by contrast the ancient oaks and chestnuts, ilex and sycamore in Mill Wood were felled, leaving the temples exposed and at the mercy of vandals. By the 1970s the Statue of Pan had been spirited away from Patcombe and taken to Castle Hill, near South Molton (Devon) and the horse monument had also been removed by the farmer. The other absentee of Sir Charles's landscape is the Druid's Temple, destroyed in the 1950s. Everywhere else, however, the scene is of derelict garden buildings and intensive farming practices.

In 1985 the house was sold to new owners and the latest chapter of Halswell began. Initially, the new owners intended to live in the house themselves, perhaps opening it to the public. But eventually the house contents were sold and planning permission granted for a change of use to offices for the 1689 block of the house. Ambitious plans to repair the garden buildings foundered when one of the joint owners was declared bankrupt. The mortgagors then repossessed the property. Meanwhile, the local authorities had become increasingly concerned over the ruinous condition of the Temple of Harmony and threatened the owner with a Repairs Notice. Publicity in 1993 over this course of action attracted Cricket St Thomas Wildlife Park near Chard to offer to buy the temple and re-erect it. This was not the first time such a venture had been put forward; in 1958 Pevsner reported that "*the Temple is to be re-erected at Portmeirion, Mr Williams-Ellis's estate in Wales*".

Galvanised into action by the local community, the District Council refused listed building consent for the removal of the temple. A repairs notice was served on the understanding that if the District Council proceeded with compulsory purchase, the Somerset Building Preservation Trust would accept the building, undertake its repair and open it to the public. This decisive course of action proved conclusive and with the help of grants and loans from the County and District Council, English Heritage, the Architectural Heritage Fund and other contributions, work eventually got underway in 1995 and the Temple of Harmony was painstakingly repaired, opening to the public in May 1996.

The Building Preservation Trust established a new charitable trust: the Halswell Park Trust. The Park Trust was set up to mastermind the restoration of Halswell Park and, as such, took into its care the day-to-day responsibility for the temple. Meanwhile, the Building Preservation Trust had been given Robin Hood's Hut and begun the lengthy process of repairing this structure. Following the offer of a substantial grant from the Heritage Lottery Fund, work on site commenced in June 1997.

All this time the house has remained empty and although wind and weather tight is slowly deteriorating. Ownership has again changed but no interest has been expressed in putting the house into use. The condition of the Rotunda and Rockwork Screen have become a matter of concern and the early-seventeenth-century dovecote suffered a serious collapse of a section of cob walling.

For its part the Halswell Garden Trust have commissioned an historic landscape survey and management plan with funding from the Countryside Commission's Countryside Stewardship Scheme (now administered by the Ministry of Agriculture, Fisheries and Food). Plans are well advanced on a feasibility study for submitting a second bid to the Lottery to acquire the area known as Mill Wood, and thereby commence the long-term objective of reuniting the ornamental buildings with the landscaped parkland.

In the mean time English Heritage have encouraged the Trust to pursue lottery funding, rather than make further grants from their own funds, and have turned their attention to the vacant and deteriorating Grade I house. One of the most ambitious options put forward in the Trust's management plan for the estate suggests that all the buildings and their original parkland should be brought back into one ownership. Such a course of action could only be realised by funding from the National Lottery.

This comprehensive option has perhaps greater potential for success than the current piecemeal approach which is constantly threatened by uncertainties over funding, vested interests and a protracted timescale.

opposite: Fig. 10.7
A plan of HALSWELL PARK *showing the locations and state of the temples and follies.*

Fig. 10.8
The statue of TERPSICHORE, *the muse of song and dance, by John Walsh of London. In her left hand is a zither and in her right hand a pair of compasses. In the eighteenth century architecture, mathematics and music were considered as one harmonious whole. A copy of the statue stands in the Temple of Harmony.*

Case Study 2

HESTERCOMBE
by Philip White

The history of Hestercombe can be traced back more than sixteen hundred years to a Saxon charter of 682, when it was known as *Haegsteldescumb*. For nearly five hundred years, from 1391, Hestercombe had belonged to the Warre family whose ancestor Sir John Warre had accepted the surrender of the King of France at the battle of Poitiers in 1356.

Ironically, the earliest reference to a garden at Hestercombe is "*pulling down garden hedge*" from the accounts of Sir Francis Warre in 1698. The garden figures in the accounts again with mention of the drawing up of plans for the garden in 1720, 1728 and again in 1731, during the period when considerable alterations were being made to Hestercombe House by John Bampfylde, son-in-law of Sir Francis Warre.

The site of these gardens and the extent to which these designs were acted upon is still unclear. The only evidence, so far, for an early garden is a portrait of Coplestone Warre Bampfylde, John's son, painted in the early 1740s which shows an obelisk on the skyline that may have formed part of an early designed landscape.

The first specific reference to work in what became the landscape garden was "*for doen the pond head in Easter combe*" in 1698 followed in 1700 by "*making a grate for the pond*". We have to wait until 1761 for the first detailed description of Coplestone Bampfylde's pleasure grounds which was provided by his brother-in-law, Edward Knight, when he came to visit Coplestone and his wife Mary in June of that year. He recorded in his miniature diary:

> "*Hestercombe C B's*
> *View up the Valley of Cascades*
> *Water and Root House*
> *Octagon Summerhouse, Taunton Vale*
> *Terrace and Chinese Seat*
> *View down the Water to Taunton Vale*
> *Rock - Lawn and Beeches -*
> *Gothic seat views into the*
> *Vale from east to West*
> *Witch or Root House confined*
> *View of Taunton and the Vale.*
> *Tent open view of Taunton the*
> *Vale etc. - Mausoleum 18 feet*
> *Arch 7 feet wide and 7 high -*
> *Piers 12 feet urns on the tops.*"

Much of this work had probably been achieved in the eleven years since 1750, when Coplestone had inherited the estate on the death of his father. The garden continued to be developed and it was after a visit to William Shenstone in 1762, according to Richard Graves, that Bampfylde decided to construct the magnificent Great Cascade.

The Doric Temple, now so much a part of the garden design, was not recorded by Arthur Young when he visited in 1771, although it appears in Bampfylde's watercolour of the Pear Pond painted later in the 1770s. Bampfylde's final addition to his garden appears to be the memorial urn erected in 1786 to the memory of his great friends Sir Charles Tynte of nearby Halswell and Henry Hoare of Stourhead. Gardens are, by their nature, dynamic, a point noted even during Bampfylde's lifetime by Edmund Rack, who wrote to John Collinson, author of THE HISTORY OF SOMERSET: "*We shall on this occasion adopt the following animated and just description of [Hestercombe] written by A. Young Esq, with some little variation which the progress of growth in the plantation renders necessary.*"

Following Bampfylde's death in August 1791 the estate passed to his nephew John Tyndale, who took the name Warre and lived at Hestercombe until his death in 1819, a few months before the forced sale of the estate. The family managed to negotiate the sale of the reversion of the estate to Lord Ashburton, which enabled John Tyndale Warre's daughter, Miss Elizabeth Warre, to continue to live on the estate until her death in 1872. After her death and sale of the contents of the house the Ashburtons sold their interest to Viscount Portman.

The effect of these financial upheavals on Miss Warre was to cause her to live very frugally and, although she died in possession of a large quantity of cash, she was never tempted to improve on Bampfylde's original design. Rather she appears to have acted as guardian of Bampfylde's legacy by collecting together his watercolours and opening his garden to the public every Thursday. Public access was attended by problems all too familiar today. It was reported in the TAUNTON COURIER on 21st August 1822 that "*Four young men, apprentices to respectable tradesmen of this town, were on Wednesday last summoned for wantonly and maliciously throwing down and defacing an ornamental urn in the pleasure grounds of Hestercombe House on the proceeding Sunday. Dismissed with reprimand.*" After her death the Rev. Hugo, a local antiquary, described the neglected state of the landscape garden: "*dark, deep, silent woods, solemn avenues and winding walks by silent pools, a dashing cascade and shady arbours, a shadowy thing of the past rather than a reality of the living and breathing present. For more than half a century little has been done even to preserve what was once so regularly ordered and exactly arranged. The woods have about them a primeval aspect. The lawns are overgrown with varied vegetation, the paths, where a hundred years ago the feet of fair ladies wandered amid a very paradise of delights, are now in some places all but obliterated, while those which are tended the best have entirely lost that courtly care which was once so lavishly and lovingly expended on them. The visitor has oftentimes to gaze on landscape beauties through an umbrageous screen which all but hides them from his view and to investigate the works of its old possessors, where his foot is impeded at every step and the air is dense with sylvan odours and heavy with the atmosphere of the forest and its verdure.*"

The Portmans appeared content to leave the landscape garden as they concentrated their efforts on remodelling the house, building a new stable block and creating model farms on the estate. In Bampfylde's garden they reroofed the Temple and Mausoleum, built a paved carriage drive through the valley, rebuilt the sluices on the dams and used the streams to feed a water supply system commensurate with the needs of a modern Victorian gentleman's residence. Luckily, they only toyed with the garden, planting azaleas and a magnolia in front of the Mausoleum and bamboo in the Valley of Cascades.

When Lord Portman's son, the Hon E. Portman, eventually turned his attention seriously to gardening it was to commission Edwin Lutyens and Gertrude Jekyll to create the now famous garden to the south of the house between 1904 and 1906 and Bampfylde's garden escaped further attention.

The Hon E. Portman died in 1912, predeceasing his father, the Viscount, and putting an end to large-scale improvements on the estate. As a result of heavy death duties incurred by the deaths of several Lords Portman the 10,500 acre Taunton estate, including all of the Hestercombe estate, was sold in 1944, to the Crown Estates. Like Miss Warre before her, Mrs Portman continued to live at Hestercombe

House until her death, in 1952. Unlike Miss Warre, Mrs Portman allowed no staff and few visitors into the landscape garden but maintained the valley as her own private preserve - another accident of fate which helped to protect the garden's integrity. After her death the house, now leased to Somerset County Council, became the headquarters of the Somerset Fire Brigade.

In 1962 the Crown Estates embarked on a misguided exploitation of the Hestercombe woodlands by clear-felling all the valuable eighteenth-century parkland trees. Despite many representations at the time from people all too aware of the importance of Bampfylde's designed landscape the Crown allowed felling to continue and a great work of English landscape art was largely destroyed.

Fig. 10.9
View of the PEAR POND,
Hestercombe Gardens.

Fig. 10.10
The Charcoal Burner's Camp.

Fig. 10.11
The Mausoleum.

Laurie Fricker responded pithily in the *The Landscape Journal*: "*Recently [Hestercombe] has been remodelled by a hand not unaware of at least one aspect of twentieth century art, for the taste of the Crown Commissioners has clearly been formed by a close study of Paul Nash's work as official artist to the '14-'18 War. By sacking the temples, felling and burning most of the timber and so exposing the vertical outcrops of rock, they have created a convincing evocation of Passchendaele Ridge.*"

The valley was replanted between 1963 and 1964 as commercial forestry and the remains of the eighteenth-century landscape disappeared from view, engulfed by impenetrable scrub and laurel.

I first became aware that there was something buried in the woods when I started work at an office in Hestercombe House and in 1992 resolved to restore the garden, even though at that stage I had little understanding of its design or extent. I was encouraged by officers of the Countryside Commission to commission an historical survey and feasibility study which they three-quarters funded, the balance coming from Taunton Deane Borough Council and Somerset County Council. The final report by Johnny Phibbs of Debois Landscape Survey was a model of academic research and continues to provide the basis of the restoration plan.

Discussions with the Crown continued and David Usher, head gardener of the Lutyens garden, and I set up the Hestercombe Gardens Project Ltd, through which we eventually signed a thirty-year lease with the Crown on 28th February 1995, the 275th anniversary of Bampfylde's birth.

The garden was by now in a sorry state and to the uninitiated there was little or no evidence of its previous glory. Three of the four lakes had almost completely disappeared and the fourth, the Pear Pond, was two-thirds silted up. We decided early on in the restoration that it was essential to get all the main features of the garden restored as soon as possible in order that we could open the garden to the public and generate revenue income. Unfortunately this also meant that our greatest expenditure would occur in the first two years.

In June 1995 we started clearing the trees that were growing over the tops of the silted ponds: a difficult job over dangerous substrata. On July 4th Graham Burton was appointed project officer and given the daunting task of ensuring that the restoration plan was enacted; he has remained our only full-time member of staff.

On 23rd July, Pond Management Services moved their machinery on site and the restoration began in earnest. The same week David Usher and I were in London hanging an exhibition of Bampfylde watercolours at Christie's in King Street. The exhibition opened on July 28th to very good reviews and David and I spent the next fortnight alternately manning the exhibition and keeping an eye on the lakes at Hestercombe. Our greatest concern was that the lakes had been clay - or, even worse, stone-lined - and that the smallest damage might cause them to leak. As it was, Bampfylde had constructed them directly on to the natural clay of the valley floor.

I had not realized the ability of the digger drivers to feel the base of the ponds with their buckets and was amazed that they were able gently to lift the lowest silt layers, exposing the blackened leaves that had first fallen in the ponds two hundred and fifty years previously. The Reservoir Pond contained over twelve feet of silt and the four ponds together were cleared of an estimated seventeen thousand tons of silt. The diggers worked five days a week for four weeks with five large dump trucks carrying the silt up the valley to a neighbouring farm. The silt was spread over the corn stubble fields, returning the topsoil that had been eroded over the centuries.

The biggest surprise was to discover that the Pear Pond had been constructed in two phases. The original pond, which had been impounded by Sir Francis Warre in 1698, had acted as a reservoir for the Mill Pond directly below, to which it was connected by a sump plugged with a tapered oak bung on an iron bar. You may imagine our delight when we literally pulled the plug and the water emptied from the lake, as if it were a bath, after a gap of nearly three hundred years.

Bampfylde had, by the simple expedient of raising the height of the dam with a stone retaining wall, more than doubled the extent of the lake, making the attractively-shaped body of water that we see today. After clearing the ponds our first priority was to restore the dams on the top two lakes, both of which had been destroyed by the Crown in order to drain them prior to tree planting. When the four lakes were finally completed and holding water we were at last able to appreciate the basis of Bampfylde's design.

Having cleared the lakes our next priority was to restore the 300-yard-long brick leat which fed the waterfall from the Reservoir Pond. Although still visible on the ground, the leat had been badly damaged when the trees had been felled and the waterfall had not run consistently since Mrs Portman's death in 1952.

The Great Cascade was designed as the centrepiece of the garden and the most theatrical of all its elements. Approaching through a dark wood, the visitor entered a woodland clearing with the magnificent waterfall crashing down a rock cliff; the only intrusion into this dramatic scene was a gothic seat, now gone, from which to enjoy the picturesque view.

We started the restoration of the leat in September 1995 and the work continued right through the autumn, finishing just before Christmas. At the same time Graham started to rebuild the retaining revetment wall that extended almost the whole length of the leat. To construct this dry stone wall, which was approximately three feet high, he scavenged all over the valley in an effort to find sufficient stone to join up the few remaining pieces of original wall. As he said, "It's like joining up the points in a dot-to-dot drawing."

On April 2nd, 1996 the Great Cascade was officially opened by the Mayor of Taunton accompanied by a horn player playing eighteenth-century hunting calls. This served the purpose of disguising the four and a half minutes that it took the water to flow the length of the leat and happily echoed Bampfylde's watercolour which shows a man with a hunting horn at the base of the waterfall.

Water features generate their own problems and 1996 saw us coping with several of them. First of all, the reservoir sprung a large leak and lost a considerable amount of water before a diver could be traced who was willing to plug the hole. Then the summer showed that the leat, which ran well enough when there was a good volume of water, leaked through its base, causing the water gradually to disappear along its length, leaving the waterfall literally high and dry. One of the main priorities of 1997 will be to build sluices into the dams to give us greater flexibility over controlling water flow. This was not a new problem; Richard Graves's character Columella (for whom

we might read Coplestone) instructs his man Peter: " *'Do you go down now towards the forest seat, you know where I mean, and wait till we come.'* *This was a hint for Peter to give the principal cascade a little additional flash to entertain his friends. For although there was a constant stream, yet at this time of the year the water was somewhat low, and required same little accumulation to give it a proper effect.* "

Financing these capital works has been fairly straightforward. The Countryside Stewardship scheme had already identified the capital cost of the dredging and the restoration of the leat which they fifty per cent grant-aided and, more by good luck than judgement, we were able to raise the balance from charitable bodies.

Our main project in 1996 was the restoration of the two remaining buildings in the garden: the Doric Temple and the Mausoleum. Early indications from English Heritage were that a high level of grant aid was likely to be forthcoming, but after various vicissitudes we were eventually told than none would be available. Much to their credit the Countryside Stewardship scheme, by now taken over from the Countryside Commission by the Ministry of Agriculture, were able to step in and offer support for the restoration of these buildings.

Our architects suggested that the cost of the building together with other capital works, including rebuilding the badly leaking Pear Pond dam, would leave us with a shortfall, after grant, of some £60,000. Although our initial appeals had been successful, it was apparent that many charities are only able to give to other charitable bodies, and in January 1997 we eventually set up the Hestercombe Gardens Trust in conjunction with Somerset County Council. The stated objectives of the charity underline the importance of the whole site which it is committed to supporting and developing.

The landscape garden was opened on April 22nd, 1997 and followed a few days later by a television documentary that had been following the progress of the restoration. Opening the garden and its attendant publicity will undoubtedly bring forth more evidence which will shed further light on Bampfylde's original intentions. This is only the beginning of a story which, as they say, will run and run.

BIBLIOGRAPHY

Edmund Rack's manuscript notes on Hestercombe, c1785, for COLLINSON'S HISTORY AND ANTIQUITIES OF SOMERSET (1791).

Hugo, Rev. Thomas, Hestercombe', *PSANHS* Vol. 18 (1872), ii, pp 136-76.

L. Fricker, Gardens at Hestercombe House, Somerset, JOURNAL OF THE INSTITUTE OF LANDSCAPE ARCHITECTS (Feb 1963), pp.8-11.

TAUNTON COURIER, 21 August 1822.

Richard Graves, COLUMELLA OR THE DISTRESSED ANCHORET (1779?)

This is the sorry story of Orchardleigh Park, which is an historic garden registered by English Heritage. The park contains a collection of historic buildings and structures, most of which are listed. These include Orchardleigh House, its terraced garden, lodges, stables, church, boathouse and ornamental bridges - in fact, all you would expect to find in a country park and an asset to be treasured by the nation.

Orchardleigh lies to the north-east of Frome in rolling countryside typical of that part of Somerset. The name makes its first appearance in the Domesday Book as 'Horcerlei' when it was held by the Bishop Geoffrey of Coutances. By 1285 it had been conveyed to Sir Henry de Merlaund, who may have been responsible for creating the park from what was then the great forest of Selwood.

Henry is also likely to have built the church of St Mary's which stands on an island at the western end of the lake and which is still worshipped in regularly today. In 1318 the estate was described thus: *"There is a capital messuage with a garden worth yearly 5s., a dovecote worth yearly 7s., 160 acres of arable land worth 53s. 4d. price 4d. per acre, 20 acres of meadow for mowing, which are in common after mowing, worth yearly 30s. price 18d. per acre, a pasture worth 6s. 8d., 5 acres of wood whose profits are worth yearly 5s. price 12d per acre, rents of free tenants 23s. 5d., rent of two customary tenants 4s., each of the said customary tenants holds a cottage and 2 acres of land; rents of cottars holding at will 5s., pleas and perquisites of court worth yearly 12d. Henry Merland, son and heir of the foresaid Henry de Merland, is his next heir and of 30 years and more."*

Descendents of Merland married into the Champneys family, who remained the freeholders of Orchardleigh for over 400 years. It can be seen that at this time the park was not that extensive, stretching to no more than about 150 acres, and no formal landscaping took place until the early eighteenth century. There is evidence that some trees have survived from before the eighteenth century but for the most part Orchardleigh is a nineteenth-century creation, showing major plantings in about 1800 and again when the Duckworth family bought the estate in the 1850s.

Orchardleigh is situated in a valley whose two flanks are of different forms. The northern flank is gentle and accommodates the house on its crest, while the southern flank rises quite steeply beyond the lake to a ridge known as the Down. The underlying geology is from the Jurassic period and is known as Forest Marble, which is a combination of clay with Oolitic Shelly Limestone. This stone is used in the Frome area for building and can be seen in the lodges of Orchardleigh. A stream runs past the church, feeds the lake and passes over a spillway at the dam to join the River Frome on its journey north to meet the Avon. The planting in the park is dominated by oak, either in copses or as individuals, with associated ash, horse chestnut and some lime and beech. Large woods used for timber and game create a dense boundary to the open parkland to the north and west. The park is dominated by the house overlooking the lake in views from the south but is partially hidden from view as it is approached along the main drive from the west.

Little is known about the park before the eighteenth century but in the 1740s it is clear that Richard Champneys was enlarging and beautifying the gardens. The gardens at that time were probably of limited extent, concentrated around the house which at that time was very near the church at the western end of the lake. The northern and eastern parts of the park as we find it today did not exist at that time and were probably in the original Selwood forest. The Champneys failed to manage the estate effectively, fell into debt and mortgaged it in the late eighteenth century. The family tenuously held the land into the early part of the nineteenth century and had serious designs to improve the park and improve the old house, commissioning Sir Jeffry Wyatville to draw up plans in about 1808. These were not implemented and the house fell into further decline. Wyatville did design the entrance lodges at Murtry and at Gloucester Lodge, which is the eastern entrance to the park. It is thought that Humphry Repton may also have worked at Orchardleigh at the same time that he was designing landscapes at Longleat. The owners of many local houses such as Bowood and Ston Easton had advice from him and certainly some of the elements of Orchardleigh, including the lake, boathouse and planting, show evidence of Repton's style.

The main influences on Orchardleigh are undoubtedly those of the Duckworths in the nineteenth century and it is the work of the first owner, William, which has had a lasting effect on the park.

In 1849 the estate was offered for sale and the sale particulars included: *"The park ... upwards of 616 acres of which about 107 acres are ornamental plantations, woods and underwoods, full of very superior thriving oak timber. The remainder is rich grazing land, beautifully undulating and studded with large and noble oak elm and other trees.... Large serpentine lake of about 24 acres.... On the margin of the lake stands an elegant erection designated the Temple intended as a retreat for the enjoyment of fishing and commanding rich and enchanting views.... on an elevation in a large wood stands a highly ornamental and delightful summer retreat called Wood Lodge."* The Temple stands above the boathouse and Wood Lodge still exists and is used as a shooting bothy.

In 1854 William Duckworth of Beechwood in Hampshire bought the estate for £96,000. He was not enamoured of the house and decided to build a new one on elevated land above the lake. He asked Thomas Henry Wyatt to design it for him and simultaneously appointed William Page, who had worked for him in Hampshire, to set about designing a new parkland planting that would be orientated towards the house that was being built. As well as specifying planting for the park, Mr Page laid out the terraces in front of the house. By August 1857 these were *"brilliant with flowers and the conservatory, only ten days old quite cheerful with creepers"*.

The estate became more prosperous under the Duckworths' patronage and Mr Page and later a William Thomas continued to improve and modify the park. The position of the house dictated new approach drive arrangements and other houses such as Temple Lodge and Keepers Cottage were built in the grounds while a new boathouse was erected at the eastern end of the lake.

The park was probably at its most splendid towards the turn of the nineteenth century and was described in suitably gushing terms in *Country Life* in 1901: *"The park covers nearly the whole are of the parish and is a pleasant, picturesque and well wooded expanse with a spacious lake and ponds. Here in ancient times spread the forest of Selwood and the sylvan character still invests the land. The River Frome runs on the south side and with the woods, meadows and orchards completes the rustic*

Fig. 10.12
An aerial view of
ORCHARDLEIGH PARK *today*
showing the damage done to the
character and quality of the
landscape after the creation of
a golf course.

charm.... Seclusion and great beauty have marked the place for their own. An indefinable English charm is found here. The genius loci is found here. A breath of the South may seem to have suggested a nude Cupid on his pedestal or the turn of a pergola, but the spirit is that which belongs to the English shires. Fortunate it is, as an ancient dwelling of substantial men, in its regeneration to the state to which it stands and rich it is in the glory of its green and beautiful surroundings. Long may change be averted from places such as Orchardleigh."

The Duckworths lived at Orchardleigh until the last owner, George Arthur, died in 1986. Much of the landscape had started to age by this time and the park suffered badly in the gale of October 1987. Arthur Duckworth had done little tree management in his later years except to clear away major fallen trees and a survey carried out by Durston Woodlands in 1990 showed that as many as 65 per cent of all the trees in the park needed some remedial treatment. On Arthur Duckworth's death, his daughters decided that none of them wished to live at Orchardleigh and so the estate was sold in 1987. A consortium bought the 2000 acres to which Orchardleigh had stretched and then broke it up. Land around the margins was taken by local farmers and woodland was acquired for forestry and game management. This left a residual 200 acres in the centre of the park which was retained by Clarendon Properties for development. In early 1988, against the advice of their officers, English Heritage and amenity groups, Mendip District Council gave approval for an 18-hole golf course, and clubhouse. Permission was also given for 32 time-share units around the walled garden and the conversion of the stable block to six dwellings.

Clarendon then sold the site to Meadrealm Ltd, which was a subsidiary of the Baron Hotel and Leisure Group. The chairman of this group later achieved notoriety as Britain's greatest personal bankrupt when his empire collapsed at the end of the boom in 1990. However, in the mean time Meadrealm had added to its landholding in the core

Fig. 10.13
ORCHARDLEIGH HOUSE,
showing much of the original planting with kitchen gardens and stables set apart from the main house.

of the historic park and obtained consents for a further 18 holes of golf stretching around the lake and away over the Down, together with consent for a new hotel. Meadrealm was at this time advised by the former Ryder Cup golfer Brian Huggett, who envisaged a championship course which would attract many thousands of spectators. Many of the conditions applied to the consents anticipated this intensified use so that a new road junction was required to be built at Murtry and the access drive was altered to provide passing bays to deal with the high volumes of vehicles which were expected to arrive on tournament days.

Work started apace in 1989 and the park appeared devastated as heavy earth-moving machinery remodelled the landscape. The Council had anticipated some difficulties of control over tree felling and had imposed a tree preservation order over the whole estate. This was a blanket area order which was intended to be used as a holding action but work continued at such speed that it was very difficult for Council officers to verify tree positions and any losses. At this time Mendip District Council had no specialist tree officer and it was left to the planning officer to oversee this work. Understandably local people who had walked the park in the past were outraged at what was happening and many meetings took place on site to try to sort out the problems.

Meadrealm collapsed in 1990 and all work stopped. The American course contractors departed for their next job in Portugal, leaving a scarred landscape all over the park, in particular in front of the house, around the lake and worst of all on the Down. The earth-moving plant had removed the thin topsoil in many places to expose the limestone below and at its worst the estate looked like a moonscape.

In 1990 there was another great gale and more trees were lost in the park, increasing the devastation throughout the estate. The Countryside Commission set up an initiative called Task Force Trees to try to deal with storm damage across the country, a problem which had not been helped by the increasing drought conditions in the summer. In 1992 Mendip District Council obtained grant aid from the taskforce to review the situation at Orchardleigh, make recommendations for landscape restoration and mitigate the worst effects of the development which had been approved.

Land Use Consultants Ltd were commissioned to carry out this work and their report was published in August 1993. It concluded that the planning approvals for the golf course in particular had been very damaging to the character and quality of the historic park and that certain remedial work should be carried out, both in terms of planting and also to renegotiate the terms of the planning consents if possible. Receivers had been brought in by the creditors to manage the estate and to attempt to find a buyer, but this was hard to achieve in a depressed market. It appears that the grandiose plans for time-share and large leisure hotel uses did not attract any takers and the park lay in limbo for a long time while successive prospective purchasers sought to alter the planning consents to residential. The Council has consistently resisted this approach.

The report showed that the golf course had been built without due regard to the historic significance of the landscape. It stated that vistas had been disrupted, boundary plantings have been broken through, parts of ha-has destroyed and orchards totally removed. The need to maintain a lowered water level in the lake because of structural problems with the dam meant that the boathouse had lost its context. Land Use Consultants also produced an alternative layout for the golf course with a view to this being used as a negotiating tool but this has not been taken up by the receiver. It should be possible to incorporate some of these components into any revised schemes which are put forward for completing the golf course over the Down.

The receiver quite rightly claims that his first duty is to his creditors; he is not keen to spend a great deal of money in the estate, so it has been a slow haul over the last five years to effect any amelioration in the park. The condition of the houses and lodges is kept under review and a phased programme of landscaping has been agreed and carried out based on the recommendations of the Task Force Trees study. An 18-hole golf course has been laid out and a clubhouse has been built to the north-east of Orchardleigh House. Planting has been carried out to reinforce traditional park planting and some copses and shelter belts that had become degraded, but most of this is concentrated around the north of the house and, while the receiver contemplates what to do about the proposed second 18 holes, the lake margins and the Down have not yet received any attention.

Golf has altered the grass management of the park, for where previously there was rough grazing and annual mowing now there is regular mowing which retains the grass at different heights. While it is acknowledged that rough areas remain, for the most part the golf course has reduced the habitat value by cutting down the number of native wild plants that are allowed to flower. This has a knock-on effect on insects, birds and bats in the park.

There is no doubt that Orchardleigh was undervalued as an historic park at the time that the development proposals were put forward. The would-be developers of golf in the estate wanted an instant high-quality landscape with mature trees and pretty views both within the course and from it. This has certainly been achieved, but at considerable cost. Orchardleigh has taught Mendip Council and many other local authorities some lessons about intensification of leisure uses in historic parks: first, the Task Force Trees report on the historic significance of the park should have been carried out before the planning permissions were granted, not after; second, the full implications of golf-course landscaping in terms of mounding and bunkers should have been made clear; and, finally, a policy should have been agreed that would have directed the golf course to other, less sensitive, areas, where landscaping and tree planting could have helped to improve the habitat diversity and the appearance of the rural landscape and benefited farmers seeking diversification.

Selected Bibliography

Full references to the present text have been quoted at the end of each chapter. There is now a vast literature on the history of parks and gardens, but the following books provide a valuable introduction to the subject.

General References

Mavis Batey & David Lambert, *The English Garden Tour: a View into the Past* (John Murray, London, 1990).

Julia S. Berrall, *The Garden: an Illustrated History* (Viking Press, New York, 1966).

J.H. Bettey, *Estates and the English Countryside* (B.T. Batsford, London, 1993).

Richard Bisgrove, *The National Trust Book of the English Garden* (Penguin Group, London, 1990).

Jane Brown, *The Art and Architecture of English Gardens* (Rizzoli, New York, 1989).

Laurence Fleming & Alan Gore, *The English Garden* (Michael Joseph, London, 1979).

Alastair Forsyth, *Yesterday's Gardens* (Royal Commission on Historical Monuments, England; London, 1983).

Richard Girling (ed.), *The Making of the English Garden* (The Sunday Times/ MacMillan, London, 1988).

Miles Hadfield, *A History of British Gardening* (3rd edn, John Murray, London, 1979).

Anthony Huxley, *An Illustrated History of Gardening* (Paddington Press, New York, 1978).

Edward Hyams, *The English Garden* (Thames & Hudson, London, 1964).

Gervase Jackson-Stops & James Pipkin, *The Country House Garden: a Grand Tour* (National Trust/Pavilion Books/Michael Joseph, London, 1987).

Geoffrey & Susan Jellicoe, Patrick Goode & Michael Lancaster (eds), *The Oxford Companion to Gardens* (Oxford University Press, 1991).

David Joyce (ed.), *Garden Styles: an Illustrated History of Design and Tradition* (Pyramid Books, London, 1989).

Susan Lasdun, *The English Park* (André Deutsch, London, 1991).

Anthea Taigel & Tom Williamson, *Parks and Gardens* (B.T. Batsford, London, 1993).

Christopher Taylor, *The Archaeology of Gardens* (Shire Archaeology no.30, Princes Risborough, 1983).

Christopher Thacker, *The History of Gardens* (Croom Helm, London, 1979).

Christopher Thacker, *England's Historic Gardens* (Headline Book Publishing, London, 1989).

Roman Gardens

Elisabeth B. MacDougall & Wilhelmina F. Jashemski (eds) *Ancient Roman Gardens* (Dumbarton Oaks Colloquium on the History of Landscape Architecture no.7, Washington D.C.,1981).

Medieval Gardens

John Harvey, *Mediaeval Gardens* (B.T. Batsford, London, 1981).

Sylvia Landsberg, *The Medieval Garden* (British Museum Press, London, 1995).

Elisabeth B. MacDougall (ed.), *Medieval Gardens* (Dumbarton Oaks Colloquium on the History of Landscape Architecture no.9, Washington D.C.,1986).

Teresa McLean, *Medieval English Gardens* (Collins, London, 1981).

Formal Gardens, c.1500-1740

John Anthony, *The Renaissance Garden in Britain* (Shire Garden History Series no.4, Princes Risborough, 1991).

David Green, *Gardener to Queen Anne: Henry Wise (1653-1738) and the Formal Garden* (Oxford University Press, 1956).

David Jacques & Arend J. van der Holst, *The Gardens of William and Mary* (Christopher Helm, London, 1988).

Roy Strong, *The Renaissance Garden in England* (Thames & Hudson, London, 1979).

18th Century Landscape Parks

Miles Hadfield, *The English Landscape Garden* (2nd edn, Shire Garden History Series no.3, Princes Risborough. 1988).

Gwyn Headley & Wim Meulenkamp, *Follies: a National Trust Guide* (Jonathan Cape, London, 1986).

Thomas Hinde, *Capability Brown: the Story of a Master Gardener* (Hutchinson, London, 1986).

John Dixon Hunt & Peter Willis (eds), *The Genius of the Place: the English Landscape Garden, 1620-1820* (Paul Elek, London).

Edward Hyams, *Capability Brown and Humphry Repton* (J M Dent & Sons, London, 1971).

Barbara Jones, *Follies and Grottoes* (Constable & Co, London, 2nd edn, 1974).

Tim Mowl & Brian Earnshaw, *Trumpet at a Distant Gate: the Lodge as Prelude to the Country House* (Waterstone, London, 1985).

Dorothy Stroud, *Capability Brown* (4th edn, Faber & Faber, London, 1984).

Dorothy Stroud, *Humphry Repton* (Country Life, London, 1962).

David C. Stuart, *Georgian Gardens* (Robert Hale, London, 1979).

Michael Symes, *The English Rococo Garden* (Shire Garden History Series no.5, Princes Risborough, 1991).

Tom Williamson, *Polite Landscapes: Gardens and Society in Eighteenth-Century England* (Alan Sutton, 1995).

P. Willis, *Charles Bridgeman and the English Landscape Garden* (A Zwemmer, London, 1978).

Gardens of the 19th and 20th Centuries

Mavis Batey, *Regency Gardens* (Shire Garden History Series no.7, Princes Risborough, 1995).

Richard Bisgrove, *The Gardens of Gertrude Jekyll* (Frances Lincoln, London, 1992).

Jane Brown, *Gardens of a Golden Afternoon, the Story of a Partnership: Edwin Lutyens and Gertrude Jekyll* (Van Nostrand Reinhold, New York, 1982).

Tom Carter, *The Victorian Garden* (Bell & Hyman, London, 1984).

Joan Morgan & Alison Richards, *A Paradise out of a Common Field: the Pleasures and Plenty of the Victorian Garden* (Random Century Group, London, 1990).

George Plumptre, *The Latest Country Gardens* (Bodley Head, London, 1988).

David Stuart, *The Garden Triumphant: a Victorian Legacy* (Harper & Row, New York, 1988).

Nurseries, Kitchen Gardens, Glasshouses and Garden Plants

Roy Genders, *The Cottage Garden and the Old-Fashioned Flowers* (Pelham Books, London, 2nd edn, 1983).

Richard Gorer, *The Development of Garden Flowers* (Eyre & Spottiswoode, London, 1970).

John Harvey, *Early Nurserymen* (Phillimore, Chichester, 1974).

Penelope Hobhouse, *Plants in Garden History* (Pavilion Books, London, 1994).

Charles Lyte, *The Kitchen Garden* (Oxford Illustrated Press, 1984).

F A Roach, *Cultivated Fruits of Britain: their Origin and History* (Basil Blackwell, Oxford, 1985).

David C. Stuart, *The Kitchen Garden: an Historical Guide to Traditional Crops* (Alan Sutton, Gloucester, 1987).

May Woods & Arete Warren, *Glass Houses: a History of Greenhouses, Orangeries and Conservatories* (Aurum Press, London, 1988).

Local Studies

Michael Aston (ed.), *Aspects of the Medieval Landscape of Somerset* (Somerset County Council, 1988) (see especially John Harvey's chapter, 'Parks, gardens and landscaping').

Susan Chivers & Suzanne Woloszynska, *The Cottage Garden: Margery Fish at East Lambrook Manor* (John Murray, London, 1990).

Gillian Clarke, *Prior Park: a Compleat Landscape* (Millstream Books, Bath, 1987).

Margery Fish, *We Made a Garden* (W.H. & L. Collingridge, London, 1956).

Michael Havinden, *The Somerset Landscape* (Hodder & Stoughton, London, 1981).

Penelope Hobhouse, *On Gardening* (Francis Lincoln, London, 1994) (mainly concerns Tintinhull).

John Sales, *West Country Gardens* (Alan Sutton, Gloucester, 1980).

Garden Conservation and Restoration

John Harvey, *Restoring Period Gardens from the Middle Ages to Georgian Times* (Shire Garden History Series no.1, Princes Risborough,1988).

INDEX

SUBSCRIBERS

Bernard and Ruth Adams, Taunton, Somerset

Canon and Mrs Ian Ainsworth-Smith, Milverton, Somerset

Roxanna Albury, Lander University, Greenwood, South Carolina

P.H.B. Allsop, Charlton Mackrell, Somerton, Somerset

John Anthony, Spalding, Lincs

Professor Mick Aston, Sandford

Joella and Dane Baird, Belmont, MA, U.S.A.

Adriaan H. Bakker, Taunton, Somerset

John Ball, Hinton St George, Somerset

Tanis Ballerini, East Lambrook, Somerset

Bath Preservation Trust

Dora E. Beale, Cheltenham, Gloucestershire

Geoffrey M. Beale, Maidstone, Kent

Mrs H. and Mr A. Beatt, Deane Drive, Galmington, Taunton

Revd Alan and Mrs Shirley Beck, Creech Heathfield, Somerset

Dr and Mrs G.T. Bell, Beaconsfield, Bucks

Miss A.F. Benson, Long Sutton, Langport, Somerset

Janet Bickerstaff, Blagdon Hill, Somerset

Keith Billinghurst, Bleadon, Somerset

Mrs Priscilla Boddington, Taunton, Somerset

Reverend David Bond, Cotterstock, Peterborough

J.R.E. Borrow, Near Sawrey, Cumbria

Jennifer Bou, New York, U.S.A.

George Breeze, Cheltenham, Glos.

James Brockmann, New York, U.S.A.

Dr Diana L. Brown, Glastonbury, Somerset

John F. Brown, Weymouth, Dorset

John R. Brunsdon, Glastonbury, Somerset

Wreford Buttle, Camberley, Surrey

Michael and Hilary Cansdale, Wells, Somerset

Anthony and Stella Capo-Bianco, Clock House, Cowfold, W. Sussex

Ann Carter, York, Yorkshire

David Cawthorne, Taunton, Somerset

Steven Champlin, Washington DC, U.S.A.

Mr H.J.T. Channing, Padstow, Cornwall

Peter and Anna Channing, Guernsey, UK

Mr D.M. Child, Lytham, Lancs

Mrs Mary C. Clarke, Doccombe, Devon

Pauline Clark

Ralph Clark, Street, Somerset

Mr E. Clifton-Brown, Nr Glastonbury, Somerset

Mrs J.M. Colledge, Buckland St Mary, Chard, Somerset

Dr K.G. Collins, Portishead, Bristol

Sheila Cotterell, Bruton, Somerset

Allen W. Cotton, West Bradley, Somerset

Michael G. Cousins, Brentwood, Essex

Mrs R.A. Cowell, Hatfield Peverel, Essex

Gordon Cox, East Horrington, Somerset

M.A. and C.M. Cox, Birmingham

Phyllis Cram, Winscombe, Somerset

Gill Cramer, Whitefield, Wiveliscombe, Somerset

Stephen Croad, Hounslow, Middlesex

Joseph, Charlotte and Megan Croft, Wiveliscombe, Somerset

David Croom, Low Ham, Somerset

Michael I. Cullen, Clevedon, Somerset

Mr and Mrs Roger Curtis, North Curry, Somerset

Mike Cushing, North Hills, California

Carol David, Arnold Arboretum, Jamaica Plain, U.S.A.

Graham Davies, Fifehead Neville, Sturminster Newton, Dorset

Mr E. Dennison, Beverley, East Yorkshire

Pierre Deville, Chineham, Basingstoke, Hants

Brian Dix, Northampton

Laurence Dopson, Taunton, Somerset

I.C.M. Douthwaite, Taunton, Somerset

Tom Down, Waterlake, Tatworth, Somerset

Muff Dudgeon, Chagford, Devon

Mrs M.L. Eade, East Grinstead, West Sussex

June Eckhart, Wellington, Somerset

Mrs M.G.M. Ede, Ilminster, Somerset

Dr Howard Edington, Orlando, FL, U.S.A.

Richard N. Emeny, Goathurst, Somerset

Joy Etherington, Downderry, Cornwall

Mrs Anne Evans, Benenden, Cranbrook, Kent

G.E. Evans, Cardiff, Wales

Piers Feilden

Elizabeth J. Ferriss, Ilminster, Somerset

Mrs Elaine L. Flemons, Bath, Somerset

Alan Fletcher, Royston, Herts

Sidney Franklin, Sanderstead, Surrey

Betty Fraser, U.S.A.

Eric and Diane Freeman, Curry Mallet, Somerset

Flora Constance Alice Fricker, Southsea, Hants

Rob Froud

Ann Gardner, Sketty, Swansea

Bob and Florence Gatten, U.S.A.

Shirley Gazzard, Sussex

Gill Gibson, Shepton Mallet, Somerset

Jeremy and Caroline Gould, Street, Somerset

Sue Greaves, Bristol

Miss Patricia Hadland, Barrington, Somerset

Roger A. Hagley, Taunton, Somerset

F.R. Hamp, O.B.E., T.D., Taunton, Somerset

Michael Harris, Kent

Mr and Mrs Robin H. Harris, Horton, Somerset

S.J. Hartree, Deerleap, Bleadon

Joan Hasler, Wookey, Wells, Somerset

Rene Hatfield, Barrington, Ilminster, Somerset

Mrs Jean Hayman, Ilminster, Somerset

Mrs A. E. Leslie Heard, Holmbury Park, Bromley

Cecily M. Heaton, Wells, Somerset

Ann Heeley, Butleigh, Somerset

W.J. Highnam, Gillingham, Dorset

R.W. Hobbs, Langport, Somerset

Hermione Hobhouse, F.S.A., Westcombe

Penelope Hobhouse, Bettiscombe, Bridport, Dorset

Keith A. Honess, Winchester

Elizabeth Hord, Bruton, Somerset

Mrs Diana M.P. Huggill, Taunton, Somerset

Mrs Mary Humphries, Wiveliscombe, Somerset

Jean Hunter, Dulverton, Somerset

Fay Hutchcroft, Glastonbury, Somerset

Prof. S.P. Hutton, Southampton, Hants

T.B. Hutton, Birmingham

Mr C.W. Jackman, Bishops Lydeard, Taunton, Somerset

Mr and Mrs P. Jessop, Langport, Somerset

Ann E. John

Simon Johnson, Middle Chinnock, Crewkerne, Somerset

W.D. Johnson, Crewkerne, Somerset

Carolyn J. Keep, Woodbury, Devon

Norma Knight, Backwell, Somerset

John and Diana Knott, Birmingham

Rev. P.C. and Mrs F. Lambert, Langport, Somerset

John Lawrence-Mills, Stogumber, Somerset

Mrs Elizabeth Leggatt, Woodstock, Oxon

Mr R. Lillford, Taunton, Somerset

Jennie E. Llewellyn, Taunton, Somerset

Mrs Madge D. Long, Cole, Bruton, Somerset

The Library, Long Ashton Research Station, Bristol

Joan Loraine, Porlock, Somerset

Lordleaze Hotel, Chard, Somerset

Jonathan Lovie, Rugby, Warwickshire

Mr and Mrs B.G. Luker, Wookey, Wells, Somerset

Mr David Machin, London, WC1R 5AZ

Mrs Margaret Maddison, Newcastle-upon-Tyne

Mrs P. Mallet-Harris, Curry Mallet, Taunton, Somerset

Freda Marsden, Pilton, Somerset

Mark McDermott, Trull, Somerset

Michael McGarvie, Frome, Somerset

The Mendip Society

R.W. Millard, Bridgwater, Somerset

The Miller Family, Minehead, Somerset

Mr and Mrs D. Mitchell, Brent Knoll, Highbridge, Somerset

Irene R. Mitchell, M.B.E., Templecombe, Somerset

Susan Monaghan, Street, Somerset

Beryl N. Moore, Felton, Nr. Bristol

Mrs Camille Mowat, Curry Rivel, Langport, Somerset

Dr Timothy Mowl, Bristol

Ann Norman, Chard, Somerset

M. Norris, Reading

Mrs S.A.B. O'Neil, Bath

John G. Page, Brent Knoll, Somerset

Jill Parker, Holcombe, Bath

Liz and Bill Pearce, Liskeard, Cornwall

Max Perry, Milverton, Somerset

The Revd and Mrs D.E. Pett, Tresillian, Truro

Reva B. Phillips, U.S.A.

Michael and Marianne Pitman, Cleeve, North Somerset

Richard J. Pitts, Ashprington, Devon

Mary and John Priddle, Shepton Mallet, Somerset

R. Priddle and K. Seviour, Buckland Dinham, Somerset

Lesley K. Pring, Roadwater, Watchet, Somerset

D. and S.M. Rabson, Nynehead, Wellington, Somerset

Ian and Susan Rands, Glastonbury, Somerset

Mrs R.J. Ray, Exford, Minehead, Somerset

Jo Rees, Westbury-sub-Mendip, Somerset

Dr C.R. Riches, Shipham, North Somerset

Hazel Riley, Exeter, Devon

Mrs C. Rimell, Sonning, Berks

Nancy and Howell Roberts, U.S.A.

Dr Warwick Rodwell, Downside, Somerset

Bernadette Rowe, Ford, Wiveliscombe, Somerset

Miss C. Rutter, Edinburgh, Scotland

Marilyn Sadler

Dr Andrew Sclater, Cambridge

Jennifer and Richard Sheldon, Pilton, Somerset

Abigail Shepherd, Bath

Mr and Mrs A.B. Siddons, Wells, Somerset

Mrs A. Sims, Bristol

Margaret and Chris Skidmore, Walton-in-Gordano

Dr T.R. Slater, University of Birmingham, Birmingham

Peter and Christine Smedley, Ston Easton Park

D.L. Smith, London

Merilyn Smith, Wadstray House, Dartmouth, Devon

Somerset Environmental Records Centre, Bishops Lydeard, Taunton, Somerset

Somerset Studies Library, Taunton, Somerset

Isabel B. Stanley, Johnson City, Tennessee, U.S.A.

Elaine M. Steele, Stamborough, Somerset

Georgia P. Steiger, Sebring, Florida, U.S.A.

Shirley Stirling, Exhall, Warwickshire

F.E. Stoakley, Churchinford, Taunton, Somerset

Roger Stoakley, Adsborough, Taunton, Somerset

Mr and Mrs Simon Stoye, Enmore Castle, Somerset

Sir Roy Strong, F.S.A, Much Birch, Herts

Joyce and Bryan Sullivan, Cannock Wood, Staffordshire

Mr M. Symes, Wallington, Surrey

Mrs B. Tacchi, Minehead, Somerset

Judith B. Tankard, Newton, Massachusetts, U.S.A.

Patrick Taylor, Cudworth

Mary Terry, Abbots Leigh, Bristol

Ms Bobbie Thompson Roth, Tucson, Az, U.S.A.

Roy A. Thorne, Harringay, London

Dr Kate Tiller, Oxford University, Oxford

Mrs Toomey, Bridgwater, Somerset

J.H. Townson, Taunton, Somerset

David Tudway Quilter, Wells, Somerset

John Turner, Taunton, Somerset

Sir Ferrers Vyvyan, B.C., Helston, Cornwall

Paula C.V. Ward, Taunton, Somerset

Phil Waterman, Plymouth, Devon

Dr. J. Waymark, Petts Wood, Kent

D.H. Whiffen, Stogursey, Bridgwater, Somerset

Diana M. White, Cardiff, Wales

Joan M. Whitelegge, Cricket St Thomas, Somerset

Mrs Pamela M. Wilcock, Australia

Betty Wilkins, Sidmouth, Devon

Mr Chris Wiltshire, Dursley, Gloucestershire

Denys Wingfield, Long Sutton, Langport, Somerset

Colin G. Winn, Winchester, Hants

Elizabeth K. Winzinger, New York, U.S.A.

S.M. Wood, Stroud, Glos.

D.M. Woodford, Bozeat, Northants

Daphne Woods, Goathurst, Somerset

Mrs Eunice Woods, Malmesbury, Wilts

Mr E.G. and Lady Sarah Wright, Stogursey, Bridgwater, Somerset

Mrs David Wrightson

Archaeology Library, Yeovil College, Yeovil, Somerset

M. Young, Exebridge, Dulverton, Somerset